FORGOTTEN
Patriots

FORGOTTEN
Patriots

THE UNTOLD STORY OF AMERICAN PRISONERS DURING THE REVOLUTIONARY WAR

EDWIN G. BURROWS

A Member of the Perseus Books Group
New York

Published by Basic Books,
A Member of the Perseus Books Group

Books published by Basic Books are available at special discounts for
bulk purchases in the United States by corporations, institutions, and
other organizations. For more information, please contact the Special
Markets Department at the Perseus Books Group, 2300 Chestnut
Street, Suite 200, Philadelphia, PA 19103, or call (800) 810-4145,
ext. 5000, or e-mail special.markets@perseusbooks.com.

Designed by Brent Wilcox

Library of Congress Cataloging-in-Publication Data
Burrows, Edwin G., 1943–
    Forgotten patriots : the untold story of American prisoners during
the Revolutionary War / Edwin G. Burrows.
        p.   cm.
    Includes bibliographical references and index.
    ISBN 978-0-465-00835-3 (alk. paper)
    1. United States—History—Revolution, 1775–1783—Prisoners and
prisons, British.   2. Prisoners of war—United States—History—18th
century.   3. Prisoners of war—Great Britain—History—18th century.
4. Military prisons—New York (State)—New York—History—18th
century.   5. Great Britain. Army—Prisons—History—18th century.
6. New York (N.Y.)—History, Military—18th century.   I. Title.
E281.B87 2008
973.3'71—dc22
                                                      2008028093

10 9 8 7 6 5 4 3 2

For Pat, Matt, and Kate

"Too many of us have been prisoners in New-York."

—"A STEADY WHIG," 1783

CONTENTS

PREFACE

Thorburn's Lament

The idea for this book began to spread its wings many years ago when I happened across the reminiscences of Grant Thorburn, a Scottish immigrant who came to New York City about a decade after the end of the Revolutionary War. Thorburn settled in a small frame house on Liberty Street, just east of Broadway—now deep in Manhattan's downtown business district, but in those days a rather nondescript residential neighborhood of two- and three-story private homes, a few churches, and some modest shops. With one notable exception, that is: about halfway down the block, next to the Middle Dutch Church, rose a massive and mysterious five-story building, one of the largest in town, constructed of dark stone, with "small, deep windows, exhibiting a dungeon-like aspect."

This, Thorburn learned, was the infamous "Old Sugar House." Built as a sugar refinery many years earlier on what was then called Crown Street, it served as a British prison for Americans captured during the Revolutionary War. Since then the building had become a shrine of sorts for the men who somehow managed to survive its horrors. Day after day, Thorburn watched war-worn veterans, many with wives and children in tow, coming to the Sugar House to meditate upon what they endured there in the cause of independence. Often they paused to tell him stories about appalling squalor and rampant disease, about brutal guards and bad food, about daring escapes. They wept for comrades taken away every morning by the dead-cart, corpses "piled up like sticks of wood." But time passed. The visitors grew older and increasingly infirm. They came less frequently, then stopped coming altogether. In 1840, itself "grown gray and rusty with age," the Old Sugar House on Liberty Street came down to make way for dull stores and commercial buildings.[1]

Thorburn despaired. The loss of the Old Sugar House was rank historicide—a *"foul deed,"* he cried, born of "the leveling spirit of the day." Such a place should have been preserved as "a monument to all generations of the pains, penalties, sufferings and deaths their fathers met in procuring the blessings they now inherit." But now, alas, "it is probable that in the year two thousand and twenty-one there will not be found a man in New-York who can point out the site whereon stood a prison whose history is so feelingly connected with our revolutionary traditions."

Thorburn's lament for the Old Sugar House comes to us from a windy and sentimental age, when Americans were fond of patriotic bombast and disconcerted by the passing of the Revolutionary generation. Still, he had a point. I had never heard of the place. Nor, for that matter, could I recall coming across much of anything about the broader subject of captivity during the war for independence. I knew the basics: that New York had been the nerve center of British operations in the colonies, that the great majority of Americans taken prisoner had been confined in and around the city, that appalling numbers of them had died. The rest was pretty hazy. A bit of digging turned up a couple of out-of-print monographs and a small handful of scholarly articles, but that was all. Thorburn, it seemed, got it right. The Old Sugar House had indeed slipped the bonds of memory, taking with it a piece of American history that we should have remembered.

My curiosity about the Sugar House eventually blossomed into a study of all the prisons and prisoners of occupied New York. After four or five years of wandering through the sources—private correspondence, diaries, memoirs, newspapers, pension applications, and government records—I reached several conclusions that lie at the heart of *Forgotten Patriots*. First, the numbers involved are a lot bigger than I had anticipated. Before now, approximately 18,000 Americans were thought to have been captured by the British from 1775 to 1783, of whom 8,500 (47 percent) succumbed to disease and starvation. For reasons that will become clear, I think the number of captives may actually have exceeded 30,000 and that 18,000 (60 percent) or more of them did not survive—well over *twice* the number of American soldiers and seamen who fell in battle, now believed to have been around 6,800. It is a mean, ugly story. It is also a story that enlarges our understanding of how the United States was made—not merely by bewigged gentlemen who thought deeply, talked well, and wrote gracefully, but also by thousands upon thousands of mostly ordinary people who believed in something they considered worth dying for.

My second conclusion was that with very few exceptions, contemporary accounts of the British prisons in New York are quite credible. One reason we lost track of this remarkable story, in fact, is that historians have been too quick in recent years to dismiss a handful of prominent witnesses (Ethan Allen, for example) as propagandists who grossly exaggerated conditions in the prisons to enflame public opinion against a cruel enemy. But there is simply too much testimony, from too many different sources and over too many years, to be disposed of so neatly. This does not mean that Americans were correct when they alleged that the British *intended* the deaths of so many captives. My reading of the evidence is that the thousands of Americans who perished in New York during the Revolution were the victims of something well beyond the usual brutalities and misfortunes of war, even eighteenth-century war—a lethal convergence, as it were, of obstinacy, condescension, corruption, mendacity, and indifference. Although the British did not deliberately kill American prisoners in New York, they might as well have done. Did Americans treat their prisoners any better? Not necessarily, though as we will see, circumstances were such that their capacity for inhumanity in this context was never fully tested. Some at least, if only to prove that they were *not* British, attempted to set higher, more humane standards for the treatment of prisoners of war.

Third, it became apparent to me that the prisoners of New York have been forgotten more than once. On several occasions over the last 200 years, a variety of groups and individuals found reason to recall the story and tried to anchor it in public memory with appropriate memorials. That they did not succeed was partly due, as Grant

Thorburn foresaw, to the feverish transformation of Manhattan's built environment. Today, every tangible link with its Revolutionary past has been destroyed except for a chapel holding on bravely in the shadows of downtown skyscrapers, an old iron fence, and a former country house tucked into a corner of upper Manhattan. No wonder even native-born New Yorkers, let alone the millions of visitors who converge on the city every year, have trouble recalling the thousands of American prisoners of war who died there, under circumstances as dismal as any to be found in our history. Two obscure memorials to the prisoners—the Soldiers' Monument in the yard of Trinity Church and the Prison Ship Martyrs' monument in Brooklyn's Fort Greene Park—are not enough to overcome the feeling that New York City, unlike Boston or Philadelphia, has no connection whatsoever to the American Revolution.[2]

What Thorburn could not have predicted is that the story would also become a casualty of Anglo-American reconciliation. In the decades on either side of World War I, as we will discover, the death of thousands of captives during the Revolution was downgraded in American public opinion from an outrage to an embarrassment—a regrettable and minor breach in the friendship of two kindred peoples. Academic historians, eager to rescue the Revolution from flag-waving jingoism and personality cults, shelved the subject. By the 1920s it had disappeared all over again.

Forgotten Patriots is my attempt to take the story down from the shelf, dust it off, and see how it looks now, at the beginning of the twenty-first century. I have refrained from drawing parallels to contemporary events, but I will not be sorry if readers find themselves thinking about Abu Ghraib and Guantánamo Bay, about the evasion of habeas corpus, about official denials and cover-ups, about the arrogance and stupidity that can come with the exercise of great power. I hope they will also see that once upon a time, when the country was young, our own experience with prisoner abuse led us to believe that we are supposed to do better.

Northport, New York
July 4, 2008

FORGOTTEN
Patriots

1

⤜⤝

Brooklyn

THE BIGGEST BATTLE of the Revolutionary War began at the Red Lion Inn at around two o'clock in the morning of August 27, 1776. A passing cold front had put an unseasonable chill in the air, and the handful of American pickets posted nearby, sprigs of green tucked into their hats in lieu of proper uniforms, shivered and yawned while they watched for the enemy. Maybe they heard something beforehand—a muffled cough, horses blowing, the metallic ring of a sword being drawn from its scabbard—but nothing could have prepared them to see two or three hundred redcoats suddenly burst out of the shadows on the double quick, bayonets gleaming in the milky light of a gibbous moon. Mostly raw militia, and badly outnumbered, the Americans got off a few perfunctory rounds. Then, despite orders to hold their ground "at all hazards," they ran for their lives. Their commander, Major Edward Burd, was taken prisoner along with a lieutenant and fifteen privates. More Americans—many more—were about to meet a similar fate.[1]

Named after the public house where King Henry V rested after his great victory at Agincourt, the Red Lion was a small frame building close by the junction of three busy country roads on the western end of Long Island, a stone's throw from Upper New York Bay. Martense Lane, looping through a gap in the hills that formed the island's spine, brought travelers from Flatbush and other villages of Kings County. The Narrows Road came up the shore of the Lower Bay from Denyse's Ferry, the link between Long Island and Staten Island. Finally, just behind the Red Lion, the Gowanus Road led back up to the village of Brooklyn, on the Heights above New York City, skirting the mill ponds and broad tidal marshes along Gowanus Creek. Five days earlier a mixed force of 20,000 British redcoats and green-coated Hessian jaegers—German mercenaries—had come ashore at Gravesend Bay, and General George Washington expected that the Gowanus Road would be one of the routes they would take to attack the American force occupying Brooklyn Heights. This morning, however, the road was full of Burd's feckless militia.[2]

About halfway to the Heights, a mile or so up from the Red Lion, the stampeding Americans were corralled by a pair of energetic officers, roused from sleep by messengers and the rattle of musket fire. One was Colonel Samuel Holden Parsons, a Connecticut lawyer and militia officer recently awarded a commission in the Continental Army; the other was Colonel Samuel Atlee of Pennsylvania, a veteran of the French and Indian War who had brought a battalion of musketry from his state to help Washington defend New York City. The moon would be down soon, so it must have been getting difficult to see, but Parsons and Atlee somehow formed the frightened men into a line to screen the road.[3]

While they waited anxiously for the enemy to appear, General Lord Stirling, the ranking American officer in that part of Long Island, came down from the Heights with detachments of regulars from Pennsylvania, Maryland, and Delaware. By sunup, a little after five o'clock, the total number of Americans on the scene had grown from a few score to 2,100 or more. Massed just down the road from them by now were two full brigades of redcoats and at least part of the kilted Forty-second Royal Highland Regiment (the fabled Black Watch), plus a detachment of Royal Artillery and two companies of local Tories—something like 7,000 men in all, with more on the way. At their head was Major General James Grant, a tough career officer who had famously assured Parliament only the year before that Americans would "never dare to face an English army, and didn't possess any of the qualifications necessary to make a good soldier."[4]

The fighting resumed in earnest at around seven, as Grant funneled the first of his columns into the Gowanus Road by the Red Lion, drums beating the march step and regimental colors snapping

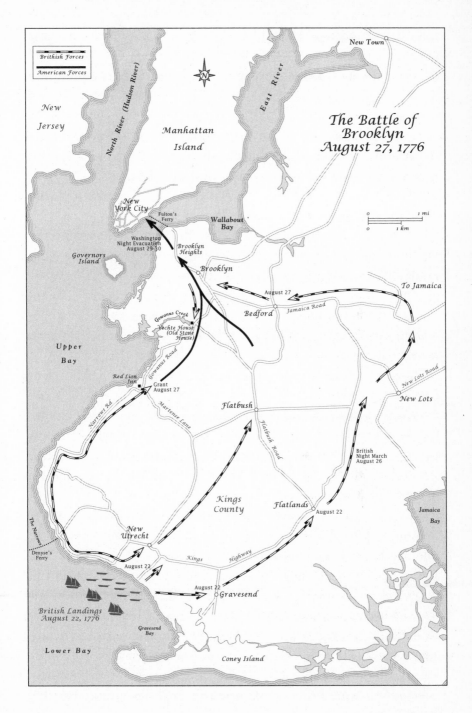

The Battle of Brooklyn August 27, 1776

Brithish Forces
American Forces

New Town

East River

New Jersey

North River (Hudson River)

Manhattan Island

0   1 mi
0   1 km

New York City
Fulton's Ferry
Wallabout Bay

Washington Night Evacuation August 29-30

Brooklyn Heights

Governors Island

Brooklyn

To Jamaica

August 27

Gowanus Creek

Bedford

Jamaica Road

Vechte House (Old Stone House)

Upper Bay

Gowanus Road

New Lots Road

Red Lion Inn

Grant August 27

New Lots

Martense Lane

Flatbush

British Night March August 26

Flatbush Road

The Narrows

Kings County

Flatlands

Jamaica Bay

Denyse's Ferry

New Utrecht

August 22

August 22

Kings Highway

Flatlands

August 22

August 22

Gravesend

British Landings August 22, 1776

Gravesend Bay

Lower Bay

Coney Island

in the bright morning air. Stirling, still getting his defenses set up, sent Atlee's musketeers forward to delay the enemy at a spot where the road narrowed to cross a patch of marsh. Grant deployed for battle, but the Pennsylvanians held steady, braving a hail of grapeshot until Stirling pulled them back to a wooded slope near the road. For the next several hours both sides blazed away with muskets, rifles, mortars, and cannon, rarely more than 100 yards apart. "The balls and shells flew very fast, now and then taking off a head," declared one Maryland soldier. "Our men stood it amazingly well, not even one shewed a Disposition to shrink."

When it looked as though Grant might try to circle behind the American positions, Stirling sent Parsons to occupy a prominent hill east of the Gowanus Road, on the left flank of the American line. Parsons took several hundred men, including a part of Atlee's battalion, and held the hill despite three ferocious assaults that left the slopes littered with enemy dead and wounded. One of Atlee's officers boasted that the Americans had "mowed them down like grass."[5]

It was now early afternoon, and although Atlee's men had not slept or eaten in nearly twenty-four hours, they continued to fight tenaciously in the increasingly oppressive August heat. Then they discovered something worse than hunger or fatigue: they had fallen into a trap and were about to be surrounded. In Atlee's words, the "Grand Body of the British Army" was not in front of them, as they originally believed, but at their backs.[6]

Only later would the Americans tumble to the fact that Grant's move up the Gowanus Road from the Red Lion had been a diversion. So was a second thrust, spearheaded by the jaegers, who had started up the road from Flatbush to Brooklyn around nine or ten in the morning, pushing back 800 defenders under General John Sullivan of New Hampshire. The main enemy force, perhaps 14,000 strong, had actually slipped out of their Flatlands camp the night before in a long column led by General William Howe, commander-in-chief of His Majesty's forces. Completely undetected, the enemy swung east through New Lots and up to Jamaica. By daybreak on the twenty-seventh they had come down the road from Jamaica to Brooklyn as far as Bedford and proceeded to descend on the unsuspecting Americans from behind, cutting them down almost at will. "The Hessians and our brave Highlanders gave no quarters," gloated a British officer. "It was a fine sight to see with what alacrity they dispatched the rebels with their bayonets, after we had surrounded them so they could not resist. Multitudes were drowned and suffocated in morasses—a proper punishment for all Rebels." One report had American riflemen spitted to trees with bayonets.[7]

From east to west, the American lines collapsed in waves of confusion and panic. Along the Gowanus Road, where Atlee and Parsons had managed to hold the British at bay for hours, organized combat degenerated into random clashes and running firefights. By early afternoon, the American army had broken into isolated parties of officers and men trying to reach the safety of the American camp in Brooklyn Heights, plunging through woods and fields to avoid enemy cavalry on the roads. A Pennsylvanian, Lieutenant James McMichael, recalled the slow destruction of his battalion as the men were driven from place to place, skirmishing with the enemy until they finally made it back to the lines at half past three, utterly spent. Eighteen-year-old Michael Graham, also from Pennsylvania, remembered "the confusion and horror of the scene. . . . Our men running in almost every direction, and run which way they would, they were almost sure to meet the British or Hessians." Graham narrowly avoided capture by wading across a swamp. Colonel Parsons and a handful of his men fought their way past the enemy six or seven times, then hid out in heavy woods and returned to their lines at around three o'clock the following morning.[8]

Many surrendered or, disoriented and demoralized, simply dropped their weapons. Frederick Nagel, a Pennsylvania soldier then only fifteen or sixteen years old, recalled that when the enemy captured his colonel after hours of fighting, "we all fled in confusion into some briars and high grass, along a pond. About sunset the British and Hessians came upon us and took us prisoners." Jabez Fitch, a thirty-nine-year-old lieutenant in Parsons's Connecticut brigade, sought cover in a swamp with some companions—only to be surprised on the other side by Hessians, who let go with two heavy volleys that sent the Americans reeling back into the swamp again.

Emerging a second time, close to where they had begun, they were engaged by yet another enemy force. Eventually recognizing that they were surrounded, they agreed to let every man fend for himself. Fitch went north and was soon captured by regulars of the Fifty-seventh Regiment. Later that afternoon, having survived "various Struggles, running thro' the Fire of many of the Enemy's detachments," Colonel Atlee and several dozen weary men surrendered to soldiers of the Seventy-first Highland Regiment. Hessians found General Sullivan in a cornfield, waving a pistol in each hand. General Stirling, too, fell prisoner, but not before organizing a rear-guard action against redcoats now advancing *down* the Gowanus Road. His heroic stand at Nicholas Vechte's stone farmhouse afforded many fleeing Americans time to reach their lines on the far side of Gowanus Creek.[9]

Surrender did not put a man out of harm's way, however, as many Americans quickly found out. A Hessian lieutenant admitted that his troops routinely beat rebels who knelt and begged for quarter. Lieutenant Jonathan Gillett (or Gillet), a farmer from West Hartford, Connecticut, later told his wife that when he gave himself up, enemy soldiers stole his watch, buckles, and other personal possessions, then clubbed him senseless with the butts of their guns. "I never shall forget the Roberys, blows and Insults I met with as well as hunger," he declared. The Hessians who captured Thomas Foster, a Pennsylvania rifleman, stripped him of his clothes, then "put a cord about his neck and hanged him up to the limb of a tree, where they suffered him to remain until he was almost strangled." Eventually, they cut him down and revived him with a little rum—then strung him up again, cut him down, and strung him up a third time. He counted himself lucky to have survived this macabre sport, as the redcoats assured him that Hessians had murdered a number of Americans this way after they had thrown down their weapons. Colonel Atlee's captors marched him off toward Bedford, showering him and a large group of other prisoners with "the most scurrilous and abusive language" and vowing they would all be hanged. On their arrival, the British provost marshal, "one *Cunningham*," confined Atlee and sixteen officers in a mere soldier's tent, so small they had no room to lie down at night.[10]

Also squeezed into that tent in Bedford was Lieutenant Robert Troup, a native New Yorker and recent graduate of King's College (now Columbia University). Troup had been one of only five men assigned to watch the narrow gorge where the road from Jamaica to Bedford cut through the wooded hills of eastern Kings County—the very route, as luck would have it, that the British took to get behind the American lines. Around the same time that Grant's redcoats charged the American pickets at the Red Lion, Troup and his party were scooped up by an advance patrol of dragoons, who rushed them off for interrogation while the main body of General Howe's forces swept through Bedford to fall on the American rear. Howe himself threatened to hang the five prisoners, and the redcoats reportedly amused themselves by seating the Americans on coffins, draping nooses around their necks, and carting them off as if to the gallows. In January 1777, after he had been exchanged, Troup testified that throughout this terrifying ordeal, the British continually berated him and his comrades "with the grossest language" and did so—a real indignity—in the presence of common soldiers. At Bedford, the provost marshal, a British officer he too knew only as "Cunningham," appeared in the company of "a negro with a halter . . . telling them the negro had already hung several, and that he imagined he would hang some more . . . calling them rebels, scoundrels, villains, robbers, murderers, and so forth."[11]

What happened to Atlee and Troup squares with Lieutenant Jabez Fitch's version of events, laid out six months later in a 12,000-word manuscript rather awkwardly entitled "A Narative of the treatment with which the American prisoners were Used who were taken by the British & Hessian Troops on Long Island York Island &c 1776. With some occasional Observations thereon." After surrendering, Fitch wrote, he and a large body of other prisoners were herded off to New Utrecht, passing through a gauntlet of curses and threats from enemy soldiers, while one of the army's camp followers, a woman whose husband had been killed in that day's fighting, pelted them with rocks. When they finally reached New Utrecht, several hundred enlisted men, some gravely wounded, were locked in a barn. Fitch and twenty-odd officers went off to a nearby farmhouse, where they

spent the next two days confined to a "very durty" room. British officers came by to question them, often "with mean & low lived Iso-
lence, Despising & Rideculing the mean appearance of many of us
who had been strip'd & abused by the Savages under their comd:
[command]." Not all their captors behaved this badly, to be sure. The
major in charge treated them with "the greatest Civility & Comple-
sance." Even General Grant, despite his widely publicized contempt
for Americans, presented the officers with a side of mutton and several loaves of bread. But those were the exceptions. For Fitch, captivity was above all else a revelation of inhumanity on a scale he had
never imagined possible among civilized peoples. That the British
and their Hessian allies could beat, rob, and even murder men who
had laid down their arms was so unexpected—so *bewildering*—that at
first he did not know what to make of it.[12]

Not two months after the Declaration of Independence, the Battle of
Brooklyn—a label it acquired almost immediately—dealt the American cause a potentially fatal blow. In its first head-on test against sea-
soned professional soldiers, the ill-trained and poorly equipped
Continental Army had been routed with ease. What remained of it by
sundown on August 27 was huddled miserably on the Heights, waiting for Howe to finish the job and wondering what would become of
comrades led off into captivity. Never again would Washington risk
an encounter on such a scale. Without Brooklyn, moreover, he had
lost any realistic hope of holding on to New York, the new nation's
largest city after Philadelphia. Whether the loss of New York would
in turn end the dream of independence remained to be seen, but
things looked very bad. As Major General Nathanael Greene glumly
reported, "The Country is struck with a pannick."[13]

No one was entirely certain about the number of casualties. The
British may have lost as few as 63 killed and 314 wounded or missing.
Of the 9,000 or so Americans pitted against them, at least 300 died,
though people returning to New York City after the battle seemed to
think the number was much higher. One reported that "the fields and
woods [of Brooklyn] are covered with dead bodies." So did Ambrose
Serle, personal secretary to Admiral Lord Richard Howe, the gen-

eral's older brother, who toured the scene of the fighting only days later. "Putrid dead Bodies" lay everywhere, Serle noted in his journal, and residents of the village could not enter the nearby woods owing to "the Stench of the dead Bodies of the Rebels." Apparently, the British were unable—or unwilling—to clear the battlefield of corpses, as one visitor still noticed the smell in the summer of 1777, nearly a year later.[14]

But by all accounts the most astonishing result of the battle was the number and quality of American captives—three generals (Stirling, Sullivan, and Nathaniel Woodhull), three colonels (including Atlee), four lieutenant colonels, two majors, nineteen captains, and a thousand or more enlisted men. One British officer, flush with victory, believed His Majesty's forces had taken as many as 2,000 prisoners; Earl Percy thought 1,500; Ambrose Serle, 1,200. By contrast, the British netted thirty Americans at Bunker Hill in June 1775, and several hundred more after the failed attack on Québec in December of that same year. Never before, in other words, had so many Americans been taken in arms—"so many," Serle mused, "that we are perplexed where to confine them."[15]

"Perplexed," but not for lack of experience. Thanks to the rising frequency and scale of warfare between the great powers of Europe, the detention of large numbers of enemy captives had become a predictable result of every successful campaign conducted by His Majesty's fleets and armies—predictable enough, at any rate, that a bureaucracy of sorts was already in place to deal with them.

Decades earlier, at the beginning of the War of the Spanish Succession (1702–1713), the Admiralty assigned the business of caring for prisoners of war, military as well as naval, to a temporary Commission for Sick and Hurt Seamen. Shortly after the "War of Jenkins' Ear" (1739–1742) erupted with Spain, the commission became a permanent body commonly referred to as the Sick and Hurt Board. The board's work, as well as its staff and budget, expanded significantly during the War of the Austrian Succession (1744–1748), then again during the Seven Years' War (1756–1763), both of which brought thousands of French and Spanish prisoners to England for detention.

When the latter conflict ended, the Sick and Hurt Board may have had as many as 40,000 enemy captives under close confinement in English jails, old castles and country houses, a converted barracks, an abandoned pottery works, and the like.[16]

In March 1776, expecting that he would soon capture large numbers of American insurgents, General Howe had appointed a Boston Tory named Joshua Loring as his commissary general of military prisoners.* Loring, who reported (in theory, anyway) to the Sick and Hurt Board in London, possessed two unbeatable qualifications for the job: a settled conviction that men who took up arms against their sovereign deserved no mercy, and a beautiful wife, to whom the general had taken a fancy (Loring "fingered the cash," quipped the Tory historian Thomas Jones, while "the General enjoyed madam"). It was now Loring's responsibility to arrange food and shelter for the Americans seized on Long Island. Although his task may have looked rather modest compared to the one faced by the board during the Seven Years' War, he had to contend with the fact that Kings County was plainly unsuitable for incarcerating large numbers of prisoners.[17]

According to a census taken as recently as 1771, the county's entire population barely exceeded 3,600 souls. Brooklyn, the largest village, consisted of only a few score houses and single-story wooden buildings, plus a church. Flatbush, the county seat, was even smaller. New Utrecht, Bedford, New Lots, and Gravesend were little more than rustic hamlets clinging to country lanes and wagon roads. Most of the inhabitants were fourth- or fifth-generation descendants of Dutch and Walloon colonists who came to New Netherland in the middle of the previous century, drawn by some of the most beautiful and fertile farmland on the east coast of North America. Though not caring much for the British, they remained staunchly loyal to the Crown in

---

*Loring's responsibilities did not extend to Americans captured at sea, and we shall see that as their numbers grew, the British would also appoint a commissary for naval prisoners. Etymologically, "military" and "naval" refer to two distinct and separate kinds of power or activity—one taking place on land and concerning soldiers, the other taking place on water and concerning seamen. The difference between them was still quite sharp in eighteenth-century usage, and I have tried, within reason, to respect it in the pages that follow.

large measure because they had prospered under British rule, producing a good part of the grain and cattle that New York City merchants processed and shipped out to feed the slaves on West Indian sugar plantations. Along the way the Dutchmen had acquired slaves of their own—so many that by the middle of the eighteenth century, one of every three people in Kings County was black, proportionally more than any other county north of the Mason-Dixon Line. That British authorities had never hesitated to use force to suppress slave resistance and revolt gave the white master class still further reason to remain loyal.[18]

Hence Loring's dilemma. He really had nowhere to put a mass of prisoners other than in the houses and barns of local farmers or the occasional church. But taking over houses and barns and churches— or pulling them down for materials to construct barracks and stockades—would play havoc with one of the most bountiful agricultural regions in America and one now certain to be a vital source of provisions for the Royal Army and Navy. It would also antagonize one of the few places in the colonies not up in arms against the king.[19]

Washington simplified things for Loring on the night of August 29, when he evacuated Brooklyn Heights and brought the remnants of his army back across the East River into New York City. This celebrated stroke, carried off under the very noses of an unsuspecting foe, spared the Americans a second and undoubtedly terminal confrontation with Howe. It also left the British in nominal control of Queens and Suffolk counties, which were at once placed under martial law and scoured by light horse. Several thousand male residents of the island signed a loyalty oath, swearing their "utter abhorence [sic] of congresses rebellions etc." Others gathered their belongings and fled across Long Island Sound to Connecticut. Suffolk militiamen blustered for a while about putting up a fight, then decided they were better off at home and threw down their weapons.[20]

But Long Island—better than 100 miles from end to end and as much as 20 wide—was far too extensive ever to be entirely pacified by the forces at the disposal of General Howe or of Brigadier General Oliver De Lancey, the Tory boss of those parts of the island not garrisoned by regulars. East of the village of Jamaica, British authority thinned out rapidly, and it was generally conceded that the residents submitted only because they had no alternative. What was more, raiding parties from Connecticut and Rhode Island were soon shuttling back and forth across Long Island Sound in whaleboats, stealing or killing livestock and kidnapping prominent supporters of the Crown. One notably aggressive young officer, Lieutenant Colonel Henry Beekman Livingston, reported to General Washington at the end of September that he had just undertaken "a little excursion upon Long Island" and returned with 3,500 head of sheep and cows from the Shinnecock Hills; give him more men and he would strike the enemy camp at Jamaica itself.[21]

Trying to detain a large quantity of prisoners in such close proximity to what was shaping up as a semi-lawless no man's land and with every prospect of more prisoners to come was clearly asking for trouble. Staten Island, as yet the only other part of America controlled by His Majesty's forces, did not seem safe, either, because it lay too near the rebel-controlled mainland. The rebel general Hugh Mercer led a raid on Richmond village in mid-October that underscored the danger.[22]

As soon as the magnitude of the British victory at Brooklyn became apparent, Loring and Howe therefore did the only thing that made sense under the circumstances: they began transferring their prisoners from Long Island to a handful of the numerous vessels that made up the British invasion fleet. Only the most severely wounded were left behind; they remained in the Flatbush and New Utrecht churches for another six to eight weeks.

On the afternoon of August 29, in a driving rain, armed guards rounded up two dozen American officers and some 400 men in New Utrecht and marched them down to the shore, hands tied behind their backs, and loaded them into flat-bottom boats. Their destination was the *Pacific*, a large transport lying in the Narrows off Staten Island. Once aboard, her captain—Jabez Fitch called him "that son of perdition"— threw them into the hold with "many vile Curses & Execrations" and arranged two cannon to spray them with grapeshot if they made trouble. The *Pacific*'s crew meanwhile taunted them with news that Washington's army had been destroyed, that Congress "was broak up with great Confusion," and that "we were to be sent home to Europe in Confinement," presumably to be tried and executed for treason.

Commissary General Loring himself showed up the next day, taking down everyone's name and rank and chatting affably. "He treated us with Complasance," Fitch recalled, "& gave us Encouragement of further Endulgence." It was all just talk, however, and a day or two later the Americans were switched to the *Lord Rochford*, half the size of the *Pacific* and thus so overcrowded that more than a few officers decided to sleep under the stars on the quarterdeck. Her captain, another of those "very Sovereign & Tyranacal" Englishmen in Fitch's lengthening gallery of rogues, promptly ran her down through the Narrows to Gravesend Bay, where she dropped anchor near three other ships—the *Mentor*, the *Whitby*, and the *Argo*—holding the rest of the Long Island prisoners. Four hard days later, Fitch and about ninety other officers were moved again, this time to the *Mentor*, captained by yet another "worthless lowlived fellow." It dawned on Fitch that putting all the officers together on one ship would make it easier for British recruiters to lure enlisted men into the king's service.[23]

Among the officers now sharing quarters with Fitch on the *Mentor* was Lieutenant Robert Troup. Following his capture at the Jamaica pass, Troup had spent two nights in Bedford and was then removed to Flatbush, where he and a number of other captives passed the next week cooped up in a farmhouse. Its Dutch owner, no friend to the American cause, fed them only biscuits and a little salt pork; they survived, Troup said, only because kindhearted Hessians occasionally gave them some apples and fresh beef. More of the same followed when he and seventy or eighty American officers were marched down to Gravesend Bay and thrown aboard the *Mentor*. Like Fitch, he described her as a filthy, reeking cattle ship ruled by a blasphemous skipper who cursed the Americans as "a pack of rebels" and subjected them to great hardships. He forced them "to lay upon the dung and filth of the cattle without any bedding or blankets." He allowed them each only six ounces of pork and a pint of flour per day and made them drink bilge water. He refused them soap and fresh water to bathe or wash their clothes, though they became "much afflicted with lice and other vermin"—a detail that Fitch too remarked upon. "Very

few of us have been perfectly free from live Stock," was the New Eng-
lander's rather sardonic way of putting it.[24]

In the month that Fitch, Troup, and their fellow officers spent together on the *Mentor,* they whiled away the hours comparing notes
about the disastrous events of August 27 and recounting, in Fitch's
words, "the perticular Circumstances of our first being Taken, & also
the various Treatment, with which we met on that occasion." They
had plenty of stories to pass around, too, some of them not much better than battlefield rumors—like the one about the Hessians who
used a wounded American prisoner for target practice.[25]

The most troubling story, however, concerned the death of General Nathaniel Woodhull, commander of the Suffolk County, New
York, militia and president of the New York Provincial Congress. In
his "Narative," Fitch wrote that when enemy cavalry captured Woodhull in Jamaica, "those Bloodthirsty Savages cut & wounded him in
the head, & other parts of the Body, with their Swords in a most Inhuman manner." Troup also claimed in his affidavit that Woodhull
had been murdered, but supplied additional details that he said he got
directly from Woodhull. The general, Troup said, had been taken the
day after the battle by a troop of light horse under the command of
Captain Oliver De Lancey, Jr., son of Brigadier General De Lancey.
Woodhull told Troup he had surrendered on De Lancey's personal
assurances that he would be "treated like a gentleman"—whereupon,
suddenly and without provocation, De Lancey and his men proceeded to "cruelly hack and cut him" with their swords. Carried
aboard the *Mentor* "in a shocking mangled condition," he too slept on
the bare, filthy deck. He was then moved to the New Utrecht hospital, where he received only perfunctory care and soon died of his
wounds. Even if Fitch and Troup knew that some on the American
side had doubts about Woodhull's devotion to the cause (and it is difficult to imagine how they could have known), the fact remained that
one of the most prominent American prisoners had been barbarously
assaulted by the enemy. What then lay in store for the rest of them?[26]

2

⤚⤙

DESTINED TO
the Cord

O N SUNDAY, SEPTEMBER 15, 1776, Lieutenant Fitch was en-
joying his customary early-morning stroll around the deck of
the *Mentor* when he heard the thunder of big guns to the north—
followed, at about seven o'clock, by "a very Severe Canonade . . .
which lasted for more than an Hour, with great fury." He and his fellow prisoners surmised that some "Action of Importance" was under
way, but did not learn until the next day that the Howe brothers had
launched a massive amphibious invasion of Manhattan from the
Brooklyn side of the East River. In a matter of hours, the British
gained possession of New York City, captured another 20 American
officers and 300 men, and forced Washington to retreat, again, this
time up to Harlem Heights.[1]

"The bad success of our Army," as Fitch wryly termed it, gave
General Howe and Commissary General Loring what they had been
unable to find on Long Island: a secure place to house the growing
number of American prisoners. They took two or three weeks to
work out the details, mainly because of a terrible conflagration that
began in a tavern near Whitehall Slip, east of the Battery, soon after
midnight on September 21. Driven by a brisk wind, it angled northwest across Bowling Green to Broadway, engulfing whole blocks of
houses and shops and casting an eerie orange glow in the sky visible a
hundred miles away. When it finally burned itself out around dawn,
the blaze had cut a mile-long swath of destruction through the heart

of New York, claiming one of every four buildings and laying waste to much of the West Side. The British blamed American spies for starting the fire, but an official investigation failed to produce conclusive evidence one way or the other.[2]

By the end of the month, even so, all the ships with American captives had come up from Gravesend Bay to a new anchorage in the Hudson River opposite King's College, ready to discharge their human cargo. On October 5, the several hundred enlisted men on the *Argo* were deposited on the ferry wharf near the Bear Market. The officers from the *Mentor* followed two days later. Loring, who seems to have supervised this phase of the process personally, had them sign a pledge, or parole, agreeing that if released from close confinement, they would not do or say anything contrary to the interests of the king. He then split them into three groups. Field-grade officers (majors, colonels, and lieutenant colonels) received permission to find suitable lodgings on their own. Soldiers escorted the junior officers from Pennsylvania, Maryland, and Delaware to a house on William Street. Those from New York and New England were taken to a "very large" house (Fitch's description) on the west side of Broadway, just below Warren Street and directly opposite the Common, now City Hall Park. That night, his first on dry land in nearly six weeks, Fitch "slept considerably Comfortable, alth'o I have not forgot the Melancholy Consideration, that I am a Prisoner, & the Time of my Release Altogether unknown."[3]

The city in which Fitch would remain a prisoner for another several months—and where the bulk of all American captives would be held until the end of the war, seven years later—was by September 1776 a half-ruined, pestiferous shell of what it had been before the shooting started. All but a few thousand of its 25,000 inhabitants had long since fled, either to avoid the American troops who arrived in the spring of that same year or to avoid the British troops who ran the Americans out six months later. Between them, the two armies and their camp followers—the thousands of women and children who always accompanied military expeditions—had made a shambles of the place. Labor details had dug trenches across the streets, torn down shade trees to built artillery redoubts, and demolished fences to make barricades. Soldiers had broken into shuttered houses, helped themselves to the china, and

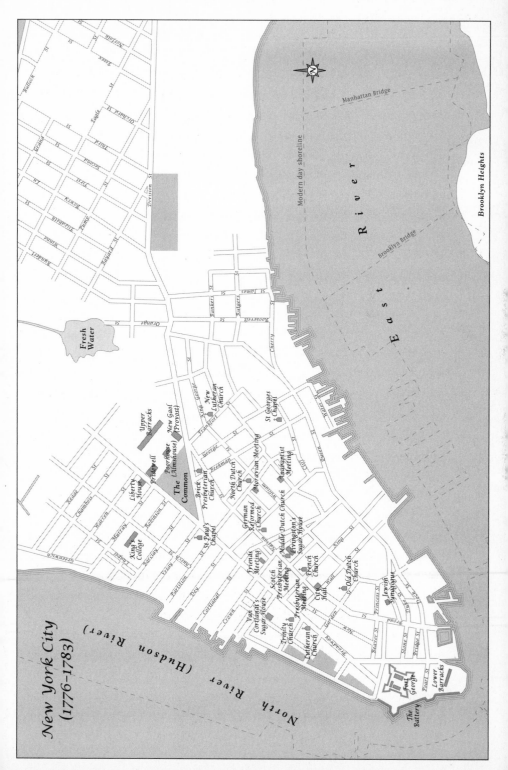

New York City
(1776–1783)

North River (Hudson River)

Fresh Water

East River

Modern day shoreline

Manhattan Bridge

Brooklyn Bridge

Brooklyn Heights

Upper Barracks
New Gaol (Provost)
Poorhouse (Almshouse)
Bridewell
The Common
Liberty St House
King's College
St Paul's Chapel
Brick Presbyterian Church
North Dutch Church
Moravian Meeting
Anabaptist Meeting
New Lutheran Church
St Georges Chapel
German Reformed Church
Middle Dutch Church
Livingsten's Sugar House
Friends Meeting
Scotch Presbyterian Meeting
Presbyterian Meeting
Van Cortlandt's Sugar House
Trinity Church
Lutheran Church
French Church
City Hall
Old Dutch Church
Jewish Synagogue
Fort George
The Battery
Lower Barracks

Pearl St
Stone St
Bridge St
Broad St
Beaver St
Princess St
Garden St
New St
Wall St
King
Crown
Partition
Day
Cortlandt
Barclay
Church St
Robinson St
Chambers St
Warren St
Murray
Greenwich
Vesey
Chapel St
Division St
Orange St
Pump St
Roosevelt St
Rutgers St
Bankers St
St James St
Cherry
Queen St
Water St
Dock
Gold
John St
Beekman
George St
Frankfort St
King George
St James St
Norfolk St
Essex St
Ludlow St
Orchard St
Eagle St
Third St
Grand St
Broome St
Delancey St
Walker St
Elizabeth St
Pump St
Hester St
Brooklyn Bridge

pulled up parquet floors for firewood. Mansions had become regimental infirmaries. The King's College building, cleared of books and equipment, had become a hospital, as had the Baptist Meeting House on Gold Street and the Lutheran church on the corner of William and Frankfort streets. Bivouacs had sprouted on the Common, on the banks of the East River, and on the northern outskirts of town by Lispenard's Meadows, which straddled what is now Canal Street. Officers had stabled their mounts in private gardens and churchyards.

Adding to the mess and confusion were the throngs of Tory refugees from every colony who now began to converge on Manhattan, joined by hundreds, perhaps thousands, of runaway slaves seeking the protection of His Majesty's armed forces. Within six months of the British takeover, this influx boosted New York's civilian population to 11,000. In another few years it would reach an unprecedented 33,000. The competition for housing became so intense that many residents wound up pitching tents in the burned-over blocks west of Broadway, a neighborhood promptly dubbed "Canvass Town." There and everywhere, overflowing privies and open pools of human waste caused widespread sickness as well as an unpleasant odor that hung over the town even in winter. Nicholas Cresswell, an Englishman who passed through town in 1777, was dismayed to see "such a number of people being crowded together in so small a compass almost like herrings in a barrel, most of them very dirty and not a small number sick of some disease, the Itch, Pox, Fever, or Flux." The effect, he wrote, "is a complication of stinks enough to drive a person whose sense of smelling was very delicate and his lungs of the finest contexture, into a consumption in the space of twenty-four hours." Complaining about poor sanitation (or anything else) was pointless because there was no one to complain to: once the British had control of the city, Howe had proclaimed martial law, suspended the civilian government, closed the courts, and appointed a commandant, Major General James Robertson, who exercised more or less dictatorial power in the city.[4]

Before the war, the "very large" house on Broadway where Jabez Fitch found himself sequestered with other northern officers had served as the headquarters of the New York Sons of Liberty. The

Sons had named it Liberty House, or Hampden House, after John Hampden, a seventeenth-century English libertarian. British authorities confiscated the building as rebel property after the city fell on September 15, and by the time of Fitch's arrival, it already held a number of New England officers captured during the American retreat. Continued skirmishing in upper Manhattan during October and November 1776 would bring a steady trickle of newcomers, and Liberty House was soon home to upwards of two dozen men.

How they all fit into the two downstairs rooms and the one "long room" upstairs is a mystery. They could walk around the tiny outside yard, though under the terms of their paroles they were honor-bound to go no further without a pass from Commissary General Loring. When inclement weather kept them all inside, the lack of space must have been almost unbearable. At least once, desperate for a bit of privacy, Fitch climbed up into the garret, or attic, "where I spent some Time very agreably in Retirement, more than I had had for a long Time." As bad as the overcrowding, though, was the mind-numbing boredom, one empty day blurring into the next, broken only by the occasional visitor, by arguments among the increasingly short-tempered prisoners, or by rumors from the battlefield. "All things seem to go on in the old wearisom Channel," Fitch wrote dejectedly toward the end of October. "The Time now hangs heavy. . . . How much longer the painfull Sceene will continue, God only knows."[5]

Harder to endure than either overcrowding or boredom was the chronic, aching hunger. By custom, prisoners of war in the eighteenth century were entitled to receive two-thirds the weekly rations of regular soldiers on duty, which in the British Army (according to General Howe) consisted of seven pounds of bread and seven of beef, supplemented by what were called "small species"—four ounces of butter or cheese, eight ounces of oatmeal, three pints of peas, and perhaps a few ounces of rice, if available. On average, such a diet would provide 2,460 calories per day, no more than adequate for active men (see Appendix A). Thus, prisoners of war should have received 1,640 calories per day. Even if he always got every scrap allotted him, a completely sedentary prisoner weighing 160 pounds would lose about one pound of body weight per week.[6]

The difficulty was this: The Howe brothers commanded an expeditionary force of better than 33,000 men—not merely the largest ever
seen in North America, indeed the largest such operation ever
mounted thus far by a European state, but larger than the prewar pop-
ulations of either New York or Philadelphia, the two biggest urban
centers in the colonies. Every day, day after day, this mobile military
metropolis consumed prodigious quantities of stores, including thirty-
two *tons* of food. Local farmers and stockmen alone could not feed so
many mouths, not even under the most favorable conditions. British
authorities had therefore cobbled together a system for contracting,
collecting, and transporting food as well as equipment from home,
across 3,000 miles of open ocean. It worked well, on the whole, but
never well enough to make up for the losses caused by bad weather,
privateers, dishonest contractors, careless inspectors, and corrupt
quartermasters. Quite often stockpiles shrank to the point that the
army itself had to go on short rations. When that happened, prisoners
inevitably got less food and got the poorest food—if they got food at
all. Because malnutrition impairs the body's immune function, they
became easy prey to typhus, dysentery, and other infectious diseases of
the skin, lungs, and gastrointestinal tract. The lack of fresh fruit and
vegetables in their diet led to a chronic vitamin C deficiency, guaran-
teeing that many would also experience the bleeding gums, open
sores, tooth loss, and listlessness that were the symptoms of scurvy.[7]

Although Fitch and the other residents of Liberty House had permission to buy additional provisions, Loring would not allow them to
shop every day and they often had to get by on rather meager fare—
a saucer of chocolate for breakfast, a flour pudding for dinner, a dish
of "Pease Butter & Rice" for supper—not enough to stay healthy for
very long. They survived thanks in large measure to the generosity of
a few city residents, who often had too little to eat themselves. "It was
the poor & those in low Circumstances only, who were thoughtfull of
our Necessitys," Fitch recalled, and "their unparallel'd generosity,
was undoubtedly the happy means of preserving many Lives." Robert
Troup made a similar point. Except for the addition of one ounce of
butter per week per man, plus a little rice, provisions were no better
than they had been on the *Mentor*; compounding their misery, Loring

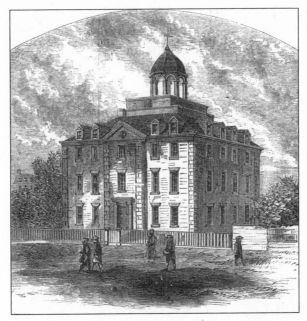

The Provost. Erected on the Common in 1759, it
served for many years as the municipal jail. Some of its
rooms held French prisoners during the Seven Years'
War. From 1776 to 1783 the British provost marshal
filled it with captured American officers as well as
civilians charged with abetting the rebellion. One
prisoner, Captain Alexander Graydon, remembered it
as "that engine for breaking hearts."

supplied them with only enough fuel for three days of every week.
Many became sick and would have perished, Troup wrote, "if they
had not been supported by the benevolence of some poor persons and
common prostitutes, who took pity of their miserable situation and
alleviated it."[8]

As tough as things got in Liberty House, they were by all accounts a
lot tougher in the provost marshal's jail—known as the "provost
guard" or "Provost," for short—a three-and-a-half-story stone building that stood on the east side of the municipal Common, facing
Chatham Street, now Park Row. Originally designed to serve as the
municipal jail, it had six cells on each of its top two floors and three

large vaults in the cellar, which functioned as dungeons. A guard room occupied one corner of the ground floor, the balance of which was taken up by the office and living quarters of the provost marshal.[9]

Although it continued to hold the usual assortment of felons and debtors, the Provost's most conspicuous occupants after the occupation began were high-ranking American officers and "state prisoners"—civilians accused of supporting the rebellion. Their numbers fluctuated widely during the war, sometimes dropping to a comparative handful, sometimes rising to sixty or more. At the upper end it would have been even more oppressively crowded than Liberty House, with an average of ten men locked up day and night in a cell that probably measured twenty feet by thirty and held little or no furniture other than the "necessary tubs" in which they relieved themselves. (One of the state prisoners once shared a cell in the Provost with *twenty* men.)[10]

Those discomforts paled, however, alongside the studied brutality of Provost Marshal Captain William Cunningham, the same officer Atlee and Troup had encountered in Bedford after the Battle of Brooklyn. Adrian Onderdonk, a leading Queens County patriot who had been arrested by dragoons shortly after that debacle, spent four harrowing weeks in the Provost. When his friends finally got him out, feeble and emaciated, he told them of Cunningham's penchant for patrolling the halls with "Richmond," his black servant, threatening to hang prisoners who annoyed him and kicking over bowls of soup left outside their cell doors by charitable townsfolk. A Captain Birdsall asked Cunningham for pen and paper to write his family, only to have the provost marshal call him "a damned rebel" and run him through the shoulder with his sword. Another prominent Queens County patriot, blind old Elias Baylis of Jamaica, who had been severely beaten by his British guards while imprisoned in the New Utrecht church, was then hauled to New York and turned over to Cunningham, who had him beaten some more. He languished there for two months, consoling himself, it was said, by singing the 142nd Psalm: "Listen to my cry, for I am in desperate need; rescue me from those who pursue me, for they are too strong for me. Set me free from my prison, that I may praise your name." When finally

Van Cortlandt's Sugar House. Trinity Church is visible in the background.

released, Baylis was in such poor health that he died crossing the East River en route to his home.[11]

In time, as stories like these began to circulate around the colonies, it was said that Tories could terrify a rebel into submission merely by threatening to have him locked up in the Provost—without the inconvenience of a trial, naturally, as General Howe's proclamation of martial law had closed the courts. Not that Cunningham's brother officers always approved of his methods. With some embarrassment, one of them confided to Captain Alexander Graydon of Philadelphia, disapprovingly, that Cunningham would, in the evening, "traverse his domain with a whip in his hand, sending his prisoners to bed, with the ruffian like *Tattoo* of, *Kennel ye sons of bitches! Kennel, G–d damn ye!*"[12]

Upwards of 1,000 enlisted men had meanwhile been crammed into buildings whose owners were identified with the rebellion in one way or another. The vast majority, as many as 700 or 800 men in all, were confined to the Old North Dutch Church on William Street between Ann and Fair (now Fulton). The remainder appear to have been sent to two of the city's five sugar refineries, called "sugar houses"—arguably its most massive and foreboding structures: Van Cortlandt's on the

Livingston's Sugar House on Liberty (formerly Crown) Street. "*Till within a few years past, there stood in Liberty-street a dark stone building, grown gray and rusty with age, with small, deep windows exhibiting a dungeon-like aspect. . . . It was five stories high; and each story was divided into two dreary apartments, with ceilings so low, and the light from the windows so dim, that a stranger would readily take the place for a jail. . . . There is a strong jail-like door opening on Liberty-street, and another on the southeast, descending into a dismal cellar, scarcely allowing the mid-day sun to peep through its window gratings. When I first saw this building–some fifty years ago–there was a walk, nearly broad enough for a cart to travel around it . . . where, for many long days and nights, two British or Hessian soldiers walked their weary rounds, guarding the American prisoners.*" Grant Thorburn, 1845.

northwest corner of Trinity churchyard, and Livingston's on Crown Street (now Liberty Street), next door to the Middle Dutch Church. (After Van Cortlandt's was closed as a prison in 1777, people began referring to Livingston's as *the* Sugar House.)[13]

Conditions in these prisons made the Provost look almost comfortable. Frederick Nagel remembered that he and about 700 other American soldiers were "all put together in one large church, and kept in the church with the window-shutters shut, for about ten days, and fed on nothing but green apples, and drank water out of old pork barrels. . . . At the end of ten days we got some bread." A Lieutenant Catlin from Connecticut, captured on September 15, told of receiving nothing to eat for forty-eight hours, then struggling to survive on scraps of spoiled pork, wormy bread, and brackish water. Predictably,

The North Dutch Church on William Street. In September 1776, to accommodate hundreds of American prisoners, the pews were removed and planks laid between the balconies to create an upper floor. The building was demolished in 1875.

illness followed swiftly on the heels of malnutrition and overcrowding. Toward the end of October, Jabez Fitch learned from Mrs. Archer—one of the sympathetic women who regularly brought food and news to Liberty House—that the imprisoned American soldiers "grow Remarkably sick & Die very fast."[14]

The next few days brought more such reports, and on or about November 3, Colonel Samuel Miles and Colonel Atlee took it upon themselves to write General Washington about the "truly deplorable" circumstances of the prisoners and pleading for help. "Their being confined so long upon salt Provisions, and the common pump Water, which in New York is very bad, and their exceeding great want of Cloathing, has rendered them so very unhealthy that unless something is shortly done for them, they almost invariably perish." Although "General Howe has been good enough to order each man a Shirt," they continued, "unless a speedy exchange takes place, or some Method fall'n upon to furnish them with Cloathing, Death must relieve them from their present miserable Situation."[15]

Because their letter had to be approved by General Howe's staff before going out under a flag of truce, what Miles and Atlee told Washington soon became common knowledge around British headquarters. Captain Mackenzie of the Royal Welch Fusiliers resented the implication that American prisoners were being mistreated. He agreed that their condition had become "really dreadful, and their dirty, unhealthy, and desponding appearance enough to shock one." But, he declared with all the hauteur of an eighteenth-century officer-gentleman, none of that was the fault of their captors:

> With respect to their provisions they have no real cause of complaint, as they are served with the same kind of provisions issued to The King's troops, at two third allowance, which is the same given to The King's troops when on board Transports. They certainly are very Sickly, owing to their want of Clothing and necessaries, salt provisions, confinement, foul air, & little exercise. They are confined principally in the Churches, Sugar houses, and other large buildings, and have the liberty of walking in the yards. But they are such low spirited creatures, particularly the Americans, that if once they are taken sick they seldom recover.[16]

Captain Mackenzie might have added that a "real cause for complaint" was of no consequence anyway, since the British were under no formal obligation to take better care of their prisoners. The rise of nation-states in early modern Europe had brought a degree of predictability to the conduct of war and valorized certain precepts and customs bearing on the treatment of prisoners—that disarmed adversaries should not be executed, humiliated, tortured, or mutilated; that they should not be denied ransom, prosecuted as criminals, or enslaved; that they should not be denied appropriate food, clothing, and shelter. But none of this had been codified in multinational treaties or conventions, nor would it be for more than a century. The "rules of war" or "law of arms" explicated by classicists and jurists were largely theoretical and essentially unenforceable. They were not rules or laws at all, strictly speaking, merely optimistic guidelines for mitigating the severity of armed conflict between purportedly civilized princes. Whether they even applied in cases of domestic insurrection or rebellion was (and still is) open to question.[17]

There were, on the other hand, supposed to be significant *social* constraints on the conduct of officers. Despite the creation of the Royal Naval Academy in 1732 and the Royal Military Academy in 1741—both evidence of an emerging post-feudal professionalism—military rank in Britain remained intimately connected to inherited property and privilege. Only someone entitled by birth to the deference of others was believed capable of leading men in war: gentility, not expertise, constituted the foundation of an officer's authority. Or as Benjamin Thompson, the future Count Rumford, would have it: "Men cannot bear to be commanded by others that are their superiors in nothing."[18]

This was no theoretical abstraction. In Britain, army officers purchased their commissions, typically at prices so steep—£1,500 for a captain, £3,500 for a lieutenant-colonel, £5,000 for a full colonel—that the service essentially belonged to the few hundred wealthy families who ran the country. (The purchasing power of £5,000 in 1777 was roughly comparable to $880,000 in 2006. An income of £70, the pay of a lowly ensign, would be equivalent to about $12,300. A man could not climb very high on that kind of money.) The navy was rather less aristocratic as well as more professional than the army, and naval commissions were not supposed to be for sale. Even so, they played a large role in the patronage and corruption that bound men with power to men with ambition—besides which the first lord of the admiralty, who kept a mistress with expensive tastes, was not above accepting money in return for plum appointments.[19]

As gentlemen, British officers were expected to exhibit a genteel appearance, polished speech, graceful manners, and perhaps even a smattering of education. Always their most urgent task, however, was the cultivation and defense of their "honor." That powerful word summoned to mind an ensemble of chivalric virtues—candor, integrity, manliness, devotion to king and country, courage under fire, fortitude, and the good opinion of others—any of which could be jeopardized by a careless word, a broken promise, or the merest hint of cowardice. By the same token, honor was a guide for evaluating and acknowledging the conduct of others. Showing disrespect to an honorable man was tantamount to physical assault, and no less dangerous, because a man who failed to defend his honor to the last extremity did not deserve it anyway, hence the close connection between honor and dueling. Of course, some men felt this obligation more strongly than others. Although all men could behave honorably, the honor of a gentleman was somehow more precious and exquisite, more finely tuned, more sensitive, than that of lesser men. A gentleman carefully calibrated his relations with others, seeking to be respectful as well as respected, neither offending another's sense of honor nor permitting offense to his own. Men of coarser sensibilities, oblivious to nuance and complexity, were irrelevant.[20]

Inasmuch as the propertied classes throughout eighteenth-century Europe fussed and fretted endlessly over honor, officers naturally grew to see themselves as members of an exclusive international fraternity, or guild, of warriors. Though divided by language and allegiance, they shared a code that prescribed the honorable way to negotiate truces, lay sieges, offer parlay, accept surrender, and forage for supplies. (There are certain basic maxims, General John Burgoyne remarked to General Horatio Gates, "upon which all men of honour think alike.") Importantly, the code enjoined officers to behave with "complaisance" toward prisoners. It also allowed for the release of captured brother officers on "parole," their solemn promise not to rejoin the fight by word or deed until exchanged. Common soldiers did not qualify for parole because they were not gentlemen and could not be counted on to keep their word.[21]

However well this code of officers and gentlemen worked elsewhere to ensure the reasonably decent treatment of captives, it rapidly unraveled in the American Revolution. At times mere exigency was the culprit. Consider, for example, an unusual scene recorded in the diary kept by a seventeen-year-old private, Jeremiah Greenman of Rhode Island, one of the Americans captured outside Québec. One day in June 1776, General Guy Carleton, the governor of Canada, came to talk with Greenman and other prisoners still confined there. Had they fared well? Carleton asked. Uncertain where this was going, the prisoners answered with caution: "We told him we had fared well for ye Stayshon we was in." To their astonishment, the governor then offered to release them on parole! They assured him he could depend on their "fidelity" and eagerly signed a pledge to take no further part in the fighting until exchanged for British prisoners of war. But after seven months of confinement in a "hole not fit for dogs," Greenman added candidly, "we would [have] sign'd any thing thay brought to us if that would carry us home." Six months later, back in Rhode Island, he broke his parole and enlisted for another tour of duty with the Continental Army.[22]

The problem was that paroling ordinary soldiers—men not bred up, like proper gentlemen, to fear the disgrace of faithlessness—subverted the assumptions and expectations that permitted parole in the first place. In the short run, Carleton's action certainly benefited everyone involved, as the Americans got to go home and he no longer had to provide them with food and shelter. Yet in the long run, by weakening the hold of established martial norms on officers and men alike, that same action increased the likelihood that the treatment of later American captives would be guided by nothing more than the convenience of their captors—which, absent a clear and enforceable body of international law governing prisoners of war, could have disastrous consequences. Besides, Carleton's sense of honor as an officer and gentleman had not prevented him from treating his prisoners worse than dogs; if he then extracted their promises not to take up arms again, who could fault them for playing along until they were safely out of his reach? Promises extracted under duress are promises made to be broken.

Exigency was only one reason for breaking the rules, however. Another stemmed from the widespread impression that the American army—at least at the beginning of the war—was an undisciplined rabble led by men without the social status necessary for genuine officers. The Americans themselves admitted as much. General Richard Montgomery had remarked before the invasion of Canada in 1775, "I wish some method could be fallen upon of engaging *gentlemen* to serve; a point of honor and more knowledge of the world, to be found in that class of men, would greatly reform discipline, and render the troops much more tractable." Opinions changed as the war developed, but it remained a nice question as to whether men who in civilian life had been merchants and tradesmen, even plain farmers, deserved the courtesies ordinarily due real gentlemen in uniform—and if captured, whether it was appropriate to exchange them, rank for rank, as if they were social equals. When Captain Frederick Mackenzie of the Royal Welch Fusiliers heard rumors that an exchange of officers might take place after the Battle of Brooklyn, it appalled him to think "we should treat with them as if on an equality."[23]

Indeed, the very sight of "men calling themselves officers" (Lord George Germain's tart phrase) could provoke acts of flagrant intimidation and violence against captured Americans that would have been condemned in Europe—which accounts for that gauntlet of insults, robberies, threats, and beatings experienced by many American prisoners, especially officers, after the battle of Brooklyn. One incredulous Hessian remarked: "Among the prisoners are many so-called colonels, lieutenant colonels, majors, and other officers, who, however, are nothing but mechanics, tailors, shoemakers, wigmakers, barbers, etc. Some of them were soundly beaten by our people, who would by no means let such persons pass for officers." A Lieutenant Bardeleben likewise observed that "prisoners who knelt and sought to surrender were beaten. . . . Most of their officers are no better dressed and until recently were ordinary manual laborers." General Sullivan, a country lawyer from New Hampshire, escaped a thrashing, but his captors relieved him of his valuables and "treated him so roughly" that he complained personally to the Hessian commander, General Leopold Philip von Heister. Despite General Stirling's claim to a lapsed Scottish earldom—or perhaps because of it—soldiers ransacked his baggage, made off with his camp furniture (valued at better than £500), and stole two of his horses. Sullivan and Stirling soon found themselves being wined and dined by Lord Howe aboard his flagship, the *Eagle*, but the gesture had less to do with a regard for their rank than with the desire of the Howes to use them as emissaries to Congress. Ambrose Serle, the admiral's secretary, snidely referred to the two American officers as "Ld. Stirling (so called) & Mr. (called Genl.) Sullivan."[24]

The obligations and expectations of honor were not the only sources of resentment against American prisoners. No less important was the peculiar vulnerability of the emerging British state to provincial unrest. When George III came to the throne in 1760, "Great Britain"—formed by the union of the kingdoms of England and Scotland, in 1707—had only just begun to command the hearts and minds of his subjects. They were still learning the words to "God Save the King" and "Rule, Britannia," new anthems for a new, broadly based sense of national pride and purpose. New patriotic societies and civic organizations were springing up to advance the nation's commerce and manufactures, and new steps were being taken, such as the founding of the British Museum and the launching of the *Encyclopedia Britannica*, to promote national learning and culture. Yet it was too soon to take either stability or unity for granted, and the rich men who ran the country were not at all certain that this new patriotism, full of populist possibilities, should be encouraged. Urban rioting and rural discontent were endemic, exacerbated now by the brutal hardships of what later generations called the Industrial Revolution. Old uncertainties over Parliamentary supremacy and the Protestant Succession to the throne continued to flicker on the horizons of public life. Beyond the borders of England proper, the authority of the government in London, let alone any sense of "Britishness," often felt contingent and fragile.[25]

It was particularly significant that England's Gaelic-speaking periphery had a long history of instability and upheaval. Ireland, with twice the white population of the North American colonies, still experienced cycles of violence against landlords and officials. The Scots, slow to accept Union, rose in 1715. They rose again in 1745 behind Bonnie Prince Charlie, pretender to the English throne, and when his army crossed the border, advancing perilously close to London itself, rumors flew that France would send him 10,000 troops and that

Wales, too, stood poised to take up arms. To put the rebellion down, the government had to bring in Dutch, Swiss, and German auxiliaries, and though the bloody massacre at Culloden Moor put an end to the "Forty-five," the English capital had been treated to a lesson in the dangers of provincial rebellion it was not soon to forget.[26]

After the middle of the eighteenth century, if not earlier, colonial Americans grew accustomed to thinking of themselves as an integral part of this far-flung, "British" nation. They spoke and dressed and furnished their homes according to British standards. They cheered the victories of British fleets and armies, they boasted of their growing importance as a market for British manufactured goods, and they rejoiced in the accession of George III (the first Hanoverian monarch to address his subjects in English rather than German). In 1770, at a cost of £1,000, the residents of New York City even raised a gilded equestrian statue of the king in Bowling Green. The following year, a pair of Princeton undergraduates, Hugh Henry Brackenridge and Philip Freneau, completed "The Rising Glory of America," an epic patriotic poem that foresaw a day when the Union Jack would wave from the Atlantic to the Pacific.[27]

It was not inconsistent for Americans to revel in their Britishness even while defying Parliament's repeated attempts to tax them without their consent: the way they saw it, taxation without representation made a mockery of their expectation of full and equal membership in a greater "Britain." On the other side of the Atlantic, however, a decade of colonial defiance—from the Stamp Act crisis of 1765 to the meeting of the First Continental Congress in 1774—only made Americans seem *less* British. It reawakened the specter of provincial separatism, kindled national pride, and prompted increasingly strident demands that the government arrest all the American "rebels" and haul them back to England for trial on charges of sedition and treason.[28]

After he became prime minister in 1770, the amiable and accommodating Frederick North (better known by the courtesy title of Lord North) tried to steer a course between intransigence and outright capitulation to colonial protest. Within a few years, however, he too succumbed to the rage for punitive action. Early in 1775—setting the stage for the clashes that followed at Lexington and Concord—Lord North's government instructed General Thomas Gage, Howe's predecessor as commander-in-chief, to round up the principal troublemakers in Massachusetts. Doctor Samuel Johnson fanned the flames with *Taxation No Tyranny*, a famously successful warning against leniency. "Nothing can be more noxious to society," Johnson wrote, "than that erroneous clemency, which, when a rebellion is suppressed, exacts no forfeiture, and establishes no securities, but leaves the rebels in their former state." Besides, as he had said previously, the Americans were "a race of convicts, and ought to be thankful for anything we allow them short of hanging."[29]

The king, too, wanted "decisive exertions." In August 1775, responding to the outbreak of a shooting war between colonists and redcoats in New England, he issued a belligerent Proclamation for Suppressing Rebellion and Sedition. It referred darkly to "dangerous and ill-designing" Americans who were "traitorously preparing, ordering, and levying War against Us," and he enjoined his loyal subjects throughout the realm to put down "all traitorous Conspiracies and Attempts against Us, Our Crown and Dignity." Lurid predictions began circulating on both sides of the Atlantic about the grief that awaited Americans captured in arms against their lawful sovereign. Holt's *New-York Journal* reprinted one particularly emphatic warning, taken from a recent London newspaper: "As every rebel, who is taken prisoner, has incurred the pain of death by the law martial, it is said that Government will charter several transports, after their arrival at Boston to carry the culprits to the East Indies for the Company's service. As it is the intention of Government only to punish the ringleaders and commanders *capitally*, and to suffer the inferior Rebels to redeem their lives by entering into the East India Company's service." At the end of December 1775, Parliament fell into step behind the king with the American Prohibitory Act. Essentially a declaration of war, the act embargoed all commerce with the American colonies on the grounds that the colonists there "have set themselves in open rebellion." American ships found at sea in violation of the embargo were to be seized, their cargoes declared forfeit, and their crews forcibly impressed into the Royal Navy.[30]

No one approved these draconian measures more heartily than the North administration's new colonial secretary, Lord George Germain. From the time he took office in November 1775 to his resignation six years later, Germain proved a more ruthless and unyielding advocate of force than either the king or the prime minister. Born George Sackville, Lord Germain had grown up in Ireland, where his father, the Duke of Dorset, ruled as lord lieutenant. In 1737, then twenty-one, Sackville purchased a commission as captain of cavalry; just two years later, he became a lieutenant colonel and won commendation for his zeal in helping to crush the Forty-five at Culloden. Over the next twenty years, rising to the rank of major general, he acquired a reputation for both personal bravery and unbearable arrogance. His military career ended abruptly in 1760 when a court martial found him guilty of disobeying orders at the recent battle of Minden. He then made his way into Parliament and began to rehabilitate his career as one of Lord North's staunchest allies. In 1770, the same year his patron became prime minister, Sackville assumed the title of Lord Germain; by 1775, when he entered the cabinet, he was already well known for denouncing Americans as "rebellious scoundrels" and expressing his wish to see them swinging alongside other malefactors on the gallows at London's Tyburn Prison.[31]

Lord Germain's arrival on the scene is a reminder that Ireland and Scotland loomed large in the backgrounds of the soldiers and politicians bent on suppressing the American rebellion. Up to 15 percent of the House of Commons—as many as fifty or sixty members at a time—held commissions in the regular army or navy. Many had had firsthand experience with the turbulent Irish and Scots—certainly many more than knew anything at all about the American colonies or their inhabitants. Moreover, a third of the "British" officers who served in the colonies during the Revolutionary War were Scots by birth. Behind them streamed regiments of men who probably spoke better Gaelic than English—such as the highlanders of the Black Watch who drove the Americans back from the Red Lion on that August morning in 1776 and cut them down in the hills above Flatbush when they tried to surrender. For after Culloden, ironically, no one had become more devoted than the Scots to the new British state, and

Lord George Germain.

General Sir William Howe.

to their own advancement in it. They knew about rebellion. They knew it should be met with unflinching, humiliating retribution—or at least that had been their experience.[32]

But not everyone in Britain saw colonial defiance as a threat to national unity and stability. Opposition spokesmen in Parliament often objected that it was misleading and inflammatory to apply the term "rebel" to people engaged in the defense of their traditional rights as Englishmen. "The Americans are resisting acts of violence and injustice," explained the Duke of Richmond. "Such resistance is neither treason nor rebellion but . . . perfectly justified in every possible political and moral sense." That was also the view of David Hartley,

Benjamin Franklin's friend. "I shall never call these men rebels, nor their cause rebellion," Hartley declared, "but a justifiable resistance." None of this went unnoticed in the colonies. Many years later, in a shrewd meditation on the power of language in politics, John Adams recalled how "the Word Rebellion" was used to work the people of England into "a Pitch of Passion and Enthusiasm" for war. "It is only necessary to let loose a single Word to stir up Armies, Navies and nations to unlimited Rage," Adams wrote. "The Word Rebellion [was] too often repeated from the Throne, and echoed from both Houses of Parliament: too often repeated in the Prayers of the Church; in News Papers and Pamphlets, in private Conversation, and in the dispatches of our Generals and Admiralty, not to have had its Full Effect."[33]

By 1775 or 1776, the officers of His Majesty's armed forces in America had also succumbed to "unlimited Rage." Bloodied at Lexington and Concord, then bloodied again at Bunker Hill, they were straining at the leash—impatient, as a captain in the King's Own Regiment put it, "to scourge the rebellion with rods of iron." Americans were "upstart vagabonds, the dregs and scorn of the human species," he declared, and if reestablishing British authority meant "almost extirpating the present rebellious race," so be it. Admiral Samuel Graves, commander of the Royal Navy's squadron in Boston, agreed that "burning and laying waste the whole country" was just the ticket (and then proved he could do it by firebombing Falmouth, Maine, in October 1775). And given the climate of opinion back home, who could doubt that a Culloden-style war of extirpation would be wildly popular? Politicians and pamphleteers had successfully marginalized the Americans as rebels, the king had pronounced them outlaws, and the new colonial secretary wanted them strung up as traitors. Of course, not everyone in uniform felt this way. As in Parliament, conciliation and forbearance had their advocates, but also as in Parliament, there were never enough of them and their influence declined sharply once the fighting began.[34]

The thousand-odd Americans who surrendered during the Battle of Brooklyn thus faced a future fraught with unusual peril. Unprotected by international agreements or by the code of honor that regulated the conduct of officers and gentlemen, they were at the complete mercy of their enraged captors. As Captain Mackenzie of the Royal Welch Fusiliers wrote soon after the battle, captured Americans should not really be considered prisoners of war at all. They were nonpersons, to be used in any way that would most effectively put an end to the insurrection:

> Rebels taken in arms forfeit their lives by the laws of all Countries. The keeping all the Rebel prisoners taken in arms, without any immediate hope of release, and in a state of uncertainty with respect to their fate, would certainly strike great terror into their army; whereas now, captivity has nothing dreadful in it; and it rather encourages them to continue their opposition to the utmost extremity, when they find, contrary to every expectation, that capital punishment has not been inflicted on any of those who have fallen into our hands. Not one Rebel has suffered death yet, except in Action.[35]

Even *referring* to captured Americans as prisoners of war was out of the question, lest it appear to concede the reality of American independence and the legitimacy of Congress. Commanders in the field were especially careful on this point. As early as August 1775, a full year before the Battle of Brooklyn, General Gage had received a complaint from General Washington that American officers, captured while fighting "in the Cause of Liberty and their Country" on Bunker Hill, were moldering in the Boston jail like felons. Washington urged Gage to treat them like proper prisoners of war, both out of regard for the "Rights of Humanity" as well as the "Claims of Rank." Nonsense, Gage shot back: he recognized no rank not derived from the king; and anyhow, the men in question had been shown only "care and kindness," though they were rebels and traitors, not prisoners of war, and by law "destined to the cord."[36]

Gage, the son of an Anglo-Irish peer and yet another graduate of the Culloden school of counterinsurgency on duty in the colonies, must have relished the thought of hanging the rebels whose stout resistance to his forces in Massachusetts had by this time effectively ruined his career. Lords North and Germain, conscious that hanging rebels had a broad base of support inside the government as well as out, might well have let Gage give it a try. That they did not was due in large measure to the appearance of one Ethan Allen, a bellowing, brawling frontiersman with a taste for ideas and a genius for self-promotion.[37]

The world first took notice of Ethan Allen in the early 1770s, when he emerged as "colonel commandant" of the Green Mountain Boys, a self-constituted militia whose main purpose was keeping New York claimants out of the New Hampshire Grants (the disputed land west of the Connecticut River that became Vermont), where Allen and his brothers just happened to be major landowners. In May 1775 he and his merry band, joined by Benedict Arnold, seized Fort Ticonderoga, New York, and its valuable military stores—arguably the first premeditated act of colonial aggression against the Crown. Emboldened by this coup, he then talked both the Continental Congress and the New York Provincial Congress into backing an invasion of Canada. At the end of September, in a foolhardy attempt to capture Montreal ahead of the main American force, commanded by General Richard Montgomery, Allen and a few dozen followers were disarmed by redcoats on the outskirts of the city. "I will not execute you now," raged the British commandant, Brigadier General Robert Prescott, "but you shall grace a halter at Tyburn, God damn you."[38]

For the next several months it definitely looked like Allen was on his way to Tyburn. As he would tell the story in his immensely popular *Narrative of Colonel Ethan Allen's Captivity . . . Written by Himself*, Prescott had him shackled in the hold of a British warship and instructed the guards to treat him with "severity." Allen remained in irons for about six weeks, alternately demanding more "gentleman-like usage" and challenging everyone in earshot to fight. (Nobody took the bait, because as one of his captors observed, the American prisoner was a mere criminal, a remark that only infuriated Allen more. "I was obliged to throw out plenty of extravagant language," he conceded.) When Montgomery's army drew near Montreal in late October, Allen and the other prisoners were sent downriver to Québec. There they were put aboard a dispatch ship and taken to England to be brought up on charges of treason and rebellion. The voyage took forty days, which the Americans spent confined in a specially constructed brig between the decks. "I should imagine," Allen recalled,

> . . . that it was not more than twenty feet one way, and twenty two the other: Into this place we were all, to the number of thirty-four, thrust and hand-cuffed, two prisoners more being added to our number, and were provided with two excrement tubs; in this circumference we were obliged to eat and perform the offices of evacuation, during the voyage to England; and were insulted by every black-guard sailor and tory on board, in the cruelest manner. . . . In consequence of the stench of the place, each of us was soon followed with a diarrhoea and fever, which occasioned intolerable thirst. When we asked for water, we were, most commonly, instead of obtaining it insulted and derided; and to add to all the horrors of the place, it was so dark that we could not see each other, and were overspread with body lice.

Surprisingly, Allen added, "not one of us died in the passage."[39]

Allen's recklessness won him scant sympathy in either the army or Congress. But given the question on everyone's mind—were captured Americans going to be treated as rebels or as prisoners of war?—the way the British had chosen to deal with him could not be ignored. Montgomery complained about it even before taking Montreal and threatened to retaliate. Washington had only recently protested to Gage about the suffering of Americans held in Boston; in mid-December, he advised General William Howe, Gage's successor, that Allen "has been treated without regard to decency, humanity, or the rules of war; that he has been thrown into irons, and suffers all the hardships inflicted upon common felons." Under the "law of retaliation," Washington warned, whatever happens to Allen, "such exactly shall be the treatment and fate of Brigadier *Prescott*"—who, by a delicious twist of fate, had become an American prisoner shortly after Montgomery's forces entered Montreal.[40]

As it happened, this uproar ensured that Allen would not end his days on the end of a rope, at Tyburn or anywhere else. Near the end of December 1775 he and his fellow captives arrived in Falmouth and were marched off through a throng of curious bystanders to Pendennis Castle, where they soon found themselves locked up together "in one common apartment." Knowing that the odds-makers in London were betting on his execution, and with the guards "perpetually shaking the halter" at him, "I could not but feel, inwardly, extremely anxious for my fate." He nonetheless resolved to "behave in a daring, soldier-like manner, that I might exhibit a good sample of American fortitude." He learned only later that the prospect of retaliation against Prescott and other British prisoners had caused Germain and the king to wonder whether hanging the American was such a good idea after all. The Duke of Richmond, John Wilkes, and other members of the pro-American opposition forced the government's hand by obtaining a writ of habeas corpus, meaning that Allen would have to be formally charged in an English court or released. Not wanting a trial as yet, but not wanting to let Allen go, the government hustled all the Americans out of Pendennis Castle and put them on a ship headed back to America, safely beyond the reach of meddlesome judges.[41]

During a brief layover in Cork in early February 1776, Allen had the satisfaction of being recognized as something of a celebrity. A group of "benevolently disposed gentlemen"—gentlemen, that is, with a soft spot for provincial insurgents—took up a collection with which they purchased clothes, tea, and sugar for each of the Americans. Allen himself received "a large gratuity of wines of the best sort" and such other "grandeurs and superfluities" as a new suit, two beaver hats, chocolate, and "a number of fat turkies." The captain of Allen's ship was understandably furious. Ranting "that the damned American rebels should not be feasted at this rate, by the damned rebels of Ireland" (another of those moments that expose the fracture lines beneath the surface of early "British" nationalism), he confiscated the wine for his own use and distributed the tea and sugar to the crew.[42]

Allen's escape from the gallows was a concession to circumstances, not a change in official policy, and like most such decisions it raised more questions than it answered. According to instructions Germain prepared for Howe in February, the prisoners being returned to his jurisdiction should be used "to procure the release of such of His Majesty's officers and loyal subjects are in the disgraceful situation of being prisoners to the rebels." Howe should be careful, however, not to compromise "the King's dignity and honour" by entering into "any treaty or agreement with the rebels for a regular cartel of prisoners," standard practice between warring nations.[43]

But what exactly did this mean? That future American captives were not going to be arrested, prosecuted, and executed for the crime of rebellion? And if that were the case, what was to be their legal status and how were they supposed to be treated, as de facto prisoners of war or something else? None of this had been resolved by the following August, when Howe and Commissary General Loring were confronted with the bumper crop of American prisoners on Long Island. Before Ethan Allen came along, Germain had been more than happy to run at the head of the pack hallooing for American heads. Now that some genuine American heads were within reach, he (and evidently the king as well) discovered that things were not going to be quite so simple. Their solution, if that is the word for it, was to let Howe and his subordinates do pretty much what they pleased with their prisoners—which goes a long way to explaining the disaster that was about to occur in New York.

There was, in any event, no change whatsoever in the attitude of Allen's captors, who spoke openly of their wish to see him dead, whether Germain wanted to bring him up on charges or not. As the captain taking Allen back to America told him (no doubt fortified by Allen's wine), "The British would conquer the American rebels, hang the Congress, and such as promoted the rebellion, me in particular, and retake their own prisoners; so that my life was of no consequence in the scale of their policy."[44]

3

THE STOOL OF
Repentance

THE MONTH OF OCTOBER 1776 found Washington and the
American army hunkered down on the rocky escarpments of
upper Manhattan, waiting for General Howe to march up from New
York City and drive them off, if he could. But Howe had other ideas.
On the morning of October 12, he and his brother, Admiral Lord
Richard Howe, orchestrated their third amphibious landing in as
many months—this one depositing some 4,000 redcoats and Hessians
on Throg's Neck, a narrow peninsula poking down into Long Island
Sound from the mainland. The British plan was to bottle up the
Americans on Manhattan by striking east from the Throg's Neck
beachhead to seize Kings Bridge, the only point at which the road
from New York crossed Spuyten Duyvil Creek on its way to New
England. But when his troops ran into stiff resistance outside the village of Westchester, the ever-cautious Howe decided to try something else. On October 18, he abandoned Throg's Neck and shifted
his entire force three miles east to Pell's Point. From there the British
advanced to the village of Eastchester. Three days later they reached
New Rochelle. Another three days brought them to Mamaroneck.
This elephantine pace gave Washington all the time he needed to
take the main body of his army across Kings Bridge and retreat to the
relative safety of White Plains, twenty miles to the north. Except for
the nearly 3,000 Americans left behind to defend a stronghold named
Fort Washington, Manhattan now belonged to the British.

Howe attacked Washington at White Plains on October 28. Although the outcome was inconclusive, Washington withdrew across the Croton River to North Castle and waited for Howe to come after him. He waited in vain, however, for Howe abruptly swiveled his attention back to Fort Washington, now completely isolated from the main American army. On November 16, Howe struck the fort from three sides with over 8,000 regulars. Although the defenders fought gamely, the odds were against them. Around mid-afternoon, their commander, Colonel Robert Magaw, a lawyer from Carlisle, Pennsylvania, made the unavoidable decision to surrender. One of Magaw's terrified men said they received the news with "crying, swearing, and cursing."[1]

They had cause to be terrified. Ever since the fighting on Long Island (where many of them saw action) the American army had been awash in rumors that the enemy summarily executed defenseless captives. After its retreat from New York City in mid-September, Major Nicholas Fish reported that "all our killed were shot thro' the Head which induces the belief that they were first taken Prisoners & then massacred." A subsequent clash on Harlem Heights gave rise to the story of how one burial detail came upon the bodies of a dozen Americans with their heads split open, allegedly after they had surrendered to the Hessians. Nor could it have escaped the Fort Washington defenders that under the rules of war (such as they were) Magaw's refusal to capitulate without a fight meant that they all could have been put to the sword. Under the circumstances, Captain Mackenzie observed brightly, anything short of execution constituted humane treatment.[2]

The mayhem that followed was anything but reassuring. "Our capitulation engaged to us our lives, baggage and side arms," explained Ensign Isaac Van Horne of the Fifth Pennsylvania, "but as soon as the enemy took possession of the fort the abuse and plunder commenced; side arms, watches, shoe-buckles, and even the clothes on our backs were wrested from us; very few, if any, of the officers but were stripped of their hats. In the evening we were marched to Haerlem, strictly guarded, and threatened hanging as rebels." A Hessian chaplain cheerfully agreed that "the prisoners received a number of blows."

Especially comical, I watched the treatment handed out by a Hessian grenadier. One of the rebels being led through looked around proudly to the left and right. The grenadier grabbed him on the ears with both hands, and said, "Wait a bit, and I'll show you the big city." Another tied him with his scarf. Two others hit him on the sides of his head. A third gave him a kick in the rump, so that he flew through three ranks. . . . The poor guy never knew what hit him, nor why he had been hit.[3]

Lieutenant Samuel Lindsay of Pennsylvania, already wounded in the leg, received a blow on the head "from the butt end of a musket" that took out his left eye and nearly blinded him in the right. Major Henry Bedinger, a Virginian, was appalled not only by the rampaging soldiers but by the evident complicity of their officers in the business—hardly the conduct Americans expected from honorable British gentlemen. "Instead of being treated as agreed on, and allowed to retain baggage, clothes, and Side Arms," he later wrote, "every valuable article was torn away from both officers and soldiers: every sword, pistol, every good hat was seized, even in the presence of Brittish officers, & the prisoners were considered and treated as *Rebels*, to the king and country." The fear of the American captives was palpable.[4]

Fear, and—at least for John Adlum, a seventeen-year-old private from York, Pennsylvania—a gloomy feeling of inadequacy as well. En route to Harlem, he badgered one of the guards, an Irish veteran, to tell him whether the Americans "behaved tolerably well" before surrendering. Yes, the Irishman allowed, "considering your numbers and the badness of your cause you have done as well as could be expected." Somewhat cheered, Adlum forged on: "Then you think that we might fight pretty hard upon an occasion?" Yes, came the answer, "if you were well disciplined and commanded by British officers." But "why British officers and not our own?" Adlum asked innocently. "Because," the man replied, "there is but very few of them that appear gentleman, consequently cannot have a proper sense of honor." That was probably so, Adlum admitted with a sinking heart. "I felt the hit."

At Harlem, guards herded the long lines of American prisoners into a handful of farm buildings, where they waited in vain to be given either food or water. Samuel Young, a Connecticut soldier and one of 500 other men locked in a barn, recalled that two days passed before the guards threw "in a confused manner, as if to so many hogs, a quantity of biscuits in crumbs, mostly mouldy, and some of them crawling with maggots, which they were obliged to scramble for without any division." Next day, their third day in captivity, "they had a little pork given to each, which they were obliged to eat raw."[5]

After that miserable meal the guards formed them up for the hot and dusty ten- or twelve-mile trek down from Harlem to New York City, an ordeal that made an indelible impression on the men who endured it. Decades later, James Little of Litchfield, Connecticut, still carried with him the vivid memory of being "marched through the British and Hessian army where we were insulted, kicked, beaten with the butt of their guns. Some of us were smashed down with poles on our heads and robbed of blankets." Private Adlum could not forget how their captors hacked furiously at the Americans with swords to cut off their knapsacks, or how masses of people lined the road, jeering and cursing. They said "that we ought to or would be hanged and called us by the opprobrious name of rebel, with a damn added to it by some. The Hessian women were particularly abusive." As William Slade, a soldier from New Canaan, Connecticut, wrote dolefully in his diary, "We was called Yankey Rebbels a going to the gallows."[6]

Was that true? Were they "destined to the cord," as General Gage had promised? "I have no idea that many will suffer," one of the guards, a kindly old sergeant, reassured Adlum—none, that is, except "the principal officers and the leading men in Congress." The "privates and small fry" such as yourself "will be treated with humanity while prisoners and will be supplied with all their wants. I shall not be surprised that after you are well fed and clothed to see General Howe send you all home with more favorable sentiments toward us [the British] than you now seem to be possessed of." Unfortunately, Adlum wrote later, the old sergeant had it all wrong. "He calculated upon a humanity that neither General Howe nor his myrmidons possessed or ever felt."[7]

But of all the Fort Washington captives, none remembered the emotional turmoil of those first few days in enemy hands as vividly as

Captain Alexander Graydon. Like Van Horne and Adlum, and like his compatriots captured on Long Island, Graydon experienced or witnessed "intolerable abuse"—gratuitous violence, the theft of personal effects, insufficient food and water, volleys of profanity hurled by camp followers. Harder to bear were the humiliating encounters with His Majesty's officers, whose open disdain for their less polished provincial counterparts still rankled decades afterward. Graydon recalled one scene in particular. A British sergeant-major was compiling a list of the names and ranks of every prisoner in a Harlem barn when he came to "a little squat" fellow from Pennsylvania. "*You are an officer, sir!* said the sergeant. *Yes*, was the answer. *Your rank sir!* with a significant smile. *I am a keppun*, replied the little man in a chuff, firm tone. Upon this, there was an immoderate roar of laughter among the officers about the door." Humiliated by this display of aristocratic condescension—"I must confess I was not sufficiently republican, to be insensible of its force," he wrote later—Graydon protested. He told one of the amused officers that "the person who had produced their merriment, belonged to the militia, and that in his line as a farmer, he was no doubt honest and respectable." A brave and even foolhardy thing to say, under the circumstances, all the more so because Graydon knew full well that honesty and respectability were beside the point: the little Pennsylvania *keppun* was no gentleman and would never be admitted to the international brotherhood of officers. To them he was—for the time being—a comical imposter.[8]

Harder still for Graydon to bear was the repeated threat that he and all his comrades would be strung up as rebels. "The term rebel, with the epithet *damned* before it, was the mildest we received," he recalled. It was also the one that cut most deeply, because "in the English language, it is too much interwoven with the idea of state criminality, to be other than highly opprobrious." Graydon did not think that its widespread use was accidental, either. "I was unable to put aside the reflection," he recalled, "that we were . . . captive to an enemy, whose system it was to treat us with contempt; to stigmatize us as rebels and load us with opprobrium; and that all this was, probably, but a prelude to the impending ruin and subjugation of my country." Little wonder, then, that "my heart was ill at ease. It was the

prey of chagrin and a most afflicting uncertainty." On at least one occasion, Graydon lost his composure and "was obliged to apply my
handkerchief to my eyes. This was the first time in my life, that I had
been the victim of brutal, cowardly oppression; and I was unequal to
the shock."[9]

When the long line of Fort Washington prisoners snaked into New
York at the end of the day on September 19, the officers were confined separately in the Baptist church. Next morning, Commissary
Loring gave them the choice of having quarters assigned to them in
town or making arrangements on their own, if they could afford the
expense. Most could not, and according to Jabez Fitch, the residents
of Liberty House suddenly found themselves with a large influx of
new arrivals to contend with. Captain Graydon and Colonel Magaw,
on the other hand, elected to board with colonels Atlee and Miles and
other Pennsylvania officers in the home on Queen (now Pearl) Street
owned by a certain Mrs. Carroll—a "particular favorite" of Commandant James Robertson, Graydon remarked prudishly, and "sufficiently
young and buxom, to give probability to the imputation." Her residence was not so crowded as Liberty House, and Graydon's trunk,
soon brought down from Fort Washington, ensured him a supply of
fresh "linen, stockings, &c." plus "a better suit of regimentals."[10]

At this point, for the first time, all the American officers captured
since the Battle of Brooklyn—now numbering somewhat over 300—
were also accorded the privilege of moving freely about the town
from sunup to sundown. Graydon immediately donned his uniform
and headed out for a stroll. "My fellow-lodgers, who had been taken
on Long Island, being older and more prudent than myself, evinced
some surprise at my temerity," he wrote. They warned him that an
American officer in uniform risked "insult and abuse"; indeed, they
had rarely ventured out of doors themselves, even in civilian clothes.
But he went anyway—a small act of defiance, as he put it, "against the
design to treat us as state criminals, and to overwhelm us with the
odium attached to that condition." (Staying indoors was not entirely

safe, either. One day in October, some "Highland officers" charged into the house where Captain John Nice and other officers were boarding, beat up two of the Americans, and dragged them off to the Provost. Commandant Robertson let them out the next day.)[11]

There seem to have been other Americans willing, like Graydon, to put themselves on display and contest the enemy's control of the streets—too many others for Captain Mackenzie, who remarked in his diary that "the Rebel officers who have been taken prisoners lately, are suffered to walk about in every part of this town on their parole, and in their Uniforms. This gives great disgust to all the Loyalists." The Americans, he went on, "publickly avow their principles, and instead of appearing sensible of the crime they have committed, seem to glory in the cause in which they are engaged."[12]

Mackenzie's bafflement is understandable. Given the widespread view that Americans were rebels, not legitimate combatants, why coddle their so-called officers? Why let them wander brazenly around New York to the offense of His Majesty's true and faithful subjects? A big part of the answer, as Mackenzie surely knew, stemmed from the North government's clumsy management of the Ethan Allen matter—first hauling him to England, presumably to be hanged, then sending him back when the opposition threatened to produce an inconvenient writ of habeas corpus and it became apparent that hanging him could jeopardize any Britons who fell into American hands. In the vacuum created by official irresolution, what happened to other captured rebels was left up to Howe. Yet Howe had no idea what to do with them, either. Mostly, he hoped the display of British might would bring the Americans to their senses and the whole problem would just go away. On November 30, he issued a proclamation calling for the rebels to disperse and for Congress to disband, but offering full pardon to anyone who, within sixty days, swore an oath of loyalty to the king. Virtually no one took him up on the offer, however, and he soon had other matters on his mind—Mrs. Loring, for one, and the social whirl of occupied New York. "Toujours de la gaieté!" he cried.[13]

In truth, the slow but steady success of British arms in the autumn of 1776 made an early end to the insurgency seem very likely. A week after the fall of Fort Washington, Captain John Bowater declared the Americans as good as beaten. "I Really believe they will never stand another Attack," he wrote cheerfully to Lord Denbigh from aboard the warship *Centurion* in New York harbor. Better still, His Majesty's forces were holding vast numbers of Americans captive in the city. "All the Meeting houses belonging to the Quakers, Annabaptist, Presbyterians & other Rascally Sects are made into prisons. We have now seven Thousand on the stool of Repentance, in the very places where this horrid Rebellion was hatched."[14]

Blaming religious dissenters for the troubles in America was a convenient oversimplification, and there could not have been many more than 5,000 Americans in custody in New York at the end of November. But Bowater was certainly correct that British officials had by then commandeered and converted into prisons almost every house of worship in the city not belonging to the Church of England. Now, besides the Old North Church, there were prisoners in the First Presbyterian Church on Wall Street, Brick Presbyterian Church on Beekman Street, the Middle Dutch Church on Crown Street, the Scots Presbyterian Church on Cedar Street, the South Dutch Church on Garden Street, the French Church on Pine Street, and the Quaker meeting house on Queen Street. (Pastor Schaukirk was told to clear the Moravian chapel for 400 prisoners but at the last minute persuaded the officer in charge to squeeze them into the Old North Church instead.) Over 800 men had also been packed into the Bridewell, which stood on the Broadway side of the Common, almost directly across the street from Liberty House. This substantial red brick building, also known as the Almshouse, was the city's new house of correction for vagrants and paupers—so new that interior walls remained to be plastered, windows lacked glass, and piles of construction materials cluttered the yard outside. Both the City Hall on Broad Street and the King's College building on Park Place were briefly used to hold prisoners as well, the latter as a hospital.[15]

Another, particularly ominous, addition to His Majesty's repertoire of prisons in New York consisted of a pair of troop transports,

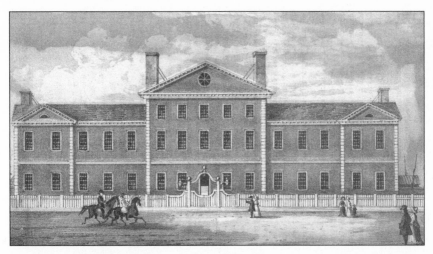

The Bridewell. Still under construction when filled with American prisoners in September 1776, it occupied the northwest corner of the municipal Common. To the left, directly across Broadway, stood Liberty House.

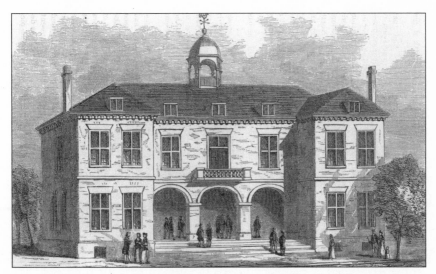

Old City Hall. The American General Charles Lee was a prisoner here in 1777. The Confederation Congress met in the building from 1785 to 1788, when it was substantially renovated to serve as the new federal capitol. It would be replaced by the new city hall on the Common in 1812.

King's College. Occupying the block between Murray and Barclay streets, it stood due west of the Common and only a block from Liberty House. The spire of St. Paul's Chapel is visible in the background. Badly damaged by redcoats in 1776, it held American prisoners until 1777 or 1778, when it became a military hospital.

the *Whitby* and the *Grosvenor.* At the end of October (a couple of weeks, that is, before the fall of Fort Washington), the Royal Navy had moved the *Whitby* to a new anchorage in Wallabout Bay on the Brooklyn side of the East River. There she was reduced to a hulk by the systematic removal of her ordnance, masts, rigging, and other reusable equipment. Around the beginning of December, probably on the orders of Commissary General Loring, she received 250 American prisoners from the city's overcrowded jails. An additional 500 were transferred to the *Grosvenor,* then lying in the Hudson River but soon brought into the East River and anchored off the Manhattan shore, about a mile north of the *Whitby.* Over the winter, or perhaps in the early spring, the navy moved her, too, into Wallabout Bay.[16]

Now known only as the site of the old Brooklyn Navy Yard, eighteenth-century Wallabout Bay was a kidney-shaped cove lying almost directly across from Corlears Hook on Manhattan, so close that people standing on either bank could shout across to one another. The shores of the bay were fringed with nearly treeless salt meadows—

thick, undulating mats of cordgrass that thrived where the brackish river water mingled with freshwater from Wallabout Creek, a lazy tributary wandering down from nearby Bushwick village. Beyond the salt meadows, broken here and there by small hummocks festooned with bayberry or chokeberry bushes, stretched broad mud flats that made the so-called bay all but inaccessible to shipping except for a narrow channel looping through its center. Europeans had first come here in the 1630s to hunt, fish, and cut salt hay for their cattle. Now, a century and a half later, the farmhouses of their descendants—Remsens, Rapaljes, Ryersons, Johnsons, Schencks, and others—perched at intervals along the thirty-foot-high sandy bluffs that circled the bay, linked by narrow paths and footbridges. Several residents had docks on the creek, suggesting that it was partially navigable (if only by rowboat); one of the Remsens had dammed a tidal pond on the south side of the bay to operate a gristmill.[17]

All in all, despite the clouds of gnats and mosquitoes that preyed mercilessly on man and beast in the summer, it was a sensible location for prison ships. They could lie close enough to the shore to be easily supplied with food and fresh water, yet sufficiently far from the city that the residents faced little or no danger from the contagions that inevitably raged among men closely confined without adequate sanitary or medical facilities. What was more, the treacherous shallows and soggy mud flats that surrounded the ships made escape exceedingly difficult, if not impossible.

This was not the first time that Britain's armed forces had relegated prisoners to hulks. They had been used for defeated rebels in Scotland in 1745, and again for French soldiers and seamen taken during the Seven Years' War. More recently, Parliament had authorized the use of hulks to resolve a looming crisis in the English penal system. It seems that the outbreak of hostilities in the colonies was interfering with the old practice of shipping convicted felons across the Atlantic as indentured servants (whence Doctor Johnson's surly description of Americans as a "race of convicts"). English courts nevertheless continued to offer "transportation" as an alternative to the gallows. But with nowhere to send them, the number of persons under detention had spiked alarmingly, along with an equally disturbing upsurge of squalor, disease, and violence in the country's teeming jails.[18]

Parliament responded, after much prodding by North's government, with the Hulks Act of May 1776, which allowed the long-term warehousing of convicted criminals on broken-down troop transports and rotting warships anchored in the Thames. News of the Hulks Act arrived in America only days before the Battle of Brooklyn, and judging by the reaction of Ambrose Serle, Admiral Howe's secretary, it met with hearty approval. Thus sanctioned by precedent, promoted by the administration, and now blessed by Parliament—and given the widespread assumption that colonists taken in arms were actually lower than common criminals—the use of prison hulks in occupied New York must have seemed eminently reasonable to Serle's masters.[19]

On the Thames hulks, moreover, it was evident from the outset that conditions left much to be desired. John Howard, the celebrated reformer, warned Parliament as early as the autumn of 1776 about spoiled food, overcrowding, and illness on the prison ships there. That captured Americans could expect even worse treatment became clear at the beginning of November, when Philadelphia newspapers reprinted an open letter to the lord mayor of London concerning the fate of the twenty-five-man crew of the *Yankee,* a captured American privateer brought in the previous summer, stripped of its rigging, and anchored in the Thames. Signed "Humanitas," the letter asserted that the prisoners had been caged "like wild beasts, in a small stinking apartment" in the ship's hold, their only supply of fresh air coming via "a small grating, over head, the openings in which are not more than two inches square." Through this same grate rose a foul, sickening stench—"putrid streams . . . so hot and offensive, that one cannot, without the utmost danger, breathe over it. . . . The miserable wretches below look like persons in a hot bath, panting, sweating, and fainting for want of air; and the Surgeon declares, that they must all soon perish in that situation, especially as they are almost all in a sickly state with bilious disorders."[20]

Even if you think of these men as criminals, "Humanitas" went on, there was no excuse for such callousness. One of the gentlemen who had recently visited the ship with him said it called to mind the noto-

rious Black Hole of Calcutta, where nearly 150 English prisoners—
men, women, and children—were driven into a small cell one night in
1756 by the Nawab of Bengal. By morning, most had been suffocated
or crushed to death. "All England ought to know, that the same game
is now acting upon the Thames," exclaimed "Humanitas." Yet a far
more terrible story lay just around the corner. [21]

To a man, the Americans who made it through the winter of
1776–1777 on the Wallabout hulks told of horrors that made the ordeal of the *Yankee*'s crew seem almost tame by comparison. On the
Grosvenor, James Little "suffered every inconvenience but death." The
ship was so crowded that the men could not all lie down at once, and
their rations barely sufficed to keep body and soul together—in the
morning, half a pint of a watery stew called "burgoo," scraps of "kennel biscuit" at night. "In the putrefied stagnated air of the hold of the
vessel crowded with vermin," he and his companions grew "pitiless
faint and feeble," and once the smallpox began its deadly work, the
mortality was just heartbreaking. Every morning, Little recalled,
"dead bodies were hoisted on deck, a cannonball fastened to them,
and they were thrown overboard with the shout of 'there goes another damned Yankee rebel.'" Little also remembered that when Isaac
Gibbs got permission to bury his father ashore in the dead of winter,
he as well as the two friends he took with him to help, none with
proper clothing, "got so chilled and frozen that they died soon after
their return. Indeed to go outside from the confined air in the hold of
the vessel brought almost instant death." At one point, Little and
about forty others with smallpox were taken off the ship and led,
"reeling and tumbling," to a hospital on shore. Only Little, Isaac
Grant, and Elisha Grant lasted a fortnight, and "we hourly expected
to follow." The three survived, however, and were paroled in February 1777. Little made his way home to Danbury, where "I soon re-
gained my health so as to be able to labor and again assist in
defending my country."[22]

In the narrative he later set to paper for his children, Ichabod
Perry—then a seventeen-year-old private from Fairfield, Connecticut—described the "outter darkness" of his first night aboard one of

the ships, when he and the other men were packed so tightly that as many as a third of them suffocated by morning. "It took us the better part of the Day to pull out the dead," he wrote. The survivors, fed rations "not fit for hogs," soon became delirious with hunger. Perry himself began to think "I could eat my own flesh without wincing." Because only a few prisoners were allowed on deck at a time, "we had no means for clenzing ourselves, our outside Clothes was glas'd over with besmear and our under Clothes was not much better, and not an hair was cut from our faces while [I] was there." One of those paroled around the first of February 1777, he somehow managed to make it home, "hardly able to Draw one foot after the other," yet eager to be exchanged "so that I cul'd be at them again."[23]

After only days on the *Whitby*, some of the captives from Connecticut managed to get a letter to Governor Jonathan Trumbull of that state, describing the more than 250 men aboard as "most wretched"—many "Sick and without the least assistance from Physician, Drugg, or Medicine, all fed on two-thirds allowance of Salt provisions, and all Crouded promiscuously togeather without Distinction or Respect, to person office or Colour, in the small room of a Ships Between Decks, allowed only to walk the main Deck from about Sun Riseing, till Sunn Sett. . . . only two at once to come on deck to do what Nature requires, and sometimes we have Been even Denied that, and been obliged to make use of tubbs & Bucketts Below deck to the great offence of every Delicate Cleanly person, as well as to great prejudice of all our healths." David Thorp, a native of Woodbury, Connecticut, recalled that four days a week his eight-man mess received nothing to eat except several pints of wormy oatmeal; on the other three days, each of them had two ounces of salt beef with a little hard biscuit. Once they had no fresh water for three days.[24]

It did not take long before the men began sinking into a kind of catatonic despondency. William Slade of New Canaan—initially held in the North Dutch Church and then transferred to the *Grosvenor*—recorded their decline in his diary:

SUNDAY, 8TH. This day we were almost discouraged, but considered that would not do. Cast off such thoughts. We drawd our bread and eat with sadness. . . . Spent the day reading and in meditation, hoping for good news.

WEDNESDAY, 11TH. Still in hopes.

FRIDAY, 13TH OF DECR. 1776. We now see nothing but the mercy of God to intercede for us. Sorrowful times, all faces look pale, discouraged, discouraged.

SATURDAY, 14TH. . . . Times look dark. Deaths prevail among us, also hunger and naked . . . At night suffer with cold and hunger.

SUNDAY, 15TH. . . . Paleness attends all faces, the melancholyst day I ever saw. . . . As sorrowfull times as I ever saw.

TUESDAY, 17TH. We are treated worse than cattle and hogs.

WEDNESDAY, 18TH. Hunger prevails. Sorrow comes on.

FRIDAY, 20TH. Prisoners hang their heads and look pale. No comfort. All sorrow.

SUNDAY, 22ND. Last night nothing but grones all night of sick and dying. Men amazeing to behold. Such hardness, sickness prevails fast. Deaths multiply. . . . All faces sad.

MUNDAY 23RD. One dies almost every day.

FRIDAY 27TH. Three men of our battalion died last night.[25]

But no one imagined things were any easier for the thousands of men left behind in New York's churches, in the Bridewell or the Provost or City Hall, or in the sugar houses. Private Thomas Boyd of West Caln, Pennsylvania, recalled wormy food, putrid water, random floggings, the gagging fetor of urine and excrement, and so much sickness that burial parties would remove ten or twenty bodies every morning. Henry Franklin, a Quaker who visited the North Dutch Church only two days after the fall of Fort Washington, testified that the men there were already fighting over scraps. "Those who were modest and backward," he added, "could get little or none." Captain Edward Boylston, snatched by Tories near his New Jersey home in January 1777, found himself in Livingston's sugar house. "Here, such was the filthy state of things, that there was not a place to lie down for rest, day nor night, but upon the excrements of the prisoners—and to sleep was almost certain death. With yellow fever, want and suffering, the prisoners were dying constantly, and it was impossible to move about without stumbling over the dead and dying."[26]

One of the Bridewell inmates who lived, private William Darlington, confirmed under oath that he and his companions were allowed, every three days, "one half pound of biscuit, half a pound of pork, half a pint of pease, half a gill of rice, and half an ounce of butter; the whole not more than enough for one good meal." They "had no straw or hay to lie on; and no fuel, but one cart load, per week, for the 800 men." Every night at nine, he continued, Hessian guards would come in to douse the fires, clubbing prisoners who failed to get out of the way fast enough. "The enemy seemed to take a kind of infernal pleasure in their sufferings," Darlington recalled. Not surprisingly, "the men began to die, like rotten sheep, with cold, hunger and dirt." Levi Whitney, confined in one of the sugar houses, purportedly gnawed the flesh of his arms to keep himself from starving to death. Colonel Joseph Barnum's son was said to have expired while trying to eat a brick.[27]

Although American officers were not supposed to communicate with the soldiers in detention, one of the first things they did after receiving permission to walk about the city was to visit the prisons. Only then, Jabez Fitch wrote in his unpublished "Narative," did he and other officers begin to grasp the "miserable Situation" of their men. "We found their sufferings vastly superior to what we had been able to Conceive, nor are words sufficient to convey an Adequate Idea of their Unparrallal'd Calamity." A New England farmer, he wrote, would have treated his cattle with greater consideration. Many had already died, their almost naked bodies thrown carelessly outside to await the dead cart. Some were said to have been "Expos'd to the unnatural Devouring of Swine & other greedy Annimals" before being buried in mass graves, loosely covered with earth. Fitch's diary, though predictably more careful in its judgments than his "Narative," leaves no doubt that he was appalled by the enemy's callousness—and that he and his fellow officers, most of whom were struggling to feed and clothe themselves, could do little to help. One of Fitch's companions, Lieutenant Jonathan Gillett (Gillet), agreed that the men were in a very bad way. "There natures are brook and gone," he wrote sadly in a letter home. "Some almost loose their voices and some there hearing. . . . I cant paint the horable appearance they make—it is shocking to human nature to behold them."[28]

Captain Graydon, too, was overwhelmed by what he saw in "these abodes of human misery and despair." Forty years later it still made him uncomfortable to think that he never returned after his first visit because he could do nothing to comfort them. "I rather chose to turn my eye from a scene I could not meliorate; to put from me a calamity which mocked my powers of alleviation." Instead, he indulged his "melancholy" by rambling through the burned-over blocks west of Broadway, meditating "on the horrors of this guilty city, where 'poor misfortune felt the lash of vice,' and thousands of my unhappy countrymen were perishing under the hand of proud, unfeeling authority."[29]

Indeed, there were no assurances that the guards would even allow outsiders to bring in provisions for the prisoners. They sometimes did, because a former inmate of one of the sugar houses never forgot the ministrations of a certain Mrs. Spicer, "a warm friend to the cause of liberty . . . esteemed by the prisoners as a mother." Lydia Robbins had no trouble with the guards, either. In 1839 she still recalled that over a period of six months she regularly brought provisions to her brothers, Henry and Benjamin Clapp, when both were confined in Livingston's sugar house.[30]

More often than not, however, attempts to get food and clothing to the prisoners turned out badly. Samuel Fraunces, a local tavern keeper employed as Commandant Robertson's cook, later recalled the trouble he had taking leftovers to the prisoners, since "the common- est Acts of Humanity was at that time Considered as a Crime of the deepest Dye." When he took food to the sugar house on Crown Street, for example, "some time the sentreys would overset it on the ground and the poor prisners would lick it up, som times the Britons they would Come past with a pice of meet or other provision kind and would hold it up to the solgers that was allmost starved to agravate them." Jabez Fitch likewise complained that the guards often turned him and other American officers away from the churches and sugar

houses, driving them off with swords and bayonets. Captain William
Gamble, a Pennsylvania naval officer, deposed that when fresh captives were brought into town, any resident who attempted to give
them food or drink was immediately knocked down by the guards.[31]

One day at the end of November 1776 the residents of Liberty House
received a surprise visit from none other than Ethan Allen, the man
with a good claim to being His Majesty's most troublesome American
captive. It was now ten months since he'd left Cork, and although his
experiences since then had nearly broken him, they had also forced
him to think about the larger meaning of those experiences.

   Off North Carolina, after a circuitous voyage across the Atlantic,
Allen and his "brother prisoners" were transferred to a British frigate
bound for Halifax. The frigate's vicious, "underwitted" captain put
them on one-third rations, and by the time they reached their destination in mid-June many of the men were down with scurvy and
Allen himself had grown "weak and feeble." Then came six weeks
aboard a prison sloop, followed by another ten in the Halifax jail,
locked day and night in one large room furnished only with excrement tubs. It was, Allen later recalled, "a time of substantial distress."
He continued to demand more "gentleman-like usage" but fell ill
with jail fever, "grew weaker and weaker, as did the rest," and came to
realize that "the malignant hand of Britain had greatly reduced my
constitution, stroke by stroke."[32]

   The once-robust, swaggering Hero of Ticonderoga was also becoming severely depressed by his inability to "play the man" in the
cause of freedom. "I thought to have enrolled my name in the list of
illustrious *American* heroes," he wrote glumly in a letter to the Connecticut Assembly, "but was nipped in the bud." On the other hand,
"the *English* rascally treatment to me has wholly erased my former
feelings of parent State, mother country, and, in fine, all kindred and
friendly connexion with them." He had never asked to be treated differently "than what the laws of arms give to prisoners between foreign nations; but instead of that, have been crowded into the most

filthy apartments of ships, among privates, where I have, almost the whole of my time since taken, been covered with lice."[33]

Around the middle of October 1776, Allen and those of his men who remained alive had been put aboard a man-of-war bound for New York City. Inexplicably, the captain "assured me that I should be treated as a gentleman, and that he had given orders, that I should be treated with respect by the ship's crew"—so "unexpected and sudden a transition, that it drew tears from my eyes." By the end of November, after several weeks at anchor in New York harbor, the men were sent ashore and confined in the city's "filthy churches." Allen was paroled and found lodgings "in some measure agreeable to my rank." He had now been in British hands for fourteen months.[34]

"The famous Colonel Ethan Allen," as a starstruck John Adlum referred to him, quickly recovered his spirits in New York and made himself conspicuous, striding about town in a blue suit and gold-laced hat given him by the gentlemen of Cork. "The enemy," Allen wrote, "gave out that I was crazy, and wholly unmanned" by his "long and barbarous captivity," but to his fellow officers he was energy and spirit and resolution personified—loud, garrulous, dramatic, opinionated, uncensored. Alexander Graydon described Allen's style as "a singular compound of local barbarisms, scriptural phrases, and oriental wildness." Adlum remembered a December dinner at Mrs. Carroll's when Allen's "history &c of his voyage to England &c and back again mixed with his observations and interlarded with anecdotes" kept the company so entertained they stayed up "pretty late" listening to him. Indeed, Adlum continued, "Colonel Allen was always a very welcome guest at our quarters. His manner of telling a story, his fund of anecdotes, his flashes of wit, and the force of his observations never failed of having an attentive and amused audience." Except for Jabez Fitch, that is, who did not care for late-night revelry and soon wearied of such scenes, griping on one occasion (to himself, of course) that "Col: Allyn came in, & Repeated to us again, the Story of his Taking Ticonarogue & also many other of his Adventures."[35]

More important than Allen's entertainment value was his ballooning rage at the abuse of American prisoners. Although it sometimes led to what might be charitably described as overheated versions of

events—as when he later reported how, after the fighting on Long Island, "a Genl. Odel, or Woodhul, of the militia, was hacked to pieces
with cutlasses, when alive" and five captured American soldiers were
hanged "on the limb of a white oak tree"—these were usually the off-
spring of rumor and Allen's willingness to believe the worst of the
enemy, not a wanton disregard for the truth. What always made him
angriest, in any event, were the horrors he now saw with his own
eyes in the prisons of New York City. "The filth in these churches, in
consequence of the fluxes, was almost beyond description," he would
write. "The floors were covered with excrements. I have carefully
sought to direct my steps so as to avoid it, but could not. . . . I have
seen in one of these churches seven dead, at the same time, lying
among the excrements of their bodies." Not only did these night-
marish scenes remind him of his own year in close confinement, but
the more he examined the matter the more he came to think "that it
was a premeditated and systematical plan of the British council, to
destroy the youths of our land, with a view thereby to deter the
country, and make it submit to their despotism." This was not war
but cold-blooded murder—"relentless and scientific barbarity"—and
it hinged on the enemy's use of the word "rebel" to describe all captives, regardless of rank. One word, Allen declared, was "sufficient to
sanctify whatever cruelties they were pleased to inflict, death itself
not excepted."[36]

What was to be done? The American officers in New York often
consulted with one another on the subject, Allen recalled. Some
wanted "to go in procession to General Howe, and plead the cause of
the perishing soldiers," then dropped the idea when it was pointed
out that Howe could not have been unaware of the situation and
would probably use such an action as an excuse to lock up the officers
as well. Allen volunteered to get up a petition instead, and actually
composed "several rough drafts," but the senior officers—colonels
Miles, Magaw, and Atlee—decided to content themselves with a letter to Howe over their signatures alone.[37]

By Christmas, meanwhile, the bodies were piling up so rapidly in
New York that burial details fell further and further behind. Twenty
or thirty Americans died every day, a Connecticut officer wrote sadly.

"They lie in heaps unburied." After one particularly cold December night, John Adlum heard a rumor that about 100 prisoners had perished and saw a wagon piled high with corpses. "They were thrown into it without any order and most of them, at least all in view on the top of the wagon, were nearly naked." Adolph Myer (or Meyer), a soldier from Harlem, New York, spent time in three different prisons before escaping from the North Dutch Church in January 1777. "No care was taken of the sick," he said afterward. "If any died they were thrown at the door of the prison and lay there until the next day, when they were put in a cart and drawn out to the intrenchments beyond the Jews' burial-ground, where they were interred by their fellow prisoners, conducted thither for that purpose. The dead were thrown into a hole promiscuously, without the usual rites of sepulchre." Sometimes, according to Private Boyd, the living would be put on the cart as well, "then thrown with the dead into the open pit." Things were no better on the prison ships, each of which reportedly disposed of ten or twelve prisoners every day.[38]

It was around Christmas, too, that Loring suddenly began releasing hundreds of rebel captives, perhaps as many as a thousand or more. Everyone knew why: these men were, by all accounts, the sickest of those still alive, and since most were not likely to survive the winter, they could do Washington no good. On December 24, for example, Oliver Babcock and 225 other New Englanders shuffled down to the Albany Pier in "Rainy icey weather" and boarded the transport *Glasgow*, bound for Connecticut. Two dozen or more died along the way. A week later, one foggy January morning, the captain of the *Glasgow* deposited the remainder on the beach at Milford. As the dazed, emaciated, and half-naked men stumbled through the streets, startled villagers took 100 of the sickest into their homes. Nearly fifty of those died over the next month, probably of smallpox, and were buried in a common grave. Numerous others, like Thomas Mayo of Brewster, Massachusetts, perished on the road home. Lieutenant Babcock made it back to his family and scribbled a final note of thanks in his little diary: "Oh that I may Live to honour and praise God all the days of my Life for his great Deliverence in Bringing me from under the Iron Rod of my enemies from the Land of Tyranny and

Bondage." But within a fortnight he too lay dead of the smallpox, followed by two of his children, who evidently contracted the disease from him. If half of the 225 prisoners on the *Glasgow* survived until spring, it was a miracle.[39]

By the end of 1776, disease and starvation had killed at least half of those taken on Long Island and perhaps two-thirds of those captured at Fort Washington—somewhere between 2,000 and 2,500 men in the space of two months, though no one will ever know for sure.[40]

The impact on local communities was crushing. Of the thirty-six men from Litchfield, Connecticut, who helped defend Fort Washington, four were killed and thirty-two taken prisoner. Twenty died in the prisons of New York, another six on the way home. Only six returned to Litchfield—six of the original thirty-six. Half a company of 100 men raised in Danbury, Connecticut, was captured at Fort Washington and confined in one of the sugar houses. Two survived. Some towns may have lost everyone. At dinner one night in April 1777, Ambrose Serle, Admiral Howe's secretary, heard of "a little Town in Connecticut" that had turned out 220 men for the American cause, every last one of whom died in battle or succumbed to disease. Many families must have been nearly wiped out. Two of Ruth Peck's three sons were taken prisoner at Fort Washington. One lost both feet to frostbite trying to walk home from New York in the dead of winter; the other returned with the smallpox and died, but not before infecting Peck's husband, who later died as well.[41]

Connecticut was not alone. Of the 130 militiamen from Northampton County, Pennsylvania, who were captured on Long Island, only forty made it out of New York alive. Colonel Thomas Hartley informed General Washington in February 1777 that of the many men from York County who fell prisoner at Fort Washington, only a handful lived "to tell the doleful Story of their Captivity and Distress." Almost all had died within days of rejoining their families. So, too, seventeen young men from Berkeley County, Virginia, took part in the defense of Fort Washington and wound up in the prisons of New York City. Fifteen did not last the winter, their names and dates of death sorrowfully recorded in the journal of the captain who had led them so far from home. Of the two ailing survivors, only one lived until summer.[42]

Stories of this kind, wrapped in bitterness and grief and pride, suffused local memory and family legend for generations. Nearly sixty years later, a newspaper editor in Amherst, Massachusetts, would give his readers a long and haunting account of how his late father, Captain Edward Boylston, was beaten and robbed by the redcoats who captured him in January 1777. After a week's confinement on an unnamed prison ship, Boylston was put in Livingston's sugar house, where "such was the filthy state of things, that there was not a place to lie down for rest, day nor night, but upon the excrements of the prisoners." It was a story, his son wrote, he could never forget. "With what intense feeling we have listened to his tale of the poor dying creatures, who in the feeble accents of expiring life, were intreating for a little water! water!" As a pensive Colonel Hartley had pointed out in his February 1777 letter to Washington, "The Influence these Things will have upon the Country will take a little Time to wear of[f]."[43]

As the winter of 1776–77 deepened—one of those gray New York winters punctuated by bouts of numbingly cold rain—Jabez Fitch restlessly prowled the streets, running errands and discussing news of the war with other officers in their quarters. Because everyone was now alarmed about the rapid spread of smallpox, his visits to the prisoners became less frequent, and he moved out of Liberty House to new quarters farther downtown. There he "began to learn to Smoak Tobacko," and at least once "took a harty wash in Sope Suds." He continued to brood, too, about the evils he had witnessed in the churches and sugar houses, and although he did not seem to agree with Allen that the British were intentionally killing their American prisoners, it grated on him that they had made so little effort to keep them alive. When he learned that General Howe had celebrated the queen's birthday on January 18 with a lavish dinner featuring over 200 dishes, Fitch's indignation overcame his usual discretion. "Query," he wrote angrily in his diary, "whether it would not have been more Honourable to the British Army, to have had (at least) part of this Extraordinary Expence, bestow'd on the poor Prisoners who have perrished for want, in such vast numbers."[44]

Fitch's life changed abruptly at the end of that same month, when Commissary General Loring sent all or most of the 300-plus captured American officers across the East River to new billets in the villages of Kings County. (Initially, the Pennsylvania officers went to Flatbush and the New Englanders to New Lots, a couple of miles to the east. Flatlands, Gravesend, and New Utrecht accommodated the overflow.) Loring offered no explanation for the action, and the Americans disagreed as to whether it left them better off or not. The self-consciously urbane Alexander Graydon, assigned to live with "an old bachelor" in Flatbush, fretted that the officers had been consigned to "dumb forgetfulness" on the outskirts of civilization—their punishment, he theorized, for failing to cringe and grovel in New York City as their captors expected.[45]

But Fitch, a Yankee farmer at heart, was relieved to find himself in the "much more agreable circumstances" of rural New Lots, a string of cottages along New Lots Road (now New Lots Avenue in the East New York section of Brooklyn). His new host was George Rapalje, the owner of a 300-acre farm that lay between the road and the high ground to the north (occupied today by Cyprus Hills Cemetery). The two got along remarkably well, considering that Rapalje was one of the many Kings County Dutchmen disposed to support the Crown. Rapalje let Fitch sleep in a featherbed and fed him a healthy (if tiresome) diet of local clams—fried clams, baked clams, roasted clams, clam chowder—supplemented with suppaun, a porridge-like mix of corn meal, milk, and molasses. (With memorable exceptions: "a fine Dinner on Rabbits & Squirrils Cook'd in a Potpie," then "an Extraordinary Dinner of Boild Bass," and once "a curious Dinner . . . of Broil'd Herren & Eales.")[46]

More important to Fitch than the featherbed or the food was the fact that the paroled officers no longer had to endure the "Malignity" of the city's Tories, redcoats, and Hessians. Better still, the Americans could move freely around the county, which gave them not only "a greater Advantage for Exercise" but also the opportunity to meet and talk together without interruption or supervision. Weather permitting, they did so on a daily basis, usually assembling in one or another of the taverns that lay within easy walking distance of their New Lots billets—up at Howard's or Field's on the Jamaica Road, or at Wyckoff's on the New Lots Road—where they drank, smoked, played cards, read newspapers, and weighed their odds of being exchanged. Fitch dubbed them the "Everlasting Club," an allusion to the London fraternity renowned for never adjourning. Ethan Allen, who boarded with a farmer named Boerum, only a stone's throw from Rapalje's, had a different image in mind. He referred to the little community of New Lots captives as "our Israel."[47]

Stirred by all the masculine camaraderie in the taverns of New Lots—and by the much reduced danger that he would be discovered and punished for violating parole—Fitch started work on a pamphlet about the handling of captured Americans in New York City. The idea may well have occurred to him back in Liberty House, or it may have been inspired by his growing admiration for Ethan Allen, who was never reluctant to share his opinions with the reading public. Either way, Fitch was soon engaged in "considerable writing" and "writing with great Industry." What emerged eight weeks later, around the beginning of April 1777, was his "Narative of the treatment with which the American Prisoners were Used who were taken by the British & Hessian Troops on Long Island York Island &c. 1776 With some occasional Observations thereon"—the first work of its kind to come out of the Revolutionary War. The manuscript, discreetly covered with "Brown paper," was smuggled out to Fitch's brother in Connecticut with an introductory letter implying that Fitch would welcome its publication, "if Divine Providence should present a favourable Oppertunity for that purpose."[48]

But Divine Providence refused to cooperate, or his brother declined to take the hint, perhaps because the manuscript left much to be desired. Fitch's preoccupation with the day-to-day minutia of captivity—his great strength as a diarist—clogged the "Narative" with superfluous, disconnected details. There was something counterfeit about the writing, too. Fitch the diarist masked his outrage at the treatment of American prisoners in plain, restrained, unpretentious sentences; Fitch the angry pamphleteer, too conscious of his audience, adopted an artificial, literary style that was by turns stilted and turgid.

More than anything else, though, the "Narative" failed because Fitch's anger did not produce a compelling explanation for the abuses he witnessed. Divine Providence, Fitch wrote, has created two kinds of people: "the Person whose mind is annimated with Sentiments of Virtue, Humanity and Friendship to Mankind," and "the Insolent Clown who knows no satisfaction, but in Acts of Cruelty, Slaughter & Rapine." The former treated captives "with Politeness humanity & acts of friendship," the latter with "the most savage Insolence, Malace & Cruelty." It all came down to individual character: good people did the right thing, bad people did not.[49]

Fitch had a point, to be sure, though when he showed the final draft of the "Narative" to Ethan Allen, it apparently got the Hero of Ticonderoga thinking. Two days later he came by Rapalje's for what Fitch described as "some peculiar conversation, & observations on Divine Providence"—which sounds suspiciously like an argument, or the continuation of an argument, over Fitch's approach to the issue of prisoner abuse. That may well have been the moment Allen resolved to write a book of his own, a book that would reveal the mistreatment of American prisoners to be the consequence of *policy*, not character.[50]

4

~

A CRY OF
Barbarity & Cruelty

A ROUND TEN O'CLOCK in the morning of Friday, December
13, 1776, Major General Charles Lee sat in a tavern outside
Basking Ridge, New Jersey, catching up on paperwork and brooding
over the inability of the American army to do anything but run from
the enemy. Lee was by all accounts the oddest and most turbulent of
Washington's commanders: a former major in the British Army who
supposedly knew his way around a battlefield, a radical intellectual
who despised monarchy, and a disheveled, overbearing, quarrelsome,
blaspheming, moody eccentric who had once married the daughter of
a Seneca chief and rarely went anywhere unless accompanied by two
or three dogs. (The Marquis de Lafayette thought "his whole appearance was entirely peculiar.")

After the American army had withdrawn from White Plains six
weeks earlier, Lee had also become increasingly certain that Congress
should have appointed him, not Washington, commander-in-chief.
He disapproved of Washington's subsequent decision to shift the
army to the New Jersey side of the Hudson, and his obvious reluctance to bring his own divisions along as Washington backed up toward the Delaware looked more and more like open insubordination.
Now, still in New Jersey a week after Washington had crossed the
Delaware into Pennsylvania, Lee was composing a letter to General
Horatio Gates (another former officer in His Majesty's army) that
lashed Washington for "damnably deficient" leadership. Just as he

General Charles Lee.

finished the letter, a British cavalry patrol galloped up and surrounded the building. It seems that a captured American officer had revealed Lee's whereabouts when the British threatened to hang him if he did not—one of the few instances when the mistreatment of prisoners can be linked to intelligence gathering. Lee's personal guard, completely surprised, put up only token resistance. Accepting the inevitable, Lee handed over his sword. "I hope you will use me as a gentleman," he reportedly said to the troopers.[1]

As news of Lee's captivity spread, Britons on both sides of the Atlantic were jubilant. The highest-ranking American officer to fall into their hands—and the only one whose abilities they took seriously at this point in the war—Lee was an even more valuable prize than Ethan Allen. Many also considered Lee a fitter candidate for the rope than Allen because they thought he had gone over to the rebels while still in His Majesty's service (not true: he had in fact resigned his commission and given up his pension). "I am happy to hear that Mr. Lee is in custody," crowed one British officer, "& I will be still happier to hear in the next acco[un]ts from New York that he has been tried as a deserter condemned & hang'd." Another, echoing General Gage's widely publicized dictum of the previous year, assured a correspondent in London that Lee was for sure "destined to the cord."[2]

The enemy held Lee in Brunswick, New Jersey, until mid-January 1777, then removed him under heavy guard to New York City. Rumors meanwhile flew on the American side that they had denied him the civilities due an officer and a gentleman—spirited him off without his hat and coat!—thrown him into a common jail!—put him in the dungeon of the Provost!—denied him parole!—intended to hang him! A worried Congress instructed Washington to find out exactly what had become of Lee and appropriated money "to render the Situation of that Gentleman as easy as possible."[3]

In fact, that gentleman was getting on splendidly. General Howe had indeed, as reported, refused to release him on parole, wondering whether Lee should be prosecuted as a deserter. But it was not an open-and-shut case. So while he waited for London to approve a court martial, Howe had Lee detained in the council chamber of City Hall. This ranked as "one of the genteelest public rooms in the City," groused the Tory historian Thomas Jones, "square, compact, tight, and warm"—much too tight and warm for a captured rebel general, even with fifty redcoats watching him round the clock. It galled Jones, too, that Lee got all the firewood and candles he needed, without charge, and enjoyed lavish dinners with whatever wine and liquor he desired, all at His Majesty's expense. No wonder, Jones snarled, the prisoner tumbled into bed "jovially mellow every night." In time, Howe even let Lee bring in his Italian manservant and one of his beloved dogs. Other than the fact that he could not go outside (and the prospect that Howe would succeed in having him hanged), Lee had nothing to complain about.[4]

While Lee got comfortable in City Hall—and while Fitch, Allen, and their brother officers adjusted to rather more spartan accommodations in Long Island farmhouses—reports about the mistreatment of other American prisoners in New York ricocheted around the country. Washington's staff got the story first, probably from the letter sent in by Colonels Atlee and Miles in early November 1776. Those two officers, it may be recalled, had written about the "truly deplorable" condition of the prisoners taken at Brooklyn and warned that without speedy relief or exchange, many would perish. In the weeks that followed, their grim prognosis was underscored by many similar reports. General Nathanael Greene heard from an informant "that our Prisoners in the City are Perishing for want of sustinance. . . . They are reduced to the necessity to beg and instead of receiveing any Charity are called damn Rebbels and told their fare is good enough." Not long after the capitulation of Fort Washington on November 16 had swelled the total number of prisoners in New York to around 5,000, General Alexander McDougall learned they "were very sickly, and died fast." Washington pressed Congress to find "some expedient" for supplying the men with blankets and clothing before it was too late. So did Colonel Miles himself, who (with General Howe's permission) made a quick visit to Philadelphia at the end of November to plead for money to assist the prisoners. Washington thought Miles extracted an appropriation of $8,000, but that seems to have been incorrect.[5]

Soon the states with citizens under detention in New York were in an uproar for action as well. When Major Levi Wells (also with Howe's permission) reported on the situation to the Connecticut legislature in early December, the members angrily decided to begin collecting sworn affidavits from anyone who had experienced or witnessed the abuse of prisoners. Governor Jonathan Trumbull fired off a letter to Washington describing the desperate condition of the many Connecticut prisoners in the city. They were "almost naked," he wrote; "their confinement is so close and crowded that they have scarce room to move or lie down, the air stagnate and corrupt; numbers dying daily." Trumbull grew even more agitated after the prisoners on the *Whitby* sent him their plea for help and after Oliver

Babcock, one of the men dumped on the beach of Milford, personally "Related the sufferings of my poor fellow prisoners at New York" to the governor and his council on January 7, 1777. Within days, the governor dispatched another letter to Washington emphasizing that voters in his state wanted those men exchanged—out of New York—right away. Ethan Allen, Trumbull added, should be the first to come home.[6]

Congress also heard from the New York State Committee for Detecting Conspiracies, which had begun its own drive to collect sworn depositions. One, given by a man who returned from New York in early January 1777, confirmed that General Lee was under heavy guard in City Hall "but in other respects well treated." The other American prisoners, however, "are most cruelly and Inhumanely treated, confined in churches without fire, and Dying in great numbers." This and similar reports prompted the New York State Convention to undertake a full-scale investigation, which produced additional allegations of abuse. On January 15, the Pennsylvania Council of Safety sent General Washington a frantic communiqué "of the Utmost Importance" claiming that no fewer than 11,000 American captives had *already* perished in New York for want of food and fuel—or so it had learned from "Persons of Veracity." The Maryland Council of Safety did not go so far, but it too was extremely concerned.[7]

American newspapers latched onto the story in January 1777, printing and reprinting the first of hundreds of letters, affidavits, and legislative documents about conditions in the prisons of New York. The *Pennsylvania Evening Post* carried a shocking report, often copied by papers around the country, that 260 American seamen, "many of whom had formerly lived in affluence," had been herded together on an unnamed prison ship in New York along with "Indians, Mulattoes, and Negro slaves." The inhumane treatment of captured American soldiers, the report continued, "has extended beyond this life, for the dead have been thrown out upon the highway and open fields, with this impious and horrid expression, 'D——n the rebel, he's not worth a grave.'" Numerous other papers ran a sobering letter from "a gentleman of honor and distinction, a prisoner in New-York," describing

the deaths of "20 or 30" prisoners every day. "Our murdered countrymen" the writer called them.[8]

The effect of these accounts on public opinion was electric. By
February 1777, according to James Thacher, a surgeon with the Continental Army, the "abominable conduct" of the British toward their
prisoners had aroused "the interest and the inexpressible indignation
of every American." Soldiers were now urged to fight to the death
rather than be taken "by British brutes, whose tender mercies are cruelty," and there were scattered indications that the stories coming out
of New York had given a much-needed boost to recruiting. Ashbel
Green later said that when some recently released American prisoners appeared at the door of his father's house in New Jersey—emaciated, wracked by "putrid fever," and covered with vermin—at least
one vowed to reenlist, if he lived, so he could do to British prisoners
what had been done to him. "This is not a good spirit," Green reflected, "but it was the expression of an indignation then popular."
General Samuel Holden Parsons, touring Connecticut to raise eight
new battalions for the Continental Army, also thought that stories
about the ill usage of captured Americans were making his work easier. Although most of the men who got out of New York detention
alive had already died, he informed Washington in mid-February
1777, "the remaining few burn with Rage against the Enemy & exceedingly desire to ingage again in the Service of their Country." Parsons's own rage against the enemy burned so fiercely that he had
started to formulate a plan for invading Long Island and liberating
the officers on parole there.[9]

In the furor, perhaps inevitably, colorful embellishments of inde-
terminate origin quickly acquired the force of settled fact. One of
the most durable—laced with just enough truth to keep it alive for
years—involved a mysterious "French doctor" who killed many
American prisoners with "poison powders." Doctor James
McHenry, one of the Fort Washington captives, identified the
Frenchman as "Louis Debute" and told Washington in June 1777
that Debute's murderous career had gone unchecked until he was let
go for beating a patient to death in one of the military hospitals
"with his stick." Jabez Fitch, out in New Lots, heard the rumor too.

In his just-completed "Narative" he told of the "Doctr Debuke" who ran a hospital in the Quaker meeting house and "often made application of his Cane among the Sick, in steed of other medecines." Yet another version had the doctor concealing his poisons in freshly baked bread.[10]

This "French Doctor" was almost certainly the same "Doctor Dubuke, Occulist and Dentist" who had trumpeted his arrival in New York toward the end of 1775 with a barrage of newspaper advertisements for miraculous pills, potions, and drops. A month or two later Dubuke was run out of town for theft. He returned when the occupation began in September 1776 and somehow obtained permission to treat rebel prisoners. Though clearly a bully as well as a quack, he had no evident motive for killing off his patients (keeping them alive being the usual mark of a successful medical practitioner). It made no sense, either, that men already dying of starvation and disease would need to be poisoned. Decades later, even so, level-headed Americans were still retelling the Dubuke legend as an explanation for the loss of thousands of lives in New York over the winter of 1776–1777. When he composed his reminiscences in the 1830s or early 1840s, John Pintard, a frequent visitor to Livingston's sugar house as well as the Provost during the war, still firmly believed that the "physics" administered by Dubuke had contained arsenic. "This," he emphasized, "is said to be a well authenticated fact."[11]

It was all nonsense, but the story of the devious French Doctor seemed credible precisely because it appeared to confirm what most Americans would conclude during the early months of 1777—that the deaths of so many prisoners in New York could not have been accidental. Exactly *why* the British would plan, or countenance, such a calamity would be explained at the end of January, when a New Haven paper, the *Connecticut Journal*, printed a remarkable 6,000-word essay on the subject. Untitled, signed only "Miserecors," and drawing heavily on the prisoners' own testimony, the essay began with a lengthy recitation of the conditions in the prisons and prison-ships of New York—the rotten food and foul water, the lack of blankets and firewood, the overcrowding, the degradation of men compelled to lie "in all the filth of nature and of the dysentery" for days on end. The principal reason for this diabolical travesty of humanity and justice, "Miserecors" then argued, was to inflict "just punishment" for the act of rebellion itself—not just to murder captives, in other words, "but to murder them by inches, to treat them ten times more cruelly than if they had hung them all, the day they took them." If, along the way, the lack of adequate food and clothing induced some captives to abandon their country's cause and switch sides—defect or die—so much the better. Such a policy, "Miserecors" reasoned, obviously did not originate in "a sudden heat of passion." It required "cool reflection, and a preconceived system."

And more: That the British could plan and implement so callous a "system" gave the lie to their boasted "politeness, humanity and compassion." It showed them, "Miserecors" continued, to be a naturally *cruel* people who "delight in torture and blood." Americans could rest assured that while they may look and talk like Britons, they were different and inherently *better*—decent, generous, and merciful. Not surprisingly, the prisoners they had taken actually thrived in captivity; in fact, "none have been so healthy, so merry, so plump and well fed." If the enemy's cruelty thus legitimated the Revolution, it also served as a warning that should they fail, all Americans would be treated like the prisoners in New York. "For cruelty runs thro' a man's whole conduct, and he that is so cruel in one part of his conduct, will be cruel throughout."[12]

"Miserecors" caused quite a stir for its time. Editors throughout New England reprinted the essay over the next couple of months, ensuring that it reached a large number of readers. European papers eventually picked it up as well. By May it had crossed Benjamin Franklin's desk in Paris. American officers paroled to the remote country villages of western Long Island likely saw it in one or another American paper at some point over the spring, though probably not soon enough to influence Jabez Fitch's musings about the meaning of prisoner abuse. It may well have made an impression on Governor William Livingston of New Jersey, however, because he was soon making strikingly similar arguments. "Cruelty and outrage are not the characteristics of America," he wrote in one of his "Adolphus" essays at the end of February. Weeks later he delivered a blistering message to the state legislature about the murder of prisoners and other "Gothic ravages" committed by the British. Such conduct, he announced, echoing "Miserecors," had "enabled us, the more effectually to distinguish, our friends from our enemies. It has winnowed the chaff from the grain."[13]

With this hue and cry building in the background, Congress and Washington became entangled in a rancorous dispute over General Lee. Though concerned for Lee's safety, Washington was far more concerned about the absence of a comprehensive agreement, or cartel, for the regular exchange of all prisoners between the British and American armies—something that European commanders-in-chief traditionally worked out among themselves in wartime. Congress, too, wanted a cartel, but its top priority was getting Lee back into service, or at least out of New York. At the beginning of January 1777, it came up with a scheme to force Howe's hand.

Congress instructed Washington to offer Howe a package of six field officers in return for their beloved Lee—five Hessians recently captured at Trenton plus a certain Lieutenant Colonel Archibald Campbell, a well-regarded young officer and MP who had been seized near Boston six months earlier. If Howe did not want a straight exchange, granting Lee a parole would be acceptable. If Howe did nothing, Campbell and the five Hessians would be locked up in retaliation until he did.

Howe did nothing. He and Washington had previously traded specific individuals in what were often referred to as partial exchanges—General Sullivan for General Prescott after the battle of Brooklyn, for example—but always rank for rank. Exchanging a general for junior officers was the kind of deal that customarily required delicate negotiations beforehand to establish a comprehensive table of equivalents between *all* ranks (how many privates for a captain, how many captains for a major, and so forth—a process called "composition"). In any case, until London clarified Lee's legal status, Howe had no intention of letting Lee out of his grasp, even on parole. So, as promised, Congress ordered Campbell and the Hessians "into safe and close custody" for the purpose of inflicting on them "the same punishment as may be inflicted on the person of General Lee."[14]

Washington did not object, in principle, to retaliation. But he also believed that Congress blundered by putting Lee's safety ahead of that of other American prisoners, inasmuch as their suffering would only increase if Howe responded in kind. When word arrived in February that Campbell had been flung into the noisome Concord jail, Washington was appalled and immediately protested to the Massachusetts authorities. General Lee, he reminded them sharply, "is only confined to a commodious House with genteel accommodations"—common knowledge by this time—whereas Campbell was subjected to conditions "scarce ever inflicted upon the most atrocious Criminals." To Campbell himself Washington sent a carefully worded note to the effect that it was all an unfortunate misunderstanding. "I shall always be happy," he declared with the orotund formality of eighteenth-century gentlemen, "to manifest my disinclination to any undue severities towards those whom the fortune of War may chance to throw into my hands."[15]

In time, Congress would order better treatment for the poor man, explaining lamely that "it was never their intention that he should suffer any other hardship than such confinement as is necessary to his security." Early in June, Congress had Campbell moved to a private house in Concord.[16]

But then came the disturbing news that Lee had been transferred to the warship *Centurion* in New York harbor, presumably in preparation for his return to England. Congress therefore adopted another resolution, threatening retaliation if anyone *in the service of the United States* were spirited out of the country for trial or imprisonment (which neatly dodged the problem of Ethan Allen, who had no commission from Congress). Lee was not assured of remaining in America, however, until early July, when American commandos snatched Major General Richard Prescott from a house near Newport, Rhode Island—the unpopular Prescott's second time around as a prisoner of war. Congress determined that Prescott made a better hostage for Lee's safety and released Campbell and the Hessians on parole.*

The Lee contretemps greatly reduced the likelihood of a cartel in 1777, but it was in fact only one of several issues blowing dense clouds of suspicion and enmity across the lines. Especially at the beginning of the war, when both Congress and the Continental Army were literally inventing themselves on the run, Washington's dealings with Howe were hampered by such irregular record keeping that he often had no idea which Americans were in enemy hands, and which of the enemy were in American hands (scores of the latter were in fact held by various state governments, who had to be wheedled and cajoled into giving them up). Embarrassingly, at one point near the end of 1776, Washington had had to ask Howe for a list of some British officers recently returned to New York, "that I may make a demand of the like Number in Exchange." Washington's inability to put his hands on information critical for negotiating a cartel would again become apparent the following year, when he and Howe found themselves at loggerheads over the approximately 1,800 captives released from New York over the winter of 1776–1777. Howe took the position that Washington owed him an equivalent number of British captives; Washington maintained that because most of those men had been so mistreated as to be unfit for further service, they ought not be counted in making up a cartel.[17]

---

*Ironically, Lee may have been flirting with treason all the while. In February 1777 he had asked Congress to send envoys to New York to hear his plan for brokering peace talks. Congress, suspecting a British trick, said no. Washington disagreed, reasoning that because Lee was so popular in the army, ignoring him would damage morale. For several weeks he tried without success to convince Congress to change its mind, both about refusing to talk with Lee as well as retaliating against Campbell. As a result, it was not until early April that Lee got the bad news. The delay may well have persuaded him that his American friends could not protect him, or did not want to, for he had by then given his captors a plan for breaking down American resistance and quashing the Revolution. There is no evidence that Howe ever knew what Lee had in mind, however. His overture was forgotten, lost in a sea of official paper, and did not come to light until the middle of the next century. Not surprisingly, the scholar who found it saw conclusive proof that the most famous American prisoner in New York at that time had turned coat to save his neck. Lee's modern biographer gives him the benefit of the doubt and speculates that he may only have been attempting to lead the British on a wild goose chase. Absent the discovery of new information, exactly what happened remains a mystery.

Yet another difficulty was that Lord North, Lord Germain, and the king refused to recognize captured Americans (Lee especially) as prisoners of war. Any exchange agreement would thus have to rest solely on the personal honor of the commanders involved and could never be endorsed by His Majesty's government. Neither Washington nor Congress was willing to negotiate on that basis, for all the obvious reasons.[18]

Any hope that the British government would take a different tack wafted away in March 1777 when Parliament adopted a measure, informally dubbed "North's Act," that suspended habeas corpus and authorized the prosecution of captured rebels for treason or piracy, as circumstances required. Opposition spokesmen valiantly denounced the act as an ominous assault on English liberty—Lord Abingdon pronounced it "shocking to humanity," while Isaac Barré warned that it would only make reconciliation with the colonies more difficult—but North and Germain reminded everyone that this was no time for timidity. The government had a rebellion on its hands, and decisive action was necessary. In any event, British forces would soon restore law and order in the colonies and the measure could be repealed. Certainly, North added soothingly, he had no intention of using the suspension of habeas corpus for "oppressive or bad purposes" at home.[19]

Also to be reckoned with was the continuing stream of American civilian detainees into the Provost. None was ever formally charged with a crime, much less tried in a court of law, and all of them remained under lock and key until someone (the provost marshal, the commissary of prisoners, or the commandant) decided to let them out. In May 1777, General Howe (now General *Sir* William Howe, his reward for victory in the Battle of Brooklyn) offered to swap captured civilians for British officers held by the United States, but Washington promptly declined because he knew that such a trade would prompt the enemy to round up even more "Inhabitants of Reputation." He as well as Congress wanted the British to stop arresting noncombatants altogether, or at the very least to exchange them on a one-for-one basis, like soldiers and officers. That promised to be no easy task, however, because no one on the American side knew for certain who or how many had been taken, for what reason, or where they were being held.[20]

Nothing, however, did more to ruin the climate for a cartel than Howe's stubborn refusal to concede that the treatment of American captives in New York left anything to be desired. Back at the beginning of December 1776, he had admitted to Washington that the sick and wounded in New York needed better "Accommodation, Refreshments, and Attendance" than he could provide. Washington had been inclined to believe him, but that was before anyone on the American side had a clear picture of the horror story unfolding in the city. The accumulating evidence of British wrongdoing soon compelled Washington to change his mind, and in mid-January 1777 he sent an angry protest to Howe, enclosing copies to Howe of the most damning affidavits recently collected from ex-prisoners. "You may call us Rebels, and say, that we deserve no better treatment," he cautioned. "But remember my Lord, that supposing us Rebels, we still have feelings equally keen and sensible, as Loyalists, and will, if forced to it, most assuredly retaliate upon those, upon whom we look, as the unjust invaders of our Rights Liberties and properties—I should not have said thus much, but my injured Countrymen have long called upon me to endeavour to obtain a Redress of their Greivances [sic]."[21]

Nonsense, Howe shot back. Perhaps "one, two, or three" bodies at a time have on occasion been laid out for burial in the morning, but nothing like the numbers alleged by Washington's informants. He knew of only *seven* Americans who had died thus far on the prison ships. Provisions for the captives are "exactly the same in Nature and Quality" as those given His Majesty's soldiers and seamen. A doctor, amply supplied with medicines, attended to the sick. If their places of confinement appear dirty, Howe added, the prisoners' own "Indolence" was to blame! Besides, no prisoner had ever complained to him or his subordinates about mistreatment.[22]

Washington ignored that absurd evasion of responsibility until the beginning of April, when he pointed out to Howe, again, that the evidence of abuse had now become simply too massive to be questioned. What came back were still more fatuous denials. Every one of the New York prisoners, Howe boasted, had received prompt medical attention as well as two-thirds of the rations allotted British soldiers ("sufficient and wholesome food" he called it). All of the men "were confined in the most airy buildings, and on board the largest transports in the fleet, which were the very healthiest places of reception that could possibly be provided for them." Why, then, did so many perish? "To what Cause a speedy Death of a large Part of them is to be attributed," Howe concluded vacuously, "I cannot determine." When Congress got a look at this correspondence, its reaction was a mixture of disbelief and outrage that made the likelihood of a cartel more remote than ever.[23]

Midway through January 1777, Congress had appointed a seven-man committee to investigate reports of the mistreatment of American prisoners as well as the profusion of atrocity stories that followed recent enemy operations in New York and New Jersey. Though chaired by Samuel Chase of Maryland, the committee's most energetic member proved to be the Reverend John Witherspoon—a rock-ribbed Presbyterian clergyman, fifty-five years old, presently in his tenth year as president of the College of New Jersey (now Princeton University). Over a period of two or three months, working mainly out of his home in Princeton, Witherspoon collected and transcribed depositions from a long procession of witnesses. As a young man in Scotland he had been imprisoned by Highlanders loyal to Bonnie Prince Charlie, and the memory of that awful experience haunted him for the rest of his life. It could never have been far from his mind when he sat down to draft the final report, which would be presented to Congress in mid-April 1777.[24]

The main points were simple and chilling: the British had engaged in "wanton and oppressive" destruction of property, they had treated their prisoners "with the greatest barbarity" and killed "multitudes," they had butchered soldiers and civilians who surrendered to them, their troops had regularly assaulted and raped women. "On the whole," the report concluded, "the cry of barbarity and cruelty is but too well founded." However, it shied away from sweeping, inflammatory conclusions of the kind drawn by "Miserecors" (and Governor Livingston, for that matter). The committee turned up no evidence, Witherspoon wrote, that the enemy *planned* any of these odious crimes in advance. It did link them, on the other hand, to the contempt for Americans, the routinized use of "opprobrious, disdainful names" for "rebels," that pervaded His Majesty's armed forces. Men taught to demonize their adversaries will become demons themselves:

> It is easy, therefore, to see what must be the consequence of a soldiery, greedy of prey, towards a people, whom they have been taught to look upon, not as freemen defending their rights on principle, but as desperadoes and profligates, who have risen up against law and order in general, and wish the subversion of society itself. This is the most candid and charitable manner in which the committee can account for the melancholy truths which they have been obliged to report. Indeed, the same deluding principle seems to govern persons and bodies of the highest rank in Britain.[25]

Congress was thrilled with the report and told the committee to print up 6,000 copies (4,000 in English, and another 2,000 in German) with all supporting documentation. Before that could be done, however, the whole thing was serialized in the *Pennsylvania Evening Post*, from which printers all over the country would take bits and pieces for their own papers in the ensuing months.

John Adams, who greatly admired Witherspoon, sent a copy of the report to Abigail, explaining wryly that it "will give you, some Idea, of the Humanity of the present Race of Brittons." Used properly, it could also be very useful to the cause. "I think We cannot dwell too much, on this Part of their Character, and Conduct," he added. A simple recitation of "the horrid deeds of our enemies" will win over public opinion in Europe and put "the Fortitude, Patience, Perseverance, and Magnanimity of Americans, in as strong a Light, as the Barbarity and Impiety of Britons." On this side of the Atlantic, it will "convince every American that a Nation, so great a Part of which is thus deeply depraved, can never again be trusted with Power over Us."[26]

Witherspoon's report was one of two accomplishments for which Congress could take credit in the spring of 1777. The other came at the end of January, when it decided to appoint a commissary general of prisoners. Besides caring for enemy captives in American hands, the commissary general would be responsible for getting food, clothing, money, and other essentials to Americans held by the enemy— ideally, by working through an agent who had permission to reside near their places of confinement. Such arrangements were customary among belligerent powers in the eighteenth century, and Washington, having repeatedly urged Congress to create both positions, was delighted. He wrote at once to Howe, proposing that Lewis Pintard, a well-known New York merchant and John Pintard's uncle, serve as resident agent to the prisoners.[27]

A commissary proved harder to find. "I want a shrewd sensible Man exceedingly for this business," Washington instructed his adjutant, Colonel Joseph Reed, but their first choice, Colonel Cornelius Cox of Pennsylvania, declined the job on the grounds that it gave an officer no opportunity for distinction. Washington then turned to a civilian, Elias Boudinot, who declined as well in early April—then relented after receiving a personal scolding from the commander-in-chief. "If men of character and influence would not come forward and join him in his exertions," Washington admonished Boudinot, "all would be lost."[28]

Boudinot and Pintard made a promising team. Pintard, nearing his forty-fifth birthday, had made a lot of money in the East India trade, aligned himself with other big merchants critical of Britain's colonial policies, and left town with his family just before Howe arrived in the autumn of 1776. Boudinot, thirty-seven, had built a lucrative legal practice in Elizabeth Town, New Jersey. He was tall, handsome, elegant, deeply religious, and well connected. (Four years earlier, his friends had discovered a bright young man from the West Indies named Alexander Hamilton, who boarded with the Boudinots in Elizabeth Town while attending the local academy; Hamilton was now a rising star in Washington's entourage.)[29]

Elias Boudinot. After resigning his position as commissary general of prisoners, he served in the Continental Congress until the end of the war in 1783. He represented New Jersey in the U.S. House of Representatives from 1789 to 1795, then spent ten years as director of the Mint. In 1816 he was elected first president of the American Bible Society.

The new commissary and his agent in fact already knew each other quite well. Both were descended from French Huguenots who had emigrated to New York and New Jersey almost a century earlier and were distantly related. They were also related by marriage. Each had wed a sister of Judge Richard Stockton, a prominent New Jersey lawyer, landowner, and signer of the Declaration of Independence. What was more, Elias Boudinot's brilliant younger sister, Annis Boudinot, was Judge Stockton's wife, and Elias first met Hannah Stockton, his future wife, while reading law in Judge Stockton's office.[30]

As it happened, Lewis and Susannah Stockton Pintard were probably living with or near the Boudinots in New Jersey at the end of November 1776, when Howe's redcoats had trashed Morven, Judge Stockton's estate near Princeton. Stockton fled but was subsequently abducted by Tories and thrown into the Provost, where he reportedly suffered violent abuse at the hands of his captors. Congress protested, and the British released him early in 1777, around the same time that Lewis Pintard, his brother-in-law, agreed to serve as agent to the prisoners still in New York. Rumors soon began to fly that Judge Stockton, health and spirits shattered, had disavowed the Declaration of Independence and taken an oath of loyalty to the Crown, as prescribed by General Howe's November 30 proclamation—which if true would make him the only Signer to have done so. There is no telling if the rumors swayed Elias Boudinot, his other brother-in-law, to take the job of commissary of prisoners, but Boudinot would certainly have heard them.[31]

Thus yoked together by blood and marriage, the two Jersey men began to create the administrative machinery for relieving the American prisoners in New York and elsewhere. It was slow going. Howe refused Pintard permission to come to the city until late April 1777, and only then with the proviso that his mission remain unofficial and informal, lest anyone construe it as recognition of the Continental Congress or American independence. Indeed, when Congress offered to appoint him deputy commissary of prisoners, Pintard declined precisely because he knew that Howe would not allow anyone with such a title to remain in the city.[32]

Boudinot was in the meantime assembling a staff and discovering what proved to be one of his most annoying problems: a congressional resolution of the previous July that urged each state to appoint a commissary of prisoners and negotiate exchanges with the enemy for its own citizens. "This resolution mitigates directly agt. my Appointment," Boudinot complained to the Board of War. One man, and one man only, should have the authority to conduct such negotiations. Washington agreed and repeatedly urged the states most actively involved in their own talks with the enemy—especially New York, Connecticut, New Jersey, and Massachusetts—to let the commissary general handle all exchanges, or at least to tell him what they were doing. They rarely cooperated, however. Although Congress, too, eventually saw the need for centralized control over the process, it never found a way to stop the wheeling and dealing or jurisdictional wrangling.[33]

No less disconcerting was Boudinot's realization that Congress had no money for him to work with, other than the nearly worthless paper currency called Continentals. At the beginning of May, it did give him a paltry £600 in bills of exchange, the idea being to have Pintard sell the bills in New York City and use the proceeds to buy provisions for the prisoners there. The bills failed to sell as well as expected, however, and—maddeningly—the little cash Pintard raised went mostly to reduce the amount due Commissary Joshua Loring for expenses already incurred on behalf of American captives, thousands of whom had by this time perished. Boudinot then asked Washington to let him take some of the clothing stockpiled for military use, but Washington said he had nothing to spare.[34]

By the end of June, if not earlier, Boudinot was already at his wits' end. "I exerted every Nerve to obtain Supplies," he would say later, "but in Vain." Instead of resigning, though, he began to dip into his own funds and borrow from friends, sinking more and more deeply into debt over the summer and fall of 1777. His extraordinary generosity enabled Pintard to begin distributing small quantities of money, food, and clothing among the New York prisoners in preparation for the coming winter. It was not much, and certainly far from enough, but it was better than nothing.[35]

Adding to the pressure on Boudinot and Pintard, the number of American captives in New York was on the rise again. Howe launched a long and elaborate campaign against Philadelphia in the summer of 1777 that yielded maybe a hundred, though after the rebel capital fell to him at the end of September he would send his prisoners there, not to New York. Even so, New York continued to receive Americans captured at sea, such as the captain and crew of the Continental frigate *Hancock*, taken off Nova Scotia in July 1777. The city also received prisoners who were swept up in routine operations within a seventy-five-mile radius of Manhattan—foraging expeditions out to eastern Long Island and through the Hackensack and Raritan valleys of New Jersey, as well as punitive raids into Westchester County and New England. There would be no big hauls like those at Brooklyn or Fort Washington; instead, the Americans were taken one or two at a time, sometimes by the dozens, occasionally by the score, and among them were a growing number of civilians.[36]

In January 1777, for example, Lieutenant Lewis J. Costigan of the First New Jersey was captured while on a one-man reconnoitering expedition into the area around Brunswick. He would spend the next three years as a prisoner in New York. In February, an expedition against American forces stationed near Sandy Hook, New Jersey, returned with seventy-two prisoners. In March, skirmishes near Kingsbridge, New York, Woodbridge, New Jersey, and Norwalk, Connecticut, yielded a total of fifty-nine American captives, including the "Chairman of a

Committee," one of numerous state prisoners. In April, General Charles Cornwallis surprised American forces under General Benjamin Lincoln near Bound Brook, New Jersey, and brought eighty-five captives back to New York City. They were said to be "the most miserably looking Creatures that ever bore the name of Soldiers, covered with nothing but Rags and Vermin." Around the same time, Captain Wynant van Zandt of the New Jersey Militia was seized by Tories, hustled back to New York, and paraded through the streets "as a show and [was] styled the great rebel." Toward the end of April, another raiding party returned from New Jersey with an especially important catch—John Fell of Paramus, prominent member of the state legislative council and "a great Tory Hunter." Only days later, forces under the command of Colonel William Tryon, the last royal governor of New York, grabbed more than fifty prisoners during the heavy fighting that followed their raid on Danbury, Connecticut; they deposited most of the Americans in Livingston's sugar house, though ten-year-old Jeremiah Sanford was reportedly put aboard the *Whitby* in Wallabout Bay, where he died two months later.[37]

On May 10, the Forty-second Highlanders beat back an assault by "1500 or 2000 of the Rebels" at Piscataway, New Jersey, killing thirty and returning to New York with twenty-eight prisoners. Long Island Tories subsequently bagged a substantial trophy of their own, the Reverend Joshua Hartt (or Hart), a 300-pound Presbyterian minister from Smithtown famous for fire-and-brimstone sermons against the Crown ("The cause we are engaged in is the cause of God!"). Like Fell and most other civilians, Hartt went into the Provost. "Forty-two Rebels came in today to be whitewashed," Nicholas Cresswell noted in his journal at the end of the month, not explaining how they had been taken, or where.[38]

On June 22, near Brunswick, New Jersey, four brigades under General Nathanael Greene clashed with a large British force commanded by General Howe; nineteen American prisoners were afterward brought back to New York, all but one of whom went straight into the sugar house. Four days later, near Metuchen, Cornwallis mauled Lord Stirling's division and came away with fifty prisoners, though a Scottish grenadier thought it was more like 150.[39]

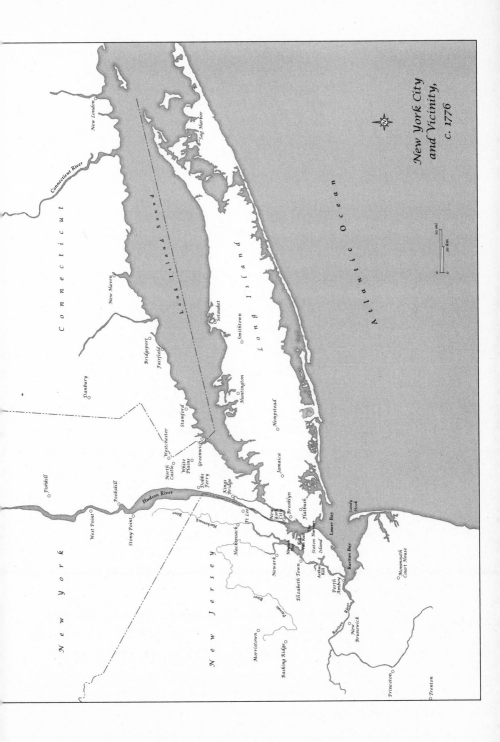

New York City
and Vicinity,
c. 1776

And so it went, through the summer and fall of 1777: five New Jersey militiamen seized on the banks of the Passaic River and hustled off to Livingston's sugar house; seventy more brought in from Amboy; about a dozen more from Woodbridge; ten from White Plains; twenty-five from New Rochelle; fourteen from Newark; seventeen from Long Island; one from Kingsbridge. On August 22, the enemy routed an American force under General John Sullivan on Staten Island, killing thirteen and capturing 172. When Forts Clinton and Montgomery, on the Hudson, surrendered to General Henry Clinton in early October, another 250 Americans were taken captive, including Major Stephen Lush, an aide to Governor George Clinton. Most wound up in Livingston's sugar house, though two dozen officers were sent to the Provost, where their only food for over a week was bread so infested with bugs that when a piece fell on the floor, one prisoner said, "it Took legs and Ran in all Directions—so full of Life." The British snagged only a single prisoner however, after a clash with Pennsylvania militia near White Marsh in December: Brigadier General James Irvine, ignominiously abandoned by his men while he lay wounded on the field.[40]

There was no letup, either, in the procession of civilian prisoners into occupied New York. A particularly notorious case involved Cornelius and Peter Van Tassel of Westchester County, seized by redcoats on the night of November 18, probably because Peter happened to be a prominent member of the local committee of safety (his relationship to Cornelius is unclear). Their houses were burned to the ground, and the two men—allegedly roped to the tails of their horses—were dragged down to Livingston's sugar house, where they would spend the rest of the war. When General Parsons complained to Colonel Tryon about this and other assaults on noncombatants, Tryon retorted that he would, if it were in his power, "burn every committee-man's house within my reach." Failing that, he added peevishly, "I am willing to give twenty silver dollars for every acting committee-man who shall be delivered to the King's troops." A man could wind up in gaol for a lot less, however. Eighteen-year-old Henry Williams, no soldier, found himself in the Provost just "for Speaking ill of the King & well of the Congress." So did Selah

Strong, a resident of Suffolk County, locked up on the all-purpose charge that he had engaged in "treasonable correspondence with his Majesty's enemies."[41]

The anecdotal and unfailingly partisan origins of this evidence make it impossible to say exactly how many new American prisoners were brought to New York during that year's campaign; there were at least 700 and maybe 1,000 or more. One thing *is* clear: this influx guaranteed that despite the best efforts of Boudinot and Pintard, the prisons of New York would remain as overcrowded, vile, and lethal as ever.[42]

In mid-March, 1777, Captain Nathaniel Fitz Randolph of Woodbridge, New Jersey, got a letter out to his wife with some decidedly mixed news: his wounds were beginning to heal and he was now "in prety good Health," but his comrades were suffering dreadfully. Words cannot describe, he wrote, "the misserys that attend the Poor Prisoners Confined in this Horrid place, they are dying dayly with (what is called here) the Gaol fever [typhus] but may more properly be called the Hungry fever." Indeed, when Admather Blodget of Massachusetts later talked with friends and family about his ordeal in Livingston's sugar house in 1777, he always mentioned that he survived only by eating garbage thrown into the prison yard from a nearby residence. Thomas Stone, a twenty-two-year-old soldier from Connecticut, likewise remembered that "old shoes were bought and eaten with as good a relish as a pig or a turkey." Over the winter of 1777–1778, Stone added, his fellow prisoners died at the rate of seven to ten per day—a mortality rate virtually identical to that of the previous winter, which had been very, very bad. Of the sixty-nine men captured with Stone in December, only fifteen remained alive six months later.[43]

Levi Hanford, also of Connecticut and only seventeen when the British captured him, recalled how the inmates of Livingston's sugar house learned to prepare their meager allotment of raw pork and wormy sea biscuit:

> The biscuit was such as had been wet with sea water and damaged, was full of worms and mouldy. It was our common practice to put

water in our camp kettle, then break up the biscuit into it, skim off
the worms, put in the pork, and boil it, if we had fuel; but this was
allowed us only part of the time; and when we could get no fuel, we
ate our meat raw and our biscuit dry. Starved as we were, there was
nothing in the shape of food that was rejected or was unpalatable.

In late October Hanford was transferred to the ill-named *Good Intent*, a transport recently converted for use as a prison ship and now
riding at anchor in the Hudson River. There he discovered 200 more
Americans crammed below decks, starving and dying like flies in the
sepulchral gloom. Within two months, half were dead. When Hanford himself fell sick, they moved him to the military hospital in the
Brick Presbyterian Church, but it was no improvement. "Disease and
death reigned there in all their terror," he told his son many years afterward, the scene still fresh in his mind. "I have had men die by the
side of me in the night, and have seen fifteen dead bodies sewed up in
their blankets and laid in the corner of the yard at one time, the product of one twenty-four hours." And worse, horribly worse:

> Every morning at 8 o'clock the dead-cart came, the bodies were
> put in, the men drew their rum, and the cart was driven off to the
> trenches. . . . Once I was permitted to go with the guard to the
> place of interment, and never shall I forget the scene that I there
> beheld; they tumbled them into the ditch just as it happened,
> threw on a little dirt, and then away. I could see a hand, a foot, or
> part of a head, washed bare by the rains, swollen, blubbering, and
> falling to decay.[44]

Hanford's two-month stint on the *Good Intent* was a sign that the
resurgent population of prisoners had compelled British authorities
to begin moving the overflow onto an assortment of vessels anchored
in the waters around New York. Over in Wallabout Bay, the infamous
Whitby, apparently taken out of service as early as April 1777, was replaced by the *Prince of Wales*, a decrepit warship, and a hospital ship
named *Kitty* (which burned in mid-October 1777, quite possibly set
ablaze by the prisoners themselves). At some point in the course of

that year, the *Judith* and the *Myrtle*, two transports anchored in the Hudson opposite Trinity Church, began to receive prisoners, as did the *Jersey* and the *Good Hope*, a pair of hospital ships hitherto reserved for the use of His Majesty's forces. American captives would also be confined in the brigs of at least nine other vessels not officially designated as prisons or hospitals: the *Eagle* (Admiral Lord Richard Howe's flagship), *Felicity, Isis, Richmond, Otter, Dispatch, York, Vigilant,* and *Mercury.* Because changing weather conditions often required them to find new anchorages, few if any remained in the same place for more than two or three months at a time. Initially, the *Good Hope* lay in the Hudson, somewhere along the city's west side, perhaps near the *Good Intent;* some reports place the *Jersey* there as well, though others find her at various locations in the East River. But when the Hudson began to freeze in December, the *Good Hope* and the *Good Intent* were brought round Manhattan to Wallabout Bay, where they joined the *Prince of Wales* and several other ships that cannot now be identified. The *Jersey* followed sometime over the winter (if she was not there already), and by the spring of 1778 she was serving as the first stop for captives destined for the prison ships anchored nearby.[45]

The agonies witnessed by Thomas Stone in Livingston's sugar house and by Levi Hanford on the *Good Hope* were described in equally graphic detail by several occupants of the Provost—none more eloquent than that of the "great Tory Hunter," John Fell, who since his arrest at the end of April had kept a daily record or "Memorandum" of his experiences as a captive of the British. His terse notations, squeezed onto each page in a minuscule script, log the emotional ups and downs of the prisoners there as they struggled with overcrowding, hunger, sickness, appalling squalor, and petty, capricious cruelties:

MAY 20. Lewis Pintard came per order of Elias Boudinot to offer me money; refused admittance.

. . .

MAY 30. Not allowed to fetch good water.

MAY 31. Bad water; proposed buying tea water, but refused. This night 10 prisoners from opposite room ordered into ours; in all 20.

. . .

JUNE 3. Capt. Van Zandt sent to dungeon for resenting Capt. Cunningham's abusing and insulting me.

. . .

JUNE 10. Prisoners very sickly.

. . .

JUNE 13. Melancholy scene, women refused speaking to their sick husbands, and treated cruelly by sentries.

A week later the prisoners drafted a letter to the sergeant, "requesting more privileges," but received no response. They then sent a "list of grievances" to the British commandant of the city, currently Major General Robert Pigot. The response was unequivocal: "Grant no requests made by prisoners." Fell's almost daily catalogue of miseries grew ever longer:

JUNE 25. Dr. Bard came to visit Justice Moore, but his wife was refused though her husband was dying.[46]
JUNE 26. Justice Moore died & carried out.

. . .

JULY 15. A declaration of more privileges, & p[risoners] allowed to speak at the windows.

. . .

AUG 1. very sick—weather very hot.

. . .

AUG 11. Freeland from Polly? Fly whipped about Salt.
AUG 12. Serj. Keith took all the pens and ink out of each room, and forbid the use of any on pain of dungeon.

. . .

AUG 26. Badcock sent to dungeon for cutting wood in evening. Locks put on all the doors & threatened to be locked up. Col. Ethan Allen brought to Provost from L.I. & confined below.

. . .

AUG 31. A.M. Col Allen brought into our room.

. . .

SEPT 4. Horrid scenes of whipping.

. . .

SEPT 10. Provisions exceeding ordinary—pork very rusty, biscuits
bad.[47]

Ethan Allen's arrival in the Provost at the end of August 1777
launched the final act in his operatic career as a prisoner of war. In the
version of events that appeared two years later in his autobiographical
Narrative, he had been arrested in New Lots "under pretext of artful,
mean and pitiful pretences, that I had infringed on my parole." In
truth, Allen had grown weary of New Lots and got into the habit of
wandering rather far afield. On several occasions he took the ferry
over to New York and strolled openly around town in broad daylight.
No matter that other American officers had done the same thing, or
that he always returned to New Lots by sundown: leaving Kings
County did constitute a violation of his parole, and he was too prominent (as well as contentious) for the authorities to let it go unnoticed.
Armed guards were therefore dispatched to bring him back to Manhattan, where he endured several days of solitary confinement in the
Provost without food.[48]

"I now perceived myself to be again in substantial trouble," he recalled dryly. As luck would have it, however, he discovered (or carved)
a small hole in the floorboards of his cell, through which he could
communicate with the occupant of the dungeon below. This proved to
be Captain Edward Travis of the Virginia Navy. How Travis became a
prisoner is unclear, but his quarterdeck bearing and manners evidently
survived the experience intact. Allen described him as "a gentleman of
high spirits," who "had a high sense of honor, and felt as big, as though
he had been in a palace, and had treasures of wrath in store against the
British. In fine I was charmed with the spirit of the man"—a kindred
soul for the Hero of Ticonderoga if ever there was one.[49]

Imagine, therefore, these two pugnacious American officers, Allen
and Travis, whispering urgently back and forth through that narrow
opening, swapping stories and stoking the hatred they shared for their
captors. No wonder that when the guards finally moved him upstairs,
Allen had more fight in him than ever. The room he now found himself in held "above twenty" officers as well as "some private gentlemen,

who had been dragged from their own homes to that filthy place by tories." One of them was the New Jersey diarist John Fell, whom Allen came to admire as "a worthy friend to America." Another was Major Otho Holland Williams of Maryland. Williams had been severely wounded and taken prisoner at Fort Washington, then paroled to Long Island with Jabez Fitch and other officers, only to be arrested and sent to the Provost on suspicion of corresponding secretly with General Washington. The major arrived a few weeks after Allen and "walked through the prison with an air of great disdain; said he, 'Is this the treatment which gentlemen of the continental army are to expect from the rascally British, when in their power?'"[50]

A third newcomer was Elias Cornelius, a Long Island native serving as a surgeon's mate with one of the Rhode Island regiments. "Doctor" Cornelius, as he came to be known, had been ambushed by Tories in East Chester at the end of August, then turned over to the regulars, who escorted him and several other captives down to New York City. "As we come into the town," he wrote in his journal, "the Hesians, Negroes, and children insulted, stoned and abused us in every way they could think of." Once their captors tired of this "show," now a well-established ritual when prisoners were brought in, the Americans were herded, "like so many hogs," into Livingston's sugar house—"the dirtiest and most disagreeable place that I ever saw," Cornelius recalled with a shudder.[51]

In charge of the sugar house was a vicious Irish sergeant named Walley (Wally, or Wolley), who allowed the prisoners far less than the two-thirds rations they were entitled to. He "gave us (13 of us) 4 pounds of poor Irish Pork and 4 pounds of mouldy bread for 4 days," Cornelius recounted. When Cornelius asked for pen and paper to petition for parole, Sergeant Walley "struck me across the face with a staff which I have seen him beat the prisoners." He then hauled Cornelius over to the Provost, where he was sequestered in a basement dungeon with three other American officers—one of them Captain Travis—along with "nine thieves murderers &c." The only thing that kept him going was the knowledge "that many of my dear country men had previously suffered greater punishment than mine; and that many of them died and bled in their countrys cause, and defense." A week or so later, he and Travis were moved upstairs to join Allen, Williams, Fell, and the other American prisoners. It was an improvement, Cornelius thought, but still onerous. "While I was in this place, we were not allowed to speak to any friend, not even out of the window," he fumed. "I have frequently seen women beaten with canes and ram-rods who have come to the Prison windows to speak to their Husbands, Sons or Brothers, and officers taken and put in the dungeon just for asking for cold water."[52]

Allen, Travis, Williams, Fell, Cornelius—some really angry men were interned in the Provost in the autumn of 1777, and they had not been together for a month before they drafted a sharply worded complaint to the city commandant, Major General Pigot. Their grievances included close confinement "without distinction of rank or character"; inadequate rations ("2 lbs. hard biscuit and 2 lbs. raw pork per man per week"); insufficient firewood; bad water; no medicine for the sick; no visits by wives or family; no pen, ink, or paper allowed for writing; and arbitrary confinement in a "loathsome dungeon." The Americans' choicest invective was reserved for the provost marshal, Captain William Cunningham, whose notoriety had been building steadily since his first appearance after the Battle of Brooklyn. Cunningham, who regularly "insulted in a gross manner, and vilely abused" the detainees in the Provost, "is allowed to be one of the basest characters in the British army, . . . whose power is so unlimited, that he has caned an officer on a trivial occasion, and frequently beats sick privates when [they are] unable to stand." (Indeed, Travis himself had already received at least one beating from Cunningham in the presence of witnesses.)[53]

At the end of September, Pintard delivered these charges to Pigot. There is no record of an answer. Sergeant Keith, Cunningham's second in command and (according to Allen) a "vicious and ill bred imperious rascal," retaliated by bolting the doors to all the rooms for a day or two.[54]

A small measure of consolation was nonetheless about to reach the Provost on the wings of what Fell termed "Glorious news from the Northward." Thanks in large part to Howe's diversion of his forces to the Philadelphia campaign, Major General John Burgoyne's invasion of

New York from Canada had ground to a halt near the Hudson River village of Saratoga, 175 miles above New York City. On October 17, American forces under General Horatio Gates cornered "Gentleman Johnny" and obliged him to surrender his entire army—some 3,200 men and officers, including 7 generals, 197 musicians, and 6 members of Parliament. When notice of Burgoyne's defeat reached the Provost a few days later (hidden in a loaf of bread, according to Major Leggett's version of the story), "the whole prison was filled with joy inexpressible!" It was no coincidence that Major General James Robertson (having resumed his duties as commandant of occupied New York) promptly sent an aide to investigate conditions there: with so many redcoats and Hessians now in American hands, the risks entailed by abusing or neglecting American captives had risen significantly. Whether anything would change was another matter entirely.[55]

Measured against the awful suffering of their countrymen imprisoned in New York, the 200-plus American officers billeted on Long Island had it easy. Few if any considered themselves really comfortable, however. They complained frequently of having too few clothes and not enough palatable food. Because New Lots, Flatbush, and the other Kings County villages remained overwhelmingly Tory in sentiment, the American officers also had to put up with a good deal of petty harassment. Captain James Morris, captured at Germantown in October 1777, lived for two and a half years in the Flatbush home of John Lott, who treated him with "great kindness." With plenty of time for reading and gardening, Morris mused, "I enjoyed my share of comfort and worldly felicity. I felt no disposition to murmer and repine in my then condition." Complaining was pointless anyway, as he and his fellow officers had no redress from the insults and abuse showered on them by unsympathetic villagers. Captain Alexander Graydon later recalled several paroled officers who learned the hard way that resistance was pointless. Meeting some Long Island fishmongers on the road one day, the Americans tried to buy part of their catch but were refused because the men would not do business with rebels—whereupon the indignant officers, "laying hold of the fish, began to bandy them about the jaws of the ragamuffins that had insulted them." The story reached General Robertson in New York, who ordered the Americans to apologize. They refused, so he sent them to the Provost for a few weeks.[56]

By the end of 1777, dozens of officers already had deserted their paroles and returned home. "The reason commonly assigned for this breach of faith," Washington explained sadly to General Alexander McDougall, "is the want of Money and necessaries. I regret this plea is too well founded." Always the fugitives would be ordered back to New York to repair the damage to their and the army's honor, though at least one of them, after giving Boudinot a particularly heartrending description of his straitened circumstances on Long Island, announced that he would rather be shot than return. His fate is unknown.[57]

But deserting parole was obviously not the typical response to vilification and hardship. Jabez Fitch, whose diary remains the fullest surviving record of any American officer on Long Island, apparently never even considered the possibility of just walking away from New Lots. He complained endlessly about boredom, about clouds of bloodthirsty "misketeers" rising out of the nearby marshes, and about all those meals involving clams. He always needed money. On one occasion he and other Connecticut officers arranged for Colonel Selah Hart to visit Hartford "for the purpose of procuring some Supplys" and to ask the state legislature to send them their long-overdue back pay. On another occasion, he walked over to Flatbush to inspect a load of "Shoes & Clothing sent from the United States"—via Boudinot and Pintard—"for the Use of the Prisoners." Tellingly, however, he saw nothing he wanted or needed, though he later found some shirts and trousers in a shipment of clothes from Connecticut. In mid-July 1777, he and some other officers even collected "several Shirts & other Articles of Clothing" for the prisoners in New York.[58]

So, too, Captain Graydon, hale and comparatively well-fed in Flatbush, coped with "the pining tediousness of our situation" by taking long, contemplative walks over the hills above the village and composing soulful poetry:

Here on the lofty summit as he stood,
His wistful eyes still sought the western shore;

There, ting'd with gold, the distant hills he view'd
Where yet her sons fair freedom's ensign bore.

"Captivity," Graydon mused afterward, creates "a peculiar sickness of the heart." For that reason, it "is justly comprehended in the catalogue of human woes; its poignancy is recognized by Shakespeare in his play of Othello, and it is among the calamities, which are particularly adverted to, in the excellent liturgy of the Church of England." Imagine, then, Graydon's relief (shaded, one hopes, with some embarrassment) when he learned in July 1777 that his mother had come up from Philadelphia and badgered General Howe into letting her take him home. Congress approved, but what Graydon's brother officers thought of this rather unsoldierly rescue can only be imagined.[59]

During the twentieth century, historians of the Revolution began to discount the litanies of brutality and degradation emanating from occupied New York as wartime "propaganda"—inflammatory, polemical, histrionic, and never to be taken at face value. But that is a mistake on several counts. Only John Witherspoon's report qualifies as propaganda, properly speaking, for it alone bore a governmental imprimatur and was circulated for the acknowledged purpose of mobilizing public opinion. (The essay by "Miserecors" comes close to meeting that standard, to be sure, as does Jabez Fitch's "Narative," which he *intended* for publication.) Given that "propaganda" has also become a code word for "misleading," even "untrue," it is worth noting that the sheer number of eyewitnesses to the mistreatment of prisoners in New York, plus the great diversity of sources from which their testimony must be extracted, make a powerful argument for their credibility. So does their very repetitiveness—story after raw story about foul water, spoiled meat, and terrible mortality. When so many people independently attest to the same facts, attention must be paid.

In May 1777, still in a lather over the enemy's treatment of American prisoners, General Samuel Holden Parsons approached Washington with a proposal: give him a few hundred men, and he would cross Long Island Sound from Connecticut to liberate the officers billeted in Flatbush, New Lots, New Utrecht, and the other villages of Kings County. Ever since the American rout in Brooklyn nine months earlier, Washington had usually given his blessing to carefully managed expeditions that "distressed" the enemy on the island by removing or destroying livestock, burning forage, kidnapping prominent Tories, and the like. Along with Governor Jonathan Trumbull of Connecticut and Lieutenant Colonel Henry Beekman Livingston of New York, among others, Washington had also toyed with the idea of a full-scale invasion to regain control of the island and its valuable resources. A raid to liberate prisoners was a new idea, however, and Washington opposed it as almost certain to make things worse. "Success in such a case would lead to unhappy consequences," he instructed Parsons. "No future prisoners, in the hands of the Enemy, would receive the same favourable indulgence, so essential to their Health and comfort, and would authorize their imposing on them a more close and severe Confinement."[60]

But Parsons did not give up easily. A famously successful American attack on Sag Harbor at the end of May showed that whaleboats launched from the Connecticut side of Long Island Sound could move sizable raiding parties to Long Island and back with ease. What was more, Howe's campaign against Philadelphia, which got under way in July, left only a few thousand regulars for the defense of Manhattan, Long Island, and Staten Island—many fewer than Washington had had the year before for the identical purpose. Consequently, the idea of a hit-and-run expedition to free American prisoners as well as to destroy enemy supplies began to look more and more feasible. So despite Washington's rebuff, Parsons shopped his plan to General Israel Putnam, his immediate superior, and this time he got what he wanted. In mid-August, Putnam ordered Parsons "to make a descent on Long Island and deplete and destroy such parties of the enemy as are found at Huntington and Setauket or other place on the Island." Circumstances permitting, Parsons was also "to retake and bring off all the officers and soldiers of the Continental Army now on Long Island."[61]

Parsons and 500 well-armed men slipped across the sound on the night of August 21. They reached Setauket the following morning—only to be driven back to their boats by a contingent of redcoats who obviously knew the rebels were coming. Despite this reverse, Parsons, along with Putnam and Governor Trumbull, continued to urge more such forays, and Parsons gave one of his colonels, Samuel B. Webb, carte blanche to harass the Long Island coast at will. In December, Webb and sixty Connecticut men would be captured when their boat, under heavy fire from an enemy sloop, ran aground off the island.[62]

No American prisoners gained their freedom as a result of these incursions. Still, the threat had been sufficiently real to worry General Sir Henry Clinton, the officer charged with the defense of New York in Howe's absence. At the end of November, when spies brought rumors of Webb's preparations, Clinton had rounded up the prisoners on Long Island and herded them onto the *Judith* and *Myrtle*. Jabez Fitch, stuffed into the hold of the *Judith* with 130 other men, found the experience a discouraging reprise of his confinement on an enemy prison ship after the fighting on Long Island. He even wrote a poem about it:

> *The meals which to our lot this day do fall*
> *Are few & corse or Rather none at all*
> *In gloomy darkness, crouded here we sit*
> *Scourg'd with excessive hunger, cold & wet*
> *This hard & disagreable adventure*
> *Resembles that on board the dirty Mentor*

After only two weeks, though, the Americans were taken off the *Judith* and returned to their billets on Long Island. Except, that is, for Fitch and two others, who received the glorious news that they had been exchanged and were free to leave.[63]

Fitch's release, as it happened, had been the handiwork of a Connecticut merchant named Joseph Webb—elder brother of the Colonel Samuel Webb recently captured on Long Island. As Connecticut's commissary of prisoners, Webb had visited the city to negotiate the exchange of Fitch and other officers from that state (exactly the sort of freelancing that infuriated Washington and Boudinot). While there he wangled permission to visit the hospitals and prisons, and what he saw left him shaken. "Death seam'd to be in Every counternance [*sic*]," he reported to Governor Trumbull in a distraught, agitated letter. "Something seriously ought to be done, or they will all die—I was in york abt. 12 days I believe there was at least Sixty buried . . . unless something is immediately done, Newyork will be their Grave." Sadly, many of the prisoners "think themselves in part Neglected by their Country" and were "much affraid I shou'd forget them when I was out but its not the Case." Ethan Allen, now going into his third year of captivity, sounded despondent. "He say's he's forgot—He's spending his Life, his very prime." Would it be worthwhile, Webb wondered, to send a letter to General Washington? "Or what is to be done?"[64]

As for Fitch, on Monday, December 15, 1777, he returned to his wife and children in Norwich, Connecticut. "I arriv'd at my own house a little after Sunset," he wrote pensively in his diary, "having been from home a Year & Eight months lacking 6 days, fifteen months & 15 days of which time I have pass'd in Captivity." For Jabez Fitch, the war was over. He always said, though, that those fifteen months left him with physical and emotional scars that never quite healed. As a local paper put it after his death in 1812: "The severities of British barbarity . . . embittered and rendered almost insupportable more than 30 years of his life."[65]

5

⤢

SWEET
Liberty

ONE WINTRY DAY early in January 1778, while the managers of New York's Theatre Royal prepared for "a numerous and splendid audience" at that evening's performance, Sergeant Walley plucked a half dozen shivering prisoners out of the Provost and marched them downtown through drifting snow to Crown Street. Their destination was his pestilential lair, the Sugar House (*the* Sugar House now because the others had been cleared of inmates by the end of 1777). One of Walley's group, nineteen-year-old Elias Cornelius of Long Island, had already spent time in the Sugar House and thought he knew what to expect. It was even worse than he remembered, however, for amid the filth and famine and disease, the strong had begun to prey on the weak without shame or mercy. "There were nearly thirty soldiers who went around to the other prisoners and stole from them, the few comforts they had," Cornelius wrote sadly in his journal, "and take the sick from their beds and take their bed clothing, and beat and kick them almost to death." Sergeant Walley not only tolerated these assaults, he openly encouraged them by supplying the perpetrators with rum in exchange for the goods they took from their helpless countrymen.[1]

But Cornelius got lucky: he quickly developed a cough and fever—he already had the scurvy, which sooner or later afflicted every prisoner—so Walley sent him up to the infirmary in Brick Presbyterian Church. This was the opportunity he had been waiting for. Early in

Brick Presbyterian Church, looking south from the intersection of
Broadway on the right and Nassau Street to the left. St. Paul's Chapel
stands on the west side of Broadway. The church was used as a prison
from 1776 to 1777 or 1778, after which it became a military hospital.

the evening of January 16, a week after he arrived, he and a few other
prisoners somehow managed to get the infirmary's solitary guard
passing-out drunk, clambered over a fence, and fled into the gathering darkness. Still so sick he could hardly stand, Cornelius headed
west, to the other side of Broadway. He circled St. Paul's Chapel,
skirted the rubble-filled lots left by the 1776 fire, then turned uptown,
past King's College, dodging sentries and keeping to the shadows
until he reached the Hudson River. His plan was to cross over to New
Jersey, only he could not find a boat. In desperation, he struck out for
the East River, on the opposite side of Manhattan, where he hoped to
find a way over to Brooklyn. "Soon the moon arose and made it very
light," he recalled, "and there being snow on the ground, crusted
over, and no wind, therefore a person walking, could be heard a great
distance." He saw soldiers everywhere and often had to crawl along
on his stomach to avoid being discovered. Dogs snarled and howled
as he passed.[2]

Eventually, miles from where he began, Cornelius came to the
East River—except he could not find a boat there, either. He spent
what remained of the night huddling miserably under some bushes.
Next morning, exhausted, hungry, footsore, and numb with the cold,

he was on his way back to town, perhaps to turn himself in, when some "friends of America" gave him food and put him up for a few days. Then they helped him over to Long Island, where he hid out in the woods with two other escaped prisoners until they were able to steal a small boat and row across the sound to Norwalk, Connecticut. From Norwalk, Cornelius and his companions set out on foot to rejoin the American army wintering at Valley Forge, Pennsylvania. They arrived seven days later, near the end of March.[3]

If anyone kept a tally of how many American prisoners escaped from New York, it has long since disappeared. There were more than a few, however, and unlike Elias Cornelius, many seem to have encountered little or no difficulty getting away. In 1777, two Jersey men, James Schureman and George Thomson, broke through the fence around the Sugar House after sedating the guard with a mixture of liquor and laudanum (how did they get their hands on *laudanum?*). The two easily located a small fishing boat and rowed across the Hudson to rejoin the American army, then camped at Morristown, New Jersey. Admather Blodget made his break from the Sugar House by borrowing a sailor's uniform, scaling the fence, and sauntering up Broadway "carelessly as if he was in the midst of friends instead of enemies." Evidently he kept right on going, without incident, all the way up to the northern end of Manhattan, where he swam across Spuyten Duyvil Creek to freedom. When Lieutenant David Marinus was allowed out of the Sugar House to buy food, he knocked down his guard and just walked away.[4]

Escaping the prison ships in New York was harder, but not impossible. Thomas Bell escaped from the *Whitby* in January of 1777 by somehow getting permission to go ashore and then disappearing; a day or so later he surfaced in Philadelphia and gave the Executive Committee of Congress a thorough report on the number and disposition of enemy forces in New York. Captain Jean Tennet, a prisoner on the *Prince of Wales*, simply jumped overboard and swam to safety. One night in December 1777, Major John "Jack" Stewart (or Steward) and several other American officers fled a prison ship moored in the Hudson by quietly lowering themselves into a boat tied up alongside, then rowing over to New Jersey before the sentries realized they were missing. Thirteen-year-old Christopher Hawkins, released from one of the prison ships to serve as a waiter on the frigate *Maidstone*, was sent ashore one day in 1778 to pick up an officer's laundry. He and a couple of other boys hitched a ride over to Brooklyn with a local dairyman, then walked the hundred or so miles out to Sag Harbor in high spirits. Friends there put him on a sloop bound for New England, and he soon reached his home in Providence, "much to the joy of my parents and not a little to myself." Once or twice on their trek across Long Island the boys had been stopped for questioning, but according to Hawkins, they were never in any real danger.[5]

The experience of Thomas Painter, on the other hand, serves as a reminder that escape attempts always involved a certain amount of risk. Painter had seen action at Brooklyn, Harlem Heights, and White Plains, then lost interest in soldiering and decided to try his hand at privateering. It did not go well. In the summer of 1778, now eighteen, he was captured off Oyster Bay in a whaleboat named *True Blue*, captained by Elisha Elderkin. After two weeks as prisoners on the *Good Hope*, then anchored in the Hudson near the Paulus Hook ferry landing, he and Captain Elderkin jumped overboard in the middle of the night and began swimming for their lives. Elderkin made it to the Manhattan shore, only to be recaptured and returned to the *Good Hope* several days later. Painter had better luck. Taking advantage of a flood tide, he swam north and came ashore, almost naked, somewhat above King's College, near the foot of present-day Chambers Street. He wandered around the outskirts of town for a few days, hungry and thirsty, sleeping under bushes and haystacks and hiding from enemy soldiers, who seemed to be everywhere. One night, in desperation, he resolved to swim across the Hudson to New Jersey. It took him until three o'clock in the morning, but he made it safely and set out for West Haven, Connecticut, "my native Village." Except for a ferry ride back across the Hudson at Stony Point, he walked the entire distance, depending on the kindness of strangers for food, clothing, and pocket money. Along the way, he figured out that "Privateering, was nothing better than Highway Robbery" and decided to join the militia again.[6]

Some attempted escapes failed completely. Thomas Stone jumped the Sugar House fence in the spring of 1778 and got all the way to the Harlem River in Upper Manhattan before soldiers caught up with him. When they brought him back to the Sugar House, "with bayonets at my back," Sergeant Walley gave Stone a caning and sent him to the Provost dungeon for a few days with "not a blanket, not a board, not a straw to rest on"—an experience he never forgot or forgave. "I thought if ever mortal could be justified in praying for the destruction of his enemies," he would later admit, "I am the man." Frederick Nagel was among a half dozen Pennsylvania soldiers captured at Fort Washington who were inexplicably taken off one of the New York prison ships and sent up to Halifax, Nova Scotia. After an abortive escape attempt there, they were locked up for six months on half rations; one of the group received 800 lashes, virtually a death sentence. "The flesh fell off his back," Nagel recalled.[7]

Outright escape was not the only alternative to prison. A group of "Gentlemen Passengers" and ship captains actually managed to talk their way off the *Judith* by kowtowing to Rear Admiral James Gambier, head of British naval operations. Gambier had just reached New York in the spring of 1778 when the Americans sent him a congratulatory note with some gauzy words of praise for a "humane and compassionate Commander in Chief." They were, they added, among a total of 197 prisoners on the ship, "45 of whom are beyond all human hopes of recovery sick with malignant putrid fevers; and about 50 other emaciated living skeletons dragging about the decks such naked miserable carcasses, that it should seem were only spared as a favour like another Polyphemus for the after sport of death"—a tortured allusion to the Cyclops, who trapped Odysseus in his cave.

> With this miserable group of unparalleled human wretchedness, your petitioners are indiscriminately drove down by the marines with fixed bayonets, and the most opprobrious language, every night between decks precisely at sun set; and as the numerous sick and infirm naturally claim a preference to occupy what is called the births [*sic*] or cabins, your petitioners . . . think themselves very

happy in securing a seat on a chest to set on; for to lay down, Sir, is an indulgence that more than 40 in number every night cannot obtain, unless they overlay each other. In this melancholy situation, the famishing, sick and dying are frequently heard to cry out for mercy's sake, in vain, for one single mouthful of water and fresh air . . . so that your petitioners have as much to dread from a general suffocation, as from the unremitting malignancy of the pestilential distemper, which continues to diminish their numbers at the rate of 3, 4 and 5 every day.

Gambier, no Cyclops and not immune to flattery, promised to have the gentlemen and masters transferred to "a large commodious ship" as soon as possible. "Another ship will be got ready," he added, "to thin the numbers on board of each prison ship." No doubt they would have preferred to be released on parole, but roomier quarters and breathable air were a definite improvement.[8]

Paroles were not customary for enlisted men and civilians, but both occasionally wangled one to get out of prison—almost always because they knew somebody who knew somebody, which was a predictable source of resentment among those left behind. John Adlum spent just a few days in the Bridewell after the fall of Fort Washington because Colonel Magaw, a family friend, asked Commissary General Loring to give him a parole. Cornelius ("Faddy") Van Vorst of Bergen County, New Jersey, a two-fisted fifty-year-old civilian, got thrown in the Sugar House for thrashing several insolent cavalry officers. General Henry Clinton let Faddy out on parole because the two had been schoolmates when Clinton's father was the royal governor of New York, decades earlier. Three Connecticut soldiers who had barely survived a stint on the *Grosvenor*—James Little, Isaac Grant, and Isaac's brother Elisha—got their paroles because Levi Allen intervened with Loring. Isaac subsequently heard he had been exchanged, so he reenlisted and spent the winter of 1777–1778 with the army at Valley Forge. When he learned almost two years later that his "exchange" had been some kind of clerical error, he went home, as honor required.[9]

There's no telling how many men, rotting away in the Sugar House or in the steaming hold of some godforsaken prison ship, decided to save themselves by defecting. They had ample opportunity, as British military and naval recruiters regularly trolled New York prisons and prison ships for able-bodied men. Washington and Congress denounced the practice with equal regularity as inconsistent with the norms of civilized warfare, and Americans often alleged that prisoners were treated harshly to make them switch sides.[10]

If so, the tactic did sometimes produce the desired result, perhaps especially among prisoners brought to New York in 1776 and 1777, when the American cause often seemed so close to disaster. Just after the Battle of Brooklyn, Jabez Fitch heard that enemy recruiters met with "Considerable Suckcess" aboard the crowded prison ships anchored in Gravesend Bay. Another diarist, Private William Slade, noted that twenty men left the *Grosvenor* one bleak day in December 1776 to join the king's service—twenty of the approximately 500 Americans brought aboard several weeks earlier. A "great number" of the Fort Washington prisoners did the same thing, according to Ensign Van Horne. The notorious Abraham Mabie, taken at Fort Montgomery in the autumn of 1777, bought his freedom by agreeing to become a British spy. Two of Mabie's fellow captives, Samuel Geek and Major Daniel Hammell (Hammill), accepted offers from General Henry Clinton to work as undercover recruiters, targeting Irish immigrants in the American army. (Hammell would claim that he had escaped from New York, but another prisoner alerted General Parsons and Hammell was arrested.) Captain Lewis Costigan, on the other hand, only pretended to switch sides. Captured in 1777 and exchanged the following year, he apparently "refused" to return to the American army, stayed in New York, and sent intelligence to Washington in letters signed "Z."[11]

Some men found ways to get out of prison that fell short of outright defection. Michael Mahoney and fourteen others got off one of the prison ships by agreeing to mine coal without pay on Cape Breton Island, where they remained until the end of the war; in fact Mahoney lingered until 1840, then returned to the United States and actually tried to collect a pension for his brief service, sixty-odd years earlier. The Pension Office turned him down. After eight months in the North Dutch Church, John Casten went to work as a tailor for

His Majesty's army. It was a decision he, like Mahoney, lived to regret. Fifty-six years later, his pension application was rejected when it occurred to the examiners that Casten had worked freely in the city almost to the end of the war without once trying to escape.[12]

And then there is the saga of Haym Salomon, arrested shortly after the British takeover on suspicion of being an American spy (he was, conspicuously, one of the only Jewish residents of the city who had not already fled). Initially consigned to the Sugar House, he was moved to the Provost around the time the Fort Washington prisoners were brought in. There he would have remained, except that General Leopold Philip von Heister, the Hessian commander, thought Salomon's knowledge of German, French, Polish, and Italian, among other languages, would make him useful as an interpreter. Evidently Salomon continued to work behind the scenes for the rebels, for he was arrested again in the summer of 1778 and this time was convicted of espionage (exactly what he had been up to is not clear). He cheated the hangman by bribing one of the Provost guards on the eve of his execution and slipping away to Philadelphia.[13]

The willingness of recruiters to take men out of prisons and prison ships indicates not only that His Majesty's forces were chronically shorthanded but also that they would not take seriously the attachment of rank-and-file rebels to the Revolution—which helps to explain why the prisoners who refused to defect always made a point of their fidelity to the cause. Ethan Allen, while visiting soldiers held in one of the New York churches, met a "large boned, tall young man" from Pennsylvania who said that he and his brother "had been urged to enlist into the British, but had both resolved to die first." The brother was now dead and the young man, "reduced to a mere skeleton," could not last much longer. Allen nonetheless urged him to save himself by enlisting and deserting at the first opportunity. "The integrity of these suffering prisoners is hardly credible," he reflected afterward. "Many hundreds, I am confident, submitted to death, rather than to enlist in the British service." Some, however, did exactly what he advised the young Pennsylvania solder to do: enlist, then desert. Private Colin Chapman, for example, enlisted after the enemy captured him at Danbury in April 1777, but voluntarily returned to the

American army in September, brimming with information about the enemy's movements and troop strength.[14]

Allen's observations square with the experience of John Adlum, who recalled that recruiters descended on the Bridewell soon after he and the other Fort Washington prisoners arrived there. After three days of "flattering promises," however, fewer than twenty of the 800 prisoners had enlisted, "and these were Irish or English and were generally servants whose masters had sent them with the militia to show their Whigism and patriotism." Just one "American-born" captive succumbed to the enemy's blandishments—a fourteen-year-old drummer boy. Major Abraham Leggett likewise rebuffed "Very Flattering offers if I would Join the British. . . . My answer was, I have put my Hand to the Plow and Cant look Back—I shall Stand by my Country." Levi Hanford recalled that it was "very rare" for any of the men held in the Sugar House to enlist with the British. "So wedded were they to their principles, so dear to them was their country, so true were they to their honor, that rather than sacrifice them, they preferred the scoffs of their persecutors, the horrors of their dungeon, and in fact even death itself."[15]

Among all the stories of escape, defection, and parole to come out of the Revolutionary War, the most puzzling may well be that of Judge Richard Stockton. Stockton, it will be recalled, was the prominent New Jersey patriot and Signer of the Declaration of Independence who enjoyed the distinction of being a brother-in-law of both Commissary Elias Boudinot and Lewis Pintard, Boudinot's agent in New York. Abducted by Tories in late November or early December 1776, Stockton spent six weeks in the Provost and was released before the middle of January 1777.

At issue are the conditions of Stockton's release. Many years later, his son-in-law, Doctor Benjamin Rush, said he had met Stockton in Princeton after the British allowed him to return home on parole—after he had promised, that is, to take no further part in the insurgency, by word or deed, until exchanged. But there are grounds for an entirely different and more ominous explanation: that Stockton received a pardon after taking the loyalty oath prescribed by Howe's proclamation of November 30, 1776. If true, he would have been the only Signer to disavow the Declaration of Independence.[16]

A rumor that Stockton had taken Howe's oath reached Congress, then sitting in Baltimore, before the end of the year. A month or so later, despite some initial skepticism, the delegates had apparently resigned themselves to the idea of Stockton's apostasy. The source or sources of their information cannot be determined, but in mid-March, a couple of months after Stockton returned to his Princeton estate, the Reverend John Witherspoon sent the following report to his son:

> Judge Stockton is not very well in health & much spoken against for his conduct. He signed Howe's declaration & also gave his Word of honour that he would not meddle in the least in the American affairs during the War. Mrs. Cochran was sent to the Enemies Lines by a flag of Truce and when Mr. Cochran came out to meet his wife he said to the Officers that went with the flag that Judge Stockton had brought Evidence to General Howe to prove that he was on his Way to seek a protection when he was taken. This he denies to be true yet many credit it but Mr. Cochran's known quarrel with him makes it very doubtful to candid Persons.

The elder Witherspoon makes a strong witness for the prosecution. He and Stockton had a close relationship, dating back to the days when Stockton traveled to Scotland to offer Witherspoon the presidency of the College of New Jersey (now Princeton University). Both lived in Princeton, they sat together in Congress, and each had signed the Declaration of Independence. Then, too, Witherspoon had just left Princeton for Philadelphia, and the two almost certainly conversed about the circumstances of Stockton's capture as well as about conditions in the Provost (not least of all because Witherspoon was at the time working on his report to Congress about enemy atrocities).[17]

If anyone knew what had happened to Richard Stockton, it would have been his friend, colleague, and neighbor, John Witherspoon. So when Witherspoon said that Stockton signed Howe's declaration, there would seem to be little room for doubt that the rumors were true: Stockton was a turncoat.[18]

On closer inspection, however, the story outlined in Witherspoon's letter does not add up. First, Witherspoon appeared to say that Stockton had taken the oath of loyalty ("signed Howe's declaration") *and also* received a parole ("gave his Word of honour"). But doing *both* makes no sense. If Stockton took the oath, it means he had recanted, ceased resistance, and sought a pardon; a parole would be meaningless. Conversely, had Stockton been released on parole it would mean that he had not recanted, that he could resume the struggle if exchanged, that he was still technically a prisoner and had not received a pardon. It must be one thing or the other, not both. Second, if Stockton had recanted, why would he return to Princeton and expose himself to the contempt of friends and neighbors like Witherspoon? Why not remain in New York, safely behind British lines, like so many others who had cast their lot with the Crown? Stockton's behavior, in other words, was not that of a man who had turned coat to get out of prison.[19]

Third, if Stockton had defected, why did Howe as well as his masters in London fail to trumpet the fact? The British press reveled in stories about this or that rebel leader's switching sides—occasionally true (Benedict Arnold), usually not (Colonel Allen, General Sullivan, General Parsons). The apostasy of a big rebel like Judge Stockton of New Jersey, the only Signer of the Declaration to fall into their hands thus far in the war, would have been front-page news in papers throughout Britain, as well as in the Tory sheets serving occupied New York City. Lord North, Lord Germain, and the government's friends in Parliament would have played the story for all it was worth, and Howe would certainly have given them the good news if he had it to give. In fact, Howe later informed Germain that no prominent rebel had yet taken the oath. Rebel newspapers did not notice or complain about Stockton's alleged defection, either. He may have been "much spoken against for his conduct," as Witherspoon told his son, but not in print.[20]

As for the mysterious "Mr. Cochran," Witherspoon was right to question the yarn that Stockton intended to "seek a protection" from General Howe *before* his abduction. Cochran's "known quarrel" with

Stockton, now impossible to reconstruct, was grounds enough for skepticism. Besides, how could Cochran, evidently a Tory refugee living in New York, have known what Stockton intended? He certainly did not hear it from Stockton. Did he hear it from Howe? Maybe—though why would Howe reveal something so important to a nonentity such as Cochran, yet make no mention of it in his dispatches to North and Germain? That Cochran remains the *only* known source for this element of the story (and a secondhand source to boot) almost guarantees that it was nothing more than a craven attempt to smear an old adversary.

So what did happen to Richard Stockton? Witherspoon's oddly muddled description of Stockton's conduct and the allusion to Stockton's poor health suggest that Stockton may have come home unable to give a coherent accounting of what he had done and why—perhaps that his captors had forced him to recant as well as ask for parole, or that his Tory abductors forced him to recant and the British then released him on parole. Either possibility could explain why Howe never reported it: a submission wrung out of any important rebel by physical or psychological abuse, particularly at the hands of paramilitary thugs, would hardly make good public relations. Nor would Stockton have been the first American to be crippled in body and spirit by a stay in the Provost—"that engine for breaking hearts," in Alexander Graydon's apt phrase.[21]

It was Graydon, too, who said that captivity caused "a peculiar sickness of the heart," and something of the sort—what might now be called posttraumatic stress, depression, or anxiety—could very well explain why Stockton then dropped out of sight for the final few years of his life. He died toward the end of February 1781, succumbing to what a Philadelphia newspaper described as "a disease peculiarly painful and tedious," reportedly throat or lip cancer. His patriotism, the paper added, had never been less than exemplary. "The nobility, dignity and integrity with which this gentleman discharged the duties of the several important offices to which he was called by the voice of his country, are well known." It was not the kind of thing one would say about a man who had willingly abandoned his country's struggle for independence.[22]

Because it delivered over 3,000 redcoats into American hands, Burgoyne's defeat at Saratoga in October 1777 ought to have made the British more careful about conditions in their prisons and prison ships. In reality, improvements in the prisons of New York and Philadelphia were small and slow in coming. Boudinot, Washington, and Congress continued to receive reports of nauseating squalor, rampant disease, and starvation—too many reports, from too many independent sources, to be disbelieved. "Our prisoners very sickly," headquarters learned in January 1778; "the Sufferings of our Prisoners is beyond Discription." Judging by John Fell's "Memorandum," not even a personal inspection of the Provost by General Robertson himself at the beginning of December made much of a difference:

> Nov 16. Jail exceeding disagreeable—many miserable & shocking objects nearly starved with cold & hunger—miserable prospect before us.
>
> . . .
>
> Nov 24. 6 taylors brought here from prison ship to work in making clothes for p[risoners] they say the people on board very sickly—300 sent on board reduced to 100.
>
> . . .
>
> Dec 3. several p[risoners] of war sent from here on board p[rison] ship, & some of sick sent to Hospital . . . p[risoners] sickly—cause, cold—p[risoners] scanty clothing in upper rooms & only 2 bush. coal for a room of 20 men, a week.
>
> . . .
>
> Dec 8. Maj: Gen: Robertson with Mayor [David Mathews] came to Provost to examine p[risoners]. I was called & examined, & requested my parole.
>
> Dec 10. p[risoners] very sick & die very fast from Hospitals & p[rison] ships.
>
> . . .
>
> Dec 14. Sunday—guards more severe than ever, notwithstanding Gen. Robertson's promise of more indulgence.
>
> . . .

DEC 16. Sent message to Mr. Pintard for wood. Cold & entirely out of wood.[23]

By this time, Fell's health was failing rapidly. As Ethan Allen explained, "The stench of the gaol, which was very loathsome and unhealthy, occasioned a hoarseness of the lungs, which proved fatal to many who were there confined, and reduced this gentleman near to the point of death." Just when Fell's comrades had steeled themselves to lose him, Allen intervened with a letter to General Robertson that moved the hardhearted commandant to change his mind. Early in January 1778 Robertson gave Fell permission to arrange for room and board with a Mrs. Marriner down on William Street, where he slowly recovered.[24]

The conditions that nearly killed Fell would probably have been far worse had Boudinot and Pintard not managed to step up the flow of food, clothing, and firewood to the prisoners in New York. By Pintard's reckoning, between November 1777 and January 1778 he and Boudinot provided the men with 796 pairs of shoes, 1,310 pairs of stockings, 787 coats, 1,253 shirts, 549 vests, 376 pairs of trousers, 184 hats, 616 blankets, and eight mattresses—still not enough, as they both knew, but no longer insignificant. (The British meanwhile lacked for nothing. As the New-York Gazette noted in mid-January, "We have had the mildest Winter that has been known for many Years, and the greatest Abundance of all Sorts of Provisions, Fuel, &c., &c.")[25]

The commissary and his agent accomplished as much as they did over the winter of 1777–1778 despite a new difficulty: after Howe took Philadelphia in late September 1777, some 550 or more Americans captured at Brandywine Creek, Germantown, and elsewhere were confined in the City of Brotherly Love. The majority were held in the jail at Walnut and Sixth streets, as many as thirty men to a cell, too crowded for them all to lie down at the same time. Others, mainly officers, were confined in the Philadelphia State House, still others in the Golden Swan and other local taverns. All were as desperate for food, fresh water, clothing, and medicine as their counterparts in

New York. "Our Friends in Captivity [are] in the greatest distress," Major John Clark wrote hurriedly to Washington in mid-November of that year. "Many have died within this few Days for want of provision—their first allowance was ½ lb. Beef & 4½ Biscuit for three Days & now reduced to ¼ lb. Salt pork & 6 Biscuit for eight Days—near 300 have lately been obliged to enlist or starve." Around the same time, a number of American officers sent a letter to Howe complaining about the "vile insulting language" of the guards and the lack of provisions; Howe breezily replied that if the food they got was not enough, they were "at full Liberty to purchase such Provisions as the Market may afford."[26]

The improbably named Albigence Waldo, a surgeon with the American army at Valley Forge, heard even more terrible stories out of Philadelphia about prisoners driven mad with hunger: "One of these poor unhappy men—drove to the last extreem by the rage of hunger—eat his own fingers up to the first joint from the hand, before he died. Others eat the Clay—the Lime—the Stones—of the Prison Walls. Several who died in the Yard had pieces of Bark, Wood–Clay & Stones in their mouths." All of which sounds a bit too much like the kind of rumor that gathers embellishments with every telling—except there is abundant evidence that a lot of captured Americans did indeed starve to death in Philadelphia over the winter of 1777–1778. Corporal John Chenoweth remembered that seven or eight men of his regiment perished every day.[27]

At least two of the Philadelphia prisoners thought another outrage deserved mention as well, and that was the enemy's refusal to support white racial privilege. "W.G.," a naval officer captured on the American frigate *Delaware*, told a Pennsylvania paper that "a certain Captain Hogshaw not only refused to punish a negro for striking one of our officers, but in direct words said that the negro was as good as any of us." In Persifor Frazer's version of the story, an American lieutenant started the trouble by ordering the black man to sweep their now-filthy cell and trying to beat him when he refused. When a British sentry made the lieutenant desist, his brother officers were furious: even rebels destined to the cord felt they were entitled to their racial prerogatives.[28]

"W.G." also named the man chiefly responsible for these over-abundant horrors: Provost Marshal William Cunningham, whom Howe had brought along from New York to deal with the Philadelphia prisoners. Cunningham displayed his talent for cruelty, "W.G." observed, when charitable residents of the city brought food to the famished prisoners and he kicked it away with a plangent curse: "Damn them, let them swallow their spittle and be damn'd!" Jacob Ritter told a similar story, in which Cunningham overturned a large tub of soup "and laughed when he saw the prisoners fall down and lick up the soup like dogs." Boudinot heard from a captured British officer that Cunningham once clubbed a sick American prisoner to death with one of the heavy keys to the Philadelphia jail.[29]

Washington complained about Cunningham in a letter to Howe midway through November. Howe promptly sent Cunningham packing—back to New York, where he resumed his abuse of Americans in the Provost there. It seems (this according to Boudinot) that Cunningham had got himself into trouble in Philadelphia only by selling off the prisoners' rations, not for brutality. Howe continued to deny that captured Americans received anything less than generous and humane treatment.[30]

In December 1777, realizing that London would not be able to replace the thousands of men who surrendered with Burgoyne, Howe agreed to a partial exchange of officers already out on parole, rank for rank. He also had some good news for General Lee, who had spent the past six months as a prisoner aboard the warship *Centurion*. Acting on instructions from Germain and the king, who had finally decided that Lee should not be tried for desertion, Howe gave Lee permission to take lodgings in New York with two British officers as chaperones. There, although Howe refused to associate with him socially, Lee resumed the high living to which he had become accustomed (he was "as easy comfortable and pleasant as possible for a Man who is in any sort a Prisoner," he assured Washington at the end of the year). When finally exchanged for Prescott in April 1778, after sixteen months of captivity, Lee left behind a bill for eight dozen bottles of port.[31]

For the Americans still in custody, on the other hand, the winter of 1777–1778 brought nothing but grief. Just before Christmas, Commissary Boudinot reported to the Board of War that only about 1,700 of the men and officers remained alive—1,200 in New York, 500 in Philadelphia—and their distress weighed heavily on his heart. For months, he sent letter after anguished letter to friends, merchants, and politicians about "our poor fellows" in captivity, "these brave but unhappy men," "our brave Country men in Bondage." Please send them a little more flour, he begged one correspondent. "I have such melancholy Accounts of their Wants."[32]

Adding to Boudinot's frustration were the requests for special favors that poured in from state governors, members of Congress, Continental Army officers, and other heavyweights. From William Livingston, for one, came an appeal to send ten barrels of flour to Ensign Meremy James Gibbons, a parolee in New Utrecht. Besides being "the only son of his Mother (who is a widow of Philadelphia)," Livingston explained, Gibbons "is a weakly Lad and an excellent little officer." In the meantime, states with prisoners in New York continued to send their own agents to the city to lobby for paroles and exchanges, undermining the commissary's efforts to rationalize the whole business.[33]

Boudinot nonetheless got one thing he wanted very badly: permission to make a personal inspection of the prisons in New York. He had suggested such a visit to Washington back in the autumn of 1777 and in early December actually tried to get into occupied Philadelphia to visit the Americans confined there. Howe sent him away. But General Sir Henry Clinton, the senior officer in New York during Howe's absence, proved more accommodating. When Boudinot asked him for permission to come to the city, he readily agreed.[34]

Loring forwarded the necessary passport, and at sundown on February 3, 1778, Boudinot's private sloop brought him to Manhattan. After breakfast next morning with a convivial Commandant Robertson—who assured him that all those "strange stories" about prisoner abuse were "damned lies"—Boudinot ventured out to see for himself. He found 191 American prisoners at the Sugar House and another

211 in two military hospitals, all held in circumstances "as decent as could be expected." Amazingly, the hospitals seemed "in tollerable good order, neat and clean and the Sick much better taken care of than I expected." The Sugar House "appeared comfortable and warm, having a Stove in each Story and Shutters to the Windows." The prisoners had ample clothing and blankets to get through the rest of the winter.[35]

The men in the Sugar House made it clear, however, that only a month or two earlier their treatment had been vastly worse. They told Boudinot that in the French Church—the Huguenot Église du Saint Esprit on King (later Pine) Street—the prisoners, "amounting on an average to 3 & 400, could not all lay down at once, that from the 15th Oct. to the lst Jany. they never rec[eive]d a single stick of wood, and that for the most part they eat their Pork Raw, when the Pews & Door & Wood on Facings failed them for fuel." Perhaps things improved somewhat after Burgoyne's capitulation, but by far the most important difference was that Pintard had been getting them food, fuel, and clothing. Now, for example, they could expect an additional two pounds of good beef and a like amount of flour or bread per week over and above their meager rations from the British. The hard-working Pintard had even hired special nurses for the hospitals and brought in fresh supplies for the sick.[36]

But things were not quite what they seemed in the Sugar House, for after that initial visit, Boudinot received an anonymous note complaining about Sergeant Walley's brutal and corrupt management of the prison. He immediately went back to investigate. Although the inmates heatedly denied that anything was amiss, the commissary began to realize (as Elias Cornelius, too, had recently learned to his sorrow) that the Sugar House was now run by "a Sett of sad villains, who rob each other of their Cloaths and Blanketts, and many of them sell their own Shoes, Blankets and even Shirts for Rum." Either because they were in cahoots with Walley or because they were simply afraid of him, anything favorable the prisoners said about conditions there would have to be taken with a grain of salt.[37]

Then Boudinot went to the Provost, where Ethan Allen and thirty-odd other American officers and political prisoners—all

"wretched beyond description"—poured out tales of "shocking barbarity" by Provost Marshal Cunningham, now back from Philadelphia. On hot summer days, they said, this blackguard used their slop
buckets to bring them drinking water, which they had to drink or die
of thirst. If they dared to complain—about anything—Cunningham
would lock them up for "10, 12, & 14 weeks" at a time in the basement dungeons, where they subsisted on an allowance of four pounds
of spoiled biscuit and two pounds of raw pork *per week*. One injured
American officer spent ten weeks in the dungeon, cleansing his
wounds himself with a mixture of rum and water. Everyone sent to
the dungeons knew, moreover, that sooner or later the sadistic
provost marshal would come down to "beat them unmercifully with a
Rattan & Knock them down with his fist."

Appalled by these revelations, Boudinot invited his British escort,
an officer, to bring in Cunningham to face his accusers. Were these
charges true?

> He, with great Insolence answered, that every word was true—on
> which the British officer, abusing him very much, asked him how
> he dared to treat Gent' in that cruel Manner, he, insolently putting
> his hands to his side swore that he was as absolute there as Gen'l
> Howe was at the head of his Army.

When Boudinot confronted General Robertson with Cunningham's stunning admission, the commandant backpedaled. He blamed
his staff for misinforming him—so much for "strange stories" and
"damned lies"—and vowed to have Cunningham punished. Boudinot
appreciated this show of "Candour and Politeness," but probably had
no idea that Robertson himself had inspected the Provost a couple of
months earlier (this on the authority of John Fell's diary) and knew
full well what was going on there. At bottom, like General Howe,
Lord Germain, and doubtless the king himself, Robertson was no
better than indifferent to the fate of captured rebels.[38]

Five days into his visit, Boudinot and Loring went over to Long Island to see the officers (235 of them now, by his count) billeted in
Flatbush, New Lots, and other country villages. "They received me

with great Joy," he scribbled in his journal. "Found them very comfortably situated." *Too* comfortably situated, in fact: "Was sorry to find
many of the officers had been very extravagant in their Clothes, getting Laces &c."[39]

The officers did, though, complain strenuously to Boudinot that
no general exchange had as yet been arranged between Washington
and Howe. Partial exchanges, they told him, were unfair and bred no
end of resentment. Who went home, and when, seemed to depend
entirely on who had the best access to Robertson, Loring, or Howe—
or on the machinations of shadowy operators like Levi Allen and
Joseph Webb, who slipped in and out of the occupied city trading
men as well as goods on behalf of their own state governments. (It
was Webb, recall, who had liberated Jabez Fitch by swapping him for
a British officer of equivalent rank.)[40]

In fact, Boudinot knew all about Webb. Only days earlier he had
encountered Webb in Robertson's office, where Webb had come to
negotiate for the release of additional Connecticut officers, including
his brother Samuel, the one just taken in a raid on Long Island.
Boudinot was furious. Congress had declared, more than once, that it
wanted no exchanges to be made without the commissary general's
approval, and as Washington had just pointedly reminded the Webbs,
the rule ought to be "to release those first, who were first captured."
Samuel must wait his turn—but here was Joseph again, negotiating
with Loring and Robertson as if no one else mattered. Small wonder
American officers on the island were upset. Happily for Boudinot, his
objections scotched the negotiations and Joseph Webb went home
empty-handed. Brother Sam was soon on Long Island, looking for a
billet in Flatbush.[41]

After bringing Webb to heel, Boudinot arranged with Loring for
the exchange of at least a dozen soldiers and a number of officers. He
got another two dozen officers paroled to Long Island, out of Cunningham's clutches (but not Ethan Allen, whom the British now considered completely untrustworthy). Besides ironing out various
problems with the purchase and distribution of supplies for military
prisoners on both sides of the lines, Boudinot also persuaded Commodore William Hotham, the senior naval officer in New York, to let

Pintard send—for the first time—small amounts of food and clothing to the men who were dying like flies on the prison ships. (Boudinot did not inspect the prison ships, for the same reason that prevented Pintard from doing so: they were under naval jurisdiction and Hotham said he had no orders to let rebel agents aboard.) Most remarkably, the ever-generous and compassionate Boudinot borrowed "near Thirty Thousand Dollars" on his own credit (the equivalent in purchasing power of $603,000 in 2007 dollars) with which he purchased clothing for 300 officers and 1,100 men, bought them all blankets, and arranged for each to receive supplemental rations of bread and beef every day for the next fifteen months.[42]

Washington had said he wanted "a shrewd sensible man" for the job of commissary general. The man he got was a saint.

Early in February 1778, just as Boudinot began inspecting the prisons of New York, Howe surprised Washington with an offer to negotiate a cartel. It could not have come at a better time. Nearly three years had now elapsed since the fighting began at Lexington and Concord in April 1775, and discontent with the prolonged detention of American captives was rippling through the army as well as Congress. (Just weeks before, Governor Trumbull had warned Washington that people in Connecticut now think "it is better to comply with Genll Hows unreasonable demands than Suffer our Distressed Soldiers to remain in their miserable and perishing Scituation without hope of Relief.") Washington eagerly accepted Howe's offer, and it was decided that each side would send commissioners to Germantown, Pennsylvania, in early March to thrash out the details. But that was the easy part.[43]

What came next was a charade that only prolonged the suffering of hundreds of captured Americans. Perhaps because Burgoyne's surrender had put it in a feisty mood, Congress began laying out new, tougher terms for a cartel. Now, besides the old demand that Lee and Allen be part of the deal, it wanted the bill for the upkeep of British prisoners in American hands to be settled ahead of time, and in coin, not paper money. It expected civilians to be included, not only military personnel, and it required that Americans who voluntarily bore arms against the United States be exchanged last, unless their home states wanted them brought back first, to be tried for treason. Not eligible for exchange were inhabitants of the United States who had aided or abetted the arrest and detention of their patriotic neighbors. If captured, such persons "shall suffer death by the judgment of a court martial, as a traitor, assassin, and spy."[44]

Knowing Howe would never agree to such stipulations, Washington was flabbergasted. Did Congress not want a cartel? True, he wrote to Henry Laurens, a cartel would help the British more than the Americans in the short run because they had the greater need for reinforcements. But that must not be the only consideration. Everybody—the public, the army, the prisoners themselves—demanded a cartel. Consider the backlash, he warned Laurens, if either Congress or the commander-in-chief appeared to have derailed the negotiations by raising new and unreasonable demands at the last minute: the honor of the nation would suffer, the army would find it increasingly difficult to attract fresh recruits, and more prisoners would be encouraged to enlist with the enemy. Hoping that Congress could be made to moderate its views, Washington asked Howe to postpone the Germantown meeting to the end of the month.[45]

Washington's impatience with Congress boiled over a day or so later, when he and the commissioners he had chosen to negotiate a cartel—Boudinot and Alexander Hamilton, plus two other officers—conferred at Valley Forge with a congressional committee. The congressmen did not mince words. It really was not in the country's best interests, they said, to exchange prisoners at the beginning of a new year's campaign; the upcoming cartel talks should be seen merely as an opportunity to placate the army and throw blame on the enemy. (Or, as Gouverneur Morris, one of the congressmen, coldly put it: the negotiators must not "suffer a Headlong Desire of releiving [sic] the Miseries of our unhappy fellow Countrymen . . . to lead them into a hasty Acquiescence in the Enemy's insidious Proposals.") Taken aback, the commissioners blasted this line of reasoning as dishonorable, and Washington angrily vowed to get every one of his men out of captivity, regardless of the consequences. The congressmen stalked away "much disgusted," returning later with a resolution that censured the commissioners for entertaining "Principles adversary to the true Interests of America &c. &c." Washington told them to ignore it and focus instead on liberating prisoners. He would deal with any political fallout.[46]

Washington's resolve brought Congress to its senses, at least temporarily, and the commissioners were allowed to proceed with the negotiations. As it happened, however, the low cunning of politicians was about to be matched by the dissembling of General Howe.[47]

The talks began on March 31, as scheduled, and continued on and off for another two weeks. Just when the Americans thought the long-anticipated agreement was at hand, one of the British commissioners confessed that the entire business was just for show: Howe never had the authority to agree to a cartel—not with rebels, anyway—and had proposed the conference to Washington purely (as Boudinot remembered the conversation) to satisfy opinion in the British Army and make the Americans appear to be responsible for preventing a general exchange of prisoners. Boudinot and his fellow commissioners declared themselves astounded "at this un-officerlike conduct in the British General"—not letting on that Congress had tried to play the same game. Instead, they persuaded their British counterparts to agree to a vague, face-saving "mutual Report" that blamed the failure of the conference on their lack of adequate authority to resolve important outstanding issues. Everyone then returned to their respective headquarters, having accomplished exactly nothing.[48]

Washington's disappointment was palpable, and he worried that a general exchange of prisoners might now be further away than ever. The only good news was that Boudinot had managed to complete arrangements for the partial exchange of fifty-nine officers, thirty-four privates, and three surgeons. Among them were the two most conspicuous and controversial American prisoners thus far in the war: Charles Lee (to be exchanged for Richard Prescott) and Ethan Allen (for Archibald Campbell).[49]

On April 21, Lee rode out of Philadelphia, where Howe had brought him some weeks earlier, toward the American camp at Valley

Forge. As he neared the lines, he was greeted with all the pomp and circumstance the little army could muster after its famously difficult winter—a marching band, long lines of cheering soldiers, mounted officers in full uniform. Washington "recd Gen Lee as if he had been his brother," Boudinot recalled, then entertained him "with an Elegant Dinner, and the Music Playing the whole time."[50]

But Boudinot was suspicious. He had met with Lee during his February visit to New York and come away deeply perturbed by the man's state of mind. Lee had railed against Congress for refusing to hear his plan to negotiate an end to the war. He had assured Boudinot that defeat was certain "under such an Ignorant Commander in Chief" as Washington. He had then revealed to the astonished commissary a plan for Congress to gather up "all the Riches of the Country" and retreat into a great western stronghold he proposed to construct at Pittsburgh. Since Boudinot was on his honor not to collect intelligence or convey secret messages, Lee had had no business talking with him about such things. Thoroughly embarrassed, and wondering whether Lee had gone barking mad, Boudinot beat a hasty retreat.

His already dim opinion of Lee was not improved by Boudinot's discovery that Lee spent his first night as a free man with "a miserable dirty hussy" he had brought out from Philadelphia—or when Lee confided to him that "Washington was not fit to command a Sergeant's Guard," that in a meeting with Howe he had described the Declaration of Independence as a mere ploy to wrest concessions from the British, or that he was going to Congress with his bizarre plan to abandon the East Coast. "All this increased my suspicions of Genl Lee exceedingly," Boudinot wrote in his journal, "and I watched him with a Jealous Eye."[51]

While watching Lee, Boudinot saw to the exchange of Archibald Campbell for Ethan Allen, now halfway through his third year of captivity. Early in May, as Allen told the story, Boudinot escorted Campbell to the headquarters of the British commander on Staten Island, where Allen waited with a party of officers who had brought him over from Manhattan. The transfer came off without a hitch, lubricated by the easy camaraderie of gentlemen at war and glasses of wine. Everyone agreed that "sweet liberty was the foundation of our gladness." When it was over, though, Allen could not resist a parting shot at his hosts: "I entertained them," he said later, "with a rehearsal of the cruelties exercised towards our prisoners; and assured them that I should use my influence, that their prisoners should be treated in future in the same manner, as they should in future treat ours." They apparently ignored the threat, for Allen was then ferried across the Kill Van Kull to Elizabeth Town Point and freedom. A month later, still basking in the glow of a cordial reception at Valley Forge (but nothing like the hoopla that greeted Lee), the Hero of Ticonderoga went back to his home in Bennington. The Green Mountain Boys gave him a fourteen-gun salute—thirteen for the United States and one for Vermont—after which, Allen deadpanned, "we moved the flowing bowl."[52]

Once he had finished with Allen, Boudinot made a quick second trip into occupied New York to complete the exchange of another forty-five American officers and men. At around the same time, Henry Clinton left for Philadelphia to replace the ineffectual Howe, under heavy fire at home for failing to support Burgoyne. Boudinot was pleasantly surprised to discover that with both Clinton and Howe out of the picture, the British in New York seemed much more willing to treat American captives decently. "Indeed," Boudinot wrote to Washington in mid-May, "their whole System appears to be changed . . . [or] at least in Confusion." Even Colonel Campbell "seems determined to interest himself in mitigating the rigors of Captivity, which he appears well acquainted with"—an understatement if ever there was one.[53]

Boudinot's return to Valley Forge followed close on the heels of even bigger news than Clinton's appointment as commander-in-chief: France had recognized the independence of the United States, and the two nations had entered into an alliance against Great Britain. These developments had important ramifications for American prisoners everywhere. The Franco-American alliance not only globalized the war and bolstered the American war effort but also, by stamping the Revolution with at least the appearance of legitimacy, put more pressure on the British government to deal with captured Americans as bona fide combatants.

The alliance also forced the British to admit that occupying the two largest urban centers in the colonies had accomplished next to nothing. In fact, Germain wanted General Clinton to get out of Philadelphia, and Clinton knew he had to leave quickly or risk being trapped if a French fleet blockaded the Delaware. To speed things along, Clinton offered to trade the hundreds of American prisoners in Philadelphia for the same number of British prisoners of equivalent rank. Washington accepted with alacrity. Hamilton as well as Boudinot conferred with Loring in early June about the specifics, and it was widely believed they had come to an agreement. At the last minute, however, and for reasons that were never made clear, Loring wrote to say that Clinton's withdrawal was under way and that the American prisoners were already on transports bound for New York. Exasperated by what looked awfully like another stroke of British duplicity, Boudinot broke off negotiations.[54]

A couple of weeks later, if it was any consolation, Boudinot received a "very entertaining" letter from Hamilton that described General Lee's poor showing as a divisional commander in the battle at Monmouth Court House on June 28. For leaving the field just when the British began to retreat, Washington denounced Lee as a "damned poltroon" in front of subordinates, then had him arrested and brought up on charges of misconduct and insubordination. Lee was convicted and eventually dismissed from the service. He spent the next few years in great personal disarray, alone with his dogs, bitter, and quite probably crazy, still dreaming of a military stronghold on the far side of the Appalachians. He died in 1782 at the age of fifty-one.[55]

As the spring of 1778 turned to summer, Commissary Boudinot had been on the job for a year—a year of "worrying myself off my Legs," he explained to Colonel Magaw. He was tired and needed a change of pace. He had also run himself to the very brink of bankruptcy by purchasing tens of thousands of dollars' worth of food and clothing for American prisoners on his own credit. On April 20, he resigned. Congress accepted, reluctantly, and dawdled for a month before naming his replacement: Colonel John Beatty, a Pennsylvania physician who had been captured by the British in 1776 and briefly imprisoned in New York.[56]

Washington, who knew a thing or two about money, urged Boudinot to join the New Jersey delegation in Congress and lobby for compensation, perhaps by laying claim to some of the $40,000 in specie recently received from Burgoyne to provision British prisoners held by American forces. Boudinot took Washington's advice, but prying his money out of Congress proved both nerve-wracking and rather embarrassing. His accounts were examined in minute detail, and a motion was made to award him almost $27,000 in specie. Which was fair enough, except miserly New Englanders then objected that since the money had been spent only on Washington's say-so, without congressional approval, Boudinot must be reimbursed only in "Continental" dollars, paper money whose value seemed to fall further every day.

This was too much, even for the usually mild-mannered Boudinot. In June, amidst an acrimonious floor fight, he leapt to his feet to announce that he would withdraw his request for compensation and declare himself insolvent. Then, as he later described the scene, "I also informed the House that even to that Moment, our Prisoners in New York were fed & cloathed on my private Credit—That I would immediately send Orders, to stop further Issues to them on my acct. in 10 Days, . . . " The dénouement came at the end of July, when Boudinot received a disturbing letter from Colonel Beatty, the new commissary of prisoners. It seems that in the short time since Boudinot closed his accounts in New York, as he promised he would do, conditions in the prisons had deteriorated sharply, the death rate had climbed, and Lewis Pintard was now in real danger of being thrown into the Provost himself for nonpayment of his debts. "With tears in my eyes," Boudinot read Beatty's letter aloud on the floor of Congress, whereupon William Duer of New York, "a man of much feeling," gave the delegates a half-hour tongue lashing for their "ungrateful Conduct"—ungrateful not only to Elias Boudinot, but as well to the prisoners who had been left to languish while the politicians dithered.

Congress promptly voted unanimously to give Boudinot a warrant for £10,000 in specie. A further £10,000 followed in August. It is unlikely, however, that he ever recovered all the money he had laid out for the prisoners in New York.[57]

In early April 1778, just as the cartel talks were breaking down, Colonel Matthias Ogden of New Jersey had approached Washington with a proposal. Reliable new intelligence from Long Island indicated that the American officers on parole there were now being watched only by small units of militia. A lightning raid could probably rescue "between twenty & thirty," Ogden reckoned, and he could do the job with only a few dozen men in three whaleboats. They would cross New York Harbor at night from Middletown Point (Matawan) to New Utrecht, a distance of eighteen miles, and be back before daybreak, "with verry little risque."

Ogden was a bold and enterprising officer—it would be his idea to kidnap Prince William Henry (later King William IV) along with Admiral Robert Digby when the two visited New York in 1782—but Washington was still opposed to liberating prisoners this way. As he had told General Parsons a year earlier, it could only make things worse for the men who remained in enemy hands. "Besides," he added, always attentive to the nuances of eighteenth-century martial etiquette, "a breach of Honor would certainly be objected against the Officers released; for it would be said, right or wrong, that they, at least, had consented to the measure, if not planned it."[58]

But the war was changing. Burgoyne's surrender and the new Franco-American alliance compelled London to abandon the notion that it could put down the revolt by methodically restoring royal control over the northern colonies. Henceforth it would concentrate on the south, rolling up the rebellion from Georgia to the Chesapeake while countering a French offensive in the West Indies. Clinton's evacuation of Philadelphia was only the first step. Although occupied New York would continue to serve as the main operational base and nerve center, controlling the city's hinterlands was now thought to be less useful than hit-and-run expeditions (like the 1777 Danbury raid) to seize or destroy rebel stores and discredit rebel governments.

Over the spring and summer of 1778, anticipating that they would be needed in the south, Clinton withdrew the regulars garrisoned in Huntington, Brookhaven, and other towns in Suffolk County, Long Island. Maintaining law and order everywhere east of Jamaica would henceforth be left to Tory militias. That autumn, additional regulars would be removed from Kings and Queens counties in preparation for Colonel Archibald Campbell's attack on Savannah and General James Grant's move against the Caribbean island of St. Lucia (both successful).[59]

The waning British presence on Long Island opened the door to privateering and pillaging on a scale that beggared anything seen in the first two years of the war. Swarming out of New Jersey, Connecticut, Rhode Island, and Massachusetts in whaleboats—locals dubbed it the "whaleboat war"—bands of rebels crisscrossed the eastern half of the island and the waters around it with impunity. Between January and December of 1778, area newspapers reported dozens of cases of robbery, arson, abduction, and murder perpetrated by armed gangs, usually but not always against residents still loyal to the crown. Some whaleboat men claimed to have commissions issued by the governments of New Jersey and Connecticut, while others appear to have been working in conjunction with units of the Continental Army. Still others sought to get friends or relatives out of detention in New York by kidnapping Tories for exchange. Many had nothing more in mind than settling old scores and stealing what they could, whenever and wherever they could, from friends and foe alike.

In August and then again in October, Major General William Tryon, now commander-in-chief of "provincial" forces in New York, led columns of Tory militia out to the East End of the island and back in a largely futile effort to restore some semblance of law and order. In September, Major General Charles ("No-flint") Grey descended on the Massachusetts coast with regulars, destroying seventy vessels, many belonging to rebel privateers, along with a mountain of stores. Grey had recently announced at a dinner party for assorted military and naval officers that "too much Refinement" had been used with the rebels thus far, and "that there was but one mode of settling anything effectually with them and that this was by the Sword." Thus the violence raged on, and by 1779 even prominent Americans, Washington included, would begin to insist that something be done to stop it.[60]

Arguably the most colorful of the whaleboat men—and one whose story intersects more than once that of the American prisoners in New York—was William Marriner (Mariner, Marrener). The details of his life are few and sketchy, but he seems to have been the same Marriner who owned the house or tavern on William Street in New York where a number of captured American officers boarded in 1776 and 1777. He was probably, or had been, a shoemaker as well. He remained in the city after the British takeover and at some point ran afoul of Mayor David Mathews, who had him committed to Cunningham's care in the Provost. In his "Memorandum," John Fell listed Marriner among the state prisoners there in the summer of 1777, noting also that a Mrs. Marriner was one of the ladies who often brought food to the prisoners.[61]

Early in 1778, Marriner was paroled to New Utrecht and billeted in the home of Rem Van Pelt. Perdurable local legend has it that Marriner and Mathews had crossed paths again in nearby Flatbush, where the mayor owned a summer house and where paroled American officers often rubbed elbows with Kings County Tories in the village tavern. Further unpleasantness ensued, after which it looks as though Marriner broke parole and fled, vowing revenge on Mathews and his ilk.[62]

Marriner went to ground in New Jersey, where he busied himself with preparations for a raid across New York Harbor to Flatbush. The goal was to get his hands on Mathews and anyone else he could find, presumably to exchange them for Americans detained by the British. Although this was around the same time that Colonel Ogden made his proposal to liberate American officers on Long Island, the two plans were quite distinct and no evidence exists of a connection between the two.

On the night of June 13, 1778, Marriner and Lieutenant John Schenck of the New Jersey militia left Middletown Point with a dozen men in two whaleboats and rowed quickly over the bay to Long Island by the light of a nearly full moon. They beached their boats near New Utrecht and were joined by some paroled American officers who apparently had advance knowledge of the raid, perhaps via Schenck, who had numerous relatives in Kings County. The combined group then took the road over to Flatbush, not three miles away, where they seized Major James Moncrieff, a British military engineer, and Theophylact Bache, a wealthy New York merchant and influential Tory.

Mathews, however, proved a more troublesome target. He barricaded himself in his house while one of the household slaves yelled for help from an upstairs window. The village was roused, shots rang out, and Marriner ordered his men back to their boats with only Moncrieff, Bache, and four slaves in tow. By six o'clock the next morning they had returned safely to New Jersey.[63]

Even if they knew in advance that Marriner was coming, only one of the numerous American prisoners billeted in New Utrecht or Flatbush elected to leave with him. That was twenty-three-year-old Andrew Forrest, a lieutenant in Captain Alexander Graydon's company, who had been taken prisoner at Fort Washington in November 1776. Even though he went with Marriner, Forrest was a reluctant escapee. What troubled him was in all likelihood what deterred his compatriots from making a break for it too: in going off with Marriner he was violating his parole, dishonoring himself and his uniform.

Soon after returning to New Jersey, therefore, the young lieutenant went over to headquarters to find out what General Washington thought. If the commander-in-chief did not approve his decision to leave with Marriner, he vowed to return immediately, as honor required. Washington, having mulled over this very issue for a year or two already, allowed that "it was a nice case," but saw no compelling reason for Forrest to give himself up. If it later seemed his "mode of release" had in fact violated military etiquette, a prisoner of equal rank could be exchanged for him.[64]

Relieved, Forrest went home to Pennsylvania. Marriner, for his part, continued to nurse his animosities, whatever they were, and like more than a few of the people living along the estuaries that feed Raritan Bay, tried his hand at privateering. It went well—so well that he soon acquired his own armed sloop, the *Enterprise,* and was able to post a £1,000 bond to get an official commission from Governor William Livingston of New Jersey and Henry Laurens, the president of Congress, authorizing him to seize British vessels and cargoes. Folks thereabouts began referring to the former shoemaker as *Captain* Marriner.[65]

On the night of November 3, 1778, *Captain* Marriner mounted a second whaleboat expedition across Lower New York Bay to Long Island. This time he went no farther than New Utrecht and confined himself to kidnapping the Cortelyou brothers, Simon and Jacques, identified by a New Jersey paper as "two famous tories in the enemy's lines." Although it was later said that Marriner targeted the Cortelyous for their mistreatment of American prisoners, an additional consideration was undoubtedly the money and goods, reportedly worth a total of 5,000 dollars, that he looted from Simon's house. That proved to be Marriner's last raid on Long Island, however. Henceforth he suspended his vendetta against Mayor Mathews and other Flatbush Tories to engage in increasingly audacious attacks on enemy shipping.[66]

By the summer of 1778, as the second anniversary of the British occupation drew near, New York City had begun to run out of food. Mostly to blame for the crisis was the long-dreaded arrival of the French fleet under the Comte d'Estaing at the beginning of July. D'Estaing's twelve mammoth ships of the line and three frigates, attended by a swarm of smaller vessels, anchored off Sandy Hook at the entrance to Lower New York Bay, preventing vital provisions from reaching Manhattan by sea. By the third week in July, bread was almost impossible to find at any price. British commissaries were giving the troops rice, peas, and oatmeal instead of flour. Famine seemed imminent, and there was hushed speculation that the city would have to be given up to the rebels. Some nervous residents reportedly "begin to send toast and butter to the prisoners by way of making fair weather for themselves" in the event of its liberation by the Americans, "which time is near at hand."[67]

Luckily, d'Estaing lifted the blockade at the end of the month, bearing off to Rhode Island just before victualing ships began to come in from Cork and Glasgow laden with hundreds of tons of urgently needed meat, flour, butter, and other essentials. Even though the threat of famine receded, however, it never quite disappeared. For one thing, as the *New-York Gazette* pointed out, the armed whaleboats infesting Long Island Sound continued to disrupt shipments of produce from Long Island farmers. For another, British foraging parties and patrols brought in new prisoners all the time, replacing those who had died or been let go. Even if they never got enough food or firewood, they were a constant drain on the occupied city's limited resources.[68]

Because the heavy fighting had now shifted to the southern theater, the new prisoners mostly arrived in small lots, rarely more than two or three at a time, often with civilians mixed in. On August 31, a British cavalry patrol under Lieutenant Colonels John Simcoe and Banastre Tarleton clashed with an American detachment in Westchester and took ten prisoners. "Sundry" residents of Huntington, Long Island, all civilians, were shut up in the Provost in early September for aiding and abetting Connecticut whaleboat men. On September 22, British cavalry bagged twenty-seven American militiamen near Englewood. At the end of the month, up near Old Tappan, "No-flint" Grey surprised a force of Continental cavalry, inflicting nearly thirty casualties and taking thirty-eight prisoners. There was some excitement in December when a Tory raiding party in New Jersey returned with a man they thought was General Artemas Ward, commander of the American forces at the siege of Boston in 1775; it turned out they had the wrong man, but another foray into the march land of Westchester County returned with "five violent Rebels & Committee Men"—all no doubt delivered into the custody of Provost Marshal Cunningham.[69]

A new round of horror stories from the prison ships confirmed that when supplies ran low, prisoners invariably received less food, and worse food, than everyone else. When transferred from the *Scorpion* to the hospital ship *Huntress*, a New Jersey seaman named John Ingersoll was told to expect a half pound of mutton per day. What the prisoners there got, he recalled, were only the severed heads of sheep. They survived by crushing the heads in water and stirring in a bit of oatmeal, producing a thick "broth" nutritious enough to keep body and soul together. The prison ship where Robert Sheffield of Connecticut spent the summer of 1778 was "a little epitome of hell":

> About 359 men confined between decks, of which about one half were Frenchmen; and he was informed that there was three more of these vehicles of contagion, which contained the like number of miserable Frenchmen also, who are treated, if possible worse than Americans. The heat so intense (the hot sun shining all day on deck) that they were all naked, which also served them well to get rid of the vermin, but the sick were eaten up alive. Their sickly countenances and ghastly looks were truly horrible; some swearing and blaspheming; some crying, praying and wringing their hands, stalking about like ghosts and apparitions; others delirious and void of reason, raving and storming; some groaning and dying, all panting for breath; some dead and corrupting. The air was so foul at times, that a lamp could not be kept burning, by reason of which three boys were not missed until they had been dead three days. One person only is admitted on deck at a time, after sun-set, which necessarily occasions much filth to run into the hole [hold], and mingle with the bildge water.

Five or six prisoners died every day, Sheffield said. Of the nineteen men taken with him, three did not survive their first week.[70]

Two years earlier, over the winter of 1776–1777, thousands of Americans detained in New York had perished from disease and starvation while General Howe gamboled with Mrs. Loring. Howe was now long gone, and with thousands of their own officers and men in American hands, British authorities responded to the food crisis by doing the sensible thing: they reduced the number of mouths to feed by releasing prisoners, some on parole, others in the expectation of a future cartel. How many they let go is not clear. A Connecticut paper rather hopefully reported five or six hundred American prisoners on their way to New Jersey as early as the end of July, though the actual numbers were probably much smaller and spread out over a period of several months. A report in mid-August that "all the American prisoners were at last sent out of the city" proved to be wishful thinking, inasmuch as another report, six weeks later, declared that "all the American Prisoners are nearly sent out of New-York, but there are 615 French Prisoners still there"—one of the earliest indications that the Franco-American alliance had put a Gallic glaze on the city's prison population. In December, with winter coming on hard, a British transport took 172 more Americans from the prison ships to Groton and New London, Connecticut. A local paper described the great majority as "in a sickly and most deplorable condition," many with severely frostbitten hands and feet.[71]

6

❦

WAR

ad Terrorem

DESPITE THE DECISION by Lords North and Germain to shift the war to the south, New York remained the center of British operations in America and a mecca for Tories from every colony. Commandant Robertson calculated that nearly 12,000 "refugees" had descended on the city within the first six months of the British takeover. More streamed in after Howe abandoned New Jersey, more still after General Henry Clinton, Howe's successor as commander-in-chief, pulled out of Philadelphia and Rhode Island in 1778.

No one knows for sure, but it is possible that by 1782 or 1783, 30,000 or more refugees had gathered in and around the city. They were a cross-section of colonial American society—deposed royal governors (five of them, in fact), a panoply of imperial functionaries and politicians, rich merchants and landowners, prominent churchmen, and a concourse of nearly destitute ordinary folks, often with families in tow, who had made the mistake of remaining loyal to their sovereign. Runaway slaves, too, were heading for the city from everywhere in the colonies, particularly after June 1779, when General Clinton promised freedom to "every Negro who shall desert the Rebell Standdard."[1]

This multitude of displaced persons, packed into little more than a single square mile on the toe of Manhattan, made New York more congested, noisome, turbulent, and expensive than ever before in its 150-year history. It also transformed the city into a veritable cauldron of Tory rancor and frustration. Nowhere else in Britain or America was the yearning for revenge more concentrated or virulent.

And nowhere would this frustration be better organized, thanks in large measure to William Franklin, Benjamin Franklin's estranged natural son. Before the Revolution, William had been his father's close companion, often accompanying him on his travels to London and assisting him with his scientific experiments. In 1763, allegedly to ensure the elder Franklin's friendship, the Crown appointed William Franklin governor of New Jersey. He served capably in that office for the next twelve years, but the widening rift between the colonies and the mother country, and his father's deepening involvement with the American cause, found the two men on opposite sides. They quarreled, openly and bitterly, and by the autumn of 1775 were no longer on speaking terms. "I have lost my son," the older man sadly informed a friend. In June 1776, only weeks before Benjamin signed the Declaration of Independence, William was arrested by the Provincial Congress of New Jersey and hustled off to prison in Connecticut. He spent over two years in close confinement, not regaining his freedom until he was exchanged for John McKinly, the president of Delaware, in October 1778.

On his release, Franklin went directly to New York, where he soon established himself as the voice of militant Toryism in the city. The Refugee Club, which he founded over the winter of 1778–1779, brought together key exiles from all over America who wanted to see the rebels in the north pursued with more vigor. Despite the influx of new prisoners over the summer and fall of 1778, Franklin and his associates considered Clinton too sluggish. They urged him to arm the Refugees and turn them loose to wage a "predatory war"—the formal term was "war *ad terrorem*"—laying waste to rebel towns and farms with the kind of crusading zeal previously directed at the Irish and Scots. "We must be prepared and not shy away from any barbarity," declared a Hessian officer sympathetic to the Refugees, "regardless of how it might be considered by a European."[2]

Clinton had no taste for that kind of thing, suspecting, correctly, that it would only broaden support for the insurgency and also undercut his authority as commander-in-chief. Quite a few of his regimental commanders liked the idea, however, among them Banastre

Tarleton of the British Legion, John Graves Simcoe of the Queen's Rangers, Sir John Johnson of the King's Royal Regiment (also known as the Royal Greens), and Lord Rawdon of the Volunteers of Ireland. The Black Brigade, a remnant of the Ethiopian Regiment raised among runaway slaves in Virginia back in 1775, was eager for action too, as were the Black Pioneers, who served the army as guides, spies, and Indian interpreters.[3]

But no one in uniform desired a predatory war more keenly than Major General William Tryon, commander-in-chief of the "provincials," units raised among the colony's Loyalist population. Some years before, as governor of North Carolina, Tryon had crushed the Regulator uprising in that colony with such ferocity that people there called him "the wolf." Named governor of New York in 1771, he soon became embroiled with the insurgents in that colony and by October 1775 had been forced to seek refuge on a British warship in New York harbor. He remained there until Howe's forces recaptured the city the following summer. Because his gubernatorial powers were suspended by the imposition of martial law, Tryon then wangled a commission in the army and made ready to wreak his vengeance on the rebels. His devastating 1777 raid on Danbury confirmed that he had not lost his lupine appetite for death and destruction.[4]

Whether Clinton would bow to the pressure for a war *ad terrorem* had not been resolved when the worst winter in living memory virtually paralyzed the city. On Christmas Eve, 1778, the first of several monster blizzards struck New York, leaving all but a handful of streets completely blocked by towering snowdrifts. Food reserves dwindled alarmingly, but the thermometer hovered at or below zero for so long that residents figured they would run out of firewood before they starved. "The storms have been terrible," declared a weary Hessian officer. "Wild geese and ducks froze to death by the thousands on the shores of Long and Staten Islands. They were most greedily eaten by the soldiers and inhabitants, for the provisions had become very low. There was no more flour, and the small amount of good oatmeal mixed with the spoiled did not make wholesome biscuits for the soldiers." One memorably cold morning, three British sentries were found dead in their guard boxes, frozen stiff as boards.[5]

Always last in line for food, firewood, blankets, and clothes, the American prisoners in New York suffered terribly. Just how terribly became apparent in early January 1779, when a British transport left New York for New London with 430 men from a single prison ship, most likely the *Good Hope*. Fifteen died along the way, and most of the rest were so weakened by cold, hunger, and disease that they had to be carried ashore. Outraged, the Connecticut General Assembly instructed each town in the state to collect depositions from the ex-prisoners as they returned home, "stating the particulars of the severe usage and sufferings" they had experienced in New York.[6]

Releasing prisoners helped reduce the pressure on the city's dwindling stocks of food and fuel. Combined with the predictably high mortality rates, it also brought down the overall numbers of prisoners there—for a while. At the end of February 1779, Commissary Beatty informed Washington that only 258 Americans were still under lock and key on Manhattan, not counting several hundred officers paroled on Long Island and another 200 men on the *Good Hope*. That added up to around 700 in all, probably the lowest total since the city fell to the enemy over two years earlier. Commissary Loring reported 286 prisoners in his care at the beginning of March, and a list of American prisoners left aboard the *Good Hope* in mid-April contained just 144 names.[7]

As the winter of 1778–1779 relaxed its grip on the city, Clinton remained firm in his opposition to arming the Refugees. He did, however, launch his own version of a predatory war by unleashing Tryon's provincials to raid the rebel-controlled hinterlands of New York—often, though not always, in conjunction with regulars. They attacked Elizabeth Town in mid-February, returning with two dozen prisoners. Private Daniel Waldo (later famous as one of the oldest surviving veterans of the Revolutionary War) spent two months in the Sugar House after his entire company, thirty-seven men in all, was captured by provincials in March.[8]

General Tryon himself brought in at least forty more captives after punitive expeditions against Horseneck (Greenwich) in February and, in July, against New Haven, Fairfield, and Norwalk. During the latter action his men looted and destroyed scores of homes, burned churches, summarily executed the wounded, and allegedly blew the heads off corpses for sport. "The existence of a single habitation on your defenseless coast," he scolded the people of Connecticut, "ought to be a constant reproof of your ingratitude." Whether his brutality had the desired effect was another matter. As one contributor to a Boston paper pointed out, the enemy's "shocking inhumanities" just made Americans more determined to fight on. Deliberate cruelty excites "only indignation and aversion," the paper said; "it awakens every motive that can animate a manly bosom, to despise every difficulty and every danger in repelling such savage invaders." Not everyone in the British army approved, either. As Colonel Charles Stuart observed sensibly, "A Rebellion is different from an other War."[9]

Clinton's war *ad terrorem* rolled on nonetheless, and the number of prisoners in New York grew apace. In June, seventy-five North Carolina troops surrendered at Verplanck's Point, on the Hudson, and Tarleton's "Legion" took thirty or forty prisoners after a clash with militia near Crompond, in Westchester County. Days later, they raided nearby Pound Ridge and Bedford, getting away with twenty-odd captives; German dragoons snatched ten prisoners in Tarrytown in August. At the end of October, Simcoe's Queen's Rangers struck Brunswick, New Jersey, where they destroyed food and forage intended for Washington's army and grabbed about thirty prisoners. On the way back to Amboy, Simcoe himself fell prisoner in a skirmish with a group of insurgents led by William Marriner, the shoemaker turned whaleboat captain.[10]

As violence cycloned around New York, the region slid into near anarchy. More than a few Refugees took the opportunity to conduct their own operations and bring in prisoners, more or less independent of either Clinton or Tryon. It was in July 1779 that a runaway slave named Colonel Tye organized a company of fifty black and white Refugees to harass rebels in Monmouth County; for the next two years, Tye and his men burned houses and barns, rustled cattle, and captured dozens of militia officers and civilians, all of whom were turned over to British authorities in New York.[11]

Tye's depredations in New Jersey had their counterparts on both sides of Long Island Sound. Refugee commandos kidnapped Brigadier General Gold Selleck Silliman and one of his sons, Major William Silliman, from the general's Fairfield, Connecticut, residence in May 1779; their captors took them to New York, where they were confined to a private house until Loring sent the general to a billet in Gravesend (his son, seriously ill, was allowed to return home on parole). Colonel Josiah Smith, a Long Island militia officer, did not fare so well as the Sillimans and served three months in the Provost after Tories surprised him at his East Moriches home in July. Still other Americans fell into enemy hands while on marauding expeditions of their own. In June, the Loyalist Hempstead militia repulsed an incursion by whaleboat raiders from somewhere across the Sound, capturing twenty-three.[12]

An increasing number of the captives coming into New York were not prisoners of war at all, but noncombatants who had drawn attention to themselves as outspoken supporters of the insurgency. In the waning days of 1778, for example, one resident of the city recorded the capture of five "violent Rebels & Committee Men" near White Plains. Judge John Covenhoven was taken the following April by a detachment of regulars on their way back to New York after a search-and-destroy expedition into Monmouth County. David Bushnell, the Connecticut inventor credited with building the world's first functioning submarine, was collared with other civilians near Norwalk in May.[13]

Conspicuous among the civilian captives were clergymen who had spoken out against the crown from the pulpit. In June 1779, Refugees descended on Greenwich, making off with cattle, horses, and thirteen prisoners—including, exulted the *Royal Gazette*, "a PRESBYTERIAN PARSON, named Burrit, an egregious REBEL." In July, a Refugee posse that included some of his former parishioners snatched sixty-year-old Moses Mather, the Congregational minister in what is now Darien, Connecticut. Mather and his sons spent five weeks in the Provost. But the good man's trials were not over. In 1781, looters from Long Island made off with his furniture and clothing; later that same year, a large party of Refugees from Lloyd's Neck surrounded his church during the Sunday afternoon service and took him down to New York again, along with about forty members of the congregation. His second stint in the Provost lasted two months.[14]

Inevitably, at least a few prisoners were probably guilty of nothing more than being in the wrong place at the wrong time. When Tories snatched Captain Nathaniel Fitz Randolph out of a Woodbridge, New Jersey, tavern in February 1779, they took the tavern keeper, Charles Jackson, back to New York as well; Jackson was apparently still in custody almost a year later.[15]

Along with the Refugees and provincial forces, the Royal Navy too was rounding up prisoners. In the spring of 1779 it began a new offensive against the privateers and whaleboat men infesting local waters, netting hundreds. The largest haul consisted of 118 Connecticut sailors who surrendered when their ship, the *Oliver Cromwell*, tangled off Sandy Hook in mid-June with a British frigate, *Daphne*. The entire crew wound up on the *Good Hope*. The *Oliver Cromwell* was then purchased by some Refugees, slyly rechristened the *Restoration*, and sent out to prey on rebel shipping in Long Island Sound.[16]

All told, it seems likely that Clinton's predatory war of 1779 brought a minimum of 600 new prisoners to New York—more than enough to make up for those who had died or had been let go during the previous winter.[17] It was certainly enough to produce a new crop of horror stories in American newspapers. When 200 prisoners from the *Good Hope* were released at Elizabeth Town in June, a local paper informed its readers, "Our prisoners on board the prison ship suffer beyond description, being turned down in great numbers below decks, where they are obliged to languish in stench and dirt, by which cruel treatment many have fallen sacrifices to diseases and the cruel hand of oppression." Of the three or four hundred said to remain, six or seven perished every day. This was roughly consistent with another report, dated mid-July, that upwards of 400 Americans had died of an unspecified contagion on the prison ships during the previous three months.[18]

Thus it must have come as quite a surprise to readers of the *Connecticut Gazette* when the paper announced, at the end of August 1779, that a British transport had just come to New London with forty-seven prisoners from the *Good Hope*, every one remarkably fit. *The Independent Chronicle*, a Boston paper, observed the following month that American prisoners in New York were being treated less cruelly than in previous years. That seemed to confirm the news from Connecticut, although another story in the very same edition recounted the arrival of 180 men, fresh off a New York prison ship, "who have undergone, since their captivity, every inhumanity conceivable."[19]

Whether things really had improved for the prisoners in New York was the subject of an unusual public disagreement among a dozen-odd men who somehow escaped from the *Good Hope* in October 1779. Captain James Prince of New Jersey was afterward heard to praise the ship's captain for "using the prisoners with a great deal of humanity, in particular to himself." But Prince's fellow escapees disagreed. According to a Norwich paper, which got the details from a correspondent in the American camp at Fishkill, they insisted that the enemy continued to mistreat captured Americans. How anyone could describe conditions on the *Good Hope* as humane was a complete mystery: "These gentlemen said, that for three days before they set off, they had no other subsistence than a scanty morsel of condemned bisquit, full of worms and oil;—That they left them only the shirts they had on, and had stripped the crew of a Spanish vessel, they had lately taken quite naked.—Thus the Britons new conduct towards their prisoners!"[20]

True or not, those rumors of greater leniency in New York fell off sharply after captured Americans were put at the mercy of a new scourge: David Sproat, appointed commissary of naval prisoners in October 1779 and destined to become one of the great villains in the prisoner-of-war story.

Sproat was a Philadelphia Tory who had emigrated from Scotland almost twenty years earlier, set himself up there as a merchant, and accumulated, by his own proud admission, "a pritty little fortune" before the war. He also became a vocal opponent of independence and eventually fled to New York to escape arrest. For this, he said later, his Philadelphia home had been ransacked and his clerk thrown into jail. He returned to the City of Brotherly Love when the British captured Philadelphia in 1777, then fled again, this time for good, when General Clinton pulled out less than a year later. January 1779 found Sproat back in New York, his affairs in ruins, casting about for gainful employment in the royal bureaucracy and aching for retribution against the rebels who had laid him so low so fast.[21]

Although occupied New York was crawling with job seekers, many as deserving of preferment as he, Sproat made no secret of his opposition to coddling rebels and rebel prisoners. As he told Joseph Galloway, a fellow Pennsylvanian and key member of Franklin's Refugee Club, men caught "in the very acts of Rebellion and Murder" had no claim to "kind treatment." That also happened to be the opinion of Admiral Marriot Arbuthnot, who arrived in the autumn of 1779 to replace Admiral Gambier as head of His Majesty's naval forces in North America. When Arbuthnot let it be known that he needed to find a new commissary for naval prisoners, Sproat was in the right place, at the right time, with powerful friends to recommend him. He got the job.[22]

The new commissary quickly discovered that he had inherited a considerable mess from his predecessors. "Our affairs were in a most wretched situation," he later informed the commissioners of the Sick and Hurt Board in London. "Not the Vestige of a Book, Paper, Return, or Precedent was to [be] found. . . . Nobody could tell how many Prisoners were here; had been exchanged; or whether the Rebels owed us, or we them." To set things right, Sproat gave orders that ships coming into port with naval prisoners must bring them to a specially designated receiving ship for proper processing, rather than the usual practice of dropping them off on whatever prison ship seemed most convenient. He instructed American naval prisoners paroled in the city or on Long Island to inform him of their exact whereabouts. By these and other measures, Sproat told the commissioners, he "reduced the business to [a] system." Though presented with plentiful opportunities to line his own pockets, he also appears to have been relatively honest—relative, at any rate, to Joshua Loring, still serving as commissary for military prisoners.[23]

That Sproat's appointment would mean no improvement in conditions on the prison ships began to come clear in mid-December, as another catastrophic winter closed in on New York—much worse, people said, even than that of the previous year. The snow fell relentlessly from December to February, piling up twelve feet deep in places. William Smith, former chief justice of the colony, said it was so cold that even when he sat by a blazing fire, the ink froze in his pen while he wrote. "We often hear of the Deaths of the Poor, frozen in their Houses," he remarked, and even "reputable People" stayed in bed all day to keep warm. By January, according to Major Baurmeister, the British Army had already lost a thousand horses for lack of forage, while the most straitened residents were chopping up boats for firewood. "In short," he wrote, "it was real misery." As the winter deepened, great stretches of the East River, the Hudson River, Long Island Sound, Upper New York Bay, and Newark Bay became solid masses of ice—thick enough to support fully loaded wagons, heavy cannon, and a troop of cavalry that galloped one day in close formation from Staten Island to the Battery on Manhattan. Residents of the city began to worry that the Americans would come swarming across the frozen Hudson and drive them off Manhattan.[24]

The suffering in the city's prisons and prison ships was dreadful. Sproat pronounced the American prisoners "comfortable," but William Webb, a soldier from Long Island on the *Good Hope*, would survive to tell his son stories of such extreme cold that "many of the prisoners froze their feet till they came off at the ankle and sometimes died there." (Because a wood-hulled vessel like the *Good Hope* was in danger of being caught and crushed in the heavy ice, she had been moved by this time from the Hudson side of Manhattan into the shallower waters of Wallabout Bay.) Thirty years later, one of the survivors declared that of 600 prisoners on the *Good Hope* when winter set in, only 250—a little better than 40 percent—lived until spring. Conditions in the Provost were no better. When John Pintard (Lewis Pintard's nephew) visited there in January, he saw many dying prisoners, including one whose frostbitten feet had turned "as black as his hat."[25]

Some French prisoners on one of the prison ships sent a frantic plea for assistance to their ambassador in Philadelphia, relating how they had been "reduced to all the extremities of misery:—Devoured on all sides, with all the impurities of nature. ... We crawl about, in the unfeeling view of our barbarous conquerors, as walking carcases. ... N.B. The American prisoners fare no better." As late as the second day of April, well after the snows had melted, one of those Americans got out a mournful letter describing conditions on the hospital ship *Falmouth*, so crowded that prisoners could not lie down to sleep at the same time. It was, he wrote, "the most shocking, horrible, infernal, cursed hole that can be thought of; beyond imagination to conceive, or tongue to paint."[26]

This frightful suffering, and Sproat's apparent indifference, might have been comprehensible if everyone else in town had been running out of provisions, as happened over the previous winter. This time, though, they were not, at least not those who were able to afford the skyrocketing prices. That became clear in mid-January 1780, when the authorities in New York mounted a lavish celebration of the queen's birthday. It was, crowed the *New-York Gazette*, an event of "uncommon Splendor and Magnificence." The town's Moravian pastor, on the other hand, was appalled. The gala ball alone, he noted in his diary, "cost above 2000 Guineas, and they had over 300 dishes for Supper"—a spectacle of piggish gorging utterly unjustified at a time when the poor were dying for lack of food or firewood. William Smith also thought the money should have been spent on fuel for needy refugees as well as the poor. Not for the first time, it was apparent that the British could have treated their prisoners better than they did, if treating them better had mattered.[27]

The prisoners themselves, predictably, had nothing good to say about Sproat, and at the beginning of March 1780 those who somehow made it through the winter on the *Good Hope* set the notorious hulk afire and cheered while she burned to the waterline. Sproat grieved extravagantly. She was the "best prison-ship in the world!" he exclaimed, and he objected bitterly when the incendiaries were merely sent to the Provost, not hanged outright. The experience only hardened his conviction that in dealing with captured rebels, the stick was preferable to the carrot. As he would later remind the Sick and Hurt Board, "It is severe, and not lenial [lenient] measures you may depend upon't that will bring these People back to a sense of their Duty."[28]

Since the collapse of the Germantown conference back in March 1778, both Washington and Congress had been under intense public pressure to reopen negotiations for a cartel, or general exchange of prisoners. Paroled officers, itching to get back into the fight, were furious that nothing seemed to be happening. Brigadier General William Thompson of Pennsylvania, for one, blasted Congress as "a parcel of *damned rascals*" because he had yet to be formally exchanged after two years as a prisoner. The officers still on Long Island grew especially short-tempered, and Commissary Beatty feared that prolonged captivity had already taken a heavy toll on their morale. "Dispondency I fear & other more serious consequences will Ensue," he warned Congress darkly. Although American and British spokesmen would in fact talk again, at Perth Amboy in December 1778 and in April 1779, those meetings, too, broke up without an agreement. After months of convoluted behind-the-scenes preparations, a third Perth Amboy conference convened in March 1780. It failed as well.[29]

These efforts invariably came to naught because each side occupied a position from which it could not afford to retreat—the Americans from their insistence on a written agreement, endorsed by both governments; the British from their refusal to accept anything that could be interpreted as de facto recognition of the United States. As General William Philips explained to Germain after the third Perth Amboy conference, the Americans sought to negotiate "on principles of nation against nation at war . . . which it may be imagined will never be suffered by Great Britain." There were other issues, too, such as the amount of compensation owed each side for feeding and clothing prisoners, and the formula for making up a cartel by "composition," but those were comparatively easy to work around. The upshot, for captives on both sides, was that until the very end of the war, if and when they were released would depend on ad hoc deals between commissaries and commanders in the field.[30]

Days after the third Perth Amboy conference broke up, Beatty resigned (to resume his medical practice, he said, though it appears he had been found engaging in illegal trade with the enemy). To succeed him as commissary, Congress picked Abraham Skinner, a native of Jamaica, Long Island, who evidently took the job with no expectation that American prisoners could be released or exchanged anytime soon. That autumn, he and Loring nonetheless managed the biggest informal exchange of military personnel so far in the war, liberating perhaps 500 privates and 200-odd officers from Long Island. By the end of October, only about 100 officers and some privates remained in detention in New York, and fewer than two dozen more on parole on Long Island. All too soon, however, their places would be filled by new batches of captives brought in by Clinton's regulars, Tryon's provincial corps, and Franklin's Associated Loyalists.[31]

At some point during the winter of 1779–1780, Sproat, too, began sending out prisoners for exchange. He stepped up the pace that spring, and within six months had reportedly released no fewer than 3,000 rebels from the prison ships in New York. If accurate, this figure suggests that the Royal Navy's efforts to clear privateers and whaleboat men from the waters around the city had continued to be highly productive. In return, Sproat obtained the release of 2,200 British seamen from American custody.[32]

Sproat's eagerness to trade captives was a response to the acute shortage of manpower now facing Admiral Arbuthnot. While crossing the Atlantic to New York in the autumn of 1779, his ships had been so ravaged by disease that 700 crewmen were said to have died and another 1,200 became so sick they had to be put ashore on arrival. His crews had then been further reduced by local captains, who lured able-bodied tars off His Majesty's ships with offers of better money and working conditions. Arbuthnot had attempted to stop the practice by fiat, repeatedly warning residents of the city not to meddle with his crews, but they paid him no heed. The next step, presumably on Arbuthnot's orders, was for Sproat to arrange the return of captured British seamen, as many as possible and as speedily as possible. At the same time, Sproat attempted to boost the recruitment of captured rebels off the Wallabout prison ships by (among other measures) taking greater pains to isolate able-bodied seamen from their officers. That effort alone, he later boasted, produced thousands of new tars for His Majesty's service.[33]

As the summer of 1780 approached, however, the fleet's need for seamen exceeded Sproat's ability to supply them by exchange or recruitment. The navy therefore resorted to its traditional, and wildly unpopular, practice of forcible impressment. In May, New York experienced the second so-called "hot press" since the war began: gangs of armed sailors from the fleet scoured every street and waterfront tavern round the clock, in search of anyone who looked like a seaman or potential seaman. It was said that they even grabbed "numbers" of Americans off the prison ships. On August 15, Captain Richard Grinnell made his escape from the *Scorpion* during another raid by the press gangs in the city. It was, he remarked, "the hottest press ever known there, they pressed about 700 men that day. . . . They not only took seamen, but all the refugees, labourers and merchant's Clerks they came across."[34]

Sproat's exchanges finally came to an end in September 1780, when Admiral George Bridges Rodney brought his fleet up from the West Indies to preempt a French attack on New York and to mount a new offensive against rebel privateers. Rodney, who outranked Arbuthnot, ordered an immediate freeze on releasing naval prisoners. The Americans, it seems, had run out of captured British sailors to trade, and the deficit against them, already up to 800 men, could only get larger. Until they made up the deficit, Rodney reasoned, continuing to release rebels who were in British hands served no purpose. But because he expected the prison ship population to rise again, and rapidly, Rodney made a point of urging Sproat to stay on as commissary. "This Man," he explained to the Sick and Hurt Board, "is the only Person I can find capable of managing the Business properly."[35]

By the autumn of 1780, it appeared that the British decision to concentrate on the southern theater was working almost to perfection. Charleston had surrendered to Clinton in May—one of the greatest British victories in the war—and organized resistance had soon collapsed throughout Georgia and the Carolinas. A second disastrous defeat followed in August, when an American army hastily gathered by Horatio Gates was destroyed by Cornwallis at Camden, South Carolina. The Americans exacted a measure of revenge in October at King's Mountain, South Carolina, butchering scores of Tory militiamen in the act of surrendering, but everyone knew that after almost six years of war, the Revolution might well have now come to the end of the road.

Easily overlooked in the dismal news from the south was the violence still raging around New York, and the hundreds of new captives it fed into the city's prisons—at least 500 by the autumn of 1780, counting civilians as well as soldiers and officers. That season's trophy prisoner was Captain William Marriner—"a great Rebel Partizan" said the *Royal Gazette*—who was bagged by a company of intrepid Tory militiamen from Queens and sent off to prison in New York along with two dozen of his men.[36]

A growing number of prisoners were not, like Marriner, taken in arms, but were snatched by Refugees or provincial troops when they wandered too far from camp or went home on furlough. That kind of carelessness became such a problem for the American army, in fact, that after Refugees captured two more officers at Elizabeth Town in November 1780, orders went out that anyone else taken "out of ye line of duty" would be put at the end of the rotation for exchange and arrested upon their return to active duty.

Plenty of civilian political prisoners remained in the mix, too. "Last Saturday Morning," ran a typical account in the local press, "Mr. Mathias Halstead, of Elizabeth-Town, was brought to this City, and lodged in the Sugar-House: He was taken out of his own House the Evening before, by a Party of Refugees from Staten-Island: He was a Justice of the Peace under Congress." Some civilians seem to have been taken for no reason at all, other than being in the wrong place at the wrong time. Several unlucky residents of Newark, innocently gathering oysters on the shore one day, were caught off-guard by provincials or Refugees and spirited away to prison in New York.[37]

Then, on top of setback after setback in the south and the apparently unstoppable drain of soldiers and civilians into the prisons of New York,

Americans got the news in late September 1780 of General Benedict Arnold's treason. Oddly enough, though long remembered as one of the most devastating blows to American morale in the entire war, the defection of this capable and energetic officer may actually have helped somewhat to contain the savagery spreading through the city's hinterlands.

It seems that William Franklin and his Refugee Club had by this time gone over General Clinton's head and persuaded both the king and Germain to sign off on their plan to arm the refugees in New York for an all-out predatory war. Clinton grudgingly accepted the verdict, but he wanted assurances that the Refugees would not operate independently of his command. In the protracted behind-the-scenes wrangling that consumed much of the summer and early autumn of 1780, Franklin found a friend and ally in Clinton's aide-de-camp, Major John André—Arnold's co-conspirator, whose accidental arrest had led to the discovery of Arnold's treachery. In October, the Americans hanged André for spying, and his death dealt a severe blow to Franklin's hopes of complete autonomy for the Refugees. When he and Clinton finally came to terms in late December, Franklin got less than he had hoped for.[38]

What Franklin did get was to all intents and purposes a private army. Known officially as the Associated Loyalists, it had the right to draw arms and supplies from the royal stores, to seize and keep rebel property, and to arrange for the exchange of any rebels who fell into its hands; it also got permission to keep them in a special section of the Provost. What it did not have—and what Franklin might have won if André had lived to fight on his behalf—was the power to act on its own, without Clinton's consent.

Even so, for the next eighteen months Franklin and his followers, four or five hundred strong, terrorized the countryside around New York from the sand dunes of the Jersey shore to the Connecticut River, trailing bitterness in their wake and ensuring a steady supply of customers for the prisons of New York. What they might have accomplished if they had been on a longer leash, or on no leash at all, is difficult to imagine.[39]

Surely one of the strangest ironies of the Revolutionary War is that while William Franklin did his best to put as many rebels as possible in prison, his father, Benjamin, was endeavoring to get them out. As the United States envoy in Paris since December 1776, Franklin *père* had learned a good deal about the mistreatment of American captives on both sides of the Atlantic, and what he heard had goaded him into action.

Initially, Franklin's efforts focused on a pair of detention centers in the south of England: Forton Prison, near Portsmouth, and Mill Prison, near Plymouth. By 1779 Forton and Mill held a total of 2,200 Americans, most of them captured on the high seas aboard merchant ships or privateers. Though never so deadly as their counterparts in New York, the two prisons were bad enough to have become a cause célèbre for English opponents of the war, who clamored about the harm done to the nation's reputation by the abuse of prisoners and conducted fund-raising drives to buy them food and clothing. In time, a shadowy network of American sympathizers and expatriates provided shelter, clothing, and pocket money to escapees. One English family reputedly assisted forty fugitives in a single week.[40]

Years before, Benjamin Franklin had become very friendly with the English scientist and reform-minded MP David Hartley. A prominent advocate of reconciliation with the colonies before 1776, Hartley had since emerged as one of the war's sharpest critics and kept up a lively correspondence with Franklin about resolving the conflict without further bloodshed. The plight of American prisoners in Britain troubled both men, and Franklin, working through Hartley, took up their cause in earnest. He arranged for unofficial inspections of both Forton and Mill and set up a system to furnish the men in each prison with small weekly allowances for the purchase of food and other necessities. He placed agents in French and Dutch ports to help escapees who managed to cross the Channel. (One of these happened to be John Witherspoon, the younger son of the New Jersey congressman and college president who had compiled the 1777 report on the treatment of prisoners in New York.) In 1778, Franklin and Hartley met face-to-face in Paris to negotiate a prisoner exchange.

Inevitably, there were complications, but partial exchanges took place in 1779 and again in 1780.[41]

As he became more aware of what was happening to American prisoners in New York as well, Franklin's anger stiffened his determination not to accept anything less than unqualified independence for the United States. "As to our submitting again to the Government of Britain," he had scolded Hartley at the close of 1777, "'tis vain to think of it. She has given us by her numberless Barbarities, in the Prosecution of the War, and in the Treatment of Prisoners . . . so deep an Impression of her Depravity, that we can never again trust her in the Management of our Affairs, and Interest."[42]

Franklin's involvement in the prisoners' cause took a literary turn at the beginning of 1779, when the dashing young Marquis de Lafayette returned to Paris for a visit. After two years of campaigning alongside Washington, Lafayette had plenty to say about the mistreatment of captives in New York. He and Franklin spoke about the matter and quickly agreed to produce an illustrated book displaying those "numberless Barbarities" to the world. Franklin's list of possible prints included graphic scenes of burning towns, bloodthirsty redcoats, terrorized women and children, and abused prisoners: "Prisoners dying in their Gaols, with Hunger Cold & want of Fresh Air"; "American Prisoners, put on board Men of War, & whips to make them fight against their Countrymen & Relations"; "American officers who as they arrive in the British Camp are insulted By an enrag'd Soldiery"; "A durty prison ship where American officers are Confin'd without Being at liberty to take the Air, and so Crowded that they Can live but a few days—British officers Come to laugh at 'em and insult at their Miseries."[43]

Unfortunately, neither man ever found time for the project. Franklin had his hands full in Paris, and Lafayette was soon caught up in preparations for a French invasion of England or Ireland. In July 1779 he asked Franklin for a progress report on "our little Book," perhaps hoping that the American had decided to do all or most of the work. There had been no progress, however. Six months later, in February 1780, Franklin lobbed a blistering letter at Hartley about the shameful treatment of American prisoners, as much as admitting that he was far behind schedule with the book project. Congress had now collected sworn accounts of "British Barbarities," Franklin wrote, and

> . . . it is expected of me to make a school Book of them, and to have 35. Prints designed here by good artists and engraved each expressing one or more of the different horrid facts, to be inserted in the Book, in order to impress the minds of Children and Posterity with a deep sense of your bloody and insatiable Malice and Wickedness. Every kindness I hear of done by an Englishman to an american Prisoner makes me resolve not to proceed in the Work, hoping a Reconciliation may yet take place. But every fresh Instance of your Devilism weakens that resolution, and makes me abominate the Thought of Reunion with such a People.

Later that same year, Lafayette returned to America and again asked for a progress report. Franklin suggested that the Frenchman find a coauthor on that side of the Atlantic. The "little book" never materialized.[44]

Like so many of his countrymen, Franklin had come to see the apparently systematic mistreatment of American prisoners as a kind of moral or psychological Rubicon: once crossed, there could be no compromise, no turning back, no restoration of the old connection between the colonies and the mother country. When the war was over and independence assured, he would look back on the refusal of thousands of ordinary men to abandon the cause while in captivity, even at the cost of their lives, as "glorious Testimony in favor of plebian Virtue."[45]

Perhaps, too, his anger at what those men endured helped to solidify Benjamin's estrangement from William, whose pursuit of predatory war was contributing materially to the suffering of so many Americans. In July 1784, after nearly a decade in which the two had not exchanged so much as a letter, William wrote his father for permission to visit him in Paris. He wanted to revive "that affectionate Intercourse and Connexion which till the Commencement of the late Troubles had been the Pride and Happiness of my Life." Could the older man understand that he had acted always in accordance with his duty to king and country? Benjamin took his time answering, then declined the offer of a visit. "Nothing has ever hurt me so much and affected me with such keen Sensations as to find myself deserted in my old Age by my only Son," he replied stiffly, "and not only deserted, but to find him taking up Arms against me, in a Cause wherein my good Fame, Fortune and Life were all at Stake."[46]

7

THE WAR OF
Words

IN THE SUMMER of 1779, a Philadelphia printer named Robert Bell began to advertise a slender volume that would transform the way Americans understood and responded to the abuse of prisoners in New York: the grandiloquently titled *Narrative of Colonel Ethan Allen's Captivity, From the time of his being taken by the British, near Montreal, on the 25th day of September, in the year 1775, to the time of his exchange, on the 6th day of May, 1778. Written by Himself.* An immediate bestseller, Allen's *Narrative* would be reprinted eight times before the end of the war and go on to be one of the most widely read books in the United States during the first half of the nineteenth century.[1]

Allen's success stemmed in part from advance publicity that most authors only dream about. Did anyone in the country *not* know by 1779 at least the general outline of Allen's career as a prisoner of war—taken during the invasion of Canada, hauled off to England in chains, thrown into the Provost in New York, and so on? His only rival as a celebrity captive was General Charles Lee, and Lee, thanks to his poor showing at the Battle of Monmouth Court House, was now in disgrace. Timing helped, too. Even though the abuse of American prisoners was not news by 1779, no one before Allen had given the reading public a full-length, firsthand, blow-by-blow account of what it was like to be caught and held by the enemy. A potential competitor surfaced in Philadelphia just months later, entitled *A Narrative of the Capture and Treatment of John Dodge, By the English at Detroit. Written by Himself.* But it was no contest. As a hero, Dodge paled by comparison to the rip-roaring, larger-than-life Allen, and Dodge's experiences, largely confined to the frontier, were only tenuously related to the suffering throngs of prisoners in New York. The Hero of Ticonderoga not only had a head start, he had a more interesting story as well.[2]

More than anything else, the popularity of Allen's book reflected its distinctive contribution to the robust tradition of captivity narratives, real and imagined, known to every literate American in the final decades of the eighteenth century. The Jews in Egypt, Christian martyrs, John Smith in Powhatan's Virginia, Robinson Crusoe, Gulliver among the Lilliputians, Mary Rowlandson in the hands of King Philip, the Black Hole of Calcutta—the list is a long one. Then, too, captivity in one form or another—not simply stories *about* captivity—was a very real part of Allen's world: think of imprisonment for debt, and the practices of coverture, indentured servitude, and chattel slavery.

In the archetypal captivity narrative, falling into the hands of one's enemies is the shameful consequence of things gone wrong—a mark of failure, personal or collective or both, that cries out for explanation and accountability. The captive's story becomes a quest for redemption. Getting to the end means re-education, transformation, even rebirth: the person who emerges from captivity is not the same person who was taken prisoner.[3]

Allen's *Narrative* works differently. His captivity is not the consequence of sinfulness or moral turpitude or incompetence, let alone cowardice. He surrendered to the enemy for the eminently sensible reason that he and his men were cornered: it's an explanation but not an apology. He committed no crime in fighting for his country. He refuses to be labeled a "rebel." He demands to be treated as "a gentleman of the military establishment." Thus his subsequent career as a captive cannot be understood as a voyage of self-discovery or moral progress, because he never has second thoughts or regrets: "The cause I was engaged in I ever viewed worthy hazarding my life for," he writes, "nor was I, in the most critical moments of trouble, sorry that I engaged in it." Indeed, instead of making him conscious of his own shortcomings, captivity awakens him to those of his enemies. His encounters with haughty, malicious officers, venal ship captains, and foul-mouthed guards teach him that British civility is a hoax. Britons, he realizes, revel in "cruelty." As "Miserecors" had written two years earlier, it is their national trait—the personality, so to speak, of tyranny—and the outrage it has already aroused across America is why there can be no peace without independence. "I know you have individuals, who still retain their virtue," he tells his captors directly, "but as a nation I hate and despise you." So when he finally regains his liberty at the conclusion of the *Narrative*, it is not because his odyssey through British jails and prison ships made him a different person but precisely because he managed to remain the same person, "a full blooded Yankee," to the end.

Less than a year after the initial publication of Allen's *Narrative*, Americans were confronted by a new horror: the prison ship *Jersey*, easily the biggest and deadliest of her kind in the Revolutionary War. She claimed so many lives during her brief time in service that for generations she would serve as the single most widely recognized symbol of British cruelty—worse than the Provost, more shocking than the Sugar House. Because of her, too, David Sproat would go down in popular lore with Provost Marshal William Cunningham as one of the biggest scoundrels of the war.

Launched in 1736, the *Jersey* had seen decades of service in the Mediterranean as a fourth-rate frigate of sixty-four guns before the navy converted her to a hospital ship around 1771. (In the Royal Navy, a fourth-rate, or large frigate, was a three-masted ship mounting fifty to seventy cannon on two decks below the main deck and carrying a crew of around 400.) She came to New York with the rest of the fleet in the summer of 1776 or shortly thereafter and as one of the largest vessels in port—41 feet at the beam, 144 feet stem to stern—her great black hull would have been a familiar sight to the residents of the city.[4]

After the *Good Hope* burned in the spring of 1780, Commissary Sproat had at his disposal only two small prison ships, *Strombolo* and

Scorpion. Both were usually at anchor in the Hudson, off the city's west side, with the hospital ship *Hunter* close by. Several other hospital ships—*Falmouth*, *Hope*, and *Jersey*—typically lay at various locations off the East River waterfront. In April or early May all five were moved to Wallabout Bay, where the *Jersey* was presumably hulked and refitted to begin receiving prisoners. *Strombolo*, *Scorpion*, and *Hunter* were in such poor condition, however, that when Admiral Rodney arrived in the fall, he had them decommissioned and ordered all naval prisoners removed to the *Jersey*.[5]

Hulking the *Jersey* for use as a prison ship began with the removal of her masts, canvas, lines, ordnance, figurehead, and rudder. Her gunports were then sealed and replaced by two rows of small square air-ports, barred with iron lattices, for the benefit of the prisoners confined on her lower decks. Aft, on the quarterdeck, a large awning or tent sheltered thirty-odd marines who watched through loopholes in a ten-foot-high barricade when the prisoners came up on deck in the mornings to exercise. ("Exercise" mostly involved walking back and forth along the gangways that connected the quarterdeck and forecastle.) On that part of the gun deck directly below the quarterdeck were the officers' cabin and various storerooms. Between the quarterdeck and forecastle lay an area of the gun deck known as the spar deck. It too was accessible to prisoners during the day, though a good bit of it was appropriated for the pens where officers kept pigs for their own consumption.

The forward part of the gun deck was reserved for the galley. Below the gun deck lay the middle deck, a cavernous, vile-smelling, vermin-infested space where the prisoners passed time, ate, and slept shoulder to shoulder. Still more prisoners dwelled like troglodytes on the dank lower deck, at or near the water line. The only way to reach topside from the holds was up a narrow ladder and through a heavy grated hatchway, which was always shut tight at sundown. "Down, rebels, down!" cried the guards after the evening gun.[6]

In Wallabout Bay, massive chain cables fore and aft anchored the *Jersey* securely in the shallow channel that looped between the mud flats. She lay about one hundred yards offshore, opposite the mouth of Remsen's mill race and sheltered from the weather by the grassy sandbanks

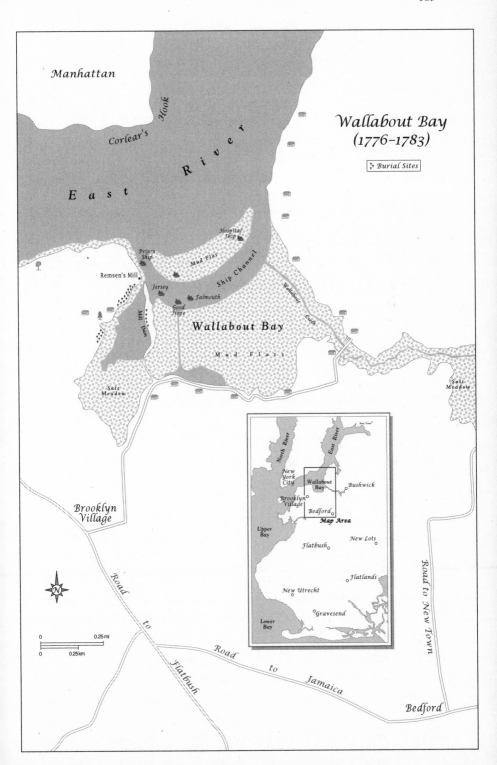

Manhattan

Corlear's Hook

East River

Wallabout Bay
(1776–1783)

Burial Sites

Hospital Ship

Prison Ship

Mud Flat

Ship Channel

Remsen's Mill

Jersey

Falmouth

Good Hope

Wallabout Creek

Mill Dam

Wallabout Bay

Mud Flats

Salt Meadow

Salt Meadow

Brooklyn Village

North River

East River

New Town

New York City

Wallabout Bay

Bushwick

Brooklyn Village

Bedford

Map Area

Upper Bay

Flatbush

New Lots

Flatlands

New Utrecht

Gravesend

Lower Bay

N

Road to

Flatbush

Road to Jamaica

Road to New Town

Bedford

0   0.25 mi
0   0.25 km

The *Jersey* as depicted for Mary Booth's *History of the City of New York* (1859).

that edged the bay to the south and east. The rising and falling tides kept the water in the channel moving, but never swiftly enough to clear away the greasy, putrescent slick that encircled her after the necessary tubs were brought up from below and emptied over the side, a daily ritual. A flock of smaller vessels usually hovered nearby, among them (though not always at the same time) the *John* and *Bristol Pacquet*, a pair of transports that sometimes also took prisoners, plus four hospital ships (*Hope, Frederick, Perseverance,* and *Falconer*).[7]

Exactly when the *Jersey* began to receive American prisoners is unclear. It may have been when she was still in service as a hospital ship—a report reached Philadelphia as early as June 1779 that 512 captives were languishing in her holds—but once she became a prison hulk, the numbers soared and conditions rapidly deteriorated. Among her first prisoners was John van Dyke, a furloughed artilleryman who had had the misfortune to be traveling on a brig that was taken by the enemy frigate *Iris*. (The fifth such experience for the brig's master, Captain Thomas Pitt, "who sat at the time on the after locker with his arms folded, and the tears running down his cheeks for sorrow," Van Dyke wrote afterward.) He and the others were taken to New York and consigned to the *Jersey* toward the end of May 1780. "When I came on board," Van Dyke recalled, "her stench was so great . . . I thought it would soon kill me." The rations he received were "so short a person would think it was not possible for a man to live on." Once, Van Dyke came back from the galley with a piece of salt pork so small that he and his five messmates had only one mouthful each and nothing else for the entire day; another time, they had only some "soup" that consisted of "brown water, and fifteen floating peas" to hold them for twenty-four hours. Each week, his mess received three pounds of flour containing mysterious green lumps along with a pound of "very bad raisins." Mashed together and boiled in a bag, it made a kind of pudding. That day became "Pudding day."[8]

Because they fell sick, or because the *Jersey* was in the process of being hulked and moved to Wallabout Bay, Van Dyke and eighty other Americans were soon transferred to the hospital sloop, *Hunter*. It was no improvement. "We drew one third allowance," he remembered, "and every Monday we received a loaf of wet bread, weighing seven pounds for each mess." After several weeks of this, Van Dyke was exchanged. He returned home to New Jersey, his health permanently shattered and images of fellow-prisoners left behind burned into his memory: "pale faces, long beards, white pale eyes, and ghastly countenances . . . this dismal sight I cannot erase from my mind as long as God permits me to retain my senses."[9]

Although Captain van Dyke's memoir would not be published until long after his death, American newspapers soon gave their readers plenty of comparable stories about the *Jersey* to worry about. Most frequently reprinted was a deposition taken from George Batterman, a prisoner on the *Jersey*, who said that when he was sent aboard in the autumn of 1780, the *Jersey* held an astonishing 1,100 prisoners—almost three times her normal component of seamen. To soften them up for Royal Navy recruiters, their rations were reduced to a pint of water and eight ounces of "condemned bread" per day, plus eight ounces of meat *per week*. American officers who urged the men to resist were thrown into the Provost, Batterman added, and just in case anyone thought of torching the *Jersey*, as had been done to the *Good Hope*, "the commanding officer on board told us, that his order[s] were, that if the ship took fire, we should all be turned below, and perish in the flames."[10]

One of Batterman's fellow prisoners that fall was Silas Talbot, a privateer captain out of Providence already well known for wreaking havoc with enemy shipping. Twenty-three years later, Talbot described a world below decks from which it is a miracle anyone emerged sane, let alone alive:

> There were no berths or seats, to lie down on, not a bench to sit on. Many were almost without cloaths. The dysentery, fever, phrenzy and despair prevailed among them, and filled the place with filth, disgust and horror. The scantiness of the allowance, the bad quality of the provisions, the brutality of the guards, and the sick, pining for comforts they could not obtain, altogether furnished continually one of the greatest scenes of human distress and misery ever beheld. It was now the middle of October, the weather was cool and clear, with frosty nights, so that the number of deaths per day was *reduced to an average of ten*, and this number was considered by the survivors a small one, when compared with the terrible mortality that had prevailed for three months before.

Contemporary accounts confirm the accuracy of Talbot's memory that prisoners on the *Jersey* were treated with unparalleled "severity and inhumanity," that they received only a few ounces of bad meat per week, that they fought "like wild beasts to get near the small air ports, that they might breathe," that "7 or 8 died every 24 hours," that hundreds had already enlisted with the Royal Navy to save themselves.[11]

Perhaps the best measure of the impact of the Wallabout prison ships on American opinion was the acclaim showered on Philip Freneau's epic poem "The British Prison Ship." First printed in 1781 by Ethan Allen's publisher, Robert Bell, it tells the story of an American taken at sea and confined in two of the New York prison ships. Its debt to Allen's revision of the traditional captivity narrative is unmistakable, both in its celebration of unwavering allegiance to the cause as well as in the hatred it evokes for a merciless enemy. Whether the poem was the product of the poet's own experience is another matter.

Philip Morin Freneau had come late to the war. When he graduated from the college at Princeton, New Jersey, in 1771, he was a scruffy, melancholic youth of poetical inclinations but no clear idea of what to do with himself. Over the next several years, he drifted dreamily from one line of work to another—teaching school in Flatbush (where he lasted all of thirteen days), studying for the ministry, failing again as a schoolmaster in Annapolis, toying vaguely with the idea of a career in law or medicine—all the while jotting down innocuous poems imitating, by turns, Milton, Dryden, Pope, and Goldsmith.[12]

The spring of 1775 found Freneau in New York, probably looking for work, when word arrived that a shooting war with the king's troops had broken out in Massachusetts. Though not awfully keen on politics, Freneau responded to the excitement with a flurry of patriotic verses that appeared in local papers over the next six months. "To the Americans," one of his more effective efforts, summoned his countrymen to "arm for vengeance" and scoffed at Gage's attempt to brand them as "rebels" destined for the cord. "This bug-bear name," he wrote, "like death, *has lost its sting.*"

But the poet himself was not ready to arm for vengeance. Wounded by Tory sniping at his work and frustrated by his inability to earn a living, Freneau quit New York at the end of 1775. The following spring he turned up in the Caribbean, where he spent better than two years shuttling around the islands as the agent for a mercantile firm in New York or Philadelphia. He kept writing, though the results were lifeless—a rhapsody on the primordial beauty of St. Croix, a fluffy elegy for a daughter of the governor of Bermuda, a gloomy adolescent meditation on the futility of ambition and work.[13]

Freneau's return to America in the middle of 1778 was a rude awakening. He arrived home in Monmouth County not two weeks after the Battle of Monmouth Court House, staggered by the ravaged

Philip Freneau.

countryside and eyewitness accounts of British predation. The war
had caught up with him at last, and Freneau rose to the occasion by
enlisting with a New Jersey militia company assigned to shore patrol
between South Amboy and Long Branch. He also began work on a
poem, "America Independent," two lines of which Bell would use as
an epigram on the title page of Allen's *Narrative:*

When God from Chaos gave this World TO BE,
Man then he form'd, and form'd him TO BE FREE.

"America Independent" was *Common Sense* set to verse. Like Tom
Paine's famous pamphlet, Freneau's poem predicted the eventual triumph of American arms. It too sang the praises of republican government and excoriated George III as a bloody despot ("the Nero of our
times"). But *Common Sense* had appeared in January 1776, when the
war was just beginning. "America Independent" came out after the
occupation of New York, after the invasion of New Jersey, after
Saratoga—after, that is, two and a half years of turmoil, destruction,
killing, bitter defeats, and miraculous victories. Where Paine had

been incredulous that anyone could fail to grasp the inevitability of independence, Freneau was appalled that the British, "led on by lust of lucre and renown," were exacting such a high price for it. What became of the many friends and neighbors consigned to the "sickly ships" and "dreary dungeons" of New York was unbearable.[14]

The next year or two brought more fiery war poems from Freneau's pen, including "On the Death of Captain Nicholas Biddle," "George the Third's Soliloquy," "A Dialogue Between George and Fox," and "The Loyalists," in which he described for a second time how the murder of American prisoners in New York had helped awaken his muse to its proper duty. Still writing, he went to sea again as the master or supercargo of vessels trading with the West Indies, the Azores, and the Canary Islands. Along the way, according to his 1832 pension application, he saw action in several "sea fights" and took "a brittish bullet in his knee."[15]

In the autumn of 1780 Freneau returned to the theme of the prisoners in New York with "The British Prison Ship." Issued by Bell the next summer as a pamphlet, it was far and away Freneau's most successful war poem. Like Allen's *Narrative*, which he had obviously read with care, "The British Prison Ship" treats the subject of captivity as an opportunity to plumb the depths of the enemy's depravity, not as a punishment for the captive's cowardice or moral turpitude. Running through the poem's four cantos (later reduced to three) is an emotional arc that begins with heady optimism, descends into the stygian caves of captivity, then rises again to a vision of ultimate victory. This progression of feeling conveys not only how Freneau understood his own life thus far but the brief life of his country as well.

In Canto I, "The Capture," the narrator sets out from Philadelphia aboard the barque *Aurora*, bound for St. Eustacia and other soft Caribbean islands, "where endless summer reigns." As the *Aurora* clears Cape Henlopen at the mouth of Delaware Bay, leaving the sight of land and plowing into the open ocean, a British frigate materializes ominously on the horizon. This proves to be Captain Dawson's vengeful *Iris*—the same frigate that captured Van Dyke—which "rush'd tremendous o'er the watery world" toward the *Aurora*, "like a starv'd lion, hungry for his prey."[16]

The captain and crew of the *Aurora* try desperately to escape, tacking about and running for land. It is, the narrator says, a pursuit straight out of the *Iliad*: "So fierce Pelides, eager to destroy / Chase'd the proud trojan round the walls of Troy." Now *Iris* closes in for the kill, her cannon belching "destruction, terror, death, and fire." The Americans return fire "to shew them we were men," but their bravery is no match for the enemy's big guns. As his ship is hammered to splinters around him, her "deck bestain'd with heart-blood streaming round," the captain of the *Aurora* surrenders. He and his brave crew, though guiltless, are now prisoners:

> *Convey'd to York the Britons lodg'd us there,*
> *Safe in their dens of hunger and dispair,*
> *Their ships are prisons, void of masts or sails,*
> *In which describing, e'en description fails.*

The second canto proceeds to explain that the narrator will nonetheless attempt to depict the "various horrors" he encountered on the hulks. Like Ethan Allen, he has no doubt the enemy's cruelty is premeditated:

> *This be my talk—ungenerous Britons you,*
> *Conspire to murder those you can't subdue;*

The question is whether, "weak as I am," the narrator has enough strength left to reveal "the dreadful secrets of these prison caves":

> *So much I suffer'd, from the race I hate,*
> *So near they shov'd me to the brink of fate;*
> *When seven long weeks in these d___'d hulks I lay.*

He resolves nonetheless to make the attempt to describe what he saw on the prison ship, because he is tormented by the memory of all those nameless young men who died for their country. At night he hears their "plaintive ghosts" pleading for vengeance.

At the beginning of the third canto, the narrator introduces four prison ships anchored off Manhattan: *Scorpion, Strombolo, Jersey,* and the hospital ship *Hunter*—"piles for slaughter, floating on the floods." He winds up on the *Scorpion,* "a dire abode" crowded with several hundred captives. The guards taunt and beat them for sport, make them drink putrid water, and keep them barely alive on "rotten pork, the lumpy damag'd flour, / Soaked in salt water, and with age grown sour." Not surprisingly, the narrator succumbs to ship-fever (typhus) and is transferred to the *Hunter.* As soon as he arrives at "this detested place," the focus of the fourth and last canto, a "wasted *phantom*" accosts him like the ghost of Hamlet's father and demands to know his purpose:

> *Why didst thou leave the scorpion's dark retreat,*
> *And hither come, a surer death to meet;*
> *Why didst thou leave thy damp infected cell,*
> *If that was purgatory, this was hell.*

Each day, the narrator discovers, at least three corpses will be removed from the ship and given a perfunctory burial on shore:

> *By feeble hands the shallow tombs were made,*
> *No stone memorial o'er the corpses laid,*
> *In barren sands and far from home they ly;*
> *No friend to shed a tear when passing by:*
> *O'er the slight graves insulting Britons tread,*
> *Spurn at the sand and curse the rebel dead.*

Sooner or later, however, these murdering vermin will be driven back to their "fatal *Islands.*" When that day comes, Americans must somehow commemorate the thousands who perished "in ships, in prisons, and in dungeons dire"—not as victims but as victors:

> *These all in freedom's sacred cause ally'd,*
> *For freedom ventur'd and for freedom dy'd;*

To base subjection they were never broke,
They could not bend beneath a tyrant's yoke;
Had these surviv'd, perhaps in thralldom held,
To serve proud Britain they had been compell'd;
Ungenerous deed—can she the charge deny?—
In such a case to triumph was to die.

"The British Prison Ship" is driven by an anger so intense and personal that Freneau is routinely assumed to have been a prisoner himself on one or more of the ships. Yet he never actually said that he had
been a prisoner—until, that is, he applied for his pension fifty years
after the fact. Then, apparently for the first time, he testified that he
was aboard the *Aurora* when she sailed from Philadelphia. He also
testified that after the *Iris* brought the *Aurora* back to New York, he
was "put aboard the prison ships Strombolo & Hunter where he remained a prisoner & endured great sufferings till Sept 25, 1780, when
he was exchanged."

Alas, though the story helped win him a pension, Freneau seems to
have remembered something that probably never happened. The *Aurora* was real enough: contemporary New York newspapers confirm
her surrender to the *Iris* on May 26 or 27, 1780, as do the records
kept by the frigate's master and captain. There is nevertheless almost
no evidence corroborating Freneau's claim that he was aboard *Aurora*
on that fateful day, much less confined on a prison ship in New York.
His dramatic rendition of the *Aurora*'s fight with the *Iris* was almost
certainly lifted from a prose narrative of that event composed by
someone else, and his description of conditions on the *Scorpion* and
the *Hunter* closely resemble the lurid stories that were by 1780 or
1781 a familiar feature of American newspapers. Equally telling are
Freneau's numerous revisions of the poem, which convey a peculiar
uncertainty about a host of fundamental details, including when the
Aurora left Philadelphia, the location of the prison ships in New York,
and the duration of his putative captivity.[17]

So, did the old poet tell a fib to get himself a pension? Maybe he
did. Or maybe, playing the story over and over in his head, decade
after decade, he had long ago forgotten that he and the narrator of his

greatest poem were in fact two different people. One way or the other, his lasting identification with the story is a measure of how completely, by 1780 or 1781, the prison ships of New York had captured the public imagination—and would do so for decades to come.

Ever since the shooting began at Lexington and Concord in April 1775, no one on the British side had bothered to contest the charge that American prisoners were mistreated, even deliberately murdered, in the prisons and prison ships of New York. Other than allowing Boudinot to visit the city in 1778 and throwing out a few contemptuous denials—General Robertson's bluster about "damned lies" comes immediately to mind—the official response had always been no response. The king and Germain ignored the subject. Parliament never talked about it. Wedded to the idea that force alone would bring the Americans to heel, no one on the British side had yet seen the need to fight for their hearts and minds as well.

That changed in early January 1781, when the outcry over conditions in Wallabout Bay, stoked by Allen's new book as well as by Freneau's new poem, prompted Congress to ask General Washington to investigate. Washington wrote at once to Admiral Arbuthnot, including a copy of the Batterman deposition as evidence of the "truly calamitous and deplorable" treatment of Americans held on the *Jersey*. He also asked Arbuthnot to allow an American officer to inspect the *Jersey*, much as Boudinot had done several years earlier for the prisons in New York City. What that request triggered, however, was a war of words in which British officials made their first concerted attempt to defend themselves publicly against the charge that they abused American prisoners.[18]

Arbuthnot was just then at sea, so the task of replying to Washington fell to Captain George Dawson of the *Iris*. Perhaps still smarting from Freneau's depiction of what happened to the Americans captured after his fight with the *Aurora*, Dawson convened a court of inquiry consisting of himself and three other officers. They visited the *Jersey* on February 2, interrogated the prisoners, and found them—to a man!—perfectly satisfied that "their situation was made at all times as comfortable as possible, and that they were in no instance oppressed or ill treated." Their weekly rations were no different, in quality or quantity, from those provided to the ship's skeleton crew or the guards. They "have never been and are not now crouded," the officers observed, adding that two or three of each rank have been allowed to go on shore to New York every day to purchase whatever additional supplies they or their comrades might wish. As for "the sickness at present among the prisoners," it "arises from a want of Cloathing and a proper attention in themselves to their own cleanliness." Six of the principal American officers on board attested to the report's accuracy. Captain Dawson forwarded a copy to Washington at the beginning of February. He noted, however, that he would absolutely not allow an American officer to visit the *Jersey*.[19]

Over the next couple of weeks, the city's two Tory newspapers, James Rivington's *Royal Gazette* and Hugh Gaines's *New-York Gazette*, printed a bundle of additional materials backing up Dawson's court of inquiry. Mayor David Mathews produced affidavits from a half dozen navy bureaucrats and the captain of the *Strombolo*, all swearing that American prisoners were well fed and comfortable. David Sproat wrote an open letter to Commissary Abraham Skinner, attacking the allegations in Batterman's deposition as lies concocted to inflame public opinion as well as to justify the mistreatment of prisoners held by the rebels. Were captured Americans dying on the *Jersey?* "That very many of them are sick, and die, is true," Sproat conceded, "but I will not allow that their disorders proceed from any other cause than dirt, nastiness, and want of clothing." Batterman's description of their rations was untrue, Sproat asserted: prisoners always received the "full quantity of good, sound, wholesome provisions" to which they were entitled; spoiled food was invariably replaced. Nor was the *Jersey* overcrowded. She had ample room for the men to move around as well as special quarters for officers. "I sincerely sympathize with the poor prisoners on both sides in distress," Sproat finished, but, he said, he had always done everything in his power to make them as comfortable as possible and to address any grievances brought to his attention.[20]

Among the British in New York, the reaction to this counterattack by Dawson, Mathews, and Sproat played well, perhaps especially among officers impatient with the slow pace of the war. Major Baurmeister, for one, applauded Dawson for exposing American talk of prisoner abuse as nothing more than a ploy "to stir up the rebellion so much more." Although little or none of this appeared in American papers—unsurprisingly—it motivated Congress to continue accumulating testimony from current and former prisoners about the "severe treatment" they met with aboard the *Jersey*. In mid-June 1781 Congress adopted a resolution referring darkly to the prisoners in New York as victims of "unrestrained barbarity and malice" and musing about "a new species of violence . . . exercised by the King of Great Britain, as unauthorized by the laws of nations, as it is derogatory to the honor and undoubted independence of these United States." A committee chaired by Elias Boudinot looked further into the matter. Its report, submitted at the end of the summer, found no justification for the outrageous mistreatment of captured Americans, "it being contrary to the usage and custom of civilized nations, thus deliberately to murder their captives in cold blood."[21]

The ensuing months yielded further evidence, from too many different sources to be the result of an organized attempt to deceive, that the *Jersey* and other prison ships were every bit as bad as the Americans said. Toward the end of August, the *Boston Gazette* excerpted portions of a letter from an unidentified prisoner still confined "on board the Jersey (popularly called HELL) PRISON SHIP." Death or enlistment with the enemy are the only two choices we have, he said. Many of his friends had chosen to enlist. Of those who remain, "we bury 6, 7, 8, 9, 10, and 11" every day, and every day 200 more take sick with "yellow fever, small pox, and in short every thing else that can be mentioned." One other thing: "I had almost forgot to tell you that our morning's salutation is, *'Rebels! turn out your dead!'*"

In another report, Major Andrew Brown, who escaped from the *Jersey* around the first of September, put the number of prisoners still aboard her at 700. "The officers and men," Brown wrote, "are indiscriminately drove under the hatches at sun-setting, and there kept in that suffocating condition 'till after sun-rising, when they are let up to wash the decks." November brought news that "the fever and small-pox raged to such a degree" aboard the *Jersey* that "great numbers" had already perished.[22]

Christopher Vail's unpublished narrative, composed years later but based on a journal he kept during the war, corroborates the published accounts of overcrowding, hunger, sickness, and hellish filth on the *Jersey*. Vail, a young sailor from Southold, Long Island, spent only two weeks on the *Jersey* in September 1781, but was haunted for the rest of his life by what he had seen. "There was only one passage to go on deck in the night," he recalled, and the guards would only allow two men up at a time. "Many of the Prisoners were troubled with the disentary and would come to the steps and could not be permitted to go on deck, and was obliged to ease themselves on the spot, and the next morning for 12 feet around the hatches was nothing but excrement." As bad as the nauseating stench was the noise: "There was all kinds of business carried on," Vail wrote, "some playing cards, others swearing, stealing, fighting some dying &c." *Many* dying, in fact: death visited the lower decks so often that the men handled corpses as casually as they would sacks of grain or animal carcasses:

> When a man died, he was carried up to the forecastle and laid there until the next morning at 8 o'clock when they were all lowered down the ships sides by a rope round them in the same manner as tho' they were beasts. There was 8 died of a day while I was there. They were carried on shore in heaps and hove out the boat on the wharf then taken across a hand barrow, carried to the edge of the bank where a hole was dug 1 or 2 feet deep and all hove in together.[23]

A strikingly similar picture of conditions aboard the *Jersey* was later drawn by Vail's fellow prisoner Christopher Hawkins. In his autobiography, Hawkins wrote of the rampant dysentery that left him and others covered with "bloody and loathsome filth" by morning, of fisticuffs between demoralized prisoners, of savage whippings, of one man so hungry he ate the lice from his shirt. A third captive,

The *Jersey* as depicted for the *Revolutionary Adventures of Ebenezer Fox* (1838). Because there are no contemporary images of the *Jersey*, nineteenth-century artists and illustrators were often called upon to re-create her dark, menacing appearance.

Ebenezer Fox, a seventeen-year-old seaman, aptly described the *Jersey* in the late summer of 1781 as a "floating Pandemonium."[24]

Then came miraculous news. In the early summer of 1781, disregarding instructions from Clinton to hold the Carolinas, Cornwallis had recklessly taken the British Army north, into Virginia. September found him holed up in Yorktown, on a narrow peninsula between the York and James rivers. Washington and the Comte de Rochambeau, commander of the French expeditionary forces now in America, quickly brought their armies down from New York and laid siege to Yorktown while a French fleet blocked access to Chesapeake Bay. On October 17, 1781, Cornwallis surrendered his entire army, better than 8,000 men. A British band is said to have played a spirited tune, "The World Turn'd Upside Down," for so it was.

In London, the king and his hawkish American secretary, Lord George Germain, vowed to continue the fight—perhaps, Germain suggested, by turning Manhattan into an impregnable, Gibraltar-like fortress that could hold out indefinitely against the rebels. But support for the war was now crumbling fast. Early the following February,

Germain resigned in disgrace, and Parliament, by a comfortable majority, voted to end offensive operations in America. Then it was Lord North's turn to step down, while the king himself began to make noises about abdicating. In March, a new government, headed by the Marquis of Rockingham, announced its intention to begin peace talks and sent Sir Guy Carleton to New York to replace Clinton, now blamed by everyone for the Yorktown debacle.

On March 25, 1782—almost exactly seven years after fighting erupted in New England—Parliament adopted as one of the preliminaries to those talks a measure repealing North's Act of 1777 and recognizing captured Americans as legitimate prisoners of war, no longer rebels destined for the cord. "This seems to be giving up their Pretensions of considering us as rebellious Subjects," Franklin mused in a letter to John Jay, "and is a kind of Acknowledgment of our Independence." Two months later, the Rockingham government unilaterally released over 800 Americans from Forton and Mill prisons and put them on transports bound for America. In July the king recognized the independence of the United States.[25]

As this incredible news dribbled into New York, residents of the city were by turns thunderstruck, indignant, and justifiably apprehensive about what now lay in store for them. Thousands resigned themselves to the prospect of permanent exile and put their houses and furniture on the market at fire-sale prices. Some allegedly collected money to buy clothing and blankets for Americans held in the Sugar House, hoping, in the words of a New Jersey man released over the winter of 1781–1782, "to make atonement for their political offences by acts of kindness & liberality to the poor prisoners."[26]

Yorktown brought no relief to the prison ships, however. When 130 men paroled by Sproat arrived in New London in January 1782, a local newspaper observed, "It is enough to melt the most obdurate heart of any one (except a Briton) to see these miserable objects continually landing here . . . sick and dying, and the few rags they have on covered with vermin and their own excrements." Skinner had already warned Washington that the prisoners on the *Jersey* are "really miserable . . . as many of them are almost naked and have not a blanket to lay on." In February, after large numbers perished in another bout of brutally cold weather, Skinner went to New York to talk with Sproat about what could be done. It did no good, and the *Jersey* in particular remained a floating deathtrap. One of her prisoners got out a letter at the end of April with word that "we are in number upwards of 700, exclusive of the sick in hospitals, who die like rotten sheep." Around the same time, a report out of New London said that about 1,000 prisoners still remained in New York, that they were "in the most deplorable condition," that about 500 had died during the last five or six months alone, and that about 300 were sick. Another report at the end of May spoke of "about 1100" Americans still aboard the prison and hospital ships in Wallabout Bay, observing that "from 6 to 7 were generally buried every Day."[27]

The war *ad terrorem* raged on fiercely as well, reaching a climax of sorts in the sensational murder of a New Jersey militia captain named Joshua Huddy. Captain Huddy had made a career of terrorizing Tories in Monmouth County—he liked to boast of having hanged several personally—and William Franklin's Board of Associated Loyalists in New York was eager to even the score before the war ended. Late in March 1782, an expedition of Associators (as they were now called) ran Huddy to ground near Toms River. After a fierce fight, they brought him and eleven others back to New York, lodging them first in the Sugar House and then in the Provost. Several weeks later, in mid-April, a Captain Richard Lippincott, allegedly acting on Governor Franklin's orders, removed Huddy from the Provost, took him back to New Jersey, and lynched him in retaliation for the death of a prominent Associator, Philip White. Lippincott and his men left the body swinging from a makeshift gallows as a warning to the rebels.[28]

Word of what happened to Huddy spread quickly. Howls of indignation rose in the American press, in the army, and in Congress. Not once since the war began had a prisoner in British custody ever been summarily executed. Men had been cut down trying to surrender, or killed while lying wounded on the battlefield. Thousands already had been left to rot in squalid prisons. But Huddy's death was an act of premeditated, officially sanctioned murder—exactly what Americans had always feared the British would do to their captives, and all the more disturbing because the end of the war now seemed so near. "AN OFFICER HAS BEEN TAKEN FROM HIS CONFINEMENT AND MURDERED," roared Tom Paine in the latest installment of his series, *The Crisis*. "To destroy the last security of captivity, and to take the unarmed, the unresisting prisoner to private and sportive execution, is carrying barbarity too high for silence."[29]

Washington was outraged. In a sulphurous protest against "the most wanton, unprecedented and inhuman Murder that ever disgraced the Arms of a civilized people," he demanded that Clinton surrender Lippincott. Clinton refused but promised to have Lippincott tried for murder by a British court-martial. The Associators, who did not want a trial at all, objected indignantly that the military had no jurisdiction because Lippincott was technically a civilian commissioned by the Board of Associated Loyalists.

When Sir Guy Carleton took over from Clinton as commander-in-chief at the beginning of May 1782, he resolved to proceed with the court-martial and warned the Associators against further marauding without his approval. As a gesture of goodwill, Carleton released a relatively recent addition to the Provost's collection of rebels: Lieutenant Colonel Henry Brockholst Livingston, son of the New Jersey governor as well as the personal secretary and brother-in-law of John Jay, just then beginning peace negotiations with the British in Paris.

Washington was unmoved. He still wanted Lippincott, and he raised the stakes by ordering the execution by hanging of an equivalent British prisoner if Carleton failed to produce the officer for trial. The choice fell upon twenty-year-old Captain Charles Asgill of the Grenadier Guards, who was sent to the American encampment near Morristown for his rendezvous with the gallows.[30]

Asgill's aristocratic pedigree and connections saved his life. When the British court-martial acquitted Lippincott in June, the fate of the young British officer became an international cause célèbre. His mother, Lady Sarah Asgill, sent a moving plea on his behalf to the king and queen of France, who in turn urged Washington through diplomatic channels not to proceed with the execution. Washington readily consented, good relations with the French being a priority at the moment—quite apart from the fact that he had never really wanted to execute an innocent officer and gentleman anyway. In November, after an acrimonious three-day debate, Congress voted to let Asgill return to England but concluded that the real culprit was the head of the Board of Associated Loyalists, William Franklin.[31]

There was virtually no likelihood that he would be turned over to the Americans and tried for Huddy's death, but Franklin decided to take no chances. He sold his furniture and in mid-August sailed for England. Carleton promptly disbanded the Associated Loyalists and pledged to stop further raids into American territory. "I cannot help hoping," Washington confided to General David Forman, "that the savage kind of desultory War which we have long experienced is at an end."[32]

Commissary Sproat was still in New York, however, and still trying to fend off accusations that the prisoners in his care had been mistreated. At the beginning of June 1782, he advised Commissary Skinner that conditions on the *Jersey* were getting steadily worse. "The very great increase of prisoners, and heat of the weather," he wrote, "now baffles all our care and attention to keep them healthy." Although he had put five additional vessels into Wallabout Bay to reduce overcrowding and had already paroled "a great number" of prisoners, the many who remained were in dire need of fresh clothing. Ultimately, he told Skinner, the only sure way to save them was via a general exchange, making no distinction between soldier and seaman. To put additional pressure on the Americans, Sproat allowed some of the *Jersey* prisoners to send Washington a petition pleading with him to accept a soldier-for-sailor trade.[33]

The British had offered such a trade before, most recently in April, when representatives from both sides met at Elizabeth Town, New Jersey, in yet another unsuccessful attempt to negotiate a cartel. At first glance it seemed like a reasonable idea. After Yorktown, the Americans held far more military than naval prisoners, and because most of the latter had been captured by privateers operating under licenses granted by the states, Congress had no authority to exchange them even if it wanted to. Thanks to the vast superiority of the Royal Navy, on the other hand, the British had a hefty (and growing) surplus of naval prisoners, few of whom belonged to the small Continental Navy. Clearly, exchanging them man for man, without regard to service, would save hundreds, even thousands, from needless suffering and death.[34]

Yet Sproat could not have expected Skinner to accept a deal on those terms. It was common knowledge by this time that Congress never authorized military negotiators to exchange naval prisoners—much less naval prisoners held by the states—in addition to which a soldier-for-sailor trade would obviously benefit the British, putting thousands of redcoats back into action before the war officially ended while the American army came away more or less empty-handed.

In reality, Sproat's proposal had less to do with saving lives than manipulating public opinion on both sides of the Atlantic. With Asgill's execution looming in the background, Washington's refusal to give up soldiers to liberate suffering seamen would make the rebel leaders look even more cynical and hardhearted than they already did, nor would that decision be likely to play well before the war-weary American population. Six or seven years after the fighting began, rampant inflation and chronic shortages had sapped morale, eroded confidence in Congress, and left the army seething with discontent over inadequate provisions and missing pay. Telling the *Jersey* prisoners to sit tight until such time as the United States had more of the enemy's naval prisoners to bargain with—how could that not put Sproat and his masters on the moral high ground?

Sproat moved quickly. He arranged with James Rivington to have his correspondence with Commissary Skinner published in the *Royal Gazette*, along with a public plea for help from the *Jersey* prisoners themselves:

> *Friends and fellow-countrymen of America*, you may bid a final adieu to all your friends and relations, who are now on board the Jersey prison-ship at New-York, unless you rouse the government to comply with just and honourable proposals, which has already

been done on the part of Britons, but alas! it is with pain we inform you, that our petition to his Excellency General Washington, offering our services to the country during the present campaign, if he would send soldiers in exchange for us, is frankly denied.

What is to be done? are we to lie here and share the fate of our unhappy brothers who are dying daily, *No*, unless you relieve us immediately, we shall be under necessity of leaving our country, in preservation of our own lives.[35]

Days later, twelve American ship captains and one doctor signed a statement that the naval prisoners in New York were well-fed, comfortable, and content: "any thing said to the contrary," they declared, "is false and without foundation." The statement commended Admiral Robert Digby, now commanding His Majesty's fleet in New York, for his "humane disposition and indulgence to the prisoners." Doctors cared for the sick "in wholesome clean ships . . . every man furnished with a cradle, bed, and sheets made of good Russia linen to lie in; the best of fresh provisions, vegetables, wine, rice, barly, &c." Commissary Sproat and his subordinates "conscientiously do their duty with great humanity and indulgence to the prisoners, and reputation to themselves."[36]

Sproat's attempt to control the prison ship story does not stand up to close scrutiny. Careful readers at the time surely noticed that the Americans' over-the-top testimonial (*good Russia linen!*) contradicted Sproat's initial letter to Skinner, which glumly warned that the summer heat and overcrowding had "baffled" his efforts to keep the prisoners healthy. And how, exactly, did the captains know what they said they knew? Admiral Digby, they explained, had just enlarged their paroles to let them go home, at which point six of their number—"being anxious, before our departure, to know the true state and situation of the prisoners confined on board the prison-ships and prison hospital-ships"—received permission to conduct their own inspection. In other words, none of the thirteen had even set foot on the ships until *after* Digby gave them permission to leave New York, and seven of them never did so at all—a suspicious provenance, to say the least. A few weeks later, in fact, several of the captains in question

reportedly admitted that they did not write, or even read, the statement. They signed it only because Sproat threatened to rescind their
paroles and lock them up on the *Jersey* if they refused. The six captains who did go aboard her stayed only a few moments and never
ventured below. An American seaman named John Cochran, present
during the visit, confirmed "that none of them went, or attempted to
go below decks to see the situation of the prisoners, nor did they ask
a single question respecting that matter." None of the sick, he added
pointedly, enjoyed "sheets of Russia or any other linen."[37]

As Sproat's public-relations ploy came apart, Carleton proposed
that the two sides trade sailors for sailors until the American supply
ran out, at which point the British would take soldiers in exchange for
sailors. Redcoats liberated in this fashion, he added, would not serve
in or against the United States for a year. Washington liked the idea,
but Congress came up with so many qualifications and conditions
that when a conference on the matter was finally held at Tappan, New
York, at the end of September, no progress could be made.[38]

Skinner had in the meantime issued a statement of his own,
chastising Sproat for his disgraceful mendacity. As always, though, the
most effective and enduring rebuttals came from the prisoners themselves, whose accounts of what they endured in the summer and fall
of 1782 make no mention of fresh vegetables or clean Russia linen.
The *Chance*, an American privateer out of Providence, was brought
into New York toward the end of May and her crew imprisoned;
within weeks, seventeen of her fifty-seven crewmen lay dead and
three others were dying in hospital. Of the twenty-five eventually sent
home, one died along the way and only three or four were able to
walk without assistance. Midshipman Alexander Coffin, consigned to
the *Jersey* in October, was explicit: "There never were provisions
served out to the prisoners that would have been eatable by men that
were not literally in a starving condition." As the winter came on, an
anonymous junior officer wrote of "deplorable" conditions and frequent death on the prison ship: "The Captains, Lieutenants and Sail-
ing-Masters are gone to the provost, but they have only got out of the
frying-pan into the fire. I am left here with about 700 miserable objects, eaten up with lice, and daily taking fevers, which carry them off

fast." It was later reported that twenty men from the *Jersey* were buried on Christmas Day alone. "This is the awfullest place I ever saw," said a Massachusetts seaman in an anguished letter to his wife. "Indeed it is one of the worst places in the world."[39]

During the negotiations that preceded the capitulation of Yorktown, Washington had assured Cornwallis that his men would receive "the Benevolent Treatment of Prisoners which is invariably observed by Americans." The British had heard this sort of thing often before. Since the war began, in fact, Americans had been congratulating themselves for handling enemy captives with "tenderness," with "every mark of respect," with "the most remarkable tenderness and generosity," with "moderation and humanity." The Rhode Island Council boasted that prisoners "have been fed on all occasions with wholesome and plentiful food, lodged comfortably, suffered to go at large, within extensive tracts of country, treated with liberal hospitality," and so on.

"Humanity to Prisoners of War," declared Elias Boudinot, "has ever been the peculiar Characteristic of the american Army." It was the flipside of British "cruelty"—another way to express the insurmountable differences between two outwardly similar peoples.[40]

But Washington and Boudinot, of all people, surely knew better. Neither could have forgotten the egregious mistreatment of Archibald Campbell in Massachusetts, but they had also fielded numerous other complaints over the years from enemy prisoners about bad food, squalor, and physical abuse. "I am close confined within the square of a Damp room, with double doors, iron grates & bars, even the window sashes naild down," a British officer wrote from the Philadelphia jail in 1776, "so that I have not a breath of free air, by which means I have often been near sufficated with smock, besides many other Disagreeable inconveniences arising from the needful necessaries that a person close shut up must have." Thomas Wileman, of the Seventeenth Dragoons, testified that when the Americans captured him, they pilfered his clothes, watch, money, and books, then locked him up for four days without food. He also reported hearing that rampaging rebel soldiers had attacked defenseless British prisoners with bayonets, killing eight and wounding eighteen. Lieutenant Michael Bach of the Hesse-Hanau Artillery, seized at Bennington in 1777, complained of being brutalized and "completely plundered" by American soldiers, then hustled off to a prison camp where he and his comrades were forced to eat "Negro food." The New Jersey militiamen who captured Lieutenant John Troup (Robert's Tory brother) beat him savagely, chained him in a hog pen, forced him to march long distances in his bare feet, and subjected him to a mock execution before he managed to escape. After his graphic account of the experience appeared in Rivington's *Royal Gazette*, Washington conceded—privately—that Troup had indeed been "marched backwards and forward till he was naked and almost eaten up with Filth and Vermin."[41]

Arguably the most conspicuous tale of neglect involved the 3,200 Hessians and redcoats taken at Saratoga in 1777—soon dubbed the "Convention Army" after the controversial "convention" signed by Gates and Burgoyne. After spending the next year in camps near Cambridge and Rutland, Massachusetts, they were sent by Congress on an overland odyssey that, by the end of the war, took them down to Virginia, then up to Maryland, into Pennsylvania again, and finally back to Rutland. Almost every step of the way they contended with meager rations, shortages of fuel, inadequate accommodations, and physical violence. For Baroness Frederika von Riedesel, the wife of General Friedrich von Riedesel, the 600-mile trek from Massachusetts to Virginia was a gauntlet of hostility from local residents, who refused her food and expressed the hope that she and her children would die of starvation. Ensign Thomas Anburey remembered the encampment outside Charlottesville when he arrived as "truly horrible."[42]

Certain state governments had particularly bad records of prisoner abuse. In New York, so many refractory Tories had been crammed into the basement of the Kingston courthouse that when the state convention began meeting upstairs in 1776, Gouverneur Morris proposed that the members be allowed to smoke to cover the appalling stench. The "prison" created at West Point for Lieutenant James Moody, a notorious Tory partisan captured in July 1780, was in reality a fetid hole roofed by ill-fitting planks that left plenty of room for the rain to get in.

> It had no floor but the natural rock; and the water, with the mud and filth collected, was commonly ankle-deep in every part of it. Mr. Moody's bed was an old door, supported by four stones, so as just to raise it above the surface of the water. Here he continued near four weeks; and, during most of the time . . . no food was allowed him but stinking beef, and rotten flour, made up into balls or dumplins, which were thrown into a kettle and boiled with the meat, and then brought to him in a wood bowl which was never washed, and which contracted a thick crust of dough, grease, and dirt.[43]

But then maybe Moody was lucky. Had he been captured in Connecticut, he might have found himself even further underground, in the clammy darkness of an abandoned copper mine near Simsbury (now East Granby). Dubbed Newgate after the infamous British prison, the mine's tunnels and caverns held dozens of notorious Tories at a time under conditions that can only be imagined. According to their Anglican chaplain, himself a fire-eating advocate of resistance to Congress, the inmates called the place Orcus, after the Roman god of the underworld.[44]

Connecticut, as it happens, was also one of four states—New York, Virginia, and Massachusetts being the others—that operated prison ships at various times during the war. New York had three, anchored together in the mouth of Rondout Creek, just above Esopus. Collectively nicknamed Fleet Prison, an allusion to the ghastly London jail reserved for debtors and bankrupts, the ships held as many as 175 "artful and designing persons" at a time. Cadwallader Colden, Jr., a leading Ulster County Tory, thought he would prefer the fleet to the stinking dungeon in Kingston. Once the rebels moved him there, however, the bad water, skimpy provisions, overcrowding, and larcenous guards quickly disabused him of that notion. One of Colden's shipmates pleaded with the legislature to let him out of his irons only long enough for him to clean himself.[45]

It is hardly surprising that in a long, increasingly chaotic civil war, both sides would treat their prisoners harshly, or that each would try to cover its tracks with denials and dissembling. No doubt, too, pre-modern fighting men were already well acquainted with dismal accommodations, bad food, primitive medical care, dysentery, and typhus; what they experienced as prisoners of war was worse, but not appreciably worse, than what they ordinarily endured in camp or aboard ship. Think of Valley Forge in the awful winter of 1777–1778 or of Admiral Arbuthnot's fleet crossing the Atlantic to New York in the summer of 1779, a voyage that reputedly took the lives of 700 men and required the hospitalization of 1,200 others on arrival.[46]

Despite these instances of outrageous cruelty, there are grounds for believing that British and Hessian captives really did fare better on the whole than their American counterparts. Partly this was a simple matter of circumstance. Because they were not confined for long periods in a few central locations but scattered all over the map, in literally scores of camps and small communities, prisoners held by the Americans mostly escaped the devastating contagions that killed as many as seven of every ten captured rebels in New York. Death traps like the Bridewell, the Sugar House, or the *Jersey*, overflowing with hundreds of sick and starving men, had no equivalent in the experience of enemy prisoners. What is more, congressional and state commissaries routinely arranged for enemy captives to earn money for food and clothing by hiring themselves out to local farmers. Hessians in particular were encouraged to give up soldiering, buy land, and settle down; thousands evidently did so. Additional thousands of all ranks and nationalities took advantage of lax or even nonexistent supervision to get away and return to New York, where they rejoined their old units. One such escapee noted in his diary that the prison camp in Albemarle, Virginia, was so casually guarded that the prisoners could come and go as they pleased.[47]

It is unnecessary, in other words, to accept rebel professions of moral superiority to conclude that enemy prisoners got on comparatively well. Indeed, if the jury-rigged system with which Congress and the states managed enemy captives had worked better, the picture might have been a good deal uglier. In this context, it is sobering to come across Samuel Blachley Webb's outburst when he learned that prisoners were escaping one of the Connecticut prison ships at will. "Your Dam'd Prison ships ought to be better guarded," he exclaimed in a letter to his brother-in-law. "Let them die as ours do in New York, from three to Eight a day,—if no other way follow the example of our Enemy shut them close under deck at sunset and starve them on two oz. of pork by day. Cruelty is oftentimes productive of the best consequences and terminates in humanity." Luckily, men like Webb did not yet possess the means to take out their rage and frustration on helpless prisoners. Confusion, inexperience, and inefficiency have nothing to do with humanitarianism, though they can produce similar results.[48]

Also worth keeping in mind is that there were tangible differences in how the two sides believed they *should* handle captives. Although no responsible person in the British government or its armed forces ever seriously proposed killing rebel prisoners en masse, the chest-thumping threats and saber-waving that preceded the war created a climate in which, as we have seen, it became impossible to think of them as anything other than disposable nuisances. Washington, by contrast, devoted himself to the strict observance of established military standards and protocols. The abuse of prisoners such as Archibald Campbell worried him profoundly, if for no other reason than that it would make the Americans look like an undisciplined rabble to other men of honor. Even Governor William Livingston of New Jersey, famously tough on Tories and never one to shrink from the idea of retaliation, believed that failing to take proper care of prisoners was counterproductive, morally inexcusable, and inconsistent "with the honour of the American nation whose glory it has hitherto been to triumph over its Enemy not only by force of arms but by the virtues of humanity." That deep-seated humanitarianism fit nicely with the charitable instincts of the American commissaries—John Beatty and Abraham Skinner, as well as Elias Boudinot—whose instructions to subordinates in charge of the camps set up for enemy prisoners demonstrate over and over again their determination to get them adequate food, clothing, and medical care. One searches in vain for their equal in the sorry parade of arrogant British commanders and corrupt bureaucrats.[49]

Nor was there anything on the British side comparable to the trial of Colonel David Henley, the American officer in charge of the Convention Army prisoners at Cambridge. Early in January 1778, against a background of nasty altercations between the detainees and American guards, General Burgoyne accused Henley of "behavior heinously criminal as an officer, and unbecoming a man; of the most indecent, violent, vindictive severity against unarmed men; and of intentional murder." Not only did General William Heath, commander of the Eastern Department, convene a court-martial to try Henley, but the court's presiding officer allowed Burgoyne to present evidence and cross-examine witnesses as if he were a prosecutor. That was astonishingly irregular—prosecution in a military court is the judge advocate's responsibility, certainly not that of an enemy officer—and Burgoyne took full advantage of the opportunity to harangue the tribunal for days about Henley's atrocious brutality.

But what, exactly, had Henley done? Prosecution witnesses testified that while attempting to disperse a hostile crowd of prisoners the American officer "pricked" a drunken British corporal with a bayonet. On another occasion he "made a lunge" with his sword at a British soldier who refused to return to his barracks when ordered. No one died, little or no blood was spilled, and no evidence was presented that Henley or his men intended or attempted to massacre prisoners. Unsurprisingly, the court exonerated him of any wrongdoing. Perhaps the whole thing was a bit silly, but then no British officer was *ever* charged with mistreating American prisoners, though the evidence against Provost Marshal Cunningham, for one, certainly warranted a court-martial.[50]

As for its frequent threats to retaliate against enemy prisoners for the outrages taking place in New York and elsewhere, Congress was always uneasy about stooping to such tactics. The stories of Colonels Campbell and Charles Asgill are instructive cases in point, but there are others. After 1778, Congress did occasionally order the commissaries to cut rations for enemy prisoners and lock up some officers. But it also let the commissaries decide when to relent, which they usually did rather quickly. In 1779, Congress instructed its Marine Committee to confine captured enemy seamen in prison ships, supplying and treating them "in all respects in the same manner as the crews of vessels belonging to these United States and captured by the enemy, are supplied and treated," then reversed course a few months later and told the committee it did not have to do that after all. Two years later Congress instructed Washington to "give immediate orders to the commanding officers at the different posts to take particular care that the British prisoners receive the same allowance and treatment, in every respect, as our people, who are prisoners, receive from the enemy"—but pointedly struck down a motion approving the use of prison ships. Neither the king nor Parliament ever troubled themselves with such matters.[51]

8

〜

DEAD
Reckonings

AND THEN IT WAS OVER. In November 1782, nearly eight
wearying years after the first shots were fired at Lexington and
Concord, representatives of the United States and Great Britain
signed a preliminary peace treaty and agreed to the prompt repatria-
tion of all captives. In fact, that process was already well under way.
Cartel ships with over 800 Americans liberated from English prisons
had reached Boston and Philadelphia during August, and as early as
December 1781, a large contingent of men freed from Canadian prisons had made it down to Springfield, Massachusetts—walking home.

In New York, General Carleton was discharging captured rebels by
the hundreds. As of February 1783, only forty-one remained on the *Jersey*, none of whom had been there more than six months. The two remaining Americans in the Provost, Abraham Hammond and George
Briggs, both civilians accused of "treasonable practices," went home before the end of March. By the time official notification of the peace
reached the city on April 6, 1783, so few prisoners were left to celebrate
their release from captivity that the event passed almost unnoticed. Elijah Fisher, one of the two dozen Americans still aboard the *Jersey*, noted
in his journal that the men gave "three howzas," and that was that.[1]

Fisher and his comrades left New York quietly, slipping away into
the fog of time unheralded by fireworks, parades, or welcoming committees of dignitaries, but their suffering left an enduring mark on international law. Between 1782 and 1787, American diplomats

negotiated treaties of amity and commerce with foreign powers that took unprecedented steps toward mitigating the evils of war. Agreements struck with the Netherlands, Sweden, and Morocco, among others, required negotiation before the use of force, curbed privateering, and regulated the exercise of search and seizure on the high seas. Most important, the treaty with Prussia negotiated in 1785 by Thomas Jefferson, John Adams, and Benjamin Franklin included provisions designed specifically "to prevent the destruction of prisoners of war." Among other things, the parties stipulated that in the event of armed conflict between them, captives taken by either

> . . . shall not be confined in dungeons, prison-ships, nor prisons, nor be put into irons, nor bound, nor otherwise restrained in the use of their limbs; that the officers shall be enlarged on their paroles within convenient districts, & have comfortable quarters, & the common men be disposed in cantonments, open & extensive enough for air & exercise, and lodged in barracks as roomy & good as are provided by the party in whose power they are for their own troops; that the officers shall also be daily furnished by the party in whose power they are, with as many rations; & of the same articles & quality as are allowed by them, either in kind or by commutation, to officers of equal rank in their own army; & all others shall be daily furnished by them with such ration as they allow to a common soldier in their own service.

No matter that the conduct of their own countrymen had sometimes fallen well short of acceptable during the recent conflict with Britain; the three American negotiators understood that the new nation must pledge itself to treat future prisoners of war with the decency and humanity never accorded them by the British—that what set it apart from the former mother country was *only* this commitment to basic human rights. Just words on a piece of paper, to be sure, but an enduring tribute nonetheless to the tens of thousands tormented by close confinement, hunger, and disease in British prisons and prison ships.[2]

One of the great mysteries of the Revolutionary War is how many of those thousands remained forever in New York, their bodies carelessly interred in trenches on the outskirts of the city or hastily covered with a few shovelfuls of sand on the beaches of Wallabout Bay. "Too many of us have been prisoners in New-York," declared a correspondent of the *New-Jersey Gazette* only months away from the end. But how many was too many? And how many of those never came home? American record keeping was too rudimentary to provide an answer, and except for some surviving logs from the *Jersey*, generations of researchers have found little or nothing useful in British archives.[3]

Nevertheless, we do have tantalizing bits and pieces of information bearing on the numbers who perished on the New York prison ships. In the summer of 1782, a Connecticut newspaper, citing "lists and returns of the prison ships at N. York," put the body count in Wallabout Bay at 4,000. The following March, the *Massachusetts Spy*, a Boston paper, received information that, on average, fifty prisoners had died every week on the prison ships and reported that "there has been 7000 or 8000 of our countrymen buried under one bank on the Long-Island shore."[4]

The most interesting report came around the same time that prisoners from New York were showing up in towns and villages throughout New England and the middle states. On April 17, Boston's *Continental Journal* ran a notice, signed by "an AMERICAN," that grabbed everyone's attention. It announced that "ELEVEN THOUSAND SIX HUNDRED AND FORTY-FOUR, American Prisoners" perished on the *Jersey*. The basis for this figure was not explained, but judging by the number of times the notice was reprinted in newspapers from New Hampshire to South Carolina, it caused a sensation. (Very few other news items circulated so widely so quickly in Revolutionary-era American papers.) Ezra Stiles, the president of Yale, gave an Election Day sermon in early May that alluded to it as evidence of British perfidy. Several weeks later, General William Heath saw a copy at the American camp in Fishkill, New York, but assumed the number 11,644 included *all* the Americans who died aboard the prison ships *and* in the prisons of New York, not just those claimed by the *Jersey*.[5]

> To all Printers of Public News-Papers.
> TELL it to the whole WORLD, and let
> it be publifhed in every News Paper
> throughout AMERICA, EUROPE, ASIA and
> AFRICA, to the everlafting difgrace and infa-
> my of the Biitifh King's Commanders at
> New-York.
> That during the late War, it is faid
> ELEVEN THOUSAND SIX HUND-
> RED AND FORTY FOUR American Pri-
> foners, have fuffered death by their inhuman,
> cruel, favage and barbarous ufage on board
> the filthy and malignant *Britifh Prifon
> Ship* called the Jerfey, lying at New-York.
> Britons tremble left the vengance of Heaven
> fall on your Ifle, for the blood of thefe
> unfortunate victims !
> An AMERICAN.

"An American." From the *Continental Journal* (Boston), April 17, 1783: The debut of a notice soon reprinted in papers from New Hampshire to South Carolina.

A few years later, Thomas Jefferson produced a remarkably similar estimate of the prison ship dead. In the summer of 1786, now the American ambassador in Paris, Jefferson took a deposition from one Richard Riddy, a Philadelphia merchant living in Nantes. Riddy swore that in January 1783 he had been taken prisoner at sea and taken to New York. While there, "David Sproate Commissary general of prisoners to the British army informed him that upwards of eleven thousand prisoners had died on board the prison ship the Jersey, and shewed him the registers whereby it appeared to be so." What prompted Jefferson to take Riddy's statement is not clear. While making corrections to Jean Nicolas Démeunier's draft article about the United States for the renowned *Encyclopédie Méthodique*, he and Démeunier had discussed the experiences that led to the special provisions for prisoners of war in the recent treaty with Prussia. Jefferson prodded Démeunier to include "facts of cruelty" from the Revolutionary War in the article, and he probably wanted Riddy's deposition as supporting evidence.[6]

Especially noteworthy is Riddy's assertion that Sproat possessed "registers" showing the deaths of more than 11,000 Americans on the *Jersey* alone. Other than the 1782 newspaper reference to the "lists and returns" of the prison ships, this seems to be our only clue to the existence of such a document or documents—all of which have long since disappeared. Riddy almost certainly erred in believing that Sproat's "registers" reflected deaths exclusively on the *Jersey*, which would imply that others remained to be accounted for elsewhere. Because the *Jersey* was supposed to be the first stop for all naval prisoners brought into port, and because the sickest or most contagious of them would subsequently be sent away to end their days on one of the nearby hospital ships, it is a safe bet that the number Riddy said he got from Sproat ("upwards of eleven thousand") represented *all* deaths in Wallabout Bay. In light of the fact that "an AMERICAN" made the same assumption three years earlier in announcing 11,644 fatalities on the *Jersey*, Riddy might have been the source of that information as well. It is more likely, however, that Sproat showed the books to other people besides Riddy, and that one of them launched the story on its whirlwind career through American newspapers.[7]

Thus we have two presumably unrelated contemporary sources claiming the deaths of over 11,000 American prisoners in Wallabout Bay, one of which attributes that figure directly to documents in Sproat's possession. Spread over a little less than four years—roughly the length of time the *Jersey* received prisoners—a total 11,000 deaths averages out to around 230 per month, fifty to sixty a week, or between seven and eight per day. That falls comfortably in line with contemporary testimony, which ranged from five or six fatalities every day to ten or more, depending on the season. It is worth noting, too, that Sproat—always ready to blow smoke around American objections to conditions on the *Jersey*—never troubled himself to deny that so many men perished on his watch. If his "registers" told a different story, he kept it to himself.

Unfortunately, neither of the two sources in question gives us the *total* number of Wallabout Bay prisoners. The best we can do here is to fall back on what the prisoners themselves said about the mortality rate, which rarely if ever fell below 50 percent on the prison ships and in really bad weather soared as high as 70 percent. Assuming 11,000-plus deaths, a mortality rate in the 50 to 70 percent range would put the total number of prisoners somewhere between 15,700 and 22,000. By comparison, the mortality rate among Union prisoners at Andersonville was roughly 35 percent. (In World War I, only 3.6 percent of U.S. prisoners died in POW camps. In World War II the figure rose to 11.3 percent, and in Korea, to 37.8 percent.) In the case of Wallabout Bay, assuming a mortality rate as low as 35 percent would boost the total number of prisoners there to an improbably large 31,400. Even 22,000 total prisoners (at a 50 percent mortality rate) seems too many in light of the anecdotal evidence. Put another way, unless we are prepared to believe that the British confined significantly more Americans on their prison ships than the available sources suggest, the mortality rate on those ships must have been ferociously, breathtakingly high—perhaps twice as high as in any other war in our history.[8]

And what of the prisoners, military as well as civilian, held in the Provost and elsewhere in the city? No contemporary estimates like those for naval prisoners have come down to us, but the evidence presented in the previous chapters, though sketchy, suggests a total of between 9,150 and 10,000.[9]

If, for the sake of argument, we again assume a mortality rate of between 50 and 70 percent—the same as in Wallabout Bay—it would mean that anywhere from 4,575 to 7,000 rebel captives perished in the city's prisons during the Revolutionary War. Altogether, then, the British may well have interned between 24,850 and 32,000 Americans in and around Manhattan during the war. Assuming 11,000 prison ship deaths, the grand total of captives who died in and around the city falls in the range of 15,575 to 18,000.[10]

American prisoners died elsewhere as well, but in far smaller numbers—probably not more than 1,000 or so. After taking Savannah at the end of 1778, the British crammed over 400 rebels into prison ships so foul that the corpses of ten or twelve were allegedly thrown overboard every day. When Charleston fell in 1780, an additional 3,300 Americans were consigned first to stockades scattered around that city and then to four reeking, scandalously overcrowded prison ships. Hundreds, well aware by this time of what was happening to rebel prisoners in New York, enlisted with the enemy to avoid an almost certain death. Of those who elected to remain, 800 reportedly succumbed to disease or malnutrition in the weeks that followed. Still more deaths would occur among American prisoners subsequently brought to Charleston as the British Army worked its way north toward defeat at Yorktown. In the meantime, small groups of rebels had also been interned at Detroit, on an island in the St. Lawrence River, on St. Lucia and Antigua in the West Indies, and even in Senegambia, a British colony on the west coast of Africa. How many survived is unclear. At Forton and Mill prisons in England, the mortality rate seems never to have exceeded 5 percent, meaning that only 125 of the 2,500 American detainees failed to make it out alive.[11]

These figures are much larger than previously recognized and put the Revolutionary War in a rather new light. According to the most recent investigation, 6,824 Americans were killed in action and another 10,000 succumbed to wounds or disease in camp. The number of those who breathed their last as prisoners in New York was thus *between two and three times* the number of those who met their deaths in battle and at least 50 percent greater than the number who died in camp. To put it a different way, as many as 35,800 patriots died in the Revolutionary War of all causes; roughly *half* of these deaths were in the prisons and prison ships of New York City. However we measure it, more Americans gave their lives for independence there than anywhere else in the country.[12]

To fully appreciate the magnitude of what happened in New York, however, we also need to consider that those 32,000 Americans held prisoner in and around the city were drawn from a population that now seems almost impossibly small. According to the federal census of 1790, the United States had 3,930,000 residents—3,170,000 whites and 760,000 blacks. Nine-tenths of the latter were southern slaves. The white population included 1.6 million males, of whom 813,000 were sixteen years of age or older. (The tally of black males was not broken down by age.) In other words, white males over sixteen made up half the white male population and one-fourth the total of all whites. The Census Bureau's compilation of the extant prefederal data indicates that ten years earlier, in 1780, the population of the thirteen colonies consisted of 2,205,000 whites and 575,000 blacks, for a total of 2,780,000.

Assuming that the age structure of the population did not change between 1780 and 1790, one-fourth or 551,000 of the whites in 1780 would have been men over the age of sixteen. Not all of them would have been eligible or willing to bear arms. Some were too old or infirm. Others, chiefly Quakers, would not serve for reasons of conscience. There must have been still others, a few anyway, who did not care about the outcome one way or the other and kept to themselves. All things considered, therefore, the pool of white fighting men probably did not exceed 500,000. Of that number, between 200,000 and 250,000 are thought to have fought with the rebels. Because it was not uncommon for a man to sign up for more than one tour of duty in a conflict that lasted nearly eight years, the lower of the two numbers is likely the more accurate. An additional 50,000 fought for the Crown.[13]

How many African Americans participated in the Revolutionary War and how many became prisoners is extremely difficult to gauge. Thousands—some estimates range as high as 15,000—served with British forces. On the rebel side, both General Washington and Congress initially opposed the recruitment of either slaves or freedmen, though they quickly changed their minds after the fighting began in earnest, partly because many states had already adopted the practice anyway, and partly because the reluctance of white men to join up left no alternative. As early as 1778, perhaps 10 percent of the 7,600 men fit for duty in the Continental Army consisted of black volunteers and bondsmen substituting for their white masters. One famous Rhode

Island battalion consisted entirely of former slaves. Privateers operating from northern ports typically carried crews that were about 10 percent black. For instance, when the *Royal Louis*, out of Philadelphia, was taken by the *Amphion* in the autumn of 1781, she had a crew of 200, of whom twenty were black; all of those onboard soon found themselves consigned to the *Jersey* in New York. Assuming that the enemy captured blacks no more or less frequently than whites—and that rebel forces relied more and more heavily on blacks as the war dragged on—between 2,480 and 3,200 prisoners held in New York may have been African Americans, leaving a balance of between 22,360 and 28,800 whites.[14]

In sum, then, approximately 1 percent of the overall white population and 0.5 percent of the overall black population were held captive in New York City during the Revolutionary War. In proportion to the current population of the United States—over 304 million, as of this writing, about 80 percent of whom are white and 15 percent black— that would represent almost 2.7 million prisoners of war—substantially more than the 2.3 million people currently behind bars in the country. That is something to think about.[15]

It is not enough, however, to ponder the meaning of all those prisoners in New York solely in reference to the number of Americans who supported and fought for independence. The Revolutionary War was in many respects a civil war, during which an estimated 50,000 Tories took up arms to maintain British rule. They too must be factored into our calculations.

Consider, to begin with, that the 6,824 men who died in combat on the rebel side represented about 3.4 percent of the estimated 200,000 who fought. On the convenient but risky supposition that the percentage of Tory combatants killed in action was the same as that of their rebel counterparts, it is possible that 1,700 died in combat.

Estimating the number who died in rebel prisons is even trickier. On the rebel side, those 6,824 combat deaths accounted for 19 percent of the 35,824 who died of all causes during the war. If the same held true on the Tory side, it would indicate around 8,900 total fatalities of whom 7,200 died in prison or camp. However, as explained earlier, mortality rates among prisoners held by the rebels never approached those in New York, and 7,200 is much too high—the question is: How high? If, for the sake of argument, we cut it in half, the total number of Tory fatalities would come to 5,300. That, in turn, would push the total number of American deaths on *both* sides to about 41,100.

All of this is wildly speculative, of course—conjectures wobbling atop assumptions—but it suggests that as much as 1.5 percent of the country's 1780 population might have died in the Revolution of war-related causes. That is well short of the 2.0 percent killed in the Civil War, but greatly exceeds the 0.12 percent slain in World War I or the 0.28 percent in World War II.[16]

None of those conflicts, on the other hand, involved the permanent exile of a substantial part of the American population. By Evacuation Day, upwards of 30,000 Tories and 4,000 or more runaway slaves had fled the former colonies through the port of New York alone, borne away from their native soil on 175 vessels of every description. And that was only New York. Altogether, the flood of emigrés is thought to have reached 80,000 men, women, and children—some authorities say 100,000. If we count that massive exodus along with the tens of thousands who perished in prison, the human toll of the Revolutionary War easily reached 140,000, or 3.6 percent of the 1780 population—well above what the country experienced in the Civil War. If such comparisons must be made, the conflict that gave birth to the United States entailed proportionally more suffering than any other in its history.[17]

9

FORGOTTEN
Patriots

IN THE SUMMER of 1785, a half dozen members of Congress found lodgings together in a boardinghouse on Brooklyn Heights, directly across the East River from New York City and not far from the site of Washington's famous nighttime retreat less than a decade earlier. It was a splendid location, commanding glorious views of the harbor yet only a short ferry ride from City Hall, where Congress had been meeting since January. But it wasn't perfect. "There is something that damps our spirits and casts a gloom over the whole," Congressman Joseph Cooke of Connecticut wrote in a letter to his son:

> At about half a mile distance from our lodgings lies the wreck of a ship which was the Jersey Prison ship, from which so many thousands of our poor Countrymen, who had the misfortune during the late war to be taken prisoners were thrown. . . . The Banks near which this Prison ship lay are high & sandy: the dead bodies of our friends only wrapped up in old blankets were laid at the bottom of the bank, and the sand drawn down over them. Soon after we came to live upon Long Island several of us took a walk that way, and were struck with horror at beholding a large Number of human bones, some fragments of flesh not quite consumed, with many pieces of old blankets lying upon the shore.

On a motion by Rufus King of Massachusetts, Congress instructed the secretary at war to have the bones gathered up and properly buried. It also urged the governor of the state to find out how many Americans died on the *Jersey*, "to the end that some plain monument be erected to the Memory of these unfortunate men."[1]

This was not the first time Congress had contemplated erecting memorials to Americans who died in the Revolutionary War. In 1776, even before declaring the country independent, it had appropriated money for a carved stone cenotaph in New York honoring the memory of General Richard Montgomery, killed outside Québec during the failed American invasion of Canada. Although it took nearly a decade to complete Montgomery's cenotaph, the delays and expense did not deter Congress from approving memorials to a string of other fallen officers: Joseph Warren, Hugh Mercer, David Wooster, Francis Nash, Count Casimir Pulaski, William Davidson, Nathanael Greene, Baron de Kalb, and Nicholas Herkimer. In each instance, the idea was that an expression of public appreciation would set an example for future generations of Americans. As John Hancock explained to Governor George Clinton of New York: "Every Mark of Distinction shewn to the Memory of such illustrious Men as offer up their Lives for the Liberty & Happiness of their Country, reflects real Honour upon those who pay the grateful Tribute; and by holding up to others the Prospects of Fame and Immortality will animate them to tread in the same Path."[2]

But there would be no monument to the *Jersey* victims, not yet. The idea of a memorial failed to gain traction in Congress or in the state government, and judging by the silence of local newspapers on the subject, it generated no interest among the public at large. Almost overnight, after years of outrage about British cruelty, the thousands of American patriots who succumbed to starvation and disease in enemy prisons and prison ships seem to have been completely forgotten. Today, more than two centuries later, the erection of monuments to the dead has become so predictable a part of how we remember war that this silence—this apparent indifference—seems almost perverse. It compels us to look more closely at how the story of those prisons and prison ships played out in the years after independence

Montgomery Monument, St. Paul's Churchyard, New York (1787). The first Revolutionary War monument in the city, and one of the first in the United States, it was largely the work of Jean-Jacques Caffieri, sculptor to Louis XVI of France. Among the eclectic mixture of elements are the obelisk (Egyptian symbol of heroic death), the Grecian altar (a symbol of martyrdom), and the Roman victory column.

and why, from time to time and for a variety of motives, people would attempt to resuscitate it.

One reason that a "plain monument" to the *Jersey* victims never materialized involves what might be called republican iconoclasm—a nagging suspicion that elaborate statues, obelisks, shrines, medals, and other commemorative devices were inherently monarchical and inappropriate for the new United States. Thus one Congressman had opposed the Montgomery cenotaph because "the General is already embalmed in the Heart of every good American," and when it was finally unveiled in the yard of St. Paul's Chapel in 1787, the monument's elaborate ornamentation drew heavy fire. This way of thinking proved so tenacious, in fact, that few Revolutionary War memorials of any kind would be erected in the United States for the next fifty years or more, including those recommended by Congress to honor fallen officers. Some republicans even thought that stamping coins with Washington's image smacked of monarchism.[3]

The exigencies of reconstruction also stood in the way of a monument to the dead prisoners of New York. After seven years of military
occupation and a pair of calamitous fires, the city was a shambles. In
the burned-over district west of Broadway, the shell of Trinity
Church loomed menacingly over a dozen rubble-strewn blocks.
Many private houses were unfit for human habitation. Churches and
public buildings, commandeered by the British for use as prisons or
hospitals or stables, needed cleaning and repairing. Trenches and redoubts blocked major streets. Wharves and warehouses on the East
River waterfront crumbled from neglect. No other city in the United
States had suffered such grievous destruction during the war, and
people in town worried that without access to markets in the British
West Indies, closed to American trade after 1783, its prospects did
not look good.[4]

For moderate and conservative patriots like Alexander Hamilton,
the key to rebuilding and recovery was political reconciliation. Everything hinged on recognizing that the Revolution was finished, Hamilton said. The popular committees and ad hoc associations that had
proliferated during the war must now yield to regular, orderly government by gentlemen of property and standing. Wartime wage and
price controls must be rolled back. Most important, the thousands of
Tories who fled at the end of the war must be allowed to return without fear of retribution. Their money, connections, and know-how,
Hamilton reasoned, were the foundation of everyone's prosperity, ordinary tradesmen and artisans no less than deepwater merchants.[5]

This conciliatory program made such rapid headway among city
voters that two or three years after Evacuation Day ex-Tories were
popping up everywhere, one as cashier of the new Bank of New York,
another as president of the Chamber of Commerce, still another as
rector of Trinity Church. By 1787 the legislature had repealed every
statute discriminating against Tories and restored full citizenship to
all those not banished by name during the war (and this group got
permission to come back in 1792). Radical patriots grumbled, but
there was no real outcry—not even when Robert Lenox reopened his
store on Maiden Lane, though Lenox had been conspicuous during
the occupation as an assistant to his uncle, Commissary David Sproat,

and offered an especially attractive target for anyone nursing old grudges. Although no one said so openly, this was not the time to build memorials to murdered prisoners of war.[6]

Whether Hamilton's strategy was the reason or not, New York's phoenix-like resurgence in the late eighties and early nineties made it all the more difficult to remember the horrors of the Sugar House or the Provost. The 1790 federal census found over 33,000 inhabitants in the city, an all-time high, but only the beginning of a demographic upsurge that would drive its population past the 100,000 mark before 1820 and beyond 500,000 by 1850. For a few years after the war, local boys playing on a hill west of Broadway near Franklin Street often found the bones of Sugar House prisoners. But the ensuing construction boom soon erased this and every other site where the bodies of American captives might have been interred (with one controversial exception, as we will see) and pushed the built-up area of town into the woods and pastures north of the Common. The old Anglo-Dutch fort, a fixture of the Battery for 150 years, came down. City Hall, where Major General Charles Lee had whiled away his time as a prisoner of war, got a complete makeover to house the federal government after ratification of the Constitution, while a new Trinity Church rose on Broadway. The damage to Livingston's sugar house on Crown Street—the one that everyone knew as *the* Sugar House— was quickly repaired. Van Cortlandt's sugar house, also damaged during its brief time as a prison, was back in business as early as 1785, advertising "all kinds of refined sugar of the best quality," along with molasses and "New-York distilled rum."[7]

In such a busy, forward-looking place, who had time to dwell on the past?

But over in Brooklyn, slower to urbanize than its neighbor across the East River, the past would not be scrubbed away so easily. For many years after the end of the war, the sandy beaches of Wallabout Bay remained littered with the bones of men who died in the prison ships— one resident of the area described skulls lying about as thick as pumpkins in an autumn cornfield—while the abandoned black hulk of the *Jersey* slowly broke up out in the mud flats beyond. In 1792, some residents of Brooklyn village talked about re-interring the bones in the graveyard of the Dutch Reform Church, only to be thwarted by a developer who had recently acquired land on the south side of the bay and said that all the remains belonged to him.[8]

The outbreak of war in Europe later that same year nonetheless kept the controversy boiling. Americans disagreed, passionately and often violently, over which of the combatants deserved the country's support—Britain, where George III still sat on the throne, or France, where the Revolution had just toppled Louis XVI. Secretary of State Thomas Jefferson, seeing the chance to strike another blow against British tyranny, urged President Washington not to renege on the Franco-American alliance of 1778. Treasury Secretary Alexander Hamilton countered that the United States had no duty to support the revolutionaries in France and that another war with Britain would be ruinously expensive. In 1793, Washington declared neutrality. The rancor in his cabinet, however, soon spawned the new nation's first political parties, the pro-French Democratic-Republicans and the pro-British Federalists. It did not take long for the organizers of New York's fledgling Democratic-Republican organization to conclude that all those bones of the prison ship dead in Brooklyn could serve as talismans of popular resistance to British aggression on both sides of the Atlantic—sacred relics, not merely of "unfortunate men," as Congress had described them a decade earlier, but of *martyrs* in the struggle against oppression and injustice.

Perhaps the earliest indication of this shift in perception came from an up-and-coming Republican operative named Matthew Davis. In 1794, Davis proposed erecting a monument on the shores of Wallabout Bay, near the "neglected and unhonored" bones of the thousands who died there during the Revolutionary War. It would stand "as a grateful memorial of the services which those heroes rendered their country; and transmit to posterity, a sense of the virtue and merits of their ancestors, that thus they may know the value of liberty, and view with abhorrence, the schemes of tyranny and arbitrary power." Davis's idea received much wider attention in 1800, when Jonathan

Russell, a rising young Republican orator in Rhode Island, proposed building "one vast ossory [*sic*]" as a permanent memorial to the 11,000 "willing martyrs" murdered on the *Jersey*. Or, if not an ossuary, then "a Colossal Column whose base sinking to Hell, should let the murderers read their infamy inscribed upon it; and whose capital of Corinthian laurel ascending to Heaven, should show the sainted Patriots that they have triumphed."[9]

The partisan value of the Wallabout bones came into still sharper focus over the spring and summer of 1802, when the Society of the Cincinnati—an elite fraternity of former Continental Army officers that was openly Federalist in orientation—began a fund-raising drive to erect a statue of George Washington in New York City. Construction of the Naval Shipyard on the south side of Wallabout Bay had just got under way, uncovering many more remains, and Democratic-Republicans were quick to complain that thousands of dead prisoners of war deserved a memorial as much as the former commander-in-chief. "Go, fellow citizens, to the Wallabout," one said excitedly, "and view the remains of the patriot, the hero and friend, who nobly died to save his country." Give them all a proper burial, and if there must be a statue of Washington, place it over their common grave by the bay: "They were companions in life, and in arms, in one common cause. Let them not be forgotten in death—they were all worthy and deserving."[10]

When the Tammany Society jumped into the fray, things really began to heat up. Established back in the mid-eighties, the "Saint Tammany Society, or Columbian Order," was an organization of master craftsmen and small merchants who loathed Alexander Hamilton as ardently as they loved Thomas Jefferson. In the election of 1800 their support was instrumental in winning New York City for the Republicans, putting Jefferson in the White House (once Congress broke the tie between Jefferson and Burr in the Electoral College). Now, a year after Jefferson's inauguration, Tammany petitioned Congress to build a "solemn depository" for the Wallabout bones—"precious relics of *these victims for the nation*"—adjacent to the Navy Yard. The site should be marked by a monument "neither lofty, nor sumptuous, nor magnificent" but sufficient to remind posterity that "an immense multitude of men" perished nearby in their country's cause. Happily, land for that purpose had already been donated by John Jackson, a Brooklyn property owner and Tammany bigwig. Although the proposal died in committee, a casualty of Jeffersonian frugality, Tammany men continued to collect the bones uncovered almost every day along the shores of Wallabout Bay. By 1805, they reportedly had twenty hogsheads full.[11]

Tammany's agitation for a memorial had nonetheless tweaked the recollections of men who survived captivity during the war, several of whom would come forward over the next few years with memoirs that kept the prison-ship story percolating furiously. In the spring of 1803, local papers announced the publication of *An Historical Sketch, to the End of the Revolutionary War, of the Life of Silas Talbot.* Recently retired as commander of the USS *Constitution* ("Old Ironsides"), Talbot gave the reading public its first look inside the *Jersey* since the end of the war, twenty years earlier. (John Blatchford's autobiographical *Narrative of Remarkable Occurrences* had come out in 1788 but said nothing of his brief stint on the *Jersey*.) Talbot's stomach-turning descriptions of "filth, disgust and horror" on the *Jersey* undoubtedly stoked the Anglophobia of New York Republicans. They must have been gratified, too, by Talbot's timely remarks on the state of affairs in Wallabout Bay as excavations continued for the Navy Yard. "The human bones and skulls yet bleaching on the shore of Long Island, and exposed by the falling down of the high bank, on which the prisoners were buried, is a shocking sight," he wrote, "and manifestly demonstrates that the Jersey prison ship had been as destructive as a field of battle."[12]

Nathaniel Fanning, a naval gunboat captain stationed in Charleston, South Carolina, was never a prisoner in New York, but he had been captured by the British several times while on privateering voyages, and two of his brothers wound up on the *Jersey*. One of the pair was killed in an escape attempt; the other became so gravely ill that he was released on parole and never entirely recovered. Their experiences left Fanning with such a ferocious hatred of the British that when he heard of the campaign for a monument to the prison ship martyrs, he dedicated his just-completed memoirs to John Jackson—the very Tammany stalwart who had donated the site overlooking

Wallabout Bay. Published in New York in 1806, Fanning's *Narrative of the adventures of an American navy officer* also made the point that stories about the *Jersey* had been a subject of fearful discussion among prisoners everywhere. When he was in Dartmoor prison, Fanning recalled, a rumor went around that the British were poisoning prisoners. The men speculated that "the same game was playing here, as had been done on board the old Jersey [where] we had heard thousands of our countrymen had died." To their immense relief, the rumor proved false. "However," Fanning added, "it is hoped by the compiler of these sheets, that this, as well as the conduct of the British relative to the old Jersey, will be had [held?] in eternal remembrance by the citizens of the United States, so long as the British shall exist as a nation!!!"[13]

In September 1807, one of the most vivid reminiscences ever published of the *Jersey* appeared in the form of an open letter from Captain Alexander Coffin to Doctor Samuel Latham Mitchill, the renowned scientist and Republican politician who had championed Tammany's memorial campaign in Congress. Mitchill immediately published it with an eye-catching title that reflected his interest in the miasmatic theory of disease:

The DESTRUCTIVE OPERATION of FOUL AIR, TAINTED PROVISIONS, BAD WATER, and PERSONAL FILTHINESS, upon HUMAN CONSTITUTIONS; exemplified in the unparalleled Cruelty of the British to the American Captives at New-York during the Revolutionary War, on Board their Prison and Hospital Ships.

Coffin's readers, however, were probably much more likely to be attracted by the unusual sensory density of his story—the appalling sights and sounds and smells that assailed him during the six weeks he had spent aboard the *Jersey* in the late autumn of 1782. Thoughtful readers would have marked the fact, too, that when he returned in early 1783, having been captured again, "very few" of the men he remembered from his first visit were still there. Some had escaped and others had been exchanged, but most were dead—deliberately murdered, he believed.[14]

In addition to rousing old navy hands such as Talbot and Fanning and Coffin, and despite congressional inaction on the Wallabout monument, appeals to remember the prison ships now became a standard rhetorical tactic for Republicans and Tammany men everywhere—gleefully covered by New York papers such as the *Public Advertiser* and the *Republican Watch-Tower*. While participants in the 1807 Tammanial Festival in New York toasted "The Martyrs to Freedom, who perished in the *Jersey prison ship*," the Republican Greens of Philadelphia lifted their glasses to the memory of "the Jersey prison ships [*sic*], in which 13000 Americans perished." The *Petersburg Republican*, a Virginia paper, promised that true Americans will never forget the suffering of their countrymen captured during the Revolutionary War: "The horrors of the English prison ships and dungeons are recorded in the black annals of British oppression." One writer, casting a wider net, recalled "the cruelties committed on our farmers during the revolution, the poisoning of thousands of farmers in the Jersey prison ships [*sic*] at Newyork." Do Federalists "feast their eyes with the bleached bones of our *farmers* and farmer's sons at the Wallabout?"[15]

By 1807, moreover, the policy of neutrality enunciated fourteen years earlier by President Washington had been strained to the breaking point. Europe was engulfed by renewed fighting between Britain and France, and the Royal Navy had blockaded the Continent, seizing American merchant ships on the high seas and forcibly impressing American seamen. In November, with Anglophobia in the country at a fever pitch, New York papers announced the publication of Joel Barlow's *Columbiad*, a bloated epic poem about the discovery and settlement of the New World illustrated with a dozen plates by the English artist Robert Smirke. After nearly 200 pages of deep historical references and classical allusions—so deep that he equipped the poem with explanatory notes and an index—Barlow found his way to the topic of the British occupation of New York. There, he wrote, the proud, unfeeling enemy, "on torture bent," proceeded to worship the goddess Cruelty, who actually takes up residence on "the black Prison Ship." Crouched over the hatch, "Her cords and scourges wet with prisoners' gore," she feasts on the cries of misery and woe from

"Cruelty Presiding over the Prison Ship," one of the plates engraved by Robert Smirk for Joel Barlow's epic poem, "The Columbiad" (1807). It was the first artistic attempt to evoke the suffering of Revolutionary War prisoners.

below while "Disease hangs drizzling from her slimy locks." For true republicans, the message could not have been plainer: Cruelty was again stalking the seas, yet still the bones of her victims from the Revolutionary War lay scattered along the beaches of Wallabout Bay, shamefully neglected by an ungrateful posterity.[16]

Barlow's readers were still slogging through the *Columbiad* when President Jefferson made a decision that pushed the Wallabout bones to the top of the New York Republican agenda. In December 1807, he persuaded Congress to adopt an embargo, shutting down virtually all American trade with foreign nations. It was a well-intentioned attempt to maintain American neutrality, but the impact on seaports up and down the coast was catastrophic. The American economy collapsed, and New York City came to a standstill.[17]

Mindful that an anti-embargo backlash would bolster the Federalists, especially among unemployed sailors and tradesmen, the Tammany Society redoubled its efforts to resurrect the prison ship dead as archetypes of plebeian resolve. In February 1808 its newly created Wallabout Committee, chaired by John Jackson, announced that the society would re-inter all the bones collected thus far and mark the site with a suitable monument. Judging by the number of times it was reprinted by editors around the country, the announcement prompted the first truly national conversation about memorializing the tens of thousands of Revolutionary War dead in New York and elsewhere. A New Hampshire paper predicted that Tammany would have the thanks of "every individual whose heart recoils from cruelty, and who feel a generous glow of sensibility for the sufferings experienced by those patriots who assisted in the achievement of independence."[18]

Caught off guard by this fervor, Federalist writers groused about Tammany's transparent cynicism and tried to cast doubt on the authenticity of the remains at Wallabout—maybe some of the bones belonged to Hessian soldiers? perhaps even to animals? But Federalist skepticism only gave Tammany and the Republicans more ammunition. "To cause eleven thousand five hundred of our revolutionary veterans to perish in heaps in the hold of a nasty stinking prison ship, for want of the common necessaries of life, is too black a crime for republicans to cherish," declared one Republican writer hotly, yet it is now "nursed and supported by those who esteem the British conduct and policy better than our own."[19]

By April 1808, fortified with private donations and a grant of one thousand dollars from the state legislature, the Wallabout Committee had completed preparations for the first of two elaborately choreographed public ceremonies to commemorate the prison ship martyrs. At noon on April 6, a crowd of nearly 2,000 assembled at the Brooklyn Ferry landing and marched over to the plot donated by Chairman Jackson, directly above the Navy Yard (near what is now the intersection of Hudson Avenue and York Street). Assorted officials, led by Benjamin Romaine, the grand sachem of the Tammany Society and himself a former prisoner of war in New York, then laid the cornerstone of the tomb intended to hold the bones collected on the nearby beaches.[20]

"The most profound silence prevailed," reported the *American Citizen*. "It was a moment big with patriotic, and exalted and enthusiastic feeling. It seemed that the recollections and sensibilities of America were concentrated—and that the debt of gratitude to the memory of 11,000 of her brave but unfortunate defenders which it belonged to the nation to discharge, was about to be canceled." A company of Marines and an artillery detachment fired "a national salute," after which Joseph D. Fay, a New York lawyer who later became active in the cause of penal reform, gave a long and impassioned address on "the sufferings of the heroes and martyrs of American liberty" during the Revolution. The many veterans present wept unashamedly.[21]

When the polls opened for state and local elections at the end of April, it was clear that the cornerstone ceremony had made a powerful impression on Republican voters, especially when a noisy throng of sailors converged on one waterfront polling-place "calling out— No Jersey PRISON SHIPS—no WAR—no TORIES—no FEDERALISTS—*our country forever!*" But an even bigger event lay just ahead. Work on the vault had gone quickly, and early in May, Tammany's Wallabout Committee announced plans for a "Grand Funeral Procession" on the twenty-fifth of that month to inter the bones of the martyrs. As the day approached, Republican papers kept their readers on edge with news and instructions—about the arrival of out-of-state participants, about the order of march, about assembly points for each participating group. The city council decreed that May 25 would be a public holiday and recommended that churches and ships toll their bells at sunrise. The *Public Advertiser* printed excerpts from Freneau's poem, "The British Prison Ship."[22]

Tammany's Grand Funeral Procession (put off until May 26 because of rain) would be remembered as one of the great civic pageants in the postwar history of New York—"superior to anything witnessed in this city since the national rejoicings on the adoption of the federal constitution" twenty years earlier, the *Republican Watch-Tower* assured its readers.[23]

The festivities got under way in midmorning, when thousands of marchers moved out of the Common (now City Hall Park) and proceeded down Broadway toward Wall Street. Leading the way was a trumpeter mounted on a fine black charger, the banner on his trumpet emblazoned with the motto "Mortals avaunt!—11500 spirits of the martyr'd brave, approach the tomb of honor, of glory, of virtuous patriotism." Behind him came a herald, an escort of light horse, a band playing "The Grand Wallabout Dead March," and members of the Tammany Society carrying thirteen open coffins, one for each of the original states in the union, filled with bones from Wallabout Bay. Behind the coffins came a float bearing the "grand national pedestal," atop which sat a young man in white robes representing "The Genius of America," described as the "chief mourner for her martyr'd sons in a contemplative posture." Each of the pedestal's four sides bore a patriotic inscription:

Americans! Remember the British.

Youth of my country!
Martyrdom prefer to slavery.

Sires of Columbia:
Transmit to Posterity the cruelties practiced
on board the British prison ships.

Tyrants dread the gathering storm—
While freemen, freemen's obsequies perform.

After the pedestal marched 300 sailors, various dignitaries, and representatives of the trades—shipwrights, coopers, masons, tailors, hatters. At the end of the column were citizens, "each with a small branch of cypress in his hand," another band playing "solemn music," then more cavalry.[24]

At Wall Street, the procession swung across town toward Pearl Street, where it turned north and proceeded along the waterfront, each group of participants peeling off when it came to the wharf where it was to meet a special ferry for the trip across the East River. "The day was one of devotion," said the *Republican Watch-Tower*. "Business was suspended," and "the concourse of spectators in the streets, the houses and upon the house tops, was immense. It seemed as if every man, woman and child in the city, was anxious to view this scene of national piety." On the Brooklyn side of the river, the marchers reassembled and processed behind the trumpeter to what was now being called the Tomb of the Martyrs. There, observed by a hushed crowd of 30,000—including hundreds of visitors from Connecticut, Pennsylvania, and other states, it was later reported—Tammany pallbearers deposited the thirteen coffins in the vault. After a "dignified, pathetic and eloquent" oration by Doctor Benjamin De Witt, a chemistry professor at the College of Physicians and Surgeons, the marchers returned in good order to New York.

Like the cornerstone-laying ceremony six weeks earlier, the Grand Funeral Procession of May 26 grabbed the attention of Republicans around the country. Residents of Sag Harbor, on the far end of Long Island, even staged a pageant of their own to honor the Wallabout dead.[25]

But this revival of interest in martyred Revolutionary War prisoners, though deeply felt and colorful, was less than universal. Federalists continued to jeer, dismissing the funeral procession as "nothing but the old farce of the Jersey Prison ships [sic] got up again by a set of hypocrites to answer some political purpose." An essay in *The Balance*, a paper published in Hudson, New York, termed it "a solemn farce"—"a burlesque of grief." Nor did it go unnoticed that prominent elements of the community, among them the clergy, the Society of the Cincinnati, and military officers, absented themselves from the line of march even though invited to take part. "Few persons of real character attended this cavalcade," scoffed a British intelligence agent several days afterward. The whole thing was "ridiculous," "an Electioneering trick" designed "to revive the ancient enmity to Great Britain."[26]

As was to be expected, Republicans vigorously defended the purity of their motives. "It is *false, basely false*, that the solemn display was intended for party purposes," huffed the *Daily Advertiser*. In July, the Wallabout Committee responded to the critics by publishing its *Account of the Interment of the Remains of 11,500 American Seamen, Soldiers and Citizens, Who Fell Victims to the Cruelties of the British, on Board their Prison Ships at the Wallabout*, a collection of eyewitness reports, speeches, and background information that would be advertised in Republican papers for most of the next year. There was more talk of erecting a "granite column" over the vault, and at meetings of the Tammany Society or the General Society of Mechanics and Tradesmen, the "Wallabout Dead March" became as regular a part of the ceremonies as "Yankee Doodle."[27]

Big crowds did not translate into big donations, however, and Tammany failed to raise the money necessary for a permanent memorial. One drag on the project was that Benjamin Romaine, a driving force behind the 1808 festivities, became implicated later that same year in a municipal corruption scandal and was forced to step down as the society's grand sachem. Bitter personal and ideological differences, complicated by the Madison administration's confused attempts to avert war with Britain, splintered New York Republicans into hostile factions. By 1812, the year war did finally break out, memorializing the Wallabout dead, let alone the rest of New York's Revolutionary War prisoners, was the last thing on anyone's mind.[28]

Tammany's interest in the prison ships revived somewhat after the war, when the state legislature, at the request of General Montgomery's widow, had his remains removed from Québec and reburied near his cenotaph at St. Paul's Chapel. The ceremony that unfolded in July 1818, organized by the Society of the Cincinnati but actively supported by the Tammany Society, was reminiscent of the Grand Funeral Procession ten years before—masses of spectators lining Broadway from the Battery to Chambers Street, cannons booming, and a long column of marchers winding through the city.[29]

Some months later, the New York State Assembly received the first of several proposals to give the Tammany Society $1,000 for erecting the long-delayed monument over the Martyrs' Tomb in Brooklyn. When a bill to that effect finally reached the floor of the Assembly early in 1821, it ran into stiff opposition, partly because the Tammany Society's treasurer was none other than Benjamin Romaine, long since restored to the organization's good graces. The bill did pass eventually, but the monument never materialized. What happened to the money was anyone's guess.[30]

Oddly, although public interest in commemorating New York's Revolutionary War prisoners seemed to evaporate after 1821, the next two decades proved to be a time of almost obsessive fascination else-

where with the country's founding generation and its impending disappearance. Newspapers tracked the health and whereabouts of old
patriots. Politicians wrangled over whether a grateful republic should
provide pensions for veterans and on what basis—as vexing a question
as whether to erect monuments in their honor. Biographies, autobi-
ographies, histories, memoirs, and collections of letters poured into
bookstores. Historical societies sprang up to preserve documents and
artifacts from what now felt like a rapidly receding heroic age. The
deaths of both John Adams and Thomas Jefferson on July 4, 1826,
fifty years to the day after the promulgation of the Declaration of Independence, imparted a sense of real urgency to the belief that surviving witnesses to the nation's birth must be sought out, like ancient
oracles, for interrogation and consultation.[31]

Between 1828 and 1838, against this background, four old salts
who survived the *Jersey*—Andrew Sherburne, Thomas Dring,
Thomas Andros, and Ebenezer Fox—produced narratives of their experiences that reveal how, at the outer margins of living memory, the
prison ship story was being reorganized and invested with new and
different meaning. Two of these accounts in particular remind us that
"memory" is not always what it appears to be, for the stories that one
generation remembers are not necessarily the same stories that earlier
ones forgot.

What Sherburne and Andros recalled of the prison ships was fil-
tered through the evangelical fervor of a religious upheaval known as
the Second Great Awakening. Sherburne's *Memoirs* (1828), for example, describes how an unchurched, blaspheming, grog-swilling young
sailor of eighteen survived the horrors of the *Jersey* over the winter of
1782–1783 only through the "merciful interpositions of Providence."
He looks back on the ordeal without anger or blame or rancor: he
does not see the *Jersey* as a showcase of British cruelty or an en-
durance test of American patriotism but rather (like the older tradition of Indian captivity narratives) an opportunity to accept his need
for God's saving grace. In retrospect, the ordeal was only the beginning of a lifelong spiritual odyssey that led him to become an itiner-
ant minister of the Gospel, wandering from New Hampshire, across
New England and upstate New York, and west into Ohio.[32]

Similarly, the Reverend Thomas Andros, author of *The Old Jersey Captive* (1833), recalled captivity as God's punishment for his career as a privateer during the Revolutionary War. "O Lord God, thou art good, but I am wicked," he reflects, with a submissiveness that would never have occurred to a tough Yankee like Ethan Allen. "Thou has done right in sending me to this doleful prison; it is just what I deserve." But like Sherburne, he begins to understand that captivity is God's way of testing him. Through "a remarkable and unexpected interposition of Providence," Andros escapes from the *Jersey* in 1781 and treks across Long Island to Sag Harbor, dodging military patrols and suspicious Tories, sleeping in barns, and cadging food from kindly strangers. It makes him uneasy that he must "frame a story that might serve to prevent my being seized and returned back to captivity," because it means lying, and "lying is entirely inconsistent with obedience or trust in God." It gradually dawns on him that the practical Christianity of ordinary folks, their willingness to feed and clothe a needy stranger, their instinctive humanity, represents the true religion of Jesus and the salvation of mankind.[33]

As in Sherburne's *Memoirs* (which Andros could well have read beforehand), there is no railing about British cruelty in *The Old Jersey Captive*. Andros was in fact the only survivor to suggest that the prisoners themselves may have been at least partly to blame for their suffering. They were given brushes and buckets of vinegar to clean the ship, he remarks at one point, "but their indolence and despair were such that they would not use them, or but rarely." He certainly saw no reason to condemn an entire nation for the miseries he experienced on the *Jersey*. "It is indeed a blot which a thousand ages cannot eradicate from the name of Britain, but no doubt, when the pious and humane among them came to know what had been done, they utterly reprobated such cruelty. Since that time, the nation has so greatly improved in Christian light, feeling and humanity, they would not now treat even rebels with such barbarity." Besides, he adds, with a spiritual detachment that must have had Ethan Allen turning over in his grave, "I have since found that the Old Jersey was not the only abode of inhumanity and woe; but the whole world is but one great prison-house of guilty, sorrowful, and dying men, who live in pride, envy, and malice, 'hateful and hating one another.'"[34]

How Sherburne and Andros came to terms with their time on the *Jersey* does not make them better or worse observers than other prisoners. Both supply supporting details that are corroborated by numerous contemporary witnesses. Sherburne's account contains particularly vivid and believable descriptions of foul water, disgusting food, absurd overcrowding, vermin, disease, and grievous suffering (such as the man whose feet were so badly frozen that when the dressings were changed, "I saw the toes and bottom of his feet cleave off from the bone, and hang down by the heel"). Andros writes convincingly about the terror he felt at night as a prisoner, confined in utter darkness with hundreds of other sick and desperate men—men fighting over scraps of food, men driven mad by ship fever, men dying.

Not so evident is the truthfulness of Albert Greene's *Recollections of the Jersey Prison Ship; taken . . . from the original manuscript of the late Captain Thomas Dring* (1829). Greene's preface explains that in 1824, the retired captain had begun jotting down his memories of the *Jersey*. After Dring's death the following year, Greene—a Providence antiquarian, poet, and collector—acquired his memoranda. He saw the potential for a book, but because Dring's material consisted of "interesting facts, thrown together without much regard to style or to chronological order," he first had to rewrite and reorganize everything, taking "full liberty . . . with the language and arrangement of the narrative" yet (he said) altering nothing of significance. The result of these labors was what has since become a standard source of information about the *Jersey*, reprinted at least a half-dozen times over the past 175 years. On close inspection, however, the book looks more like an exercise in the artful elaboration of memory, far enough removed from the events it describes that its veracity was in little danger of contradiction.[35]

Greene's arrangement of Dring's material owed much to Freneau's epic poem, "The British Prison Ship." After organizing Dring's notes into twenty-one chapters, Greene introduced almost all of them with stanzas from Freneau's work and then, like Freneau (and indeed Allen), presented Dring's captivity as an instructional rather than transformational experience. Grinding hunger, squalor, disease, and brutality do not change the American: he remains a patriot from first to last, true to the cause, steadfast and unbroken. What sees him through is not God's abiding love but the anger and resentment he cultivates for the "cruel tyrants, to whose petty sway we were subjected on board this hulk," none worse than Commissary Sproat, "universally detested for the cruelty of his conduct and the insolence of his manners."[36]

Yet Greene also injected Dring's story with an evangelical sensibility that was utterly foreign to Allen or Freneau and probably intended to find favor with the same readers who bought Sherburne's *Memoirs*. In the chapter on "our orator," for example, Dring supposedly recalls a sailor named Cooper, who delivered impromptu Sunday morning sermons to the prisoners assembled on the spar deck. Cooper lectured the men about the necessity of cleanliness and warned them about the sins of drunkenness and theft. He also told the men "that our present torments in that abode of misery were a proper retribution for our former sins and transgressions; that Satan had been permitted to send out his messengers and inferior demons in every direction to collect us together; and that among the most active of these infernal agents was *David Sproat, Commissary of Prisoners*." There is nothing remotely like this in Freneau or Allen, for whom the rigors of captivity are a manifestation of British cruelty, not divine displeasure, and the enemy is barbaric but never *satanic*. Moreover, no other prisoner on the *Jersey* ever mentioned this young sailor from Virginia or his preaching. Sherburne and later Andros would surely not have forgotten such a character, or anyone remotely like him. It is highly suspicious, too, that the "orator" concludes his sermon by prophesying that the bones of those who had already "paid the debt of nature" would be gathered up and properly buried, their grave site marked by a monument. "I have myself lived to see his predictions verified," Dring then asserts solemnly. "Those bones have been collected; those rites have been performed; that monument has been raised." No such monument existed, of course, outside the dreams of old Tammany hands who could remember the Grand Funeral Procession of 1808.[37]

Additional reasons to question the authenticity of Dring's "memory" can be found in his description of how her prisoners drew up and enforced a code of laws "chiefly directed to the preservation of personal cleanliness, and to the prevention of immorality." Alexander Sherburne, who had also spent time in Mill prison, said that the Americans there "adventured to form themselves into a republic, framed a constitution and enacted wholesome laws, with suitable penalties." Other Mill prisoners also mention the existence of this "constitution." Yet of the many surviving accounts of life on the *Jersey*, only Greene's *Recollections of the Jersey* credits her prisoners with managing their internal affairs in such a manner. Dring had died before Sherburne's book appeared, but Greene could well have come across it before finishing his work with Dring's disorganized notes, and the odds are that he liked the idea of prisoner self-government too much to pass up.[38]

Some details concerning the layout of the *Jersey* and (as of 1782) the prisoners' daily routine almost certainly reflect Dring's own experience rather than Greene's literary ambitions. Dring has a lot to say, too, about the Working Party, twenty-odd men detailed every day to empty the waste tubs, swab the decks, go ashore for fresh water, and bury the dead. Only someone speaking from firsthand knowledge would think to mention that this was a coveted assignment because it gave the men more opportunity to move around and set foot on dry land, even briefly. Also credible, and for similar reasons, are the narrator's remarks about the "thievish" nurses who attended the sick, about the "continual noises" at night of men quarreling and dying, about the "nauseous and putrid atmosphere" below the hatches, about the lice covering their clothes and bodies.[39]

That *Recollections of the Jersey* probably borrowed bits and pieces from Sherburne seems especially ironic because the autobiographical *The Adventures of Ebenezer Fox, in the Revolutionary War* (1838) borrows liberally in turn from Greene's work. Though in his mid-seventies, Fox claimed to have a perfect memory for his experiences during the war. Yet the fifty-odd pages he devotes to his months aboard the *Jersey* follow Dring like a shadow—virtually word for word in places. The results sometimes verge on the comical. At one point, Fox

unwittingly appropriated lines of verse most likely written by Greene
to dress up Dring's manuscript. At another, he repeats Greene's mis-
informed history of the *Jersey*. At still another, he paraphrased Dring's
story of how the prisoners drafted a memorial to Washington, pleading with him to exchange military for naval prisoners—an event, it
may be recalled, that did not take place until June 1782, at least six
months *after* Fox left the ship.[40]

Even if Fox's memories of the *Jersey* were often secondhand, however, a careful reading of his *Revolutionary Adventures* will discover little details clearly drawn from his own experience. Thus he reports
how, to eat the old biscuits that passed for food, he writes, the prisoners learned to rap them sharply on the deck first in order to dis-
lodge the worms. His lively descriptions of several semi-successful
escape attempts—one of which left him with a permanent scar from a
guard's cutlass—also have the solid ring of authenticity. More con-
vincing yet was his pained explanation of how he got off the *Jersey* by
enlisting with the enemy. Although Greene has Dring declare that he
"never knew a single instance of enlistment from among the prisoners of the *Jersey*," Fox ruefully admitted that "high sentiments of
honor could not well exist in the poor, half-famished prisoners." After
much discussion, he and other young men resolved to enlist. "Situated as we were," he remembered, "there appeared to us to be no
moral turpitude in enlisting in the British service"—a decision they
regretted for the rest of their lives. "We thought the end justified the
means," he wrote sadly, the shame of it still hot fifty years later. "How
often did we afterwards lament that we had ever lived to see this hour!
how often did we regret that we were not in our wretched prison-ship
again or buried in the sand at the Wallabout!"[41]

In New York City, the impulse to preserve the memory of the prisons
and prison ships of the Revolutionary War quickened again after
1830, revived this time by the inexorable elimination of houses,
churches, and public buildings connecting residents to their history.
An early casualty of the process had been the old city hall at the intersection of Broad and Wall streets, which came down shortly after
completion of the new City Hall in 1812. The provost marshal's gaol,

which stood at the northeast corner of what residents now called City Hall Park, was completely rebuilt in 1830 to serve as the municipal Hall of Records. The Bridewell, which presided over the northwest corner of the park, fell to the wreckers in 1838. To the dismay of Grant Thorburn, Livingston's old sugar house on Liberty Street came down in 1840 to make way for dull stores and commercial buildings. The Middle Dutch church—first used as a prison, then as a riding academy for British officers—was gutted and renovated in 1844 to serve as the city's main post office; it finally came down entirely in 1882. Van Cortlandt's sugar house, which had also held hundreds of American captives, disappeared in 1852. Brick Presbyterian Church on Beekman Street, used both as a prison and as a hospital, followed in 1858. The North Dutch Church on William Street, yet another prison, was badly damaged by fire in 1869 and would be demolished a half dozen years later. Well before the outbreak of the Civil War in 1861, the city where thousands of Americans perished in enemy hands had all but vanished.[42]

Among Manhattan's respectable classes, the sense of displacement and loss induced by this upheaval was expressed as a deep yearning for Old New York—a tidy, prelapsarian village governed by Protestant gentlemen of Anglo-Dutch extraction, untroubled by immigrants, labor strife, or the tasteless materialism of the nouveaux-riche. The patriots who died by the thousands in the city's Revolutionary War prisons were now remembered all over again—rediscovered not as models of plebeian devotion to republicanism (the Tammany formula), still less as evidence of God's grace (the evangelical formula), but as symbols of a lost heroic era. Well-to-do residents scrambled to acquire souvenirs from old buildings that once housed prisoners. While the demolition of the Liberty Street sugar house was under way, for example, collectors and other "persons of antiquarian taste" swarmed over the site in search of mementos. Salvaged timbers were cut up for walking sticks and became artifacts to be treasured in local families like pieces of the True Cross. It was reported that one genteel scavenger, "fond of revolutionary memorials, yet keeps as a precious relic the window-shutter which his unfortunate countrymen were accustomed daily to unhinge and use as a checker-board to while away the tedious hours of durance."[43]

Bourgeois nostalgia for the forgotten patriots of New York also fu-
eled one of the earliest historic preservation battles in the city. It
began in 1852, when James Boorman, a native of England who had
become a prominent downtown property owner, spearheaded a drive
to extend Albany Street east through Trinity churchyard to Broadway.
There it would connect with Pine Street, opening up a new crosstown
link between the Hudson and East rivers—highly desirable, Boorman
argued, for relieving the congestion in Manhattan's business district
as well as pumping up the value of his own holdings nearby. The
Hudson River Railroad, of which Boorman just happened to be president, endorsed the idea on the grounds that a spur along the Albany
Street extension would give suburban commuters a quicker ride to
Wall Street.[44]

New Yorkers had never seen anything quite like the furor that
Boorman unwittingly touched off. At a City Hall rally in June 1852,
residents turned out by the hundreds to hear speakers condemn the
Albany Street extension because it would disturb the grave sites of
Revolutionary War prisoners, most of whom perished in the nearby
sugar house on Liberty Street. This is "peculiarly consecrated
ground, emphatically holy, and the many memories associated with it
truly sacred," declared one participant. A resolution was adopted urging the vestry of Trinity Church to erect a long-overdue memorial in
the prisoners' memory. The vestry readily agreed and shortly thereafter hired the architectural firm of Willis and Dudley to design a
monument. Work got under way the following year on a site in the
northeast corner of the churchyard—directly in the path of the proposed Albany Street extension. If ever there was evidence that acts of
commemoration can spring from complicated motives, this is it.[45]

Boorman denied that any Revolutionary War prisoners were buried
in the churchyard and got up a petition to the city council in support
of his proposal. Early in February 1854, the Veteran Corps of 1812
waded into the fight with a petition of its own against the measure.
When the Street Committee of the city council began hearings on the
matter, City Hall was packed with spectators for days on end, among
them "Crazy Kate," described by the *Daily Times* as a well-known
"champion for the dead." Colonel Nicholas Haight, an attorney and

head of the Veteran Corps, made a long speech claiming that a third of the signatures on Boorman's petition had been obtained by fraud. Worse yet, Haight declared, Boorman is a foreigner—rich, to be sure, but still not One of Us. "He has no relatives deposited in Trinity Churchyard; he is in no wise connected with the illustrious patriots of our Revolutionary War, whose remains he seeks to scatter to the winds of Heaven. He has not, neither can he have, national feelings in common with us Americans." Although Trinity is the final resting place of "our forefathers," echoed Peter Cutler, attorney for the church, "it is now sought to be taken from us, not by one of ourselves, but by a stranger. One to whom all the glorious associations of our land are unknown, bids us yield up the bones of our fathers to aid him as a legitimate source of profit. Shall we yield? No, no, Sir, never!"[46]

Boorman's opponents had one more card to play. At the end of March they called a meeting at the Broadway Tabernacle "to remonstrate against the violation of the graves, attempted, in the name of 'improvement.'" The cavernous auditorium was packed, and to "frequent applause," resolutions were adopted urging the mayor and aldermen to prevent the Albany Street extension because it would violate a spot "peculiarly dear and venerable to every American heart" as "the last resting place of their revolutionary ancestors." Then down the aisle swept Crazy Kate. "There were no *men* in the City," she cried, evoking loud cheers, "or they would put a stop to it." Fired up by Kate's challenge, the audience agreed to another resolution, this one summoning every "true American" to join a "body-guard to protect the monument erected in Trinity Churchyard, and the ashes of the Revolutionary Soldiers from desecration."[47]

The battle raged on through the summer and fall of 1854. Aldermen grumbled that the monument being erected by Trinity Church was a crass attempt to intimidate municipal authorities. "Their patriotism cannot be considered to be much outraged," one alderman remarked tartly, "when we remember that they have ever since the evacuation of the City by the British army, (more than seventy years ago,) allowed this matter to rest in silence." In the end, though, dead patriots prevailed over live developers. By a vote of thirteen to seven, the city council nixed the Albany Street extension, stopping

The Soldiers' Monument, New York. Erected c. 1854 in the yard of Trinity Church, its Gothic design echoes the spire of the newly rebuilt church (1846). The inscription reads: "Erected to the memory of those brave and good Men who died while imprisoned in this City for their devotion to the cause of American Independence."

Boorman in his tracks. The Soldiers' Monument in Trinity's churchyard still stands, a rather obscure reminder of the American prisoners who perished in occupied New York and the power of historical memory.[48]

The movement that blocked the Albany Street Extension in New York City had no counterpart over in Brooklyn. Although fishermen and picnickers continued to find human remains on the Wallabout beaches, the little vault built for them back in 1808, badly neglected in the interim, had all but collapsed. In 1839, the weed-choked lot on which it stood was sold for taxes to none other than Benjamin Romaine, who at seventy-seven still clung to the hope of erecting a permanent memorial of some kind on the spot. Later that same year Romaine issued an appeal for public contributions, promising his vet-

Romaine's "Antechamber" to the Tomb of the Martyrs. Built c. 1839–1840, it was eight feet square and ten high. The wall of the Navy Yard is in the background. From Benson Lossing, *The Pictorial Field-Book of the Revolution* (1859).

eran's pension of $75 per year toward that goal. To protect the vault in the interim, he covered it with a small wooden building rather grandly described as an "ante-chamber." His efforts generated little interest, however. Following the discovery of more bones at the Navy Yard in 1841, among them a skeleton "with *iron manacles still on the wrist*," a few Brooklyn residents petitioned the state legislature to find a better site for a monument. Romaine, who now wanted to have himself interred in the vault as well, refused to cooperate, stating that only the federal government could have the bones, and after he died in 1844, his executors scrupulously followed his wishes.[49]

That Brooklyn's prison ship martyrs did not entirely disappear from view at this point was primarily due to the efforts of Walt

Whitman, a Long Island native who became editor of the *Brooklyn Daily Eagle* in 1846, shortly before his twenty-seventh birthday. Whitman had grown up at a time when people on the Island still talked bitterly about British atrocities during the long occupation, and every family seemed to remember a husband, son, or father lost in the Battle of Brooklyn, aboard the *Jersey*, or in one of the sugar houses. Steeped in this oral tradition, Whitman became convinced that a permanent memorial to the Wallabout martyrs was a gesture essential to national unity because it would keep the founding generation securely linked to all those that followed. That nothing had been done was scandalous. As he observed ruefully in an ode prepared for the 1846 Independence Day festivities, "Nor prayers, tears, or stones, / Marked their crumbled-in coffins, their white, holy bones!"[50]

By the summer of 1847, Whitman seemed to be getting somewhere with his editorials calling for the erection of a martyrs' monument. A citizens committee chaired by General Jeremiah Johnson, with Whitman acting as secretary, sprang into action. It issued a statement to the effect that commemorating the deaths of more than 11,500 American prisoners in Wallabout Bay was now a matter of national significance, "as well on account of the unparalleled sufferings and glorious constancy of the deceased, as of their numbers, which far exceeded the total loss of the American arms in all the various battles of the revolution." The committee proposed that a suitable monument be located in the recently established Washington Park (now Fort Greene Park), "upon whose green height they may have gazed, as, for the last time, they trod the deck of the doomed and deadly prison ships."[51]

But Romaine's executors still refused to let go of the bones, and after Whitman left the *Eagle* in 1848, the campaign fizzled out. At least twice in the 1850s new civic organizations sprang up to resuscitate support for the monument. Again, however, nothing happened—partly, this time around, because the country was convulsed by sectional strife and rapidly descending into civil war. Romaine's "ante-chamber" was falling apart, too. Vandals had punched holes in the walls, the door had rotted away, and a number of the caskets in the vault appeared to have been broken into. Someone replaced the

The ruined "Antechamber." Already in serious disrepair when the bones were removed from the crypt in 1873, the tumble-down building had become a curiosity twenty years later. From the *Brooklyn Daily Eagle*, Nov. 28, 1897.

broken-down fence around the site to keep out vandals, but the grounds were no better than an overgrown dump—"a place of deposit for the nuisances of the surrounding neighborhood," according to one delicately worded report.[52]

When talk of the long-delayed martyrs' monument in Brooklyn resumed after the Civil War, two things had changed. One was the rapid advance of fashionable row houses and mansions up Clinton Hill toward Washington Park, now well on its way to becoming one of the city's premier residential neighborhoods. The other was the Brooklyn City Council's greater willingness to assume responsibility for municipal improvements that in years past had been either ignored or left to private initiative. In 1864, its park commission hired the renowned architects of New York's Central Park, Frederick Law Olmsted and

Calvert Vaux, to draw up a plan to beautify Washington Park, incorporating within it a mausoleum for the remains of the prison ship martyrs. Strangely, although the mausoleum was unveiled to critical acclaim in 1873, the transfer of the now-famous bones took place without ceremony or even spectators. One morning in mid-June, a pair of large wagons with ten workmen pulled up to Romaine's tumbledown, rat-infested "ante-chamber." They quickly loaded up the bone-filled coffins from the tomb below, drove over to Washington Park, deposited the coffins in the mausoleum, and left. Thus, the *Eagle* reported dryly, "the transfer of the martyrs was accomplished."[53]

For the balance of the nineteenth century, the mausoleum in Washington Park was a focal point of middle- and upper-class patriotic expression in Brooklyn. Veterans, schoolchildren, and hordes of spectators trooped into the park at the end of every May for the observation of Decoration Day, an occasion that always prompted orators to compare the Revolution and the Civil War. ("The horrors of Andersonville were but trifling compared to the sufferings endured and inflicted at the Wallabout." "The Battle of Long Island was the Bull Run of the Revolution.") Another ceremony took place every June 17, the date when the martyrs' bones were laid to rest in the mausoleum. Nothing, though, matched Brooklyn's annual Independence Day festivities, when mammoth crowds converged on the park for concerts, speeches, and all-night fireworks. The 1876 Centennial ceremony, attended by 20,000 spectators, offered such diverse attractions as a chorus singing "Hail Atlantic" in German, 100 minute guns firing an hour-long salute, and a "huge pyrotechnic piece on the crest of the hill [that] blazed out a myriad spouting jets and bouqets of flame from which appeared the motto, 'Let us Give Thanks for Liberty.'"[54]

But the Wallabout martyrs still needed a proper memorial. As it happened, a committee of prominent citizens had already been created by the mayor for that very purpose, and in 1877 they urged Congress to appropriate $50,000 for a "monumental column" in Washington Park as a symbol of national reconciliation and unity. "These patriots belonged to every State, the North and the sunny South equally contributed their sons to the sacrifice. They died side by side," the committee averred. Perhaps the experience of Civil War could succeed where nostalgia alone had failed.[55]

Congress balked, but the monument campaign steamed on under the direction of a new group, the Society of Old Brooklynites, founded in 1880. Its 200-plus members, who were required to have lived in Brooklyn for at least forty years, devoted themselves to the work of drafting resolutions, spreading the prison ship story in books and articles, and organizing patriotic events. In 1888 the society sent Congress yet another petition for the Wallabout monument, said to be a mile in length and intended to bear over 30,000 signatures. That December, every member of Congress received a copy of the society's new booklet, *A Christmas Reminder. Being the Names of About Eight Thousand Persons, a Small Portion of the Number Confined on Board the British Prison Ships During the War of the Revolution*. Compiled from the logs of the *Jersey* that survived in British archives, the names were alleged to represent "every nationality in Christendom—Germans, French, Spanish, Irish, Scotch and English and not a few Dutch. Some of the names in after years became Presidents of this republic—Adams, Jackson; others were members of the Cabinet, the Senate, congressmen, brave generals, governors, members of both houses in every State in the Union."[56]

Nothing seemed to work. Repeatedly, though always by narrow majorities, Congress declined to appropriate money for what was considered a purely local undertaking. As a result, by the mid-nineties the Old Brooklynites found themselves yielding control of the project to two bigger, more dynamic, and nationally based groups, the Daughters of the American Revolution (DAR) and the DAR's rival, the Daughters of the Revolution (DR), both of them organized in 1890 and both aggressively interested in the Martyrs' Monument. As early as 1891, the *Eagle* concluded that the DAR in particular, "this great and growing organization of noble American women," would succeed where the doddering Old Brooklynites had failed. The paper had it right. By 1896 the DAR was mobilizing national support for new appropriations bills in the state legislature as well as in Congress. Two years later the DR and DAR jointly convened a summit confer-ence of Brooklyn patriotic groups, among them the Society of Old

Brooklynites, the Founders and Patriots Society, the Little Men and Women of '76, the Sons of the Revolution, and the Sons of the American Revolution. Out of this coalition emerged an umbrella organization, the Prison Ship Martyrs' Monument Association of the United States. Though comprising men as well as women, the DAR's flagship presence was unmistakable.[57]

As luck would have it, the work of the prison ship monument association received a timely boost in January 1900 when workmen at the Navy Yard uncovered parts of better than 100 skeletons presumed to be those of Revolutionary War prisoners—the biggest such cache in nearly a century. The association immediately announced its intention to use the bones for "special patriotic observances" that would increase the pressure on Congress to fund the Martyrs' Monument. The date chosen was June 16, the 125th anniversary of the Battle of Bunker Hill and one day shy of the twenty-seventh anniversary of the 1873 interment. Demonstrating the reach of its ambitions as well as its connections, the association sent invitations to a swarm of dignitaries, among them the governors of the original thirteen states, top generals and admirals, cabinet members, and assorted members of Congress.[58]

The scene that unfolded on the appointed day was, as an *Eagle* reporter put it, "most impressive." It began at around two in the afternoon at the Navy Yard, when six flag-draped coffins full of bones were carried between two columns of Marines and lifted onto hearses. Led by the secretary of the navy and accompanied by a band playing dirges, the cortege proceeded slowly through Brooklyn Heights to the Plymouth Church on Hicks Street, where a huge crowd had gathered. After a brief service of worship and speeches, capped by the singing of the "Battle Hymn of the Republic" and "America," pallbearers of the U.S. Navy returned the coffins to the hearses waiting outside as a Marine band played "Nearer My God to Thee." The cortege, escorted by two companies of Marines and an entire regiment of the New York State Militia, then proceeded over to Fort Greene, where the caskets were placed in the mausoleum. The day's events ended with a benediction and a Marine bugler playing "Taps." Overall, the *Eagle* observed, the heavy turnout of public

Burial of the Martyrs. From the *Brooklyn Daily Eagle*, June 17, 1900.

officials and the armed forces "gave the occasion a national aspect" rather than a purely local one. "It would seem that the Prison Ship Martyrs Monument Association has at last enlisted the support of the powers that be and as a result, is likely before a great lapse of time, to secure and erect the great monument which shall fittingly honor the revolutionary dead."[59]

Two years later the Senate and House adopted a joint resolution appropriating $100,000 for the Martyrs' Monument, the funds to be released as soon as the association raised an additional $100,000 from other sources. Fast on the heels of this triumph came news that workmen at the Navy Yard had found timbers of the old *Jersey* herself, buried under fourteen feet of silt. Although recovering the ship, or what remained of her, proved impracticable, the excitement generated by the discovery got the association's fund-raising campaign off to a rip-roaring start. It met its goal by 1904 and proceeded to adopt a plan for the monument submitted by Stanford White, of the famed architectural firm of McKim, Mead and White.

White's plan required substantial, time-consuming alterations to the site laid out in 1873 by Olmstead and Vaux, but everything was

ready for the cornerstone of the monument itself to be laid in a ceremony on October 26, 1907. Stephen V. White, president of the
prisoners monument association, used the occasion to review the
"concentrated fiendishness" with which the British treated their prisoners in New York during the Revolutionary War. It was "the shame
of the Anglo-Saxon race." For Governor Charles Evans Hughes, the
soon-to-be-completed monument was a "memorial of devotion" that
will prompt future generations to show "that same spirit, that same
readiness to sacrifice, that same devotion to ideals which conquers all
thoughts of personal comfort or of individual achievement, that same
intense love of liberty and of our institutions which gave us the hero-
ism of the Prison Martyrs."[60]

The climactic moment came with the monument's formal unveiling on November 14, 1908, almost precisely 100 years after the
Tammany Society's Grand Funeral Procession. At 1 P.M., in a bone-
chilling drizzle, an enormous parade got under way from the intersection of Bedford and Division avenues, just east of the Navy Yard
near the Brooklyn approach to the Williamsburg Bridge. The line
of march included detachments of soldiers, sailors, Civil War veterans, mounted police, patriotic societies, civic organizations, and
marching bands—15,000 people in all, spilling down Bedford to
Lafayette Avenue, while tens of thousands of cheering onlookers
lined the sidewalks, oblivious to the weather. At Lafayette, the column turned west toward South Oxford Street, a mile away, then
swung up Oxford, past elegant brownstones, toward De Kalb Avenue on the south side of Fort Greene. From there it circled round
to the west and entered the park, where a crowd of some 20,000
spectators had been gathering since noon. Seated in a grandstand
near the monument itself were members of the Martyrs' Monument Association, the Daughters of the American Revolution, the
Old Brooklynites, and several grand sachems of the Tammany Society, who brought with them the *"Mortals avaunt!"* banner from
the 1808 procession. The dignitaries on the speakers' stand included President-elect William H. Taft, Governor Charles Evans
Hughes, the governors of New Jersey and Delaware, the secretary
of war, and assorted clergy.[61]

The Prison Ship Martyr's Monument, photographed for the Program of Dedicatory Ceremonies (Brooklyn, 1908).

Around three o'clock, as the rain became a mixture of sleet and snow and marchers continued to pour into the park, Taft rose to deliver the principal address. The president-elect delivered a surprisingly frank denunciation of British "cruelty and neglect, . . . outrageous and indefensible cruelty, . . . revolting to every instinct of human nature," the *New York Times* reported. Taft did not believe the death of thousands of helpless American prisoners to have been *intentional* or *premeditated*—"such a charge would make the British commanders human monsters"—but the officers in charge clearly failed in their duty "to protect the human beings whose lives, as they must have known, were being sacrificed from day to day by the awful environment in which they were compelled to live." All the more reason, then, to honor the victims of this outrage for their heroic fidelity to the Revolution. With "very few exceptions," Taft concluded, they "preferred the death which was present to them every day in their lives upon these prison ships, to the dishonor of deserting the cause of their country." The Martyrs' Monument is both a reminder to the living of the gratitude due these thousands of unknown men and "an inspiration to future unselfish and unheralded sacrifice to maintain our institutions of liberty and civilization."[62]

When Taft returned to his seat, the large flag covering the monument, a 149-foot Doric column, reputed to be the tallest in the world, slowly descended. "The people rose and men began to take off their hats. In a few seconds a great multitude of bare-headed men stood and watched the unveiling and paid no heed to the sleet that was beating down upon them."[63]

EPILOGUE

Forgotten Again

The swell of patriotic feeling at the dedication of the Prison Ship Martyrs' Monument in 1908 receded quickly. Like the Grand Funeral Procession a century earlier, it would be followed by decades during which Revolutionary War prisoners more or less disappeared from historical memory. This latest blackout stemmed, in large part, from the increasingly common assumption that the world's English-speaking peoples must rally around the values and institutions distinguishing them from the allegedly uncivilized hordes of Eastern Europe, Asia, and Africa. In time, wrote one prominent historian, we will come to see independence as "the temporary separation of two kindred peoples" and British mistreatment of American prisoners during the Revolutionary War as an unfortunate lapse. Harping on it seemed rather, well, *churlish*, even—oddly—unpatriotic. The prisons and prison ships of New York were real enough, but they also belonged to a now-closed chapter in the national narrative that only rabid Anglophobes would wish to reopen.[1]

Federalists had made a similar point very early in the nineteenth century, ridiculing Tammany's interest in the Wallabout bones as a cynical ploy to mobilize support for another war with Great Britain. Alexander Graydon, himself a Federalist as well as a former prisoner, warned on the eve of the War of 1812 that a blanket indictment of the British as "monsters of unheard of cruelty" would cause the United States "to reject the aid of the only nation upon earth which has power to rescue us from impending perdition"—by which he meant an alliance with Napoleonic France. In any event, Graydon added, even though the suffering of the prisoners in New York was no doubt "shocking to humanity," few Americans had been "so hysterically alarmed" by the experience "as to be unable to forgive" or had "incurred disgraces which can only be washed out and avenged by the common destruction of our old enemy and ourselves."[2]

Long after the Federalists left the stage, a handful of historians and antiquarians continued to worry that reviving the story of Revolutionary War prisoners might get in the way of Anglo-American rapprochement. In 1856, George Coggeshall's *History of the American Privateers* challenged the conventional emphasis on British cruelty by assuring readers that not everyone in that "great, powerful, enlightened, Christian, and brave nation" was equally to blame for what happened on the Wallabout prison ships. Ten years later, in his monumental *History of the City of Brooklyn*, Henry Stiles went so far as to propose that unruly, uncooperative American prisoners often drove their guards to acts of cruelty and were thus "accountable, to a considerable extent, for much of their own suffering." They were certainly *not* the victims of "systematic aggravations practised by a great and civilized Government." Besides, Stiles mused, "Charity forbids that Vengeance should dictate the record against those who—however harshly their actions may be judged by man—have gone to receive their judgment before a Superior Tribunal." In 1909, David Sproat's biographer pooh-poohed the evidence of abuse on the prison ships as "largely the unproved charges of early writers and tradition founded on the bitter feeling of the day." Danske Dandridge's *American Prisoners of the Revolution* (1911)—a miscellany of excerpts from contemporary sources—likewise opened with a hands-across-the-sea vow that she had no desire to continue pointless recriminations or "excite animosity against a people whose blood is in our veins."[3]

By the end of the nineteenth century, public opinion also began tilting in favor of the idea that nursing a hundred-year-old grudge against Great Britain no longer served any productive purpose. Thomas Janvier's *In Old New York* (1894), an elegiac memoir of colorful neighborhoods and buildings, acknowledged "the truly horrible cruelties" inflicted on American prisoners in the city but hastened to add that it was no longer necessary to dwell on such unpleasantness. "Sleeping dogs of so ugly a sort very well may lie," he advised. The people of New York, Janvier added, had already put the prisoner-abuse issue behind, for "whatever was the sum of this particular score against Great Britain we wrote it off the books forever on the 28th of April of the year 1893: when the sailors of Queen Victoria—marching where no armed Englishman has marched since November 25, 1783—were cheered to the echo from the doors and windows of the very building in which American patriots were dealt with most foully by the servants of that gracious woman's graceless grandfather, King George the Third."

When a British naval squadron visited New York a dozen years later, New Yorkers celebrated again. Gushed one orator: "On public buildings, in banquet halls, and upon the men-of-war, the American and British flags have inter-twined and good-fellowship and fraternal feeling have been manifested on every side." The city's Evacuation Day festivities every November, which marked the departure of the last British troops from the city on November 25, 1783, drew ever smaller crowds. In 1902, only a solitary groundskeeper hoisted the flag in Battery Park. Several patriotic organizations struggled to keep the holiday alive, but to no avail. Its last observance took place in 1916, when sixty old men dressed in Revolutionary War uniforms rode the subway down to the Battery for a brief flag-raising ceremony.[4]

On April 6, 1917, Congress declared war on Germany, and the United States, in the 141st year of its independence, became Great Britain's defacto ally. Prompted by the Anglophobia simmering among Americans of Irish or German descent, and under intense pressure from President Woodrow Wilson, Congress quickly followed up the declaration of war with passage of the Espionage Act. This harsh and sweeping measure made it a federal offense—punishable by death or by a stiff fine and up to thirty years in jail—to publish or utter anything that would tend to aid the enemy, interfere with recruiting, or promote insubordination and disloyalty in the armed forces. The Sedition Act of 1918 would extend these provisions to prohibit "disloyal, profane, scurrilous, or abusive language" about the government.

A wave of prosecutions ensued, leaving no doubt that the Wilson administration intended to suppress all antiwar and anti-British feeling in the country. Hundreds of radicals went to prison, and seventy-five newspapers, many written for German-American or Irish-American audiences, were either banned from the mails or forced to stop publishing war news. British propaganda mills meanwhile flooded the United States with lurid descriptions of German war crimes, paeans to Anglo-Saxon democracy, and amiable references to the American Revolution (one writer dubbed it "a single regrettable incident" caused by "the most muddle-headed ministry that ever mismanaged the affairs of Great Britain"). In books, pamphlets, lectures, and college classrooms, leading academic historians encouraged Americans to see that their ancient animosity for the British stemmed from "ignorance and prejudice." Publishers scrambled to "correct" the nation's history texts accordingly, rewriting passages that seemed critical of Britain or had good things to say about Germany. In New York, the annual observance of Evacuation Day was quietly discontinued.[5]

The danger of recollecting British atrocities during the Revolution became apparent only a month after the U.S. declaration of war, when a fourteen-reel epic film, *The Spirit of '76*, premiered in Chicago. Robert Goldstein, the film's producer, had envisioned it as an ultra-patriotic blockbuster comparable to D. W. Griffith's *Birth of a Nation* (1915), and he foresaw nothing problematical about reminding Americans of their struggle for independence from Britain. "The modern American public," he explained, "do not connect the England of 1776 with the modern British Empire."

Despite rave reviews in the Chicago press, however, the movie's over-the-top scenes of British brutality—a baby impaled on an officer's bayonet; girls dragged off by the hair to a fate worse than death—raised questions about Goldstein's commitment to the war effort. Rumors skittered through the motion picture industry that he was in fact a German agent. Soon after the Los Angeles opening, in late November 1917, federal marshals seized all prints under the Espionage Act, then arrested Goldstein for fomenting "hatred of England and England's soldiers," interfering with the draft, inciting mutiny in the armed forces, and conspiracy to commit treason. While the hapless producer awaited trial in the county jail, his production company sued the government for return of the film. An unsympathetic district court judge, Benjamin Franklin Bledsoe, turned them down with a stern rebuke: no matter that "we were at war with Great Britain during the Revolutionary times. . . . This is no time . . . for the exploitation of those things that may have the tendency . . . of sowing dissension among our people and of creating animosity or want of confidence between us and our allies."

In April 1918, arguments in the aptly titled case of *United States v. "The Spirit of '76"* got under way in Los Angeles. Two weeks later, the jury found Goldstein guilty on all counts except conspiracy to commit treason. Judge Bledsoe sentenced the producer to ten years in a federal penitentiary and imposed a fine of $5,000. Goldstein's mistake, the judge observed caustically, was that he "sought to arouse enmity against Great Britain by seeking to prove that one hundred years ago that nation had been guilty of the same class of atrocities as are now charged against the detestable Huns."[6]

Although *The Spirit of '76* did not depict British mistreatment of American prisoners during the Revolutionary War, Goldstein's fate underscored that this was a bad time to raise so awkward a subject. The one historian who did so, Eugene Armbruster, maintained that the story had been blown out of all proportion. We can now see, Armbruster wrote in *The Wallabout Prison Ships* (1920), that what the prisoners at the time *believed* to be "intended cruelty" mostly stemmed from unavoidable circumstances. Indeed, at least some sources (Armbruster neglected to say which ones) indicate that conditions aboard British prison ships were not invariably horrible. Many contemporary reports were deliberate falsehoods, he added, and large numbers of Americans escaped by bribing their guards, who then reported them dead. All told, the number of Americans who perished on the *Jersey* and other ships could not have exceeded 7,000.[7]

Timing is everything. Had Goldstein waited until after the war to release *The Spirit of '76*, he might never have been accused of peddling enemy propaganda. In fact, he might have found vocal allies in the loose coalition of groups—old-stock patriotic societies, nativists, and the Ku Klux Klan, among others—who mobilized in the 1920s to stem the rising tide of pro-British feeling in the country. Their primary targets were what they considered "unpatriotic" textbooks such as David S. Muzzey's *An American History*, first published in 1911, which appeared to have replaced the heroic narrative of the nation's founding with falsehoods and half-truths favoring the British. No more straightforward stories about high-minded patriots and villainous redcoats. Schoolchildren now learned that complex social and economic "forces" pushed the colonies toward independence; that the English actually invented many of the ideals embodied in the Declaration of Independence and the Constitution; that the Founding Fathers were not demigods but real men with real shortcomings. The purpose of these heresies, critics said, was to reverse the outcome of the Revolution, promote Anglo-American union, and bolster the interests of the "international money power," Cecil B. Rhodes, and the Carnegie Foundation. Besides, as an investigatory committee in New York remarked with perfect aplomb, "Truth is no defense to the charge of impropriety."[8]

In 1927, one of the most prominent American historians under attack for Anglophilia, Claude H. Van Tyne, responded to the furor with "The Struggle for Truth About the American Revolution," a lecture he delivered in (of all places) the House of Lords. The issue, as Van Tyne framed it, was clear-cut. On the one hand, "certain racial groups" in America—he meant the Irish and Germans—cling to "the old, unreasoning hate of England," as do "born fundamentalists," who say that "we must not let die the old tradition about barbarous British 'redcoats,' a tyrannical King George, and a wicked Lord North." They all wanted the story of the Revolution to be told "much as the contemporaries had told it, bitterly, with no effort to be impartial or judicial."

On the other hand, Van Tyne continued, "trained researchers" on both sides of the Atlantic, burrowing through the archives in pursuit of objective truth, have now come to "approximate agreements" on the main points and can "discuss all the vital questions in a most harmonious spirit." They agree that "much of the traditional ill-feeling against Great Britain was groundless." Independence was not wildly popular, George III was no tyrant, and the facts "revealed not barbarous cruelty and tyrannous oppression, but divergent influences that shaped the ends to which each country, England and America, was moving." As for the thousands of Americans imprisoned by the British in New York, "Impartial study made it clear that British prisoners-of-war in American hands fared quite as badly as American prisoners in British prison hulks." If both sides were equally guilty of abusing their captives, neither had any grounds for complaint and historians should find better things to talk about.[9]

The textbook wars dragged on for years, but Van Tyne's verdict on the prisoner-of-war story reflected the emerging consensus among his professional colleagues that it was old news, interesting only to narrow-minded *Über*-patriots who recoiled at the idea of Anglo-American comity. Within several years of his address in the House of Lords, two new studies of New York in the Revolution barely mentioned the prisoners' presence in the city at all. In fact, for the next forty years the subject seemed to vanish into some kind of historical wormhole, popping out only when summoned by scholars to demonstrate the baneful effects of "war propaganda." Or as Samuel Eliot Morison wrote dismissively in his biography of John Paul Jones: "The unpleasant subject of the treatment of American naval prisoners during the war afforded fuel for American Anglophobes for a century or more, and there is no point in stirring it up again."[10]

A modest revival of interest in the subject occurred among academic historians in the 1970s, but judging by frequent declarations that the British did no wrong, most if not all writers continued to think of it as highly radioactive. "The British were not guilty of excessive disregard of the welfare of prisoners," one ventured carefully—was there an *appropriate* level of disregard?—"and the conduct of the royal military authorities did not border on criminal action. The traditional view of the British action toward prisoners as being vicious is not just or fair." Another offered: "These men were faced with a number of unpleasant things, but they did not 'suffer' at the hands of the 'British tyrants.'" Contemporary eyewitness reports in newspapers and pamphlets were thrown out of court as completely untrustworthy. Narratives by Jabez Fitch, Ethan Allen, and others were said to be marred by such gross and willful distortions of the truth that they had only limited value as historical sources.[11]

This is a good time, then, to be reminded that the prisons and prison ships of occupied New York City were not in fact the figments of overheated insurgent imaginations—mere war propaganda calculated to inflame public opinion and silence the voice of reason. We hear much nowadays about the wisdom and virtue of the "founding fathers," but the story of those dreadful places obliges us to keep in mind that the success of the Revolution depended on the unheralded spirit, selflessness, and humanity of thousands of people not so very different from ourselves. They were not, for the most part, people inclined to oratory or pamphleteering. Few of them, so far as anyone knows, were especially well off or well read. Many probably did not own enough property to vote. Some were in fact the property of others. Only a handful, one suspects, had ever traveled very far from home before the Sugar House or the Provost or the *Jersey* swallowed them up forever. They rarely spoke more than a word or two about why they fought, or what cause they were so willing to die for, except to say that it was to defend "their country" against a mighty and proud invader that held them in utter contempt. The nation they created in that war has changed profoundly since they were here—not least of all because its great wealth and power have put us at risk of becoming the kind of enemy they laid down their lives to overcome.

ACKNOWLEDGMENTS

Nothing lightens the load of research and writing more than the friends who can be imposed upon to read and critique drafts in various stages of disrepair. On my list are Laura Chmielewski, Kevin Dreyfuss, Mary Gallagher, Don Gerardi, Andy Goodspeed, Graham Hodges, Peter Hoffer, Bob Mutch, Marilyn Pettit, Barney Schecter, Gunja Sen Gupta, David Troyansky, and Jocelyn Wills. Mike Wallace, though immersed in writing the sequel to *Gotham*, was exceptionally generous with his time, encouragement, and unrivalled knowledge of New York City history. I am much indebted to Paul Goodspeed, who read several incarnations of the manuscript with great care and gratifying enthusiasm. Special thanks as well to Josephine DeCicco, my very capable research assistant, for her dedication and hard work. All of these folks did what they could to make *Forgotten Patriots* a better book, and I hope they will recognize the fruits of their labors.

For their continued interest, advice, and willingness to field queries without complaint, I am also deeply grateful to Kathleen Axen, Cathy Ball, Swapna Banerjee, Dan Conaway, Bob Doyle, John Duffy, Chris Ebert, Firth Fabend, Robert Fippinger, Bunny Gabel, Dan Gabel, John Glynn, Ken Hannigan, Toby Harshaw, Irma Jaffe, Ann Kaplan, Richard Mooney, Phil Napoli, Kristen Nyitray, Stuart and Nancy Rabinowitz, Linda Reno, Jessica Roe, Alexander Rose, and Nadezhda Williams. Sherry Warman, interlibrary loan supervisor of the Brooklyn College Library, proved extremely helpful by tracking down innumerable hard-to-find books and articles. I am thankful as well for the help I received at the David Library of the American Revolution, the Brooklyn Historical Society, the William L. Clements Library, the New York Public Library (Rare Books and Manuscripts Division), the New-York Historical Society, the Museum of the City of New York, the Henry Sheldon Museum of Vermont History, the Hofstra University Library, the Smithtown (New York) Public Library, and the Northport (New York) Public Library. I am also pleased to acknowledge that my research and writing was facilitated by an NEH Summer Stipend as well as by a grant from the Wolfe Institute at Brooklyn College.

Lara Heimert, my editor at Basic Books, deserves special notice for the wonderful acuity, determination, and good humor with which she steered the manuscript through final revisions. Brandon Proia, Lara's assistant, and Sandra Beris, the project manager, get a tip of the hat as well for keeping everything moving along, on time and on course. I am also profoundly indebted to Sam Stoloff of the Frances Goldin Literary Agency for his steady commitment to the project and watching my back when it needed watching.

Forgotten Patriots is dedicated to my wife, Pat Adamski, and to our two children, Matt and Kate, whose love and support make everything worthwhile.

APPENDIX A

Counting Calories

British officials always insisted that American prisoners received two-thirds of the rations provided British seamen and soldiers. In a letter to Washington on January 19, 1778, General Howe declared that his troops consumed seven pounds of bread and seven of beef per week, supplemented by what were called "small species"—four ounces of butter or cheese, eight ounces of oatmeal, three pints of peas, and perhaps a few ounces of rice, if available (*The Papers of George Washington* 13: 280–282). The energy potential of such a diet comes to roughly 2,460 kilocalories per day:[1]

	Full Ration/Week	*Kcal/Gram*	*Total Kcal/Week*
Bread	7 lb. (3,175g)	2.54	8,064
Beef	7 lb. (3,175g)	2.00	6,350
Butter	0.25 lb. (113g)	6.78	766
Oatmeal, uncooked	0.5 lb. (227g)	4.17	947
Peas, uncooked	3 pints (800g)	0.84	672
White rice, uncooked	0.25 lb. (113g)	3.70	418
TOTAL			17,217
			(2,460/day)

Obviously it is impossible to measure the energy content of these foods with precision, as their composition and quality necessarily varied by season, region, and supplier. Bread made of oat bran, for example, has less energy potential (2.36 kcal/gram) than wheat bread (2.54 kcal/gram), whereas rye bread has more than

251

either (2.58 kcal/gram). I assumed that soldiers were more likely to eat bread made of wheat. In the case of beef, the energy content varies so widely—from, say, lightly trimmed shoulder (1.59 kcal/gram) to a blade roast (2.54 kcal/gram)—that I have arbitrarily adopted a middle-range figure of 2.00 kcal/gram. In any case, all these figures are probably high, because the freshest, highest-quality foods were likely as not reserved for officers or were appropriated by cooks and quartermasters—or never reached the army in the first place. Small wonder that soldiers without the means to buy additional food in local markets often resorted to stealing from civilians.

In theory, then, a prisoner on two-thirds rations could expect to consume no more than 1,640 kcal per day, at best. If that prisoner were twenty-five years old, stood five feet seven inches tall, and weighed 160 pounds, he would need 2,186 kcal every day to maintain his weight when completely sedentary. Bearing in mind that one pound of body weight represents 3,500 kcal, the deficit—roughly 550 kcal per day—would result in the loss of about one pound of body weight per week. If that same prisoner were very active, he would need to consume as much as 3,323 kcal per day to maintain his weight. In that case, the deficit—1,680 kcal per day—would cause him to lose more than *six* pounds a week. Taller and heavier prisoners, having higher energy needs, would lose weight even more rapidly, as would prisoners who were ill or recovering from injuries. But because caloric requirements decline with age, older prisoners would lose weight less quickly. A sedentary fifty-year-old man, standing five feet seven inches tall, needs only 1,895 kcal/day to maintain a weight of 160 pounds.

Even two-thirds of the rations described by Howe were better than the meager provisions supposedly received by the men confined on the *Jersey*, however. As Captain Dawson informed Washington in 1781—and Dawson, it may be recalled, was *boasting*—the weekly food allowance for naval prisoners in New York was 66 ounces of bread, 43 ounces of pork, 22 ounces of butter, and 2 pints of oatmeal (*The Papers of George Washing*, Library of Congress). As before, calculating the energy potential of these foods involves a good deal of guesswork.

It is nonetheless apparent that men consigned to the Wallabout hulks fared even more poorly than their compatriots in the Sugar House or the Provost:

	Weekly Ration	Kcal/Gram	Total Kcal
Bread	66 oz. (1,868g)	2.54	4,744
Beef	43 oz. (1,217g)	2.00	2,434
Pork	22 oz. (623g)	1.98	1,233
Peas	1 1/6 pint (312g)	0.84	262
Oatmeal	2 pints (533g)	4.17	2,223
TOTAL			10,896
			(1,556/day)

Of course, as we have seen over and over again, prisoners rarely if ever received the quantity or quality of rations to which they were supposedly entitled. On the *Jersey* or in the Sugar House, all of them must have lost weight rapidly, some dangerously so. In conjunction with poor to nonexistent sanitation, rapid weight loss accelerated the spread of scurvy, typhus, dysentery, and other diseases. Men who survived even a month under these conditions would have been reduced to listless, vermin-infested skeletons. Few appear to have lasted more than six months, and it was only the rare prisoner who managed to hang on for a year or more. As I have suggested elsewhere, the overall mortality rate was almost certainly in the range of 50 to 70 percent.

APPENDIX B

Cunningham's "Confession"

On Saturday, January 28, 1792, a pair of Philadelphia newspapers, *Dunlap's American Daily Advertiser* and the *Independent Gazetteer and Agricultural Repository*, ran the same 650-word story under an eye-catching headline:

The LIFE, CONFESSION, and LAST
DYING WORDS of
Captain William Cunningham,
formerly the British Provost-Marshal,
in the City of New-York, who was
executed in London, the tenth of
August, 1791: taken from his
own mouth by the ordi-
nary of Newgate.

Captain Cunningham, it emerged, had been hanged for forgery. What was more, on his way to the gallows he admitted to the chaplain (or "ordinary") of Newgate Prison that he was also guilty of committing mass murder during the Revolutionary War in America.[1]

He was born in Dublin in 1738, he explained, the son of a trumpeter attached to a regiment of dragoons in the British Army. The end of the Seven Years' War in 1763 cut short his own career in the military, after which he spent a decade drifting from one Irish city to another, looking for work, fathering children, and trying to stay ahead of the law. At

Newry, he became a "scowbanker," a kind of con artist who enticed workingmen and country folk to emigrate to America as indentured servants. In the summer of 1774, he accompanied a number of his victims to New York, where he thought he might make a go of it as a riding instructor. That plan fell apart early the following year after he tangled with local patriots protesting Britain's colonial policies. "Rendering myself obnoxious to the citizens in their infant struggles for freedom," he told the chaplain, "I was obliged to fly ... to Boston." There, General Thomas Gage of the British Army made him provost marshal with the rank of captain, an appointment that "placed me in a situation to wreak my vengeance on the Americans." And so he did. Over the next seven or eight years, Cunningham's festering hatred led him to kill, by his own count, over 2,000 captured patriots, mainly in New York after the city was seized by British forces in 1776. The great majority were starved to death, "by stopping their rations, which I sold." An additional 275 became the victims of "private executions" that he supervised under cover of darkness outside the Provost:

> a guard was dispatched from the provost, about half after twelve at night, to Barrack-street, and the neighborhood of the Upper barracks, to order the people to shut their window shutters and put out their lights, forbidding them, at the same time, to presume to look out of their windows or doors, on pain of death; after which the unfortunate prisoners were conducted, gagged just behind the Upper Barracks, and hung without ceremony, and there buried by the black pioneer of the provost.[2]

This was the first public acknowledgment of something that Americans had already suspected for years—that the British deliberately killed prisoners in New York City during the Revolution. Not surprisingly, Cunningham's "Confession" caught the eye of editors around the country, who reprinted it so often that it eventually become a fixture of patriotic lore and legend.[3]

Unfortunately, it was a hoax. For one thing, although William Cunningham (and his "black pioneer") were real enough, the calendar of London's Newgate Prison makes no reference to the hanging of anyone named Cunningham, in 1791 or any other year. The so-called Confession does not exactly say that Cunningham *died* at Newgate—only that he told his story to the Newgate ordinary—but it does imply he had left the army by this time, and as a civilian he would not have been hanged anywhere else in London. Nor do the records of the Old Bailey, London's central criminal court, show anyone named William Cunningham brought up on forgery charges during the eighteenth century. Also noteworthy is the complete absence of other contemporary testimony about midnight executions behind the Upper Barracks in New York. Even if area residents were too frightened to say anything, the late-night disappearance of so many prisoners from the Provost—prisoners never seen alive again—would hardly have gone unremarked by their fellow inmates, a number of whom left detailed descriptions of Cunningham's brutality. And then there is the testimony of an old Irish revolutionary named John Binns, who happened to mention in his autobiography that when the British sent him to Gloucester Prison in 1799, the "governor," or warden, there was none other than ... William Cunningham, a retired army officer, "about fifty years of age, five feet seven inches high, well made and well mannered," and still very much alive.[4]

The timing of the alleged "Confession" is suspect, too. A direct voyage from London to Philadelphia in 1792 could take eight to ten weeks as winter came on, meaning that if the "Confession" appeared in print by late August or early September 1791, it might well have reached Philadelphia by, say, the beginning of December, maybe earlier. It seems improbable, though, that two American editors would sit on such a juicy item for so long, then print it on the same day almost two months later. But what if the "Confession" had just arrived and the editors printed it within a day or two? That seems even less probable. Another Philadelphia paper, Claypool's *Daily Advertiser*, revealed on January 27 (i.e., one day before the "Confession" appeared) that "navigation of the Delaware has been for some time past obstructed by ice." So if the "Confession" did not arrive by sea, did it come by land from New York, which often got the news from Europe as much as a week ahead of Philadelphia? Alas, the port of New York, too, had been shut down by ice, apparently for weeks. On January 20, Dunlap's *General*

Advertiser reported that a brig had finally reached New York bearing London papers up to November 16 of the previous year. Judging by extracts printed in the New York papers, however, she appears to have brought no news of importance.[5]

In light of all this, it is hard to resist the conclusion that Cunningham's "Confession" to the murder of American prisoners in New York was concocted by someone in ice-bound Philadelphia, who arranged for it to be published on the same date by two local papers. That someone clearly knew a good deal about Cunningham's background, however, and was also well acquainted with events in both New York and Boston before the Revolution. For example, the "Confession" asserted that Cunningham brought indentured servants to New York from Newry on August 4, 1774, aboard the *Needham*. A ship of that name did arrive in New York on that date, and her master subsequently advertised that he still had "the times of a few [indentured] servants" for sale, along with Irish beef and butter.[6]

There is no reason to believe that the servants in question had been "kidnapped" in Ireland, as the "Confession" alleged, or that they were liberated in New York "on account of the bad usage they received from me during the passage [from Ireland]." But charges of fraud and violence were often levied against recruiters for colonial land developers, and the voyage of the *Needham* was connected with schemes to populate a Champlain Valley settlement owned by the rich and influential Beekman family. Whoever fabricated his "Confession" knew that Cunningham had been mixed up in some rather unsavory business.[7]

As for the contention that Cunningham went up to Boston in 1775 because he had become "obnoxious" to the patriots in New York, that too would appear to contain at least a germ of truth. On Thursday, March 9, 1775, Rivington's *New-York Gazetteer* carried a statement, signed by Cunningham and one John Hill, complaining that the two of them had been roughed up the previous Monday by "a mob of above two hundred men" gathered near the Liberty Pole on the Common (now City Hall Park). "The leader of this mob brought Cunningham under the Liberty Pole, and told him to go down on his knees and damn his Popish King George; and they would then set him free, but on the contrary, he exclaimed, God Bless King George."

Hill did the same, and only the intervention of some passersby, the two men said, saved them from being killed. They had done nothing to deserve this savage treatment "except being on the King's side of the question in the morning"—a reference to the fracas that had erupted a few hours earlier at a public meeting called to discuss the election of delegates to the Second Continental Congress.[8]

Partisan brawls were hardly unusual in pre-Revolutionary New York, but this one seems to have left especially bitter feelings. Eight years later, only months before the last redcoats left the city, papers in Pennsylvania and Connecticut ran an anonymous warning to wealthy and influential Tories that they should depart as well. The writer singled out a pair of New York merchants, the brothers Hugh and Alexander Wallace, for their relationship with the British provost marshal: "Do you imagine," he asked, "that we have forgotten your sending to General Gage for that low-lived bloody-minded villain Cunningham, whom you sent as your gladiator to interrupt our peaceable associations in the commons, and who afterwards you procured to be a provost for the purpose of murdering, with impunity, such of your fellow-citizens as were the most obnoxious to you and your friends[?]" Later that same year, on the other hand, an attainted Tory named John Wetherhead recalled the attack on Cunningham and Hill as a perfect example of how law and order had already broken down in the city by 1775.[9]

Finally, Cunningham's alleged promise to "wreak my vengeance" on patriots in Boston is entirely consistent with contemporary reports of his conduct there. The diary of a young patriot named Peter Edes is a running account of Cunningham's sadistically abusive treatment of Americans confined in the Boston jail over the summer and fall of 1775. In addition to beating and starving the prisoners in his charge, Edes wrote, Cunningham liked to have them kneel in the yard and say, "God Bless the King"—a settling of scores if there ever was one. Of young Edes's twenty-nine cellmates, only eleven survived.[10]

In short, somebody knew enough about Cunningham's career, in Europe as well as in America, to fabricate a "Confession" plausible enough to fool more than a few people over the last 200 years. We will probably never discover his or her identity, but a prime suspect would have to be the man who initially placed it "by particular request" in the

Independent Gazetteer: that paper's colorful owner and editor, Colonel Eleazer Oswald.

Oswald emigrated to New York from England in 1770. He apprenticed himself to John Holt, printer of the *New-York Journal*, married Holt's daughter, and built connections to printers in cities and towns from New England to Virginia. When the war began, he took part in the invasion of Canada and was captured outside Québec in December 1775. Exchanged a year later, Oswald returned to the army as an artillery officer and earned high marks in action at the Battle of Monmouth Court House and elsewhere before resigning his commission in a dispute over seniority. He knew and admired General Charles Lee, and in Philadelphia, where he moved toward the end of the war, Oswald was friendly with Tom Paine, Haym Salomon, and Philip Freneau, among others. As editor of the *Independent Gazetteer*, which he founded there in 1782, he also became renowned for a bare-knuckle style of journalism, including the publication of anonymous libels and off-color parodies, that entangled him in lawsuits, near duels, and a jail sentence. It would be difficult to find anyone else in Philadelphia better equipped, by experience or temperament, to cook up Cunningham's dying "Confession." Oswald had been a prisoner of the British himself, he was in New York when Cunningham had his run-in with the crowd at the Liberty Pole, and he knew people who had plenty to say about Cunningham's career as provost marshal.[11]

Supposing that Oswald did write Cunningham's "Confession," why he wrote it when he did and why he published it in 1792 all remain mysteries for which his subsequent career yields no clues. Six months after it appeared in the *Independent Gazetteer*, he left Philadelphia to volunteer his services to the government of revolutionary France. Through Tom Paine, then in London, he wangled a commission as a colonel of artillery in the French army and later that same year saw action at Jemappes and Liège. Impressed by his zeal, the French sent Oswald on a secret mission to Ireland to investigate the prospects of revolution there. He returned to the United States at the end of 1793 and plunged into the agitation against the Jay Treaty. Two years later he died in New York of yellow fever.[12]

LIST OF ABBREVIATIONS
AND NOTE ON SOURCES

In addition to the archival and published materials identified here, various online sources allowed me to cover a lot of ground very quickly from the comforts of home. HeritageQuest Online, a division of ProQuest, has digitized the microfilm edition of *Revolutionary War Pension and Bounty-Land-Warrant Application Files* (National Archives Publications M804 and M805)—an important and still underutilized trove of information. The *Early American Newspapers Database*, Series I, part of the Readex Digital Collection, makes it possible to search hundreds of eighteenth- and nineteenth-century newspapers in minutes rather than weeks or even months, with a high degree of accuracy. Reconstructing the various efforts to commemorate the prisoners of New York would have been much more time-consuming without the online archives of both the *New York Times* and *Brooklyn Daily Eagle*.

AA Peter Force (comp.), *American Archives*, 9 vols. (Washington, DC, 1837–1853)

AHR *American Historical Review*

AQ *American Quarterly*

BF Benjamin Franklin

BIHR *Bulletin of the Institute of Historical Research*

BHP British Headquarters Papers, New York Public Library

BHS Brooklyn Historical Society

BJ Elias Boudinot, *Journal or Historical Recollections of American Events during the Revolutionary War* (Philadelphia, 1894)

BLB *"Their Distress is almost intolerable": The Elias Boudinot Letterbook, 1777–1778*, ed. Joseph Lee Boyle (Bowie, MD, 2002)

BLL [Boudinot, Elias], *The life, public services, addresses, and letters of Elias Boudinot*, ed. Jane J. Boudinot, 2 vols. (Boston, 1896)

CH *Church History*

CHSC Connecticut Historical Society, *Collections*, 31 vols. (Hartford, CT, 1860–1967)

DAR *Documents of the American Revolution, 1770–1783*, ed. K. G. Davies, Colonial Office Series 12 (Dublin, 1976)

EAL *Early American Literature*

EAS *Early American Studies*

EB Elias Boudinot
EHR *Economic History Review*
GW George Washington
GWP George Washington Papers, Library of Congress
HM *Historical Magazine*
HR *Historical Research*
HSM Henry Sheldon Museum, Middlebury, Vermont
HSP Historical Society of Pennsylvania, Philadelphia
JAH *Journal of American History* [incl. orig. series and successor to MVHR]
JCC *Journals of the Continental Congress*, ed. W. C. Ford, 34 vols. (Washington, DC, 1906) (lcweb2.loc.gov/ammem/amlaw/lwjc.html)
JHG *Journals of Hugh Gaine: Printer*, ed. Paul L. Ford. New York, 1902.
JLIH *Journal of Long Island History*
JMH *Journal of Military History*
JPC *Journals of the Provincial Congress, Provincial Convention, Committee of Safety, and Council of Safety of the State of New York, 1775–1776–1777*, 2 vols. (Albany, 1842)
JSH *Journal of Social History*
JUH *Journal of Urban History*
LC Library of Congress
LDC *Letters of Delegates to Congress, 1774–1789*, ed. Paul H. Smith et al., 26 vols. (Washington, DC, 1976) (lcweb2.loc.gov/ammem/amlaw/lwdg .html)
LIHJ *Long Island Historical Journal*
LLP *Lafayette in the Age of the American Revolution: Selected Letters and Papers, 1776–1790*, ed. Stanley J. Idzerda, 5 vols. (Ithaca, 1977)
LP *The Lee Papers, 1754–1811*, ed. Charles Lee. New-York Historical Society *Collections*, 4–7, 4 vols. (New York, 1872–1875)
MHSC Massachusetts Historical Society, *Collections*
MHSP Massachusetts Historical Society, *Proceedings*
MVHR *Mississippi Valley Historical Review*
NARA National Archives and Records Administration
NDAR *Naval Documents of the American Revolution*
NEQ *New England Quarterly*
NJH *New Jersey History*
NJGC *Selections from the Correspondence of the Executive of New Jersey from 1776 to 1786* (Newark, 1848)
NRAR *New Records of the American Revolution* (London, 1927)
NYGB *The New-York Genealogical and Biographical Record*
NYH *New York History*
NYHC New-York Historical Society, *Collections*
NYHQ *New-York Historical Society Quarterly*
NYPL New York Public Library
P&P *Past and Present*
PA *Pennsylvania Archives*
PAH *The Papers of Alexander Hamilton*, ed. Harold C. Syrett et al., 27 vols. (New York, 1961–1987).
PBF *The Papers of Benjamin Franklin*, ed. Leonard W. Labaree et al., 39 vols. (New Haven, CT, 1959) (http://franklinpapers.org/franklin/)

PCC Papers of the Continental Congress, National Archives

PGC *Public Papers of George Clinton*, ed. Hugh Hastings and J. A. Holden, 10 vols. (Albany, NY, 1899–1914)

PGW *The Papers of George Washington: Revolutionary War Series*, ed. Philander D. Chase et al., 17 vols. (Charlottesville, SC, 1985–2008)

PH *Pennsylvania History*

PHE *The Parliamentary History of England, from the Earliest Period to the Year 1803*, ed. William Cobbett and T. C. Hansard, 36 vols. (London, 1806–1820)

PMHB *Pennsylvania Magazine of History and Biography*

PRC *Public Records of the State of Connecticut*, 16 vols. (Hartford, 1894)

PRO Public Records Office, London

PTJ *The Papers of Thomas Jefferson*, ed. Julian P. Boyd et al. 34 vols. (Princeton, NJ, 1950)

PWD *Papers of the War Department*, Center for History and New Media, George Mason University (http://wardepartmentpapers.org)

PWL *The Papers of William Livingston*, ed. Carl Prince and Dennis P. Ryan, 4 vols. (Trenton, NJ, 1980)

RAM *Report on American Manuscripts in the Royal Institution of Great Britain*, Historical Manuscripts Commission, 4 vols. (London, 1904–1909)

RMP *The Papers of Robert Morris*, ed. E. James Ferguson et al., 9 vols. (Pittsburgh, 1973)

RWPA Revolutionary War Pension Applications, part of Record Group 15 of the Records of the Veterans Administration (microfilm)

RRW *Records of the Revolutionary War*, ed. W. T. R. Saffell (orig. pub. 1913; repr. Baltimore, 1969)

SBW *Correspondence and Journals of Samuel Blachley Webb*, ed. Worthington C. Ford, 3 vols. (orig. pub. 1893; repr. New York, c. 1969)

SFDL Sol Feinstein Collection of the American Revolution, David Library, Washington Crossing, Pennsylvania

SIIP Staten Island Institute of Arts and Sciences, *Proceedings*

SPL Smithtown (N.Y.) Public Library

SS *Report on the Manuscripts of Mrs. Stoppford-Sackville*, Historical Manuscripts Commission, 2 vols. (London, 1904)

TJ Thomas Jefferson

VH *Vermont History*

VMHB *Virginia Magazine of History and Biography*

WL William Livingston

WLCL William L. Clements Library, Ann Arbor, Michigan

WMQ *William and Mary Quarterly*

W&S *War and Society*

WW *The Writings of George Washington*, ed. John C. Fitzpatrick, 39 vols. (Washington, DC, 1931–1944) (http://etext.lib.virginia.edu/washington/)

NOTES

PREFACE

1. Thorburn, *Fifty Years' Reminiscences*, 9–10, 166–170. For descriptions of the city when Thorburn arrived, see Smith, *The City of New York in the Year of Washington's Inauguration*, esp. 5–52; Mercantile Library Association, *New York City*; and "Old Reminiscences of New York," *New-York Mirror*, Apr. 14, 1838. *Note*: Sources are cited here using short titles. For full biographical details, and a key to abbreviations used in the notes, please see Works Cited.

2. I am referring here to St. Paul's Chapel on Broadway, the fence enclosing Bowling Green, and the Morris-Jumel mansion in upper Manhattan. For details, see p. 323, n. 42.

CHAPTER I

1. Manders, *Battle of Long Island*, 33, 37–40, and passim; Schecter, *Battle for New York*, 126–143; Gallagher, *Battle of Brooklyn*, 141–154; and Devine, "Pennsylvania Flying Camp." Still valuable because they incorporate much original source material are Johnston, *Campaign of 1776 Around New York and Brooklyn*, 48–49, 162; Field, *Battle of Long Island*; Stiles, *History of the City of Brooklyn*, 1: 250–297; and Onderdonk, *Revolutionary Incidents of Suffolk and Kings Counties*. For the times of moonset and sunrise, see the online calculator maintained by the Astronomical Application Department of the U.S. Naval Observatory (http://aa.usno.navy.mil/data/).

2. For a description of the Red Lion, purportedly based on local tradition, see Whittemore, *Heroes of the American Revolution and Their Descendants*, xiv–xv. Although largely obliterated by urbanization, the original terrain can still be understood thanks to the beautifully detailed map drawn five years later by Lieutenant George Sproule, an engineer with the British Sixteenth Regiment of Foot, now in WLCL (see Manders, *Battle of Long Island*, 20–21). Also helpful are the Faden Campaign Map (1776) and the Holland Map (1776–1777), both reproduced and annotated in Cohen and Augustyn, *Manhattan in Maps*, 78–83. The Gowanus and Narrows roads have become Third Avenue, and Martense Lane roughly corresponds to what is now the southern boundary of Green-Wood Cemetery.

3. Manders, *Battle of Long Island*, 40; Gallagher, *Battle of Brooklyn*, 101–102, 123–127. Parsons's account of the action is contained in two letters to John Adams (see Johnston, *Campaign of 1776*, 33–36; Hall, *Parsons*, 50–58).

4. Manders, *Battle of Long Island*, 43. Grant is quoted in Jensen, *Founding of a Nation*, 579. On Stirling, see Nelson, *William Alexander, Lord Stirling*, 84–87. Stirling's claim to a lapsed Scottish earldom had not been recognized by the English House of Lords, but he used the title anyway.

5. [Atlee], "Extract from the Journal of Col. Atlee," 2 *PA* 512 (hereafter [Atlee], "Extract"). Though dated the same day as the battle, internal evidence indicates that this "extract," now in HSP, was composed at least several months later. See Atlee to John Bayard, Nov. 15, 1779, *LDC* 14: 194–197. Atlee may have continued to work on the journal, as the version printed in 5 *AA* 1: 1251–1255 is a bit more polished and richer in detail. For other reports of the action along the Gowanus Road, see Onderdonk, *Revolutionary Incidents of Suffolk and Kings*, 147, 157–158; [Anderson], *Personal Recollections*, 21–22; Moore, *Diary of the American Revolution*, 1: 295–298; Patrick Sim, RWPA: S35072; 4 *AA* 1: 107–108; 5 *AA* 1: 1193–1196, 1212, 1213, 1231–1233, 1243–1245; and [Nice], "Excerpts from the Diary of Captain John Nice," 402 (hereafter *Nice Diary*). For a British version of events, see Howe to Lord George Germain, Sept. 3, 1776, *DAR* 12: 216–218. The hill defended by Atlee and Parsons is most likely the one now known as Battle Hill in Green-Wood Cemetery.

6. [Atlee], "Extract," 2 *PA* 1: 515.

7. Manders, *Battle of Long Island*, 43–44; Gallagher, *Battle of Brooklyn*, 113–122; Johnston, *Campaign of 1776*, 206; "Journal of Col. Samuel Miles, Concerning the Battle of Long Island—1776," 2 *PA* 1: 519–522. Daniel Brodhead to _____, 1776, 1 *PA* 5: 21–23; Onderdonk, *Revolutionary Incidents of Suffolk and Kings*, 138, and 5 *AA* 1: 1259–1260. See also Atwood, *Hessians*, 68; Lowell, *Hessians and the Other German Auxiliaries*, 65–66; [Serle], *American Journal*, 77–79 (hereafter *Serle Journal*); and Fischer, *Washington's Crossing*, 97.

8. "Diary of Lieutenant James McMichael," 2 *PA* 15: 195–203; *Nice Diary*, 402–403; Michael Graham, RWPA: S8621, excerpted in Dann, *Revolution Remembered*, 48–50. For similar stories, see Wade and Lively, *This Glorious Cause*, 215; "Revolutionary Reminiscences by an Old Soldier"; Trumbull, "Journal of the Campaign at New York, 1776–7," 187; Hall, *Parsons*, 55; [Anderson], *Personal Recollections*, 22; Christian Balsley, RWPA: W7231.

9. On Nagel, see *History of Northampton County*, 240. Also [Fitch], *New-York Diary of Lieutenant Jabez Fitch*, 30–31 (hereafter *Fitch Diary*); [Atlee], "Extract," 2 *PA* 1: 513; 5 *AA* 1: 1252; *Nice Diary*, 403; Manders, *Battle of Long Island*, 43–45; Scheer and Rankin, *Rebels and Redcoats*, 188; Stirling to George Washington (hereafter, GW), Aug. 29, 1776, *PGW* 6: 159–162; Gallagher, *Battle of Brooklyn*, 123–133; Ryan, *Salute to Courage*, 38.

10. Burgoyne, *Enemy Views*, 71–72, 128; Gillet's letter, dated Dec. 2, 1776, is in Stiles, *Letters from the Prisons and Prison-Ships of the Revolution*, 3–16. On Foster, see Johnston, *Campaign of 1776*, 169–170. See also the account given by William Sterett (Sterrett) as reported in *Pennsylvania Evening Post*, Apr. 29, 1777; repr. *Connecticut Gazette*, May 30, 1777. For Atlee, see 5 *AA* 1: 1254. Howe's forces did hang at least one of the captives taken on August 27, but on the grounds that he had deserted from their army in Boston the previous year. See [Mackenzie], *Diary of Frederick Mackenzie*, 1: 44 (hereafter *Mackenzie Diary*).

11. "Robert Troup Affidavit," in Ryan, *Salute to Courage*, 66–69 (hereafter Troup, "Affidavit"); Thacher, *Military Journal of the American Revolution*, 76n. Thacher heard the mock-execution story from a friend then imprisoned in New York, presumably

one of Troup's party. Another of the men taken with Troup, Lieutenant Edward Dunscomb, gave the New York Committee of Safety an account of his captivity around the same time (Comm. of Safety to GW, Feb. 13, 1777, *PGW* 8: 326–327). See also Edward Dunscomb, RWPA: W19206; Henry Yeager, RWPA: R11928; [Johnson], "Recollections of . . . General Jeremiah Johnson," 17; and Onderdonk, *Documents and Letters*, 110, 148.

12. *Fitch Diary*, 31, 34, 78–80, 92–93, 120, 137–138, and passim (see "Narative," 136–158). Because Fitch's day-to-day diary has almost nothing uncomplimentary to say about his captors, its editor, W. H. W. Sabine, concluded that the "Narative" is less authentic and truthful—anti-British propaganda, not an honest record of his captivity. But this is exactly backwards. Fitch needed to be quite careful about what he put in the diary: a catalogue of complaints about the conduct of the enemy, especially enemy officers, could cause him no end of trouble if it fell into the wrong hands. It would undoubtedly cost him the chance to be released on parole, a privilege soon granted a few American officers who signed a pledge not to do or say anything contrary to the interests of His Majesty George III until officially exchanged. By the spring of 1777, as we will see, Fitch too was on parole and living under little or no supervision with a New Lots farmer. At that point it was much safer to speak his mind, and that is when he wrote the "Narative." As it happened, one of the first American officers to be paroled was Major Edward Burd, the American officer captured at the Red Lion in the wee hours of August 27 (Johnston, *Campaign of 1776*, 48–49, 170–171; *Nice Diary*, 399).

13. Greene to GW, Sept. 5, 1776, *PGW* 6: 222–224; Major General William Heath to GW, Sept. 3, 1776, *PGW* 6: 199–120, 207–208. On December 23, 1776, Hugh Gaines's *New York Gazette*, a Tory paper, announced the publication by James Rivington of "The Battle of Brooklyn, A Farce of Two Acts"—perhaps the earliest use of that name for the battle and one that suggests it was coined in derision. Rivington's own *Royal Gazette* used it in 1780 in an advertisement for battle maps, and in 1783 the Tory judge Thomas Jones referred to "the battle of Brookland" in his *History of New York*, 2: 297–298. The "Battle of Long Island," a name not widely adopted until the nineteenth century, may have arisen as an attempt to give the debacle a more dignified name.

14. For discrepant contemporary reports, compare *Serle Journal*, 79, 87, 91; *DAR* 12: 218; 5 *AA* 1: 1194, 1195, 1212–1213, 1215, 1221, 1231–1233, 1258; Onderdonk, *Revolutionary Incidents of Suffolk and Kings*, 136; [Cresswell], *Journal of Nicholas Cresswell*, 231 (hereafter *Cresswell Journal*); Nelson, *William Alexander, Lord Stirling*, 88; Ryan, *Salute to Courage*, 42; and GW to Hancock, Aug. 31, 1776, *PGW* 6: 177–179. Subsequent attempts to reconcile the sources include Peckham, *Toll of Independence*, 22; Manders, *Battle of Long Island*, 62; Gallagher, *Battle of Brooklyn*, 135–137; Johnston, *Campaign of 1776*, 202–206; and Clodfelter, *Warfare and Armed Conflicts*, 1: 181. On disposing of the bodies, see Stiles, *History of City of Brooklyn*, 1: 270, and Willard, *Letters on the American Revolution*, 355.

15. Woodhull was captured on August 28, the day following the battle, as were another 400 Americans, sent to Long Island (as Serle put it) "to cut the Throats of the Cattle" (Balderston and Syrett, *Lost War*, 100–101; Bolton, *Letters of Hugh Earl Percy*, 68; *Serle Journal*, 82–83; *NRAR*, 10). On prior captives, see Bowman, *Captive Americans*, 6, 8–10; Metzger, *Prisoner in the American Revolution*, 34.

16. Cohen, *Yankee Sailors in British Gaols*, 18–23; Abell, *Prisoners of War in Britain*, 92, 115, and passim; Baugh, *British Naval Administration*, 48–52, and passim; Rodger,

Wooden World, 35–36; Bowman, *Captive Americans*, 8, 17; Cogliano, *American Maritime Prisoners*, 49–55; Anderson, "Treatment of Prisoners of War in Britain."

17. Jones, *History of New York During the Revolutionary War*, 1: 351; Bernard, *Retrospections of America*, 59–60; Young, *Revolutionary Ladies*, 57–86.

18. Rosenwaike, *Population History of New York City*, 8, 12–13; [Bureau of the Census] *Statistical History of the United States*, 170–171. The beauty as well as fertility of western Long Island are noted in *Serle Journal*, 86; Dohla, *Hessian Diary*, 76–77; Burgoyne, *Enemy Views*, 70; Eddis, *Letters from America*, 218; Kipping, *Hessian View of America*, 22 and passim; [Wansey], *Henry Wansey and His American Journal*, 130–131. On the connection between slaveholding and loyalism, see Burrows, "Kings County."

19. Armbruster, *Wallabout Prison Ships*, 14, notes the lack of sufficient building material on Long Island for barracks, prisons, and the like. A small number of prisoners were detained briefly in the Flatbush and New Utrecht churches (Cornelius Brooks, RWPA: S14997). The New Utrecht church also held a number of political prisoners rounded up during or just after the battle. See, e.g., the story of Elias Baylis, the blind chairman of the Jamaica Committee of Safety (Dandridge, *American Prisoners of the Revolution*, 100–101).

20. On Washington's retreat, see Schecter, *Battle for New York*, 155–167; Gallagher, *Battle of Brooklyn*, 138–164; Johnston, *Campaign of 1776*, 207–224. For Long Island, Livingston to GW, Aug. 31, Sept. 11, 1776, *PGW* 6: 184, 282–283; Jonathan Trumbull to GW, Aug. 31–Sept. 1, 1776, and Sept. 5, 1776: *PGW* 6: 190–192, 226–227. Onderdonk, *Revolutionary Incidents of Suffolk and Kings*, 44–46.

21. 5 *AA* 3: 1233–1234, 1236; *Mackenzie Diary*, 1: 73–74; *Serle Journal*, 135; Livingston to GW, Sept. 24, 1776, *PGW* 6: 390–391; Nicholas Cooke to GW, Oct. 5, 1776, *PGW* 6: 472–473; Jonathan Trumbull to GW, Oct. 13, 1776, *PGW* 6: 559–561; Livingston to GW, Oct. 14, 1776, *PGW* 6: 566–568; Trumbull to Christopher [Lossing?], Sept. 8, 1776, SPL, Misc. Manuscripts; Buel, *Dear Liberty*, 86–87; Luke and Venables, *Long Island in the Revolution*, 27, 32–54; Mather, *Refugees of 1776*; Stone, *Letters of Brunswick and Hessian Officers*, 203; Vincitorio, "Revolutionary War and Its Aftermath." For raids on Setuaket in early November 1776, see Onderdonk, *Revolutionary Incidents of Suffolk and Kings*, 62–63; Hinman, *Historical Collection*, 91; and Rose, *Washington's Spies*, 83.

22. Mercer to GW, Oct. 16, 1776, *PGW* 6: 577–578; Devine, "Pennsylvania Flying Camp," 72.

23. *Fitch Diary*, 35–36, 39–43, and 139–143 ("Narative"); *Nice Diary*, 403. Dr. Thomas Moffat, a Scottish physician, noted in his diary that tensions between "Southern and Northern Rebels" prompted Admiral Howe to have their officers confined on separate ships, but Fitch makes no mention of such a move (*NDAR*, 6: 656). Around this time transports came in with Jeremiah Greenman and the other prisoners from Québec. They were isolated from the Long Island prisoners and later released near Elizabeth Town, New Jersey, under the terms of an agreement with Sir Guy Carleton, the governor of Canada. See Henry, *Account of Arnold's Campaign Against Quebec*, 176–181; [Nichols], "Diary of Lieutenant Francis Nichols"; [Greenman], *Diary of a Common Soldier*, 31–33. A small number of other Americans taken prior to August 27 were being held elsewhere in the fleet. Henry Hawkins, for example, spent almost a year in the brig of HMS *Phoenix*. He had been captured in May 1776 on a sloop that was en route to New York with gunpowder for the American

army (Esek Hopkins to GW, Sept. 2, 1776, *PGW,* 6: 201–202. Tradition has it that after the Battle of Brooklyn, Lieutenant Henry Scudder of Northport, New York, was confined briefly on the sloop of war *Swan,* though she was not a prison ship (see Cochran, *Scudders in the American Revolution,* 16, and Admiral Howe's report on shipping in New York waters in early November 1776: *DAR* 12: 245).

24. Troup, "Affidavit," 67–68; *Fitch Diary,* 42.

25. *Fitch Diary,* 143 ("Narative"); see also *Fitch Diary,* 46.

26. Ibid., 40, 49, 143 ("Narative"). The diary noted only that Woodhull was brought aboard the *Mentor* with multiple saber wounds and that when his condition worsened, the British removed him to the field hospital in New Utrecht. Woodhull's reputation as a Revolutionary martyr has been questioned by Sabine, *Suppressed History of General Nathaniel Woodhull,* large portions of which reappeared in Sabine, *Murder, 1776.* Sabine contended (among other things) that Woodhull may have stayed on the sidelines during the Battle of Long Island, that he may have gone over to the British shortly after his capture, that Troup's affidavit was a tissue of lies, and that Fitch took Troup's tale at face value in preparing his "Narative" because, ever the propagandist, he was overly eager to put the British in the worst possible light. Sabine's is not the only possible reading of the evidence, however. See Hayes, "General Nathaniel Woodhull and the Battle of Long Island."

CHAPTER 2

1. *Fitch Diary,* 52–54; Bliven, *Battle for Manhattan,* 18ff.; Onderdonk, *Revolutionary Incidents of Suffolk and Kings,* 161–165; Stiles, *History of the City of Brooklyn,* 1: 282–296; Schecter, *Battle for New York,* 204–209. On the number of captives, see Howe to Germain, Sept. 21, 1776, *DAR,* 12: 228. For a somewhat lower estimate, made on the day of the battle, see *Mackenzie Diary,* 1: 50; Peckham, *Toll of Independence,* 23. On September 23, one American officer and thirteen men had been taken prisoner in an abortive attempt to seize Montresor's (now Randall's) Island (*Mackenzie Diary,* 1: 63; *Serle Journal,* 112).

2. General Orders on September 15, 1776: "All Rebel Prisoners to be Kept in New York, in the Hospl or wherever M. Gl Robertson shall Think proper," quoted in Stokes, *Iconography of Manhattan,* 5: 1015. Carp, "Night the Yankees Burned Broadway", 471–511; Burrows and Wallace, *Gotham,* 241–242; Barck, *New York City During the War for Independence,* 79–82; Wertenbaker, *Father Knickerbocker Rebels,* 99–103. Captain Amos Fellows of Connecticut was subsequently captured and held in City Hall on suspicion that he had been involved in setting the fire. He was never charged, however, and died in prison several months later (*Fitch Diary,* 157; [Trumbull], *Trumbull Papers,* 2: 26 [hereafter *Trumbull Papers*]; GW to Joshua Loring, Jan. 20, 1777, *PGW,* 8: 118; Jonathan Trumbull to GW, Jan. 12, 1777, *PGW* 8: 53–54; and GW to Trumbull, Jan. 24, 1777, *PGW* 8: 151–152). Also held on suspicion of arson was Captain Abraham C. van Dyk (Dyke). As Major General Alexander McDougall explained, "He being a heavy fat man, became so fatigued in the retreat from the City of newyork, that he could not retire with that corps [Lasher's battalion], and secreted himself in the Cedars between the City and Harlem." Eventually discovered, he was put in the Provost and exchanged in 1778 (*PGW* 6: 97n4; McDougall to GW, Feb. 17, 1778, *PGW* 13: 572–573).

3. *Fitch Diary,* 120. The Bear Market stood in Greenwich Street near the foot of Fulton (now the north side of the World Trade Center site). Captain John Nice of

Germantown, Pennsylvania, said the William Street house belonged to a Mr. Mariner (*Nice Diary*, 404; see also the diary of Lieutenant William McPherson, another Pennsylvanian prisoner, in Johnston, *Campaign of 1776*, 2: 168). Alexander Graydon, one of the officers taken at Fort Washington in November, found Atlee and other field officers boarding with a Mrs. Carroll in Queen Street (Graydon, *Memoirs of His Own Time*, 224–225 [hereafter *Graydon Memoirs*]).

4. Burrows and Wallace, *Gotham*, 229, 245–261; Dunlap, *History of the American Theater*, 46ff.; Barck, *New York City During the War for Independence*, 57–58, 74–97, and passim; Wertenbaker, *Father Knickerbocker Rebels*, 70–73, 78–80, 98–109; Schecter, *Battle for New York*, 194, 272–285; *Cresswell Journal*, 244–245. General Robertson said that when he left New York in February 1777 the city's population "amounted to upwards of 11,000" (*The St. James Chronicle*, Mar. 22–25, 1777, quoted in Stokes, *Iconography of Manhattan*, 5: 1046).

5. Fitch never said exactly how many officers shared Liberty House with him, only that they were "pretty Numerous." He did say that the inmates ate in three shifts, or messes, and that his mess had six men. Assuming the shifts to have been roughly equal in size, around eighteen men lived in the house as of mid-October. New arrivals, often mentioned but not enumerated, almost certainly boosted the actual number to two dozen or more *Fitch Diary*, 55–59, 62, 64, 66–68; *Nice Diary*, 404.

6. Howe to GW, Jan. 19, 1778, *PGW* 13: 280–282; Bowler, *Logistics*, 8, 36; Bowman, *Captive Americans*, 18–19.

7. Bowler, *Logistics*, 92 and passim; Anderson, "Treatment of Prisoners of War in Britain"; Metzger, *Prisoner in the American Revolution*, 86–90. Both the army and navy relied on porter or spruce beer to combat scurvy, but prisoners rarely if ever saw either.

8. *Fitch Diary*, 146. Mrs. Archer, Mrs. Sunderland, Mrs. Lesley, and Mrs. Griffis turn up frequently in Fitch's diary as the bearers of food, fresh laundry, and news from the outside. Although Troup's affidavit says only that he was "confined in a house near Bridewell," it is apparent that he was one of the crowd in Liberty House (*Fitch Diary*, 127).

9. Hall, *Old Martyrs' Prison*; Pintard, "Old Jail"; Lucey, "History of City Hall Park," esp. 24–28, 33–35.

10. The exterior dimensions of the building are usually given as sixty by seventy feet. Making allowances for stairwells and hallways, this would permit six twenty-by-thirty-foot cells per floor. One modern scholar has concluded that the Provost "was not crowded," though it is hard to imagine that even ten men confined day and night in an area of 600 square feet would have agreed (Bowman, *Captive Americans*, 11). Fell, "Memorandum in the Provost Jail," identifies by name the twenty men in his cell on Apr. 23, 1777. Many years later, John Pintard recalled that one civilian had been held in an "upper dungeon" measuring just twelve by twelve feet. If so, the size and configuration of cells on each of the top two floors may have been quite different (see "Reminiscences of John Pintard," Bancroft Collection, v. 298 ["New York and Miscellaneous"], NYPL).

11. Field, *Historic and Antiquarian Scenes*, 14–16; Dandridge, *American Prisoners*, 100–102, 200–201. As is often the case, Dandridge's sources cannot be determined.

12. Leiby, *Revolutionary War in the Hackensack Valley*, 122; *Graydon Memoirs*, 241. See also Christopher Hawkins's 1781 encounter with a Long Island woman whose husband had recently died in the Provost ([Hawkins], *Adventures of Christopher Hawkins*, 100).

13. John Nicholas Kline, RWPA: S8796. The letter from Miles and Atlee to Washington on November 3 describes the men as confined in two churches. The other one may have been the Middle Dutch Church, as we have a report that a French priest was incarcerated there after September 16 for saying the Mass (Stokes, *Iconography of Manhattan*, 5: 1016, 1037). The other sugar houses were Bayard's on Wall Street, which had in fact become a tobacco manufactory only several years earlier; Roosevelt's on Cliff Street; and Cuyler's on Rose and Duane. The latter, better known later as the Rhinelander Sugar House, is often represented to have housed American prisoners of war, but Cuyler was a Tory and his refinery appears to have continued to operate during the occupation (Stevens, *Progress of New York*, 27; Harrington, *New York Merchant*, 147–148; Dunshee, *As You Pass By*, 83, 99; Stokes, *Iconography of Manhattan*, 4: 790; 5: 220–223).

14. For Nagel's deposition, see *History of Northampton County*, 240. Around the first of October, Nagel continued, the men were removed to a British ship, the *Juliana*, where they spent several more weeks in misery. He probably was not moved until the first of November, however, as Loring did not even begin feeding prisoners into the city until early October (*DAR*, 12: 244–245). For Catlin, see Dandridge, *American Prisoners*, 107, and *Fitch Diary*, 61.

15. Miles and Atlee to Washington, [Nov. 3, 1776]. This and a second letter from Miles, urging Washington to arrange for his parole, went out under a flag of truce on November 12 (*PGW* 7: 140–141, 190–191; *Mackenzie Diary*, 1: 103).

16. One of Howe's aides groused, "A large volume of letters to and by many prisoners must be read by us, which keeps us busy many an annoying night" (Kipping and Smith, *At General Howe's Side*, 8; *Mackenzie Diary*, I, 103–104). The "other large buildings" mentioned by Mackenzie included City Hall on Broad Street and the three-story stone building of King's College (Onderdonk, *Revolutionary Incidents of Suffolk and Kings*, 207), though it is not clear when or for how long the latter two were in use as prisons.

17. Karsten, *Law, Soldiers, and Combat*, 3–31, and Fooks, *Prisoners of War*. Cox, *Proper Sense of Honor*, 203ff., conveniently summarizes the attempts of Grotius, Montesquieu, and others to articulate standards for the humane treatment of prisoners of war. See also Strickland, *War and Chivalry*, esp. chap. 2, which emphasizes that even a successful appeal to the papacy under the canon law was almost impossible to enforce with an uncooperative prince.

18. Quoted in Weintraub, *Iron Tears*, 40. This and several following paragraphs draw liberally on the following: Geoffrey Parker, "Early Modern Europe" and Robert C. Stacey, "The Age of Chivalry," both in Howard, Andreopoulos, and Shulman, *Laws of War*, 40–58, 27–39; Barker, *Prisoners of War*, 7–10; Duffy, *Military Experience in the Age of Reason*, esp. 74ff.; Conway, *War of American Independence*, esp. 23–42; Black, *War for America*, esp. 13–19; Shy, *Toward Lexington*, 345ff.; Mackesy, *War for America*, 9–20 and passim; Higginbotham, *War of American Independence*, esp. 122–129; Higginbotham, "Military Leadership in the American Revolution," in Higginbotham, *War and Society in Revolutionary America*, esp. 84–89; Royster, *Revolutionary People at War*, esp. 86ff.; Fischer, *Washington's Crossing*, 31–80; Ian K. Steele, "Surrendering Rites, esp. 143–145; Starkey, "War and Culture, a Case Study"; Bruce, *Purchase System*, esp. 22–40; Van Buskirk, *Generous Enemies*, chap. 3.

19. In figuring the modern value of eighteenth-century commissions, I relied upon the Measuring Worth website (http://www.measuringworth.com/ppowerus/), which

offers appropriate cautions about such calculations. Also helpful were Rodger, *Insatiable Earl*, esp. 122–124, 166–192; Namier and Brooke, *House of Commons, 1754–1790*, 1: 143–145; Brewer, *Sinews of Power*, 55–59. On the price of commissions, see Thomas Simes, *Military Guide for Young Officers*, 1: 356, which pegs the price of a commission for a lieutenant-colonel of dragoons at £4,365 and an ensign of foot at a mere £405. Writing from Newport in April 1777, Charles Stuart informed his father, the Earl of Bute, that a lieutenant-colonel's commission sold for as much as £5,000, an indication that the war was beginning to drive up prices (*NRAR*, 27; Mackesy, *War for America*, 9–12). The two army corps where specialized training was required, the engineers and artillery, recruited officers from a somewhat broader cross-section of society.

20. Cox, *Proper Sense of Honor*, esp. 37–39; R. Frey, *British Soldier in America*, 123ff. Also useful in this context, though focused on the postwar period, is Freeman, *Affairs of Honor*.

21. For Burgoyne, see *New-York Gazette*, Oct. 4, 1777.

22. [Greenman], *Diary of a Common Soldier*, 29–30, 60–61. Carleton expected that paroling these men would bring about the release of some redcoats who had fallen into American hands. When that did not happen, or did not happen quickly enough, he ordered an end to all communication with "Rebels, Traitors in Arms against their King, Rioters, Disturbers of the Public Peace, Plunderers, Robbers, Assassins or Murderers." Washington was shocked (*PGW* 6: 42–43, 91–93).

23. Flexner, *Traitor and Spy*, 81; *Mackenzie Diary*, 1: 39.

24. Lowell, *Hessians and the Other German Auxiliaries*, 66; Kipping, *Hessian View of America*, 21, 32–36, and passim; *Serle Journal*, 80–81; Burgoyne, *Enemy Views*, 71–72, 124–125, 128. Germain to Mansfield, Aug. 6, 1776: *DAR* 12: 176; Nelson, *Stirling*, 87–91; GW to Hancock, Aug. 31, 1776, *PGW* 6: 177–179; Sullivan to GW, Mar. 2, 1778, *PGW* 14: 40–41, 15: 9–10. Stirling later said, however, that Von Heister "treated me like a brother when I was a prisoner." Both Stirling and Sullivan were exchanged within weeks, Sullivan reportedly saying that Howe treated him politely. "Letter from New-York, August 30, 1776," *Pennsylvania Evening Post*, Aug. 31, 1776. A proper officer's accouterments are described at length in Simes, *Military Guide*, 1: 370–371. It may be the case that many American officers represented the most respectable elements of American society; the point is that by European standards they still did not measure up (Lender, "Social Structure of the New Jersey Brigade"). The American practice of deliberately aiming at officers gave additional cause for resentment. (Jensen, *Founding of a Nation*, 648). The Hessians put some prisoners to work hauling cannon—not intentional brutality, but certainly humiliating. (Lowell, *Hessians and the Other German Auxiliaries*, 64; Manders, *Battle of Long Island*, 56n6; Atwood, *Hessians: Mercenaries from Hessen-Kassel*, 70.)

25. For this and the next several paragraphs I am heavily indebted to Colley, *Britons: Forging the Nation*; Conway, *British Isles and the War of American Independence*, esp. chap. 5, an assessment of Colley's thesis; Calder, *Revolutionary Empire*, esp. 375–382, 416–429, 430–442, 524–539, 553–564, 649–655, 672–682; Doyle, *Ireland, Irishmen, and Revolutionary America*, esp. 53–54; Gould, *Persistence of Empire*, esp. 17–18, 28–29, 77, 83–87; Black, *Culloden and the '45*, esp. 188–201; Gilmour, *Riots, Risings, and Revolution*; Richards, "Scotland and the Uses of the Atlantic Empire"; Savelle, "Nationalism and Other Loyalties in the American Revolution"; Breen, "Ideology and Nationalism"; and Wahrman, "The English Problem of Identity."

26. The long-term effects of Culloden on British colonial policy are traced in Plank, *Rebellion and Savagery*, 155–180. Rebellion was nothing new in England, but the customary punishment for all but the ringleaders had been fines, confiscation, mutilation, banishment, or imprisonment. It was the peculiarly disturbing specter of wholesale *provincial* rebellion that seems to have made war *ad terrorem* and mass executions look like the only feasible reaction (see Strickland, *War and Chivalry*, 240–247, and passim).

27. Leary, *That Rascal Freneau*, 34–35, 39; "A Poem on the Rising Glory of America" appeared as a pamphlet in Philadelphia in 1772.

28. On the increasingly hawkish climate in England after 1774, see Stedman, *History of the . . . American War*, 1: 258; Draper, *Struggle for Power*, 489–490; Guttridge, *American Correspondence of a Bristol Merchant*, 49–50, 64; Hibbert, *Redcoats and Rebels*, esp. 21–25; Guttridge, *English Whiggism and the American Revolution*, 72–84; Ritcheson, *British Politics and the American Revolution*, 157–173; Labaree, *Boston Tea Party*, 170–216; Labaree, "Idea of American Independence"; Lutnick, *American Revolution and the British Press*, 76–77 and passim; Jensen, *Founding of a Nation*, 453–460, 569–586, 645–650; Ammerman, *In the Common Cause*, 13–17; Bickham, "Sympathizing with Sedition?"; Burrows and Wallace, "American Revolution," esp. 226–234. On the popularity of punitive measures, see Gould, *Persistence of Empire*, 150–164; Gould, "American Independence and Britain's Counter-Revolution," esp. 114ff.; Sainsbury, *Disaffected Patriots*, 55–62, and passim; Conway, "From Fellow-Nationals to Foreigners."

29. Thomas, *Lord North*, 68–88; Gruber, *Howe Brothers*, 19–20, 323ff.; Alden, *General Gage in America*, esp. 233ff.; Greene, *Samuel Johnson*, 453; Hill, *Boswell's Life of Johnson*, 2: 312. Allusions to the practice of transporting felons from the mother country to America often figured in British threats to execute captured rebels. They belonged to "a scape Gallows race," observed one army officer, "the genuine progeny of their worthy Ancestors from Newgate and the Old Baily" (quoted in Bickham, "Sympathizing with Sedition?" 69).

30. Brigham, *British Royal Proclamations*, 224–229; Gruber, *Howe Brothers*, 28ff.; *New-York Journal*, Oct. 19, 1775. "Decisive exertions" is from the king's October 26 speech to Parliament in (Douglas et al., *English Historical Documents*, 9: 851). The king's belligerence is clearly described in O'Shaughnessy, "'If Others Will Not Be Active.'"

31. Valentine, *Lord George Germain*, 93–95, 100, and passim; Brown, *American Secretary*, 26–28, 37–54, 64, and passim; Gruber, *Howe Brothers*, 22–25; Mackesy, *War for America*, 47–54; Miller, *Triumph of Freedom*, 166n3; Weintraub, *Iron Tears*, 26–36. The Earl of Shelburne denounced the Prohibitory Act as "a mere wanton act of feminine revenge," a snarky allusion to rumors of Germain's homosexuality (*PHE*, 18: 1084–1085); see also the written protest entered by eight lords in *PHE*, 18: 1088–1094.

32. For the Scottish connection, see Colley, *Britons: Forging the Nation*, 101–140, and passim; Richards, "Scotland and the Atlantic Empire," 88; Gould, *Persistence of Empire*, 106–147, 153–155; Namier, *Structure of Politics*, 24–36; Namier, *England in the Age of the American Revolution*, 256ff.; Namier and Brooke, *House of Commons*, 1: 138–143; Shy, *Toward Lexington*, 352–355; Brewer, *Sinews of Power*, 44–45. Scottish influence over British policy was an axiom of American opinion throughout the Revolution, often centering on the king's former tutor and prime minister, Lord Bute. For early examples, see the *Essex Journal*, Apr. 12, 1775; *The Pennsylvania Evening Post*, Aug. 12, 1775; *Massachusetts Spy*, Aug. 30, 1775. Warnings of the Culloden-like

fate that awaited America were common in colonial papers in 1775. See Major Persifor Frazer's revealing conversation with General Grant following Frazer's capture by redcoats in 1777, as recounted by his granddaughter: "That is a Scotch name said the General (himself a Scotchman) and should not be the name of a rebel. 'England has called other men rebels besides those who resist her government in America' was the reply.—'For that answer,' said Grant, 'you shall have your horse,' and when it was brought he restored his sword also, and they rode along very pleasantly together for the remainder of the journey" (Frazer, *General Persifor Frazer*, 161.)

33. For Richmond and Hartley: *PHE*, 18: 1079, 1170; and *PHE*, 19: 554. For Adams: Hutson, *Letters from a Distinguished American*, 47. Montgomery's death at the gates of Québec occasioned yet another testy debate in the Commons over the word "rebel," during which Fox asserted "that all the great assertors of liberty, the saviours of their country, the benefactors of mankind, in all ages, had been called rebels" (*PHE*, 18: 1239–1240).

34. As quoted in Starkey, "War and Culture," 15. On Falmouth, see Daughan, *If By Sea*, 17–18, 43–46. I am indebted here to two essential essays by Stephen Conway: "To Subdue America" and "'The great mischief Complain'd of.'" See also Selesky, "Colonial America." Not surprisingly, the hue and cry for revenge often went hand in hand with assurances, such as the one made by General Grant in 1775, that the Americans would not fight back. "The native American is an effeminate thing," General James Murray informed Lord George Germain only weeks before Saratoga, "very unfit for and very impatient of war" (*SS* 1: 371). More than a year later, a British officer admitted that "most of the army have all along looked upon the enemy in a very contemptible light" (*London Packet*, Jan. 13–15, 1777, quoted in Stokes, *Iconography of Manhattan*, 5: 1039). Among the officers refusing to fight in America were Admiral Augustus Keppel and Lord Jeffrey Amherst, the conqueror of Canada. General Howe and Admiral Howe, who at first felt rather kindly toward Americans, likewise hesitated before agreeing to take the field against them (Sainsbury, *Disaffected Patriots*, 146–148; Weintraub, *Iron Tears*, 45–46; Lutnick, *American Revolution and the British Press*, 82–83; Gruber, *Howe Brothers*, 66–67, 70–71; Jones, "Sir William Howe," 45ff.)

35. *Mackenzie Diary*, 1: 39; Gruber, *Howe Brothers*, 31.

36. For a succinct discussion, see the essay on prisoners of war by Worthington C. Ford in *SBW*, 2: 19–85; also Lieutenant Colonel James Patterson's memorandum of an interview with Washington in July 1776, dismissing Washington's complaints as groundless and "easy to confute" (*RAM*, 1: 50). James Rivington, the New York printer, quickly published the documents in *The Letters of the Two Commanders in Chief*. Gage's tough talk played well back in London (see William Eden to Germain, Sept. 18, 1775, *SS* 2: 8–9).

37. Shy, "Thomas Gage: Weak Link of Empire," in Billias, *George Washington's Opponents*, 18, 21–22.

38. [Allen], *Narrative of Colonel Ethan Allen's Captivity*, 29–36 (hereafter *Allen Narrative*). Allen got a letter to Prescott in which he declared, "I expect an honourable and humane treatment, as an officer of my rank and merit should have," but Prescott ignored him (4 *AA* 3: 801–802; Bellesiles, *Revolutionary Outlaws*, 126–128; Jellison, *Ethan Allen: Frontier Rebel*, 158–160).

39. *Allen Narrative*, 39, 45, 47; Allen to Prescott, Sept. 25, 1775, 4 *AA* 3: 801–802; *Allen Narrative*, 45, 47; Jellison, *Ethan Allen: Frontier Rebel*, 161–162. The *Allen Narrative* has often been discounted as over-the-top war propaganda (see, e.g., Baxter,

"American Revolutionary Experience," 60–64; Denn, "Prison Narratives of the American Revolution," 31–33, and passim). But as Charles Jellison pointed out years ago, when checked against all the available evidence, the *Allen Narrative* "is probably an essentially accurate record of what actually happened" (*Ethan Allen: Frontier Rebel,* 161; see also Graydon, *Memoirs of His Own Time,* 243; and Bellesiles, *Revolutionary Outlaws,* 330n).

40. *New York Gazette,* Oct. 23, 1775; *New England Chronicle,* Nov. 2, 1775; *Constitutional Gazette,* Nov. 29, 1775; Moore, *Diary of American Revolution,* 1: 153n, 159–160; Jellison, *Ethan Allen: Frontier Rebel,* 160–61; Bellesiles, *Revolutionary Outlaw,* 127–128; see also Montgomery to Major Stopford, Oct. 20, 1775, 4 *AA* 3: 1134; Robert R. Livingston to John Jay, Dec. 6, 1775, *LDC,* 2: 450; and the Diary of Richard Smith, Dec. 18, 1775, *LDC,* 494. For Washington's promise to retaliate against Prescott, see 4 *AA* 3: 310–311. Howe, ever cautious, promptly wrote home for instructions (*AA* 4: 357–358; *SBW,* 2: 21–22). Congress supported Washington with its own threat to retaliate, and in early January 1776 ordered that Prescott be "safely and securely kept" (*LDC,* 2: 537–539; *JCC,* 4: 16). Prescott's case is discussed in Haffner, "Treatment of Prisoners of War by the Americans," 63–68.

41. *Middlesex Journal,* Jan. 4, 1776, quoted in Moore, *Diary of American Revolution,* 1: 190–191. Also *Allen Narrative,* 49–50, 53, 57–58; 4 *AA* 6: 508; Sainsbury, *Disaffected Patriots,* 141; Jellison, *Ethan Allen: Frontier Rebel,* 164; Cogliano, *Maritime Prisoners,* 43; and Suffolk's remarks to the House of Lords as quoted in 4 *AA* 6: 294, 296.

42. *Allen Narrative,* 61–64; "Extract of a letter from Cork (Ireland) to a Gentleman in Philadelphia, Dated January, 1776," 4 *AA* 4: 836. This and other news about Allen was widely printed in American papers (e.g., *Connecticut Gazette,* May 16, 1776).

43. *DAR,* 12: 56; Knight, "Prisoner and Parole." While Germain continued to wrestle with the niceties of the problem—should captured American privateers, who stood to profit from their actions, be treated differently than soldiers taken on land?—he did not waver in the belief that the government would have been justified in trying Allen for treason. Sending him back to America was simply the more prudent course, except for the confusion it caused. (See his correspondence with Lord Chief Justice Mansfield in *DAR,* 12: 176–180.)

44. *Allen Narrative,* 68.

CHAPTER 3

1. Fort Washington stood at the intersection of what is now Fort Washington Avenue and 183rd Street, the highest natural point on the island. GW to Hancock, Nov. 16, 1776, *PGW* 7: 162–169; David Thorp, RWPA: W15427, excerpted in Johnston, *Battle of Harlem Heights,* 195–196; Journal of Abner Everett, RWPA: W6087; Thomas Bull, RWPA: S2056; Johnston, *Campaign of 1776,* 276–286; Schecter, *Battle for New York,* 243–257; Fischer, *Washington's Crossing,* 111–114.

2. Johnston, *Battle of Harlem Heights,* 152, 155; Ryan, *Salute to Courage,* 43; *London Packet,* Jan. 1–3, 1777, quoted in Stokes, *Iconography of Manhattan,* 5: 1039; Lydenberg, *Archibald Roberson,* 112; *Graydon Memoirs,* 210; *Mackenzie Diary,* 1: 110. Judge Thomas Jones thought all the Fort Washington defenders should have been killed outright as a lesson to other rebels (Jones, *History of New York,* 2: 27).

3. Ryan, *Salute to Courage,* 51–52; "Extracts from MSS. Diary of Lieut. Oliver Babcock," in Johnston, *Battle of Harlem Heights,* 198 (hereafter "Babcock Extracts"); "Miserecors," *Connecticut Gazette,* Feb. 28, 1777; Burgoyne, *Enemy Views,* 97.

4. For Lindsay, see RWPA: X465; on Bedinger, see Dandridge, *American Prisoners*, 16–17. Howe's adjutant admitted afterward that the assaults on American prisoners had been shameful (*Kemble Papers*, 1: 100). A Hessian officer confirmed that the Americans were terrified that they would all be killed (Kipping, *Hessian View of America*, 22).

5. Hinman, *Historical Collection . . . Connecticut*, 134. Cf. Dandridge, *American Prisoners*, 108; Thomas Bull, RWPA: S2056.

6. RWPA: W8256 (the 1832 pension application by Little's widow); [Adlum], *Memoirs of the Life of John Adlum*, 77–78 [cited hereinafter as *Adlum Memoirs*]; Journal of Abner Everett, RWPA: W6087; "Revolutionary War Diary of William Slade," HSM, entry for Nov. 18, 1776 (hereafter "Slade Diary"); Perry, *Reminiscences*, 14; Testimony of William Darlington, *Pennsylvania Evening Post*, May 3, 1777; and the notice of General [then Lieutenant] Robert Brown in *History of Northampton County*, 240.

7. *Adlum Memoirs*, 81–86.

8. *Graydon Memoirs*, 206–209. The anonymous first edition of 1811 was entitled *Memoirs of a Life, Chiefly Passed in Pennsylvania, within the Last Sixty Years* (see Arch, "Writing a Federalist Self: Alexander Graydon's *Memoirs of a Life*"). My references are to the 1846 edition. For a curiously similar story, see [Hughes], *Journal by Thos: Hughes*, 57. "The Rebel prisoners were in general but very indifferently clothed," Captain Mackenzie noted in his diary. "Few of them appeared to have a Second shirt, nor did they appear to have washed themselves during the Campaign. A great many of them were lads under 15, and old men: and few of them had the appearance of Soldiers. Their odd figures frequently excited the laughter of our Soldiers" (*Mackenzie Diary*, 1: 111–112).

9. *Graydon Memoirs*, 205–207, 209, 217, 221–222.

10. *Fitch Diary*, 69 (diary), 147 ("Narative"). But Captain John Jamison said he was held for two months in the John Street Methodist Church (RWPA: W21447). "A Return of Prisoners taken by the British Army till 26th November 1776," Elias Boudinot Papers, LC, puts the number of officers at 303; see also *Nice Diary*, 405; Steiner, *Life of James McHenry*, 9–10. Doctor McHenry was another of Mrs. Carroll's boarders.

11. *Graydon Memoirs*, 224–226; *Fitch Diary*, 69, 70. For Captain Bedinger, see Dandridge, *American Prisoners*, 17. For another view of Mrs. Carroll and her establishment, see *Adlum Memoirs*, 89–91. "They went out but little and stayed much within doors," Adlum later remarked. "It was not very pleasant for gentlemen of any sensibility (prisoners) to hear frequently as they were passing through the streets from the mouths of blackguards say, 'There goes a rebel,' with a 'damn' frequently attached to it" (*Adlum Memoirs*, 128; cf. *Nice Diary*, 404).

12. *Mackenzie Diary*, 1: 112–113.

13. Gruber, *Howe Brothers*, esp. 143–147; Burrows and Wallace, *Gotham: A History*, 245–276; Jones, "Sir William Howe," 50.

14. Balderston and Syrett, *Lost War*, 108; Conway, "From Fellow-Nationals to Foreigners," 92.

15. Howe reported a total of 2,818 men and officers captured at Fort Washington; some American tallies put the figure at 2,916. Counting the 1,000-plus taken on Long Island, another 500 seized during subsequent actions, and perhaps an additional 100-odd political prisoners, a total of 5,000 seems entirely reasonable (see Hugh Gaines's *New-York Gazette*, Nov. 25, 1776, which uses the same figure). The American tally put the number of officers and men in enemy hands at 4,101 ("A

Return of Prisoners taken by the British Army till 26th November, 1776," Elias Boudinot Papers, LC; see also "A Return of Prisoners taken by the British Army, 26th Nov 1776," among the Elias Boudinot Papers at HSP, which lists 328 officers and 4,101 privates, for a grand total of 4,429). On December 3, Howe reported that he still had 4,500 American prisoners in New York (Cohen, *Yankee Sailors*, 24). Judge Jones had the completely daft idea that there were at this time "not less than 10,000 prisoners, (sailors included) within the British lines at New York" (Jones, *History of New York* 1: 351). The town certainly was crowded, in any event. With 5,000 prisoners, around 11,000 civilians, and almost 14,000 regulars, there were already more people in New York than ever before. On troop dispositions in January 1777, see *Kemble Papers* 1: 107. For the story of one political prisoner, brought to New York by Tory partisans, see Winfield, *History of the County of Hudson*, 500; "Diary of Rev. Mr. Shewkirk [Schaukirk], Pastor of the Moravian Church, New York," in Johnston, *Campaign of 1776*, 2: 121–122. Oliver Woodruff said he was one of 815 confined in the Bridewell (RWPA: S14885; see also Onderdonk, *Revolutionary Incidents of Suffolk and Kings*, 207, 209; *Adlum Memoirs*, 80, 98–99; *Fitch Diary*, 146). American prisoners sometimes referred to the Provost sarcastically as "the new City Hall."

16. William Slade's diary says the *Grosvenor* dropped anchor in Turtle Bay (now the foot of Twenty-third Street) ("Slade Diary," Dec. 8, 1776). The *Whitby*, and possibly the *Grosvenor*, had been among the ships in Gravesend where American prisoners were held after the Battle of Brooklyn. Neither appears on Admiral Howe's list of shipping in and around New York City as of early November 1776, which suggests that they were merchantmen pressed into service as transports (*DAR*, 12: 244–245). It is not clear, either, whether the *Grosvenor* was hulked. On December 10, Lieutenant Oliver Babcock brought "some Cloths to the poor prisoners" confined on the *Grosvenor* and *Dutton*, the only reference I have found to a third prison ship at this point ("Babcock Extracts," in Johnston, *Harlem Heights*, 198–199). Cornelius Brooks remembered that when he was put aboard the *Whitby*, she held 334 American prisoners (RWPA: S14997). See also the application of Isaac Grant (RWPA: R4195). Cornelius Westbrook, taken at Fort Washington, recalled that he was first confined in one of the sugar houses, then moved to "the prison ship lying between Governors Island and New York City," but he could not recall her name (RWPA: S40656).

17. Wetland ecosystems like that of Wallabout Bay once existed throughout the New York region (Barlow, *Forests and Wetlands of New York City*). Thomas Andros recalled that the bluff overlooking the bay rose at a forty-five-degree angle to as high as thirty feet in places. Andros, *Old Jersey Captive*, 26–27. See also Barnes, *Wallabout and the Wallabouters*; Dankers and Sluyter, *Journal of a Voyage to New York*, 341–342, 374.

18. Cohen, *Yankee Sailors*, 20; Abell, *Prisoners of War in Britain*, 92; Lenman, *Jacobite Risings*, 271–274 and passim; Seton and Arnot, *Prisoners of the '45*, 1: 157–165 and passim; Ekirch, *Bound for America*, 227–238. Full-scale transportation resumed in 1787, when the First Fleet departed for Botany Bay in New South Wales (Hughes, *Fatal Shore*, 41–42).

19. Campbell, *Intolerable Hulks*, esp. 5–12; Johnson, *English Prison Hulks*, 8, 84, and passim; *Serle Journal*, 75–76.

20. *Pennsylvania Evening Post*, Nov. 7, 1776; subsequently reprinted in a string of American papers, including *Pennsylvania Packet* (Nov. 12), *Connecticut Gazette* (Nov.

15 and 29), *Connecticut Journal* (Nov. 20), and *Boston Gazette* (Dec. 9). "Humanitas" was probably William Lee, a Virginia tobacco merchant living in London who had become, in company with his brother Arthur, closely associated with the pro-American opposition (Sainsbury, *Disaffected Patriots*, 119, 141–142; Riggs, "Arthur Lee"). Two of the American prisoners, Eliphalet Downer and Seth Clark, corroborated the information in "Humanitas" in affidavits given in March 1777 to Benjamin Franklin, the American minister in Paris (*NDAR*, 8: 723). On Howard, see Campbell, *Intolerable Hulks*, 17–21.

21. A "black hole" was the generic term for naval and military lockups. By the time of the American Revolution, it had become inextricably associated with the story of the Black Hole of Calcutta. The classic source of that story was J. Z. Holwell's *Genuine narrative of the deplorable deaths of the English gentlemen and others who were suffocated in the Black Hole in Fort William, at Calcutta, in the kingdom of Bengal* (1756).

22. For Little's account, see RWPA: W8256. Isaac Grant's pension application (RWPA: R4195) corroborates Little's story. The only discrepancy is that Little says their parole was arranged by "Steve Allen, formerly of Salisbury, Connecticut." Grant correctly identifies him as *Levi* Allen, a younger brother of Ethan (cf. *Fitch Diary*, 110).

23. Perry, *Reminiscences*, 15–20; RWPA: W1743.

24. *NDAR* 7: 421; 5 *AA*, 3: 1137–1138; Onderdonk, *Revolutionary Incidents of Suffolk and Kings*, 213. The version in Dandridge, *American Prisoners*, 96–97, is bowdlerized. William Gamble complained that military and naval officers alike "are huddled together between decks in a prison-ship, with Indians, Mullattoes, Negroes, &c" (*Pennsylvania Gazette*, Apr. 29, 1777; repr. *Connecticut Gazette*, May 30, 1777). John Barrett, too, objected that he and other naval officers were held in one of the sugar houses "with common Soldiers, Sailors & even Negroes & were all treated alike both as to Provisions & other Matters & indiscriminate Insolence & Cruelty" ("Deposition of Lt. John Barrett," [Aug. 4, 1777], *NDAR*, 9: 705–706). For Thorp, see RWPA: W15427, repr. in Johnston, *Harlem Heights*, 196.

25. "Slade Diary," passim. According to Samuel Young, "Great numbers died in this confinement, three and four, and sometimes more, died in a day, and one day nine." Young's account was corroborated under oath by James Shannar and William Houston. John Caryl recalled one morning when "ten were found dead" (*Pennsylvania Evening Post*, May 3, 1777; see also the statement of James Reed, RWPA: S16236).

26. For Boyd, see *Pennsylvania Evening Post*, May 3, 1777; repr. *Connecticut Gazette*, May 30, 1777. For Franklin, see *JPC* 2: 411–412. Ichabod Perry was reduced to eating wood (Perry, *Reminiscences*, 14; see also the statements of Lambert Dorland, RWPA: S42171, and "The Old Jersey Prison Ship," *Farmer's Cabinet* ([Amherst, NH], Jan. 3, 1834).

27. *Pennsylvania Evening Post*, May 3, 1777; Hinman, *Historical Collection . . . Connecticut*, 135; 5 *AA* 3: 1234. The version in Dandridge, *American Prisoners*, 108, is bowdlerized. See also Phoenix, *Whitney Family of Connecticut*, 1: 87; Hinman, *Historical Collection . . . Connecticut*, 137.

28. Thomas Bull, RWPA: S2056; *Fitch Diary*, 70, 71, 78–79, 89, 148, 149; *Nice Diary*, 405. For Gillet, see Stiles, *Letters from the Prisons and Prison Ships*, 11–12. Troup deposed that he "understood from several persons that the privates who were prisoners in the city of New York were uniformly treated with great inhumanity"— which suggests that he, unlike Fitch and other officers, never visited the jails person-

ally before he was exchanged in early December (Ryan, *Salute to Courage*, 68; see also *Adlum Memoirs*, 127, which remarks that the officers were gloomy, perhaps "owing to the suffering of the soldiers").

29. *Graydon Memoirs*, 232–233. "Poor misfortune . . ." is a line by the Scottish poet James Thomson (1700–1748), better known as the author of "Rule, Britannia."

30. Mrs. Spicer is mentioned in [Hanford], *Narrative . . . Levi Hanford*, 21–22 (hereafter *Hanford Narrative*). The testimony of Lydia Robbins is in RWPA: W22804. Lewis Pintard declared in January 1779 that "no Articles of Cloathing Provisions or other Necessaries that I have sent from time to time to the Provost for the American Prisoners of War have ever been refused Admittance." Of course Pintard was acting in his official capacity as American agent (*RAM*, 1: 366). In his diary, Oliver Babcock notes making multiple visits to the prisons with food and firewood, and one trip, with clothing, to the *Grosvenor* and *Dutton* ("Babcock Diary," in Johnston, *Harlem Heights*, 198–199). A Connecticut officer, Major Bezaleel Bebee, later said he spent "large sums of money to relieve the extream distresses of the privates" in prison (*PRC*, 2: 338). When John Adlum was buying groceries for the officers boarding at Mrs. Carroll's, the "country people" in the markets gave him a 20 percent discount because he identified himself as a prisoner (*Adlum Memoirs*, 91–92).

31. For Fraunces, see his 1785 petition to Congress in PCC, Record Group 360, M247/r49. (I am grateful to Nadezhda Williams for bringing this document to my attention.) It was probably Fraunces who told the story reported in [Fisher], *Elijah Fisher's Journal*, 23. *Fitch Diary*, 149 ("Narative"). Because Fitch also reported numerous visits to the imprisoned men, Sabine sees further reason to dismiss the "Narative" as untrustworthy. Clearly, however, Fitch was generalizing about the experience of all the American officers, and his remark is entirely consistent with the testimony of numerous others. For Gamble, see *Connecticut Gazette*, May 30, 1777. Gamble's deposition was transmitted to Washington in January by the Executive Committee of Congress, with the assurance that "his Account of their ill usage is confirmed by all the Prisoners that come from thence" (*NDAR*, 7: 877). See also *Hanford Narrative*, 18 and passim; Watson, *Historic Tales of Olden Time*, 178; and Private James Stuart's declaration in *Pennsylvania Evening Post*, May 3, 1777. Doctor James McHenry, on the other hand, later told General Washington that from November 20 to the middle of the following January, he was repeatedly denied permission to visit the sick (Steiner, *Life and Correspondence of McHenry*, 14; McHenry to GW, June 21, 1777, *PGW* 10: 95–99).

32. *Allen Narrative*, 68–82; Jellison, *Ethan Allen*, 166–169.

33. 4 *AA* 5: 860; 5 *AA* 1: 928; Duffy, *Ethan Allen and His Kin*, 1: 59–60. No one at the time would have missed Allen's appropriation of the last words of the Protestant martyr Hugh Latimer as Latimer and Nicholas Ridley were about to be burned at the stake outside Balliol College in 1555: "Be of good comfort, Master Ridley, and play the man! We shall this day light such a candle, by God's grace, in England, as I trust shall never be put out." Quite apart from what it reveals about his state of mind at this point in his ordeal, Allen's identification of patriotic sacrifice with manliness is a small clue that captivity was, or at least could be, an emasculating experience. I thank Paul Goodspeed for reminding me of Latimer's immortal lines.

34. *Allen Narrative*, 84. "This is a mutable world," the captain told him, "and one gentleman never knows but that it may be in his power to help another"—a code that

Allen honored by dissuading his fellow prisoners from attempting to seize the ship and murder its officers (*Allen Narrative*, 87; see also Allen to Washington, Nov. 2, 1776, *PGW,* 7: 79; *Freeman's Journal* (Philadelphia), Dec. 3, 1776; Moore, *Diary of the American Revolution*, 1: 346). Where Allen stayed in New York is unclear, but it was not at Mrs. Carroll's or in Liberty House.

35. *Graydon Memoirs*, 243; *Allen Narrative*, 92. As the English actor John Bernard said of Allen: "You entered his presence with reverence, and left it with wonder." Bernard also learned that Allen became "an object of amusement to the English at New York" (Bernard, *Retrospections of America*, 114, 115; *Adlum Memoirs*, 100; *Fitch Diary*, 75, 84).

36. Allen almost certainly learned the Woodhull story from Robert Troup, who was with him in New York for about a week or ten days before being exchanged in early December (*Allen Narrative*, 92–93, 109; *Fitch Diary*, 44). Allen seems to have mixed up the story of Captain Joseph Jewett, apparently killed after surrendering on August 27, with that of a Captain Amos Fellows, who was imprisoned after the British seized New York City. Sabine reports this as a typically "reckless" mistake (*Fitch Diary*, 157), but it was an easy one to make and probably did not originate with Allen. As we have seen, rumors were rife about American soldiers hanged after the fighting on Long Island. Allen's error was failing to corroborate these and other tales he heard from fellow prisoners, though it is hard to see how he could have done so (*Allen Narrative*, 93, 94–95, 96).

37. *Allen Narrative*, 101–103; cf. *Graydon Memoirs*, 235.

38. "Extract of a Letter, from a Gentleman of Honor and Distinction," *Connecticut Gazette*, Jan. 17, 1777, repr. in *Boston Gazette*, Jan. 27, 1777, and elsewhere; Hinman, *Historical Collection . . . Connecticut*, 121; "Letter from New York to a Friend in Leeds, Jan. 14, 1777," *St. James Chronicle*, Mar. 11–13, 1777: quoted in Stokes, *Iconography of Manhattan*, 5: 1044; *Adlum Memoirs*, 125. For another nearly-buried-alive story, see the Journal of Abner Everett, RWPA: W6087. On December 25, Jabez Fitch learned that no fewer than twenty-one prisoners had died during the night (*Fitch Diary*, 94). Myer's deposition is in *JPC* 2: 410–412; see also Booth, *History of the City of New York*, 512–513; Onderdonk, *Revolutionary Incidents of Suffolk and Kings*, 212–214; "Miserecors," *Connecticut Gazette*, Feb. 28, 1777; [Heath], *Memoir*, 97–98; and the deposition by H. G. Livingston, in *Calendar of Historical Manuscripts*, 1: 671. For similar observations, see John Heller, RWPA: S8702. For Boyd, see *Pennsylvania Evening Post*, May 3, 1777, repr., *Connecticut Gazette*, May 30, 1777. Private James Stuart recalled how one sick prisoner actually revived "after being thrown with the dead in the pit, and with help got out" (*Pennsylvania Evening Post*, May 3, 1777). John Pintard remembered many grave sites along the Hudson River shore from the Battery all the way up to Trinity Church. After the burial parties left, he added, the wives of British soldiers would uncover the bodies, strip them of blankets, and leave them exposed for packs of dogs to devour ("Reminiscences of John Pintard," Bancroft Collection, v. 298 ["New York and Miscellaneous"], NYPL).

39. *Graydon Memoirs*, 244. *Fitch Diary*, 90, notes the release of 200 men on December 21. *Nice Diary*, 405, has a total of twenty-five officers and thirty-four privates exchanged on December 4 and December 10. "A General Return of Prisoners," dated Philadelphia, January 10, 1778, now among the Elias Boudinot Papers, HSP, shows that Howe, presumably in the course of the previous year, had released 1,701 American captives without exchange, most of whom would have been taken on Long Island

or at Fort Washington. Oliver Woodruff put the number of dead on the *Glasgow* at twenty-eight (RWPA: S14885). A report in the *Connecticut Journal*, Jan. 8, 1777, mentions twenty dead en route to Milford, with another twenty dead shortly after the *Glasgow* arrived there. Prior to this voyage, the *Glasgow* seems to have served briefly as a prison ship (see James Lovell to Captain Proctor, Nov. 5, 1776: 5 *AA* 3: 519). On Mayo, Babcock, and others, see *History of Litchfield County*, 39; Hollister, *History of Connecticut*, 2: 289; Starr, *History of Cornwall, Connecticut*, 186; Newton, *Rev. Roger Newton*, 50–51; *Connecticut Gazette*, Jan. 17, 1777; "Babcock Extracts," in Johnston, *Harlem Heights*, 201. See also *Fitch Diary*, 93–94, 149; Backus, *Church History of New England*, 2: 317; cf. *Adlum Memoirs*, 142–143, on the many prisoners who died on the way home, spreading disease. Governor Trumbull of Connecticut was so alarmed by this that he ordered new recruits to be inoculated. "Our returning soldiers have spread the infection into almost every town in the State," he informed Washington in February 1777 (*Trumbull Papers*, 2: 43; Fenn, *Pox Americana*, 108 and passim).

40. Fitch said that half the prisoners from his regiment were dead by the end of December (*Fitch Diary*, 149 ["Narative"]). Adlum said "upwards" of 1,100 of the Fort Washington prisoners died in two months, "and a full third died on their way and after they arrived home" (*Adlum Memoirs*, 124–125). Ethan Allen put the number of dead in New York at "about two thousand" (*Allen Narrative*, 109). See also newspaper accounts in Moore, *Diary of the American Revolution*, 1: 374–379. It is all exceedingly impressionistic, but if we count prisoners who died of malnutrition or disease soon after their release, the overall mortality rate probably reached 60 or even 70 percent.

41. Hollister, *History of Connecticut*, 2: 289; Starr, *History of Cornwall*, 186–187; Hinman, *Historical Collection . . . Connecticut*, 137, 587–588; *Serle Journal*, 201; the 1832 pension application of James Little's widow, RWPA: W8256; see also the story of Cornelius Rich, a resident of Chatham, Connecticut, who had lost three of his six sons by 1779 (*PRC*, 2: 384).

42. *Adlum Memoirs*, 124. Cornelius Brooks, one of the Northampton men, declared many years later that of the nineteen soldiers from his company held on the *Whitby*, "he does not know of but two who lived to get home" (RWPA: S14997). A century ago, W. T. R. Saffell wrote that none of the thirty-six prisoners belonging to Captain George Tudor's company of the Third Pennsylvania survived captivity in New York. Private Cornelius Westbrook, however, filed a pension application in 1825 (RWPA: S40656; *RRW*, 310–311). On York, Pennsylvania, see Hartley to GW, Feb. 12, 1777, *PGW*, 8: 317–318. For Virginia, see Dandridge, *American Prisoners*, 11–32.

43. *Farmer's Cabinet*, Jan. 3, 1834.

44. *Fitch Diary*, 91, 92–97, 103, 152, and passim. His new landlord was one John Laperee, usually referred to in the diary as "The Frenchman." Sabine was unable to identify Laperee or locate his house in contemporary city directories.

45. *Fitch Diary*, 104–105, 156–157 ("Narative"); *Graydon Memoirs*, 245. "Dumb forgetfulness" is from Thomas Gray's "Elegy Written in a Country Church-yard." Graydon may well have been right, though the shortage of acceptable housing for His Majesty's officers probably came into play as well ("Examination of Mrs. Hannah White," *Pennsylvania Evening Post*, Mar. 6, 1777).

46. According to Sabine, Rapalje's farm extended from New Lots Avenue up to Jamaica Avenue and was bounded by Montauk Avenue in the west and Autumn Avenue

in the east. But see Landesman, *History of New Lots, Brooklyn*, esp. 65–74, which makes no mention of either George Rapalje or his property. It is not apparent how many paroled officers occupied billets in New Lots, but if there were two per household, on average, there might have been thirty or more. In late April, thirty-eight New England officers from the New Lots area were allowed to petition the Connecticut Assembly for support (*Fitch Diary*, 118, 122, 163–164, 179). "Samp porridge," as it was also known, seems to have been a staple of the local diet, not something inflicted solely on hapless prisoners. Graydon pronounced it "very eatable" (*Graydon Memoirs*, 247; also Furman, *Antiquities of Long Island*, 226–228; and Charles Anthon, "Anthon's Notes," *SIIP*, 114). Fitch shared that featherbed with Captain Ozias Bissell, also from Connecticut.

47. *Fitch Diary*, 103–105, 130, 157 ("Narative"), 181; Bowman, "Military Parolees"; Huguenin, "Ethan Allen, Parolee." As of mid-1778, parolees on Long Island were required only to return to their assigned quarters at sunset (Axtell to Webb, May 29, 1778, *SBW*, 2: 99–100). The 100 members of the Everlasting Club purportedly arranged matters so that when one of them was ready to leave the table, another would take his place. Joseph Addison famously described the club in the May 23, 1711, issue of the *Spectator*. Fitch's loyalty to British cultural standards can also be gauged from his habit of referring to the mosquito-infested meadows on the south side of New Lots Road as "St. James Park."

48. *Fitch Diary*, 109, 110, 113, 118, 125, 128, 136–158.

49. Ibid., 132–135, 137.

50. Ibid., 131.

CHAPTER 4

1. 5 *AA*, 1: 1368; 5 *AA*, 3: 1176, 1201–1202, 1231–1232, 1239–1240, 1294, 1377; Moore, *Diary of the American Revolution*, 1: 360; *LP*, 2: 348, 356, and passim; Alden, *General Charles Lee*, 157–159 and passim; Shy, "Charles Lee"; Fischer, *Washington's Crossing*, 147–149; Hibbert, *Redcoats and Rebels*, 145–148; Buchanan, *Road to Valley Forge*, 142–144. For a contemporary assessment of Lee, see Bernard, *Retrospections of America*, 95–103. Lafayette's observation is from his "Memoir of 1779" (*LLP* 2: 9). Lee's betrayal is described in Kipping and Smith, *At General Howe's Side*, 7.

2. British officer quoted in Alden, *General Charles Lee*, 160. See also *NRAR*, 23; Lutnick, *American Revolution and the British Press*, 96–99; Kipping and Smith, *At General Howe's Side*, 7; *Fitch Diary*, 102. According to a story first printed in Philadelphia and often copied in the American papers, Lee's captors showed "an ungenerous, nay boyish triumph, after they got him secure at Brunswick, by making his horse drunk" (*Connecticut Gazette*, Jan. 24, 1777). Second officer: 5 *AA* 2: 1293–1294.

3. GW to Lund Washington, Dec. 10–17, 1776, *PGW* 7: 289–292; Joseph Trumbull to GW, Dec. 13, 1776, *PGW* 7: 328–331; Hancock to GW, Dec. 23, 1776, *PGW* 7: 418–419; Robert Morris to GW, Dec. 23, 1776, *PGW* 7: 420–422; Hancock to GW, Jan. 6, 1777, *PGW* 8: 31–32; GW to Robert Harrison, Jan. 10, 1777, *PGW* 8: 32–33; also 5 *AA* 1: 1368; 5 *AA* 3: 1607; *JCC* 6: 1029; 7: 16, 140, and passim; *LDC* 6: 39; Onderdonk, *Revolutionary Incidents of Suffolk and Kings*, 217; *SBW* 2: 31; "Examination of Mrs. Hannah White," *Pennsylvania Evening Post*, Mar. 6, 1777; Thacher, *Military Journal*, 73–74. Judge Jones was outraged that Howe made no effort to counter the "scandalous, false, and infamous" rumors about Lee that were "industri-

ously reported throughout the revolted Colonies from one end to the other" (*History of New York*, 1: 173–175).

4. Kipping and Smith, *At General Howe's Side*, 7, 10; Alden, *General Charles Lee*, 164–165, 166–168; Howe to Germain, Dec. 20, 1776, *DAR*, 268–269. Howe did eventually conclude that Lee had given up his army pension before accepting a commission in the American service and could not be tried by court-martial for desertion (see Howe to Germain, June 5, 1777, *SS* 2: 68). What to do with Lee, as with Allen, was ultimately a political decision that only Germain and the king could make (Jones, *History of New York*, 1: 173–175).

5. Miles and Atlee to GW, [Nov. 3, 1776], *PGW* 7: 140–141; and Greene to GW, Nov. 11–12, 1776, *PGW* 7: 190–191; see also Magaw, Miles, Atlee, et al. to Howe, Dec. 8, 1776, *RAM* 1: 76; Hancock to GW, Nov. 9, 1776, *PGW* 7: 122–124; GW to Hancock, Nov. 19, 1776, *PGW* 7: 180–186; GW to Atlee, Nov. 21, 1776, *PGW* 7: 190–191; GW to Miles, Nov. 25, 1776, *PGW* 7: 211–212; GW to Hancock, Nov. 27, 1776, *PGW* 7: 223–224. Also *Mackenzie Diary*, 1: 103; 5 *AA* 3: 858; and Bowman, *Captive Americans*, 74–75. I find no reference to an $8,000 appropriation in *JCC* or *LDC*. Miles was followed, over the next month or so, by several more paroled or escaped prisoners, among them Captain William Gamble, a Pennsylvania naval officer, who supplied Congress with graphic details of the mistreatment of prisoners in New York (*LDC* 6: 46–47; *Connecticut Gazette*, May 30, 1777; 5 *AA* 3: 1193; *PRC*, 1: 86, 125; *Fitch Diary*, 74, 76, 93, and passim).

6. Trumbull to GW, Dec. 12, 1776, *PGW* 7: 322–324; GW to Trumbull, Dec. 21, 1776, *PGW* 7: 406–407; Trumbull to GW, Jan. 12, 1777, *PGW* 8: 53–54; Trumbull to GW, Jan. 14, 1777, *PGW* 8: 70–71; Trumbull to GW, Jan. 23, 1777, *PGW* 8: 140–143; GW to Trumbull, Mar. 23, 1777, *PGW* 8: 622–623; *Trumbull Papers*, 2: 28; Buel, *Dear Liberty*, 153–154; *Fitch Diary*, 94. See also the 1779 deposition by eight men from Cornwall, captured at Fort Washington in Starr, *History of Cornwall*, 185.

7. *JPC* 2: 410–412, 671; *Minutes of the Committee*, 1: 119–125. (The investigation was led by Gouverneur Morris, but after taking depositions in January and February—from Robert Troup, Henry Franklin, and Adolph Myer, among others—Morris said he was too busy and gave up. Besides, witnesses were hard to come by up in Kingston, where the Convention was then sitting). See also Pennsylvania Council of Safety to GW, Jan. 15, 1777, *PGW* 8: 74–76. For Maryland, see Captain George Cook to the Maryland Council of Safety, Jan. 19, 1777, and the petition of Captain James Campbell to the Maryland Council, Jan. 20, 1777, *NDAR* 7: 997, 1003.

8. *Pennsylvania Evening Post*, Jan. 9, 1777; "Extract of a Letter, from a Gentleman of Honor and Distinction," *Connecticut Gazette*, Jan. 17, 1777; *Boston Gazette*, Jan. 27, 1777; *Freeman's Journal* (Philadelphia), Jan. 28, 1777; *Essex Journal*, Jan. 30, 1777; and elsewhere.

9. Thacher, *Military Journal*, 74, 75; *Freeman's Journal* (Philadelphia), Feb. 2, 1777; *Continental Journal*, Feb. 13, 1777; *Boston Gazette*, Feb. 17, 1777; Parsons to GW, Feb. 19, 1777, *PGW* 8: 372; Hall, *Parsons*, 89, 94–95; Green, *Life of Witherspoon*, 164n; Davidson, *Propaganda and the American Revolution*, esp. 369ff. American newspapers printed stories about the abuse of prisoners confined elsewhere, but it was the situation in New York that grabbed everyone's attention. See, e.g., *New-Hampshire Gazette*, June 28, 1777, on the "barbarous and inhuman" treatment of 200 American prisoners on the *Lord Stanley* prison ship in Halifax. As for the effect on recruiting, Parsons eventually concluded that although stories of abuse did spur men to reenlist,

they discouraged *new* recruits (Hall, *Parsons*, 90, 92; Buel, *Dear Liberty*, 105ff.; *Connecticut Courant*, June 30, 1777). See also Colonel Thomas Hartley to GW, Feb. 12, 1777, *PGW* 8: 317–318.

10. Onderdonk, *Revolutionary Incidents of Suffolk and Kings*, 218; McHenry to GW, June 21, 1777, *PGW* 10: 95–99; GW to McHenry, July 5, 1777, *PGW* 10: 197–198; Steiner, *Life and Correspondence of James McHenry*, 10–14 (hereafter *McHenry*); *Fitch Diary*, 148–149; Stone, "Experiences of a Prisoner," 528–529.

11. Dubuke's first advertisement appeared in the *Constitutional Gazette*, Oct. 14, 1775, and continued to run in that paper as well as in the *New-York Journal* until December. The circumstances of his departure were noted in the *Constitutional Gazette* for Mar. 9, 1776. For later iterations of the legend, see "Reminiscences of John Pintard," Bancroft Collection, v. 298 ("New York and Miscellaneous"), NYPL, and Boudinot, *Journal or Historical Recollections*, 35–36. Other stories, unrelated to Dubuke, accused the British of infecting their prisoners with smallpox. See, e.g., Colonel John Chester to Colonel Samuel B. Webb, Jan. 17, 1777, quoted in *WW* 7: 3n; Davidson, *Propaganda and the American Revolution*, 370–371.

12. *Connecticut Journal*, Jan. 30, 1777.

13. See *Connecticut Gazette*, Feb. 28, 1777; *Boston Gazette*, Mar. 17, 1777; *Massachusetts Spy*, Mar. 20, 1777; and *New-Hampshire Gazette*, Mar. 22, 1777. See Dumas to Franklin, May 23, 1777, *PBF* 24: 68–69; Arrenberg to Franklin, May 24, 1777, *PBF* 24: 72; Moore, *Diary of the American Revolution*, 1: 374–378; *Fitch Diary*, 165, 183. For Livingston's address to the legislature, see *Pennsylvania Packet*, Mar. 4, 1777. On Livingston as "Adolphus": *New-Jersey Gazette*, Feb. 25, 1778; *PWL*, 2: 3–6, 239–241. Livingston remained convinced that the deaths of so many prisoners could hardly have been an accident. In 1778 he blasted Commandant Robinson for "the coolest and most deliberate kind of murder" (*Continental Journal*, Feb. 5, 1778).

14. Hancock to GW, Jan. 6, 1777, *PGW* 8: 3–4; GW to Hancock, Feb. 5, 1777, *PGW* 8: 249–252; *JCC* 7: 16, 135; *LDC* 6: 49–50, 73–74; Alden, *General Charles Lee*, 166–167, 171–172; McGeachy, "The American War of Lieutenant Colonel Archibald Campbell of Inverneill"; Knight, "Prisoner Exchange and Parole," 202–203; Haffner, "Treatment of Prisoners of War by the Americans," 151–159; *Kemble Papers* 1: 90.

15. Howe to GW, Feb. 27, 1777, *PGW* 8: 453–454; GW to James Bowdoin, Feb. 28, 1777, *PGW* 8: 461–463; GW to Campbell, Mar. 1, 1777, *PGW* 8: 468–469; GW to John Hancock, Mar. 1, 1777, *PGW* 8: 472–474; GW to Robert Morris, Mar. 2, 1777, *PGW* 8: 486–489; GW to Hancock, Mar. 6, 1777, *PGW* 8: 522–523; Hancock to GW, Mar. 17, 1777, *PGW* 8: 591–592; GW to Nathanael Greene, Mar. 21, 1977, *PGW* 8: 611; GW to Greene, Mar. 22, 1777, *PGW* 8: 617–618; Nathanael Greene to GW, Mar. 24, 1777, *PGW* 8: 636–637; Hancock to GW, Mar. 26, 1777, *PGW* 8: 626–629; GW to John Hancock, May 28, 1777, *PGW* 9: 546–548; *RAM* 1: 90.

16. See *JCC* 7: 179; *LDC* 6: 452; John Hancock to the Massachusetts General Court, Oct. 8, 1777, *LDC* 6: 496; *LDC* 7: 154–155; *LDC* 8: 78–79.

17. GW to Howe, Dec. 29, 1776, *PGW* 7: 478; GW to James Bowdoin and the New Hampshire General Court, Dec. 22, 1776, *PGW* 7: 409–410; GW to Nicholas Cooke [Governor of Rhode Island], Mar. 3, 1777, *PGW* 8: 496–497; Dixon, "Divided Authority," 28–29; Haffner, "Treatment of Prisoners of War by the Americans," 179–280, and passim. On Lee's alleged "treason," see *LP* 2: 358–359; Alden, *General Charles Lee*, 173–179; *LDC* 6: 373–375; *JCC* 7: 207; Lee to GW, Feb. 9, 1777, *PGW* 8: 289–290; GW to Lee, Apr. 1, 1777, *PGW* 9: 39–40; Lee to GW, Apr. 5, 1777,

PGW 9: 70. Also *LP* 2: 361–366; Moore, *Treason of Charles Lee*, reprinted in *LP* 4: 335–427; Alden, *General Charles Lee*, 174–179; Shy, "Charles Lee," 153–154. In July, Captain John Bowater described Lee as an "atrocious Monster . . . as perfect in Treachery as if he had been an American born," adding that he "says it is all over with them and now is the time they should treat." But Bowater did not explicitly say that Lee had abandoned the American cause, and he was in a position to know if he had (Balderston and Syrett, *Lost War*, 131, 138). For a Hessian report on Lee's attitude, see Burgoyne, *Enemy Views*, 218.

18. Knight, "Prisoner Exchange and Parole," 201–222; Metzger, *Prisoner in the American Revolution*, esp. 203–240; Bowman, *Captive Americans*, 83, 103–107, and passim; *SBW* 2: 19–85; *WW* 6: 359, 390, 410; *WW* 7: 258–259; Dixon, "Divided Authority," pp. 201–243.

19. Fooks, *Prisoners of War*, 271; Cohen, *Yankee Sailors*, 26–29; Cogliano, *Maritime Prisoners*, 43–45; *Pennsylvania Evening Post*, May 8, 1777; *Norwich Packet*, June 2, 1777; Anderson, "Treatment of Prisoners," 66. In America, North's Act was known by May (Robert Sherman to Jonathan Trumbull, May 14, 1777, *LDC* 7: 81–82).

20. GW to Brigadier General David Forman, May 15, 1777, *PGW* 9: 428–429; Bowman, *Captive Americans*, 23–27; Metzger, *Prisoner in the American Revolution*, 16–19. In the summer of 1777, New Jersey authorities declared their intention to begin jailing prominent Tories for exchange with the "honest citizens stolen and imprisoned" in New York (*Pennsylvania Evening Post*, Aug. 26, 1777). At the end of August, they had ten men in custody (William Livingston to Samuel Hayes, July 10, 1777, *PWL* 1: 15–16; WL to EB, Aug. 29, 1777, *PWL* 1: 48–49).

21. GW to Atlee, Nov. 25, 1776, *PGW* 7: 191; Howe to GW, Dec. 5, 1776, *PGW* 7: 264–265; *RAM* 1: 75–76. Executive Committee to GW, Jan. 7, [1777], *PGW* 8: 7–8; *LDC* 6; GW to Robert Morris, George Clymer, and George Walton, Jan. 12, 1777; GW to Howe, Jan. 13, 1777, *PGW* 8: 58–61. Washington wrote twice to Howe on the thirteenth. His second letter contained a copy of Captain Gamble's report to Congress on the abuse of prisoners (see note 5 above) and the dying affidavit of Lieutenant Bartholomew Yeats [Yates] of Virginia, who was shot at Princeton, then bayoneted and clubbed by British soldiers as he lay wounded. Howe replied that "the Heat of Action will sometimes produce Instances [of 'Barbarity'] that are only to be lamented." GW to Joseph Reed, Jan. 14, 1777; GW to William Livingston, Feb. 14, 1777; Howe to GW, Jan. 23, 1777, *PGW* 8: 67–68, 137–138, 335–336; *RAM* 1: 82; [Lawrence], *Brief Narrative*, 42–43.

22. Howe to GW, Jan. 17, 1777, *PGW* 8: 91–94.

23. GW to Howe, Apr. 9, 1777, *PGW* 9: 102–105; Howe to GW, Apr. 21, 1777, *PGW* 9: 228–230; GW to Howe, June 10, 1777, *PGW* 9: 661–666; *SBW* 2: 40–42. For a point-by-point refutation of Howe's claims, see James McHenry to GW, June 21, 1777, *PGW* 10: 95–99. On Howe's obstinacy, see also Metzger, *Prisoner in the American Revolution*, 93; *NDAR*, 10: 76–77; and Uhlendorf, *Revolution in America*, 130.

24. Green, *Life of Witherspoon*, 38–39; Collins, *President Witherspoon*, 1: 22–24; 2: 20–21, and passim; [Lawrence], *Brief Narrative*, 15n. The five other members of the committee were Abraham Clark, Francis Lewis, George Ross, Thomas Hayward, and William Smith (*JCC* 7: 42–43; *LDC* 6: 133–134). See also Chase to GW, Jan. 23, 1777, *PGW* 8: 136–137; GW to Chase, Feb. 5, 1777, *PGW* 8: 247; William Livingston to GW, Feb. 6, 1777, *PGW* 8: 261–262; GW to Livingston, Mar. 3, 1777, *PGW* 8: 500–502. Legend has it that soon after the Battle of Long Island, the British ransacked Lewis's home in Whitestone, Queens, and dragged his wife, Elizabeth, off

to jail in New York. Badly treated, she died several months later (Delafield, *Biographies of Francis Lewis and Morgan Lewis*, 41–44, 49). The information received by Congress, however, was only that she had been "detained" at home and denied permission to visit New York (*JCC* 6: 936).

25. *JCC* 7: 276–279; Stedman, *History of the American War,* 1: 242–243.

26. *Pennsylvania Evening Post,* Apr. 24, 26, 29, May 3, and May 10, 1777; *JCC* 7: 279; *JCC* 8: 564; *JCC* 9: 1085; *Connecticut Courant,* June 2–9, 1777; *Providence Gazette,* July 12, 1777; *New England Chronicle,* May 29, June 5, 12, 1777; *Norwich Packet,* June 9, 1777. As late as the end of May, the New York State Council of Safety was still urging Congress to distribute the report as a pamphlet to give the world "a proper idea of the spirit with which the King of Britain wages and conducts this wicked war against us" (*JPC* 1: 947). Apparently, Congress never did so, as no copies are known to exist. For Adams, see *LDC* 6: 661–662; and Butterfield, *Diary . . . of John Adams,* 2: 112, 120–121.

27. See GW to Hancock, Sept. 25, 1776, *PGW* 6: 401–402, and Dec. 20, 1776, *PGW* 7: 381–389; GW to Howe, Jan. 20, 1777, *PGW* 8: 117; Howe to GW, Jan. 29, 1777, *PGW* 8: 117, 180; *SBW* 2: 29–31; Bowman, "Lewis Pintard"; Bowman, *Captive Americans,* 68–69; *BLB,* 5, 10–11; and Haffner, "Treatment of Prisoners of War by the Americans," 11–14. To the very end of the war Congress would struggle to clarify the scope of the commissary general's authority and whether he should come under civilian or military supervision (Dixon, "Divided Authority," 28–30, 73–74, 91, and passim).

28. GW to Reed, Feb. 23, 1777, *PGW* 8: 432–433; *BJ,* 9; Dixon, "Divided Authority," 90; Boyd, *Elias Boudinot,* 33–35 and passim; *BLL* 1: 42; GW to EB, Apr. 1, 1777, *PGW* 9: 33. Washington and his staff sometimes wrote "Boudinot" as "Boudinotte," a clue to how it was pronounced (GW to Joseph Spencer, Sept. 2, 1777, *PGW* 11: 130; Hamilton to McHenry, Mar. 5, 1778: *PAH* 1: 437).

29. Mitchell, *Alexander Hamilton,* 41–49.

30. One set of Pintard's grandparents were also Boudinot's great-grandparents (Boyd, *Elias Boudinot,* 36n11; Mulford, "Annis Boudinot Stockton"; see also Mulford, *Only for the Eye of a Friend,* esp. 11–28. John Pintard, Lewis's nephew, later recalled that the two men were extremely close. "Pintard Reminiscences," NYPL.

31. *LDC* 6: 40; *JCC* 7: 12–13.

32. Loring to GW, Apr. 24, 1777, *PGW* 9: 258–259; Bowman, "Lewis Pintard," 40–41. Pintard to EB, May 19, 1777, Boudinot Papers, HSP; *SBW* 2: 46n; *BLB,* 5–7. Congress gave Boudinot his commission on June 6, backdated to Apr. 15, but he and Pintard were on the job well before then. Bowman, "Pintard," 40–41, erroneously has Pintard in New York by the end of January.

33. *BLB,* 8–9, 55–57, 69–70, and passim; Boyd, *Elias Boudinot,* 40–41; GW to Trumbull, July 2, 1777, *PGW* 10: 173–175; also GW to Joseph Spencer, Sept. 2, 1777, *PGW* 11: 130; Thomas Shaw to Trumbull, Nov. 5, 1777, *NDAR* 10: 403–404; *PGC* 2: 547–548, 550–551; *PGC* 4: 837, 844–845; *PGC* 5: 129–130, 387–388, 95; *PGC* 7: 319–320; *Boston Gazette,* July 28, 1777. See also Knight, "Prisoner Exchange and Parole," 202n; and Dixon, "Divided Authority," 29–30, 46–47, 91–94, 250–254, and passim.

34. Hancock to GW, April 26, 1777; Secret Committee of the Continental Congress to GW, May 2, 1777, *PGW* 9: 274–75, 326; *JCC* 7: 289; Bowman, "Lewis Pintard," 41; *BJ,* 10.

35. *BJ,* 9–10; Pintard to EB, Sept. 3, 20, and 24, 1777: Boudinot Papers, HSP. Boyd, *Elias Boudinot,* 35–37; *BLB,* 11, 13, 19–22, 24–25, 30–31, 32–35, 37–39, 41–42;

BLL 1: 44–48; see also Bowman, "Lewis Pintard," 41–42, which puts a somewhat more positive gloss on the situation than I think is warranted.

36. *PGW* 10: 500 (citing *NDAR*, 9: 273–724). On the Philadelphia campaign, see Schecter, *Battle for New York*, 289–292; Taaffe, *Philadelphia Campaign*.

37. For Costigan, see RWPA: S43337. For the Sandy Hook action, see *JHG* 2: 17; Peckham, *Toll of Independence*, 30; and "Battle of the Navesink," *New York Times*, Feb. 23, 1896, which includes excerpts from the pension applications of several surviving prisoners. For Kingsbridge, etc., see *JHG* 2: 22; Kipping and Smith, *At General Howe's Side*, 10. On Cornwallis and van Zandt, see *JHG* 2: 28; *Serle Journal*, 211; Leiby, *Revolutionary War in the Hackensack Valley*, 116. Fell's story can be followed in William Livingston to GW, Apr. 30, 1777, *PGW* 9: 308–309; *JHG* 2: 30; *Kemble Papers* 1: 114; Leiby, *Revolutionary War in the Hackensack Valley*, 119–120; and [Fell], *Delegate from New Jersey*, 6–8 (this journal is not to be confused with the "Memorandum" Fell kept while in the Provost). On Tryon's Danbury raid, see Grumman, *Revolutionary Soldiers of Redding*, 60–65, which has more than forty American captives; on Sanford, see Hall, *Parsons*, 422. Benjamin Banks was likewise initially first put in a sugar house and then moved to "the prison ship" (RWPA: S12954). *JHG* 2: 31 has fifty-three prisoners from the Danbury raid arriving in New York on the first of May. See also Peckham, *Toll of Independence*, 33, which reports twenty Americans killed and seventy-five wounded during the raid, but none captured. According to a description of the action in the *Connecticut Journal*, Apr. 30, 1777, the enemy "behaved with their usual barbarity, wantonly and cruelly murdering the wounded prisoners who fell in to their hands."

38. The Piscataway action is described in [Peebles], *John Peebles' American War*, 111. Here, too, Peckham's cautious reading of the sources yielded a much lower number of captives, or none at all (see *Toll of Independence*, 34). Captain von Muenchhausen put the number of captives at thirty-five (Kipping and Smith, *At General Howe's Side*, 12). Ambrose Serle said it was thirty (*Serle Journal*, 222); see also Major General Adam Stephen to GW, May 12, 1777, *PGW* 9: 404–406. For Hartt, see Fell's "Memorandum," which dates Hartt's arrival in the Provost on May 27. Onderdonk (*Revolutionary Incidents of Queens*, 154) has Hartt in the Jamaica jail on June 14, but this is clearly an error. The Hartt quote is from the draft of the sermon he preached at Smithtown on August 24, 1776, three days before the Battle of Brooklyn (Archives of the Presbyterian Church, SPL). Cresswell's remark is in *Cresswell Journal*, 224. But he may have been referring to deserters, not prisoners.

39. For prisoners taken at Brunswick, see Fell, "Memorandum"; Onderdonk, *Revolutionary Incidents of Suffolk and Kings*, 220. Peckham reports no prisoners taken in this action, however (*Toll of Independence*, 36). On the Metuchen clash, see Peebles, *John Peebles' American War*, 117. Captain von Muenchhausen thought eighty-two Americans had been taken (Kipping and Smith, *At General Howe's Side*, 20). Serle put the number at seventy (*Serle Journal*, 235). Peckham, however, has none (*Toll of Independence*, 36).

40. *JHG* 2: 38–57; Leiby, *Revolutionary War in the Hackensack Valley*, 117–119, 183; Hall, *Parsons*, 128–129; Ward, *Between the Lines*, 22–23; Ryan, *Salute to Courage*, 90–91; Peckham, *Toll of Independence*, 39; Burgoyne, *Enemy Views*, 216; [Lee], "Sullivan's Expedition." Also Brigadier General Nathaniel Heard to GW, May 14, 1777, *PGW* 9: 417–418; Major General Adam Stephen to GW, May 15, 1777, *PGW* 9: 434–435; John Sullivan to GW, Aug. 24, 1777, *PGW* 11: 57–62. Fell's "Memorandum" shows the seventeen prisoners from Long Island coming in on September 16.

They were most likely civilians, as there is no mention in Peckham of action on the island around that date. The abuse of prisoners after the fall of Fort Montgomery is vividly described in [Leggett], *Narrative of Major Abraham Leggett*, 17–22 (hereafter *Leggett Narrative*). See also Leggett's pension application (RWPA: S42859) as well as those for the widows of William Swan (W25185), Stephen Lush (W15926), and Robert Cooper (W16219). A letter in the *Pennsylvania Evening Post* of Oct. 21, 1777, reported that numerous officers and about 300 privates had been taken prisoner at Forts Montgomery and Clinton. Later that year, or early in 1778, a broadside naming 28 officers and 247 privates was published in New York over Loring's signature. Peckham, inexplicably, estimates that only 100 prisoners were taken in all these actions. At one point, according to Lieutenant Henry Pawling, he and other Fort Montgomery prisoners were put on ships supposedly "for the purpose of being sent out to the British Government for trial," but they were subsequently paroled on Long Island (RWPA: S43785). On Irvine, see Saffell, *Records of the Revolutionary War*, 309; *Pennsylvania Packet*, Dec. 17, 1777; *Connecticut Gazette*, Dec. 22, 1777. Irvine was confined briefly in Philadelphia and then sent to New York and eventually paroled to Flushing.

41. Hall, *Parsons*, 127–131; *SBW* 1: 392–393. Tryon sent Germain copies of his exchange with Parsons, in order that "your Lordship may judge of the tone I think should be held towards the Rebels" (Hall, *Parsons*, 394. *SBW* 1: 301). On Strong, see *Royal Gazette*, Jan. 3, 1778; see also Onderdonk, *Revolutionary Incidents of Suffolk and Kings*, 71.

42. *Royal Gazette*, Jan. 3, 1778; see also Onderdonk, *Revolutionary Incidents of Suffolk and Kings*, 71. Peter Williams, captured during the Danbury raid, said there were 600 prisoners in Livingston's sugar house when he got there in April 1777 (RWPA: S11829). "The Hospitals are full of the wounded," Nicholas Cresswell wrote in June, "and the prisons full of the Rebels" (*Cresswell Journal*, 232).

43. Johnston, *Campaign of 1776*, 2: 171–172; "A Sugar House Prisoner" [Blodget obituary], *New York Daily Times*, Mar. 27, 1855; RWPA: S45288. Stone, "Experiences of a Prisoner," 527–529. Henry Onderdonk's sources told him that eight to twelve bodies were removed every day from the Livingston's sugar house in the summer of 1777 (*Revolutionary Incidents of Suffolk and Kings*, 208).

44. "Incidents of the Revolution. Recollections of the Old Sugar House Prison," *New York Daily Times*, Nov. 16, 1852, portions of which also appeared in Booth, *History of . . . New York*, 516–521. *Hanford Narrative*, 14, 23, 27–28, often emends and elaborates upon the original 1852 text. A letter from Hanford to his father, written in Livingston's sugar house in June 1777, is in Stiles, *Letters from the Prisons and Prison Ships*, 24. See also *New-York Gazette*, Oct. 4, 1777; Knapp, *History of the Brick Presbyterian Church*, 70; and Cozzens, *Geological History of Manhattan*, 22. Hanford's pension application is in RWPA: S23676. Bradford Steele, captured along with a dozen other men in the summer of 1777, was also moved from a sugar house to the *Good Intent*. Two weeks later he came down with smallpox. See the report of the Senate Committee on Pensions, Feb. 23, 1832: 22nd Congress, 1st sess., 70.

45. On the *Prince of Wales*, see *Connecticut Courant*, July 28, 1777, and a Captain Jean Tennet's petition to Congress, August 30, 1777, *NDAR* 9: 302, 850–851. Other ships holding prisoners are mentioned in *NDAR* 9: 234–235; "Return of Clothing by L. Pintard to the Continental Prisoners, Nov. 1777–January 1778": Boudinot Papers, HSP; and PCC, r91/i78/v2/p. 353. Winfield, *50-Gun Ship*, 42 and passim, states that

the keel of the *Jersey* was laid in 1733 and that she was converted to a hospital ship in 1771. For her presence in New York as a hospital ship by November 1776, see *DAR* 12: 245. John Nicholas Kline, a Pennsylvania soldier taken prisoner at Fort Washington, declared in his pension application that he was put aboard the *Jersey* in December 1776. At the time, Kline recalled, she lay in the Hudson, but was then moved to a "Cove in the East River" prior to his release in early January 1777 (RWPA: S8796). Was this "cove" Wallabout Bay? Maybe. Levi Hanford remembered that when the *Good Intent* was moved to the bay in December 1777, the *Jersey* was already there. However, a shipping notice in the *Royal Gazette* for Feb. 24, 1779, has the *Jersey* anchored in the East River near Tolmie's Wharf, though Jeremiah Johnson— whose family lived on the bay and whose detailed memories of the prison ships are frequently relied upon by historians—said the *Jersey* had arrived in April 1778, almost a year earlier ([Johnson], "Recollections" Part 2, page 2). The *Jersey* did not become a *permanent* fixture of Wallabout Bay until the spring of 1780, however. As for the *Good Hope*, when Thomas Painter was put aboard her in the summer of 1778, she again lay off the lower west side of Manhattan by the Paulus Hook ferry landing ([Painter], *Autobiography of Thomas Painter*, 21 [hereafter *Painter Autobiography*]; see his pension application in RWPA: S18536). This *Good Hope* may have been a Danish vessel of the same name that was seized off Cape Henry and brought to New York as a prize in April 1778 (*NDAR* 11: 468n1; *New-York Gazette*, Apr. 13, 1778). The rumor that the *Kitty* had been set ablaze by the prisoners also comes from Johnson's ("Recollections." She was not completely destroyed, as her "remains," including "launch, anchors, and cables," were up for sale three years later (*New-York Gazette*, July 3, 1780). The fate of the *Whitby* remains a mystery.

46. This was Thomas Moore, also of New Jersey, another state prisoner (Leiby, *Revolutionary War in the Hackensack Valley*, 19).

47. Fell's "Memorandum in the Provost Jail, N.Y.," was first printed in Onderdonk, *Revolutionary Incidents of Suffolk and Kings*, 219–227; a typically bowdlerized version appears in Dandridge, *American Prisoners*, 112–122. The original of Fell's "Memorandum" is now in BHS.

48. *Allen Narrative*, 114–115; Jellison, *Ethan Allen: Frontier Rebel*, 174; *Fitch Diary*, 204–205. For Allen's letter to the Connecticut Assembly in April 1777 complaining that "this Mode of Existence is Very urksome": Duffy, *Allen and His Kin*, 1: 65–66. Jordan, "Colonel Elias Boudinot in New York City," 455. Sterling, "American Prisoners of War in New York," 387.

49. *Allen Narrative*, 115. Troublesome prisoners were routinely punished with a few days or weeks in one of the Provost's basement dungeons. Fell has Captain Travis returning upstairs at least twice, first on August 16 and again on September 12. Allen says that Travis spent almost four months downstairs, and that he himself was twice led to the dungeon "by a file of soldiers with fixed bayonets, and the serjeant brandishing his sword" (Fell, "Memorandum," 122–123; see also *BLB*, 32–33, and the deposition of Lieutenant John Barrett in *NDAR* 9: 705–706). In his essay "The Old Jail," John Pintard later regaled readers of a local paper with the story of a fistfight between Allen and Travis, but there are no other reports of such an event.

50. *Allen Narrative*, 119–120; see also Fell, "Memorandum," for Sept. 6, 1777; Fell's "list of P[risoners] in the same room with me," an addendum to his memorandum, names twenty men, including Allen, Travis, and Williams; see also *Fitch Diary*, 113, 147, 160, 176, 187, 210.

51. [Cornelius], *Journal of Dr. Elias Cornelius*, 4–6 (hereafter *Cornelius Journal*). Peckham has no report of prisoners brought in at this time. Thacher, *Military Journal*, 76, tells of four wounded American officers "put in a common dirt-cart, and conveyed through the streets of New York as objects of derision, reviled as rebels, and treated with the utmost contempt."

52. *Cornelius Journal*, 7–9. For similar comments on Sergeant Walley, see Fell's "Memorandum" and *Hanford Narrative*, 30–31.

53. Fell, "Memorandum." On June 20, the prisoners sent a "memorandum" to the commandant, General Pigot, with a "list of grievances." It was summarily rejected ("Grievances of Prisoners," Pintard Papers, NYHS). In November, Boudinot got word that a lady just returned from New York could confirm the stories about Cunningham's brutality (Jacobus Van Lundt to EB, Nov. 11, 1777, Boudinot Papers, HSP). See also "Deposition of Lt. John Barrett [Aug. 4, 1777]," *NDAR*, 9: 705–706; and "Examination of an anonymous American held as a prisoner," June 20, 1777 in *PCC* r91/i78/v2/p215).

54. Fell, "Memorandum," for Sept. 26, 28, 30, 1777. That Fell bothered to take note of Keith's way of punishing the prisoners for their protest suggests that the men were usually free to move about the upper floors of the building. Being locked up for any length of time meant, among other things, overflowing waste tubs and no access to supplies from the outside. On Keith, see *Allen Narrative*, 122–124; Keith also appears frequently in Fell's "Memorandum," and John Pintard remembered him as a complete villain, worse in some respects than Cunningham ("Reminiscences of Pintard," NYPL).

55. Sampson, *Escape in America*, 191–192, is the latest word on the numbers who surrendered. *Cornelius Journal*, 9; Metzger, *Prisoner in the American Revolution*, 34. The loaf of bread story is in *Leggett Narrative*, 67n44. On joy, see Fell's "Memorandum" for Nov. 5.

56. Johnston, *Campaign of 1776*, 2: 172–174; Bowman, "Military Parolees"; Burrows, "News from Occupied Flatbush"; *Graydon Memoirs*, 259. The fish incident led to a lively discussion of whether the officers, when they returned to Long Island, were still bound by the terms of their original parole. A board of officers was convened to discuss the matter, and Ethan Allen, one of its members, argued convincingly that they were so bound. "I have mentioned this circumstance," Graydon wrote, "principally to show, that Allen, however turbulent a citizen under the old *regime*, was not the vulgar ruffian, that the New York royalists represented him."

57. [Boudinot], *Life . . . of Boudinot*, 1: 47; Samuel Miles to Joseph Reed, Jan. 25, 1777, encl. with Reed to GW, Feb. 13, 1777, *PGW* 8: 327–329; GW to McDougall, May 23, 1777: *PGW* 9: 506–507. As of January 10, 1778, a total of thirty-eight officers had deserted their paroles on Long Island: one major and the rest a mix of captains, lieutenants, and ensigns, none identified by name. Boudinot informed Washington in early March 1778 that 235 American officers were paroled on the island. Sterling, "American Prisoners of War in New York," 382; Loring to GW, Mar. 24, 1777, *PGW* 8: 201–204; Magaw to GW, Apr. 6, 1777, *PGW* 8: 221; GW to Hancock, Apr. 18–19, 1777, *PGW* 8: 293–294; GW to Magaw, Apr. 20, 1777, *PGW* 8: 629; GW to Hancock, Apr. 28, 1777, *PGW* 9: 74–75.

58. *Fitch Diary*, 163, 164, 188, 199, 200, 201; *PRC* 1: 257; Onderdonk, *Revolutionary Incidents of Suffolk and Kings*, 214–215; Hinman, *Historical Collection . . . Connecticut*, 277. At the end of April 1777, a group of officers asked Howe to let Atlee go to Philadelphia "to obtain relief necessary to their subsistence." It is not clear whether he actually made the trip, however (*RAM* 1: 105–106).

59. *Graydon Memoirs*, 257–258, 261–269; *Fitch Diary*, 186–187; John Hancock to GW, May 20, 1777, *PGW* 9: 485.

60. Trumbull to GW, Oct. 21, 1776, *PGW* 7: 9–10; Livingston to GW, Oct. 28, 1776, *PGW* 7: 44–45; GW to Parsons, Feb. 10, 1777, *PGW* 8: 300; Parsons to GW, Feb. 23, 1777, *PGW* 8: 430–431; Parsons to GW, Mar. 6, 1777, *PGW* 8: 527–529; Parsons to GW, May 11, 1777, *PGW* 9: 389–390; GW to Parsons, May 17, 1777, *PGW* 9: 455–456. For a particularly strong argument for the "Expedition on Long Island," see William Duer to GW, *PGW* 8: 478–484; Hall, *Parsons*, 86–90, 95–96. For Washington's concerns that raiding Long Island would degenerate into mere banditry, see his letter to Parsons of Mar. 20, 1777, *PGW* 8: 605–607.

61. The overnight Sag Harbor raid, led by Lieutenant Colonel Return Jonathan Meigs, was in retaliation for Tryon's raid on Danbury. Meigs left Guilford, Connecticut, at the end of May with 170 men in thirteen whaleboats. After burning a dozen enemy vessels, destroying a large quantity of forage, and taking ninety prisoners, he returned to Guilford without the loss of a single man. Congress was impressed and rewarded Meigs with a sword (Hall, *Parsons*, 97–98, 108; Buel, *Dear Liberty*, 119; *SBW* 1: 309–310). Just prior to the Sag Harbor raid, General Parsons persuaded Washington to approve the purchase of forty additional whaleboats, which would give him a total of sixty and permit stepped-up raids on the Island (Parsons to GW, May 21, 1777, PGW 9: 494–495; GW to Parsons, May 25, 1777, *PGW* 9: 526–27; Parsons to GW, May 25, 1777, *PGW* 9: 527–530).

62. *Parsons*, 109–110, 113, 134–137; *SBW* 1: 229, 239, 310, 398–399, 410–415; *SBW* 3: 316, 334–335; *Mackenzie Diary*, 1: 174–175; cf. [Greenman] *Diary*, 34 and 54n136; Putnam to GW, Dec. 16, 1777, *PGW* 12: 617; Putnam to GW, Jan. 13, 1778, *PGW* 13: 228–230; Buel, *Dear Liberty*, 132–133; *Connecticut Gazette*, Dec. 19, 26, 1777; *New-Jersey Gazette*, Jan. 7, 1778.

63. *Fitch Diary*, 244–246; *JHG*, 57; *Graydon Memoirs*, 290; Samuel Broome to John Jay, Mar. 2, 1778, *PGC* 2: 830. Not all American officers were removed from the Island, however.

64. *SBW* 1: 402–404; Trumbull to GW, June 27, 1777, *PGW* 10: 133–135.

65. *Fitch Diary*, 256, 261. Although Fitch accepted appointment as a captain in the state militia in July 1779, he failed to recruit enough men to complete his company and resigned his commission the following June (*Fitch Diary*, 260; *PRC* 2: 355).

CHAPTER 5

1. *Cornelius Journal*, 10. The performance on January 9 was reported in the *Royal Gazette*, Jan. 10, 1778. Sixty-six years later, an obituary for James Banks, ninety-two, noted that he had been "placed by the British officers as a general super-intendant over the prisoners, with perfect freedom to go in and out at pleasure." One wonders whether Banks was part of the problem described by Cornelius, or part of the solution (*Brooklyn Daily Eagle*, June 3, 1844).

2. Cornelius had a sharp memory for details. According to the online calculator maintained by the Astronomical Application Department of the U.S. Naval Observatory, the moon rose at 9 P.M. on January 16, 1778, and was 78 percent full (http://aa.usno.navy.mil/data). A recent cold snap is reported in the *New-York Gazette* for Jan. 19, 1778.

3. *Cornelius Journal*, 11–14. The "friends" who helped Cornelius and other escaped prisoners get out of New York do not appear to have been part of an organized network, but it is clear from his account that people sympathetic to the American cause

were accustomed to encountering and helping escapees. For the oral tradition of one family's efforts to help escaping prisoners, see Field, *Historic and Antiquarian Scenes in Brooklyn*, 77–80.

4. For Schureman and Thompson, see Blake, *Biographical Dictionary*, 1118. "A Sugar House Prisoner" [Blodget obituary], *New York Daily Times*, Mar. 27, 1855; and RWPA: S45288 (s.v. "Admatha" Blodget), and RWPA: W385; Leiby, *Revolutionary War in the Hackensack Valley*, 117. Cornelius Oakley escaped from the sugar house by climbing down a rope from a third-story window ("Biography of Cornelius Oakley—A Whig of the Revolution," *Brooklyn Daily Eagle*, Dec. 7, 1849). Some men left no explanation of how they escaped from New York. See Lieutenant James Anderson, RWPA: R190; "Deposition of Lieutenant John Barrett, [Aug. 4, 1777]": *NDAR* 9: 706–706. Valentine Shoufler merely declared, "I made my escape by swimming the Hudson" (RWPA: S22506). Isaac Causten crossed the river in a small boat (RWPA: S8183). For other escapes, see RWPA: S39986 (Thomas Beatty) and S42689 (Peter Dych).

5. For Bell, see Executive Committee to GW, Jan. 9, 1777, *PGW* 8: 21–23; GW to Major General Heath, Jan. 17, 1777, *PGW* 8: 90–91. Tennet described his escape in a petition to Congress dated Aug. 30, 1777, *NDAR* 9: 851. For Stewart, see *Graydon Memoirs*, 314–315; *New-Jersey Gazette*, Jan. 21, 1778. These were the paroled officers who had been moved temporarily from their Long Island billets in anticipation of an American raid. *PGW* 14: 342n4 identifies him as John Steward of Maryland; see also [Hawkins], *Adventures*, 30–33, 47–59. Mutiny was sometimes possible on undermanned vessels. For example, in late 1777 or early 1778, the *Royal Bounty*, a British cartel ship en route from Halifax to Providence with nearly 300 American prisoners, was caught in a storm and separated from her convoy. The prisoners overpowered her small crew and brought her successfully to Marblehead (*Boston Gazette*, Jan. 26, 1778; *New London Gazette*, Feb. 6, 1778; *New-Jersey Gazette*, Feb. 25, 1778; *New-York Gazette*, Mar. 9, 1778).

6. *Painter Autobiography*, 21–50, and his pension application, S18536. See also the application of Elderkin's widow (RWPA: W17758). As a militiaman, Painter saw action again when the British raided New Haven in the summer of 1779. He then returned to the seafaring life on a succession of merchantmen and was captured twice more. The second time, in 1783, he spent two months on the *Jersey* for his trouble.

7. Stone, "Experiences of a Prisoner," 527–528; *History of Northampton County*, 240.

8. *New-Jersey Gazette*, Aug. 12, 1778. Syrett, "'This penurious old reptile'"; Willcox, "Arbuthnot, Gambier, and Graves."

9. For typical complaints about favoritism, see *JPC* 1: 806; New York Committee of Safety to GW, Feb. 13, 1777: *PGW* 8: 326–327; and *Adlum Memoirs*, 87–88. Colonel Joseph Reed believed that another Fort Washington captive, Colonel Lambert Cadwallader, was allowed to leave New York *without* giving his parole, "thro a special Indulgence on Acct of some Civilities shewn by his Family to Gen. Prescot" (quoted in *PGW* 7: 238). See also the story of a drummer boy named Abraham Ryckman, paroled through the intervention of some British officers who boarded with his mother in the city (RWPA: R9124). On Van Vorst, see Winfield, *History of the County of Hudson*, 433–434. Clinton repeated the gesture when Faddy beat up another officer for refusing to pay for repairs on his shoes. General Clinton may have been especially susceptible to personal appeals. Zephaniah Platt of Huntington was released from the Provost in January 1778 "through the personal application of his daughter Dorothea" to the general (Onderdonk, *Revolutionary Incidents of Suffolk and Kings*,

68). For a similar story later told by John Pintard, see Haffner, "Treatment of Prisoners of War by the Americans," 305. Isaac Causten, captured when the British occupied New York in September 1776, was released by Mayor David Mathews because he and Causten's father had been good friends before the war. Causten promptly escaped and rejoined the American army (RWPA: S8183). For Isaac Grant and his friends, see RWPA: R4195.

10. Bowman, *Captive Americans*, 94–97. GW to Howe, Jan. 13, 1777: *PGW* 8: 59–61.

11. *Fitch Diary*, 39, 52. Major Baurmeister reported that upwards of 100 Americans had enlisted with a single British regiment; presumably there were others (Uhlendorf, *Revolution in America*, 71); see also Stokes, *Iconography of Manhattan* 5: 1007. Lemisch, "Listening to the 'Inarticulate,'" 17, calculates that 8 percent of naval prisoners in New York switched sides, but this figure is probably too low for reasons explained in Ranlet, "British Recruitment of Americans in New York," 26–28. The largest single defection seems to have occurred after the British seized Charleston in 1780. Of the approximately 3,300 American prisoners, 500 to 600 were said to have joined the enemy to avoid prison. (See Peckham, *Toll of Independence*, 70; Boatner, *Encyclopedia of American Revolution*, 212–213; Bowman, *Captive Americans*, 10, 96; Ryan, *Salute to Courage*, 52; Richard Peters to GW, Nov. 19, 1776: *PGW* 7: 188. Also Major General Horatio Gates to GW, Feb. 14, 1778: *PGW* 13: 532–533, concerning Jonathan Hager of Maryland, taken at Fort Washington and then compelled to enlist "thr'o the cruelty of the Enemy at New York." On Mabie, see Leiby, *Revolutionary War in the Hackensack Valley*, 182–185; *PGW* 15: 189–191; *PGC* 4: 50, 51n. George Clinton to GW, Oct. 9, 1777: *PGW* 11: 458; *PWL* 2:439n1. Friederich Sheibler of Philadelphia got off one of the Charleston prison ships by signing on as a crewman with a British frigate, then ran away as soon as she reached Kingston. He wandered the West Indies for four years before managing to get home (RWPA: S23910).

12. Mayo, *Army and Navy Pension Law*, 496. For Casten, see RWPA: S12677.

13. Schwartz, *Jews and the American Revolution*, 28–31.

14. *Allen Narrative*, 97–98. Israel Putnam to GW, Sept. 16, 1777: *PGW* 11: 250–251. For John Laurens to Henry Laurens, Mar. 9, 1778: [Laurens], *Army Correspondence of Colonel John Laurens*, 149.

15. *Adlum Memoirs*, 86. Cf. Field, "Recollections of . . . General Jeremiah Johnson," part 1, p. 18, which asserts that "many of Lord Rawdon's regiment were Irishmen enlisted in prison"; *Leggett Narrative*, 23; *Hanford Narrative*, 16. See also Thacher, *Military Journal of the American Revolution*, 76, and the story of John Gray, captured with Ethan Allen at Montreal, in James Lovell to GW, Mar. 24, 1778: *PGW* 14: 294–295. Antoine-Felix de Mézieres Wuibert, a French officer captured at Fort Washington, likewise refused to enlist with the British and as of December 1776 was suffering "hard Treatment" in the Provost (GW to Howe, Dec. 12, 1776 and Putnam to GW, Dec. 12, 1776, *PGW* 7: 313–316; Stone, "Experiences of a Prisoner," 28).

16. [Rush], *Autobiography of Benjamin Rush*, 130; Hawke, *Benjamin Rush: Revolutionary Gadfly*, 180–181.

17. *LDC* 5: 641–642; *LDC* 6: 8–9; *LDC* 6: 70–71, 240–241, 247–248, 454–455; [Rush], *Letters of Benjamin Rush*, 1: 123, 125–126; Executive Committee to GW, Jan. 9, 1777: *PGW* 8: 21–22.

18. Precisely the conclusion of Bill and Edge, *House Called Morven*, 37–47, and Fischer, *Washington's Crossing*, 163–165. "Morven," Stockton's seat in Princeton, served for many years as the official residence of the governors of New Jersey.

19. Annis Boudinot, Stockton's wife, did not act as if her husband had gone over to the enemy. Several years after his release, she and fifty other New Jersey women were recognized for their "well-known patriotism" (*Pennsylvania Packet*, July 8, 1780).

20. Lutnick, *American Revolution and the British Press*, 163ff. The British eventually captured four other Signers, all commissioned officers. Colonel George Walton of Georgia was wounded and taken prisoner when the British captured Savannah in December 1778. He was exchanged the following year. Captains Edward Rutledge, Arthur Middleton, and Thomas Heyward, all South Carolinians, were captured when Charleston fell in May 1780. Heyward initially signed a parole, but it was revoked almost immediately, and he was confined with the others at St. Augustine until they were exchanged in 1781.

21. At the end of December, Doctor Rush advised Richard Henry Lee that "my much hond [honored] father in law who is now a prisoner with Gen Howe suffers many indignities & hardships from the enemy which not only his rank, but his being a man ought to exempt him. . . . Every particle of my blood is electrified with revenge" (*LDC* 5: 705–706). How Rush knew any of this is not readily apparent.

22. In July 1777 Stockton signed a memorial from the trustees of the college to Congress protesting the use of the college's main building as a barracks for Continental troops (*JCC* 8: 558; *LDC* 7: 379–380). The following December, he appeared before the New Jersey Council of Safety and took the oath of allegiance required of every New Jersey resident captured and imprisoned behind enemy lines. He did not, however, return to Congress (*LDC* 35, unpaginated; *Pennsylvania Packet*, Mar. 10, 1781). See also a similar verdict from Richard Rush in [Rush], *Autobiography of Benjamin Rush*, 147. One intriguing snippet of additional evidence comes from the diary of William Smith, a well-informed and well-connected Tory who was the last chief justice of colonial New York as well as Governor Livingston's former law partner. In 1779, his sister-in-law, Elizabeth Livingston, brought him word from Princeton that Stockton had become unpopular with the rebels and "finds a Tyranny in the Country instead of Liberty and Law." Smith's obvious satisfaction with this news suggests that he had not yet heard anything about Stockton's switching sides ([Smith], *Historical Memoirs*, 130).

23. Boyd, *Elias Boudinot*, 48–49; *BLB*, 53, 54. In October 1777 Congress was alarmed by reports that the British were using prisoners to build fortifications, but this was later proved to be incorrect (see John Hancock to GW, Oct. 12, 1777, *PGW* 11: 492–493; GW to Hancock, Oct. 16, 1777, *PGW* 11: 527; and Major General William Heath to GW, *PGW* 13: 176–177). See also the account of the arrival in Bristol, Rhode Island, of 157 American prisoners from New York in the *Connecticut Journal*, Mar. 25, 1778. Although a few American officers were paroled to Long Island after Burgoyne's surrender, the notion that it improved things for the New York prisoners generally has proved to be a particularly stubborn misconception (see, e.g., Bowman, *Captive Americans*, 71; Clinton to Putnam, Dec. 12, 1777: *PGC*, 2: 569–574; *Leggett Narrative*, 21).

24. *Allen Narrative*, 120–121. See also Fell, "Memorandum," Dec. 28, 1777, which attributes his release to Allen's letter but notes that Robertson first sought the opinion of a physician before releasing Fell—a detail that Allen, dazzled by his own prowess as a writer, neglected to mention. When Elias Boudinot visited the prisoners in February, he arranged for Fell to be given "the Liberty of the Town" (Jordan, "Colonel Elias Boudinot in New York City," 459, 461). In May 1778, health restored, Fell returned to his home in New Jersey on parole. Six months later he would be ex-

changed for Philip Skene. "Mrs. Marriner's" was probably the same as the house on William Street belonging to "Mr. Mariner," where (according to Captain Nice) officers from Pennsylvania, Maryland, and Delaware were billeted in September 1776 see *PWL* 1: 186n1; Robertson to WL, Jan. 4, 1778, *PWL* 2: 159–160; and WL to Walter Rutherford, Jan. 15, 1778, *PWL* 2: 185–187.

25. Fell, "Memorandum," entries for Oct. 10, 15, Nov. 20, Dec. 10, 18, 19, 22, and 24, 1777; *New-York Gazette*, Jan. 19, 1778; "Return of Clothing by L. Pintard to the Continental Prisoners, Nov. 1777–January 1778," BP, HSP; also PCC, r91/i78/v2/p.353. See also Boyd, *Elias Boudinot*, 49; *BLB*, 30–39, 50, 65, 85, and passim; and Bowman, "Lewis Pintard," 42–43. Some of the money to purchase these provisions was raised by shipping flour into New York City to take advantage of a severe local shortage during the winter of 1777–1778. Between September 1777 and May 1778 Pintard received 3,700 barrels of flour from Boudinot, which he then sold to local bakers and retailers.

26. Still more captives—among them "a great number of rebel officers" betrayed by area residents—would be brought in during the course of that winter (Burgoyne, *Rebel Views*, 257; John Hoope to Joseph Howell, Assistant Commissioner of Army Accounts, Mar. 11, 1786, NARA, RG93 [via PWD]; affidavit by Captain John Stotesbury's widow, RWPA: W105 and *RRW*, 816; GW to Laurens, Dec. 14–15, 1777, *PGW* 12: 604; Frazer, *General Persifor Frazer: A Memoir*, 161–162, 169–172, 176–181 (hereafter *Frazer Memoir*); "W.G.," *Pennsylvania Packet*, Dec. 31, 1777, reprinted in the *New-Jersey Gazette*, Jan. 21, 1778, and elsewhere; Rowe, "Travail of John McKinly." See also Evans, "Letters of Dr. John McKinly." McKinley's account of his capture was published in the *Pennsylvania Packet*, Feb. 25, 1779. John Laurens to Henry Laurens, Nov. 14, 1777: Simms, *Army Correspondence of . . . Laurens*, 75; Clark to GW, Nov. 17, 1777: *PGW* 12: 285. Clark's information probably came from Nicholas Sellers, whose deposition of the same date was sent to Washington by General James Potter (*PGW* 12: 310). See also Lieutenant Charles Croxall's letter "To any Continental Officer," Nov. 20, 1777, quoted in *PGW* 12: 326, and Croxall's "Prisoners in Philadelphia" to GW, Jan. 21, 1778, *PGW* 13: 307. On the number of men per cell in the Walnut Street jail, see "The Memoirs of James Morris of Litchfield" (copy), RWPA: W2035. For a sympathetic British view of the situation, see [Peebles], *John Peebles' American War*, 162; *NDAR* 10: 519–520, 591–592; *RAM* 1: 152, 154.

27. [Waldo], "Diary Kept at Valley Forge," 132. Prisoners dying "with Grass in their Mouths" is mentioned in a 1782 report by Elias Boudinot, *LDC* 18: 396–397. See also "William Ellery to General William Whipple, [December 1777]," *PMHB* 22 (1898), 502; "An Old Soldier," *National Gazette*, May 8, 1793. For Chenoweth, see RWPA: W18899.

28. "W.G.," *Pennsylvania Packet* of Dec. 31, 1777; reprinted in the *New-Jersey Gazette*, Jan. 21, 1778, and elsewhere; also *Frazer Memoir*, 172. "W.G." is corroborated by another of the *Delaware* captives, Lieutenant Luke Matthewman, whose "narrative" was serialized in the *New York Packet*, Aug. 17, 21, 24, and 28, 1787. Matthewman escaped from Philadelphia "disguised like a porter, with a bag on my shoulder, as if going for potatoes." Henry Yeager, a fifteen-year-old drummer in the American army, made the mistake of returning to Philadelphia to see his parents. He was arrested, sentenced to death for spying, and subjected to a morbid mock execution staged by Cunningham (RWPA: R11928).

29. "Incognitus," *Pennsylvania Packet*, Jan. 21, 1778; *BLL*, 85; and Foulke, *Memoirs of Jacob Ritter*, 51–52.

30. *LDC* 18: 397–398; *BJ*, 56–58; *WW* 10: 66. Cunningham may not have been permanently banished from Philadelphia, because in April 1778 he put a notice in local papers offering a reward for items recently stolen from his house there (*Pennsylvania Evening Post*, Apr. 1, 1778; *Royal Pennsylvania Gazette*, Apr. 7, 1778; *BLB*, 54; *RAM* 1: 151, 154, 155, 185, 196). See also *BJ*, 58, recalling Howe's short-lived attempt to prevent American agents from purchasing blankets and clothing for American prisoners in Philadelphia (GW to Howe, Nov. 14, 1777, *PGW* 12: 255–257 [including depositions from Joseph Cloyd and William Dewees]; Henry Laurens to GW, Nov. 19, 1777, *PGW* 12: 319; GW to Laurens, Nov. 23, 1777, *PGW* 12: 363–364; *JCC* 9: 939; Howe to GW, Feb. 5, 1778, *PGW* 13: 455–457; Howe to GW, Feb. 21, 1778, *PGW* 13: 620–628). Washington gave his correspondence with Howe to the Board of War, which reported to Congress in early December 1777 (*JCC* 9: 939, 1006–1009). Howe's letter of February 21, 1778, included a preposterous affidavit from Thomas Franklin, Jr., asserting that the Philadelphia prisoners were treated "civilly & with humanity."

31. Germain to Howe, Sept. 3, 1777: quoted in *WW* 7: 2n; see also *LP* 2: 367–368, 375–376, 382; Alden, *General Charles Lee*, 182–185; Lee to GW, Dec. 30, 1777, *PGW* 8: 71; Kipping and Smith, *At General Howe's Side*, 49; *New-York Gazette*, Feb. 9, 1778; *Connecticut Courant*, Feb. 24, 1778. In February 1778 Lee won $500 in a lottery "and immediately distributed the same among the American prisoners in that city" (*New-York Gazette*, Feb. 9, 1778; *Connecticut Courant*, Feb. 24, 1778).

32. Persifor Frazer to GW, Oct. 9, 1777, *PGW* 11: 459; Council of General Officers, [Oct. 30], 1777: *PGW* 12: 58; GW to Howe, Nov. 4, 1777: *PGW* 12: 119; Howe to GW, Nov. 6, 1777: *PGW* 12: 143–144; GW to Howe, Nov. 14–15, 1777, *PGW* 12: 255–257; GW to Howe, Nov. 23, 1777, *PGW* 12: 363; Howe to GW, Nov. 26, 1777, *PGW* 12: 412–414; GW to Laurens, Nov. 26–27, 1777, *PGW* 12: 420–422; GW to Howe, Nov. 28, 1777, *PGW* 12: 438; *BLB*, 44–45, 46–47, 53, 63–64, 65, 66, 85–87; *BJ*, 11; *JCC* 10: 74–81; Boyd, *Elias Boudinot*, 45–52.

33. *BLB*, 48, 54, 63, 85–86, and passim; Livingston to EB, Feb. 3, 1778, quoted in Pabst, *American Revolutionary War Manuscript Records*, 20. For ongoing problems with states, see *BLB* 68, 69, 70–71, 82–83, and passim.

34. *BLB*, 86–88. Boudinot's foray into occupied New York must be reconstructed from three sources that differ in minor details: (1) a journal or diary that he kept at the time, now available in Jordan, "Colonel Elias Boudinot in New York City"; (2) Boudinot's "report" in a long letter to Washington on March 2, a draft of which is printed with annotations and Boudinot's attachments in Sterling, "American Prisoners of War in New York"; and (3) Boudinot, *Journal*, which he wrote twenty years later but which was not published until 1894. In the published *Journal* Boudinot says he went first to the Provost, then to the Sugar House. But the journal he kept at the time indicates that it was the other way around—a discrepancy that seems trivial at best.

35. Since there had been no big exchanges or releases prior to Boudinot's arrival, the difference between these numbers and those he gave to the Board of War in December (assuming both sets were accurate) probably reflects the always-high mortality rate among the prisoners more than any other factor. At one point he learned of 120 deaths in a single hospital since November 1777—more than one per day (Jordan, "Colonel Elias Boudinot in New York City," 454, 464; Sterling, "American Prisoners of War in New York," 380; Boudinot to GW, Mar 2, 1778: *PGW* 14: 16–17). For "damned lies," see *BJ*, 13.

36. *BJ*, 18–19; Sterling, "American Prisoners of War in New York," 382–383. Pintard's advertisement for nurses appeared in the *New-York Gazette*, Jan. 5, 1778.

37. Sterling, "American Prisoners of War in New York," 380; Jordan, "Colonel Elias Boudinot in New York City," 455.

38. *BJ*, 14–18; Sterling, "American Prisoners of War in New York," 380–381; Jordan, "Colonel Elias Boudinot in New York City," 457. Loring told Howe that Boudinot was "perfectly satisfied" with conditions in the New York prisons, but that was obviously untrue (Loring to Howe, Feb. 7, 1778: BHP, NYPL 1: 191). Apparently, Cunningham and/or Robertson allowed Pintard to send food and firewood to the Provost prisoners, but not medical supplies or nurses. Two of the Provost's civilian inmates reported Boudinot's visit to the Provost in letters to Governor George Clinton, both distressed that the commissary had no authority to assist state prisoners (William Miller to Clinton, Feb. 6, 1778: *PGC*, 2: 721–723; 3: 275–276). Miller's letter included the names of seventeen other civilians being held with him. The charges against them included such transgressions as "being a Rebel," "giving information to ye Rebbels," and "holding Correspondence with the Rebbels." On Robertson, see Sterling, "American Prisoners of War in New York," 386. See also Klein and Howard, *Twilight of British Rule*, 38, which seems far more sympathetic to Robertson in this regard than the facts warrant.

39. Jordan, "Colonel Elias Boudinot in New York City," 460; Sterling, "American Prisoners of War in New York," 382. The problem, Boudinot reminded Pintard on his return to New York, was that money spent on "mere Ornaments" was money that ought to have been used for essential food and clothing. From now on, he instructed, limit expenditures for the officers "to plain regimental Cloathing & real necessaries, without either Lace or Epaulets" (*BLB*, 92). A "List of Officers Prisoner in the District of NY," author unknown but dated Mar. 9, 1778, puts the tally at 263 (BHP, NYPL).

40. Jordan, "Colonel Elias Boudinot in New York City," 460; Sterling, "American Prisoners of War in New York," 383.

41. *SBW* 2: 1–2, 6, 7, 8–10, 98–99; GW to Colonel Webb, Jan. 8, 1778, *PGW* 13: 184–185; GW to Heath, Jan. 9, 1778, *PGW* 13: 188; GW to Parsons, Jan. 16, 1778, *PGW* 13: 256–257; GW to Putnam, Jan. 25, 1778, *PGW* 13: 344–345; Webb to GW, Jan. 30, 1778, *PGW* 13: 417–418. Washington had already made the same thing very clear to Governor Trumbull; see, GW to Trumbull, Feb. 1, July 2, 1777, *PGW* 8: 220–221; *PGW* 10: 173–175. See also GW to Robert Morris, Dec. 25, 1776, *PGW* 7: 439–440; GW to Parsons, Mar. 6, 1777, *PGW* 8: 526–527; GW to Caesar Rodney, Sept. 24, 1777, *PGW* 11: 315; GW to Benjamin Lincoln, Oct. 26, 1777, *PGW* 12: 19–20. As Washington explained to Trumbull in his letter of February 1, 1777, he also had to deal with complaints that the British were releasing more prisoners from some states than others (Jordan, "Colonel Elias Boudinot in New York City," 453–454, 455, 458; Sterling, "American Prisoners of War in New York," 386). General Parsons, too, was pulling strings to get Webb and other Connecticut officers exchanged as quickly as possible, if necessary through the independent action of state governors (*Parsons*, 127, 135–139; Major General Heath to GW, Dec. 25, 1777, *PGW* 12: 707; Parsons to GW, Dec. 29, 1777, *PGW* 13: 45–47).

42. Jordan, "Colonel Elias Boudinot in New York City," 460, 461, 464; Sterling, "American Prisoners of War in New York," 385; *BLB*, 126–128; Boyd, *Elias Boudinot*, 56; *BJ* 1: 158–159. Boudinot's "Estimates of Expenditures & Debts due from the Com. Genl of Prisoners" in PCC—undated but almost certainly put together soon

after his return from New York—showed that Pintard had laid out £22,583 on provisions for the New York prisoners. His March 2 letter to GW suggests that most of this was raised on Boudinot's credit. On the purchasing power of Boudinot's outlay in 2007 dollars, see http://www.measuringworth.com.

43. Trumbull to GW, Jan. 14, 1778, *PGW* 13: 242; GW to Trumbull, Jan. 24, 1778, *PGW* 13: 337–338; Howe to GW, Feb. 5, 1778, *PGW* 13: 455–457; GW to Howe, Feb. 10, 1778, *PGW* 13: 498–499; Howe to GW, Feb. 14, 1778, *PGW* 13: 536–537; Howe to GW, Mar. 2, 1778, *PGW* 14, 31–32; cf. Rawlins Lowndes to Henry Laurens, Mar. 30, 1778, *NDAR* 11: 837–838.

44. *JCC* 9: 1036–1037, 1069; *JCC* 10: 74–82, 197–198, 204–205; Laurens to GW, Mar. 1, 1778, *PGW* 14: 1–13. The resolution of December 19 fixed the exchange rate at about 4.4 Continental dollars to the pound sterling, well above the actual value of the dollar, which was around 20 to the pound.

45. GW to Laurens, Mar. 7 and 12, 1778, *PGW* 14: 83–88, 114; GW to Howe, Mar. 9, 1778, *PGW* 14: 129–130; Howe to GW, Mar. 10, 1778, *PGW* 14: 130–131; GW to Howe, Mar. 12, 1778, *PGW* 14: 159–160; Howe to GW, Mar. 15, 1778, *PGW* 14: 188–189; GW to Howe, Mar. 29, 1778, *PGW* 14: 352; GW to Laurens, Apr. 4, 1778, *PGW* 14: 401–403; Laurens to GW, Apr. 14, 1778, *PGW* 14: 509–513.

46. Burnett, *Continental Congress*, 298–299; Dixon, "Divided Authority," 262–268; *BJ*, 44–45; "Draft of a Letter to Genl Washington upon the Subject of Exchange superseded by a Conference," in the hand of Gouverneur Morris: PCC, is quoted in *PGW* 14: 890; GW to Laurens, Apr. 4, 1778: *PGW* 14: 401–403; Hamilton to George Clinton, *PAH* 1: 439–442. For a more detailed account, see Knight, "Prisoner Exchange and Parole," 202–206, which notes that Congress was deeply concerned that it lacked the money for an exchange. Redeeming American prisoners would require reimbursing the enemy for their upkeep (such as it was) plus funding the half-pay pensions promised to officers. A secondary concern was that because Howe's offer omitted any reference to civilians, he probably still meant to deal with them as rebels (Camp Committee to GW, Feb. 11, 1778, *PGW* 13: 509–510). In his March 2 report, Boudinot had given Washington the most recent British tally of American prisoners in New York, which showed a total of 1,026 privates and officers on parole or in detention, not counting 46 officers who had broken their paroles and the 1,821 privates still "in dispute" (Boudinot to GW, Mar. 2, 1778: *PGW* 14: 16–24).

47. *JCC* 10: 266–268; Laurens to GW, Mar. 21, 1778, *PGW* 14: 252–253. Boudinot later learned that Congress was "so ashamed" of the censure resolution that the members had expunged it from the secret minutes. Congress continued nonetheless to wrangle over the exchange question, and there was much criticism of Washington's approach (see Burnett, *Continental Congress*, 299–309). The views of the American commissioners on a range of issues can be glimpsed in various memoranda and drafts prepared by Hamilton now in *PAH* 1: 460–472.

48. William Grayson et al. to GW, *PAH* 1: 475–478; "Boudinot's Notes of Two Conferences."

49. Joseph Webb to GW, Jan. 30, 1778, *PGW* 13: 417; Howe to GW, Mar. 27, 1778, *PGW* 14: 329–330; GW to Laurens, Apr. 18, 1778, *PGW* 14: 546–547; Boudinot to GW, Apr. 22, 1778, *PGW* 14: 583–584; *BJ*, 48–49, 74–76. The copy of Boudinot's letter in *PCC*, M247, r.168, lists the prisoners exchanged on April 20 by name. One, Colonel Thomas Bull, never forgot that his name appeared on the list right behind Ethan Allen's (RWPA: S2056); see also "Grant of Authority to the Commissioners for Prisoner Exchange," Mar. 28, 1778, *PGW* 14, 334; Boyd, *Elias*

Boudinot, 60–61; *LDC* 9: 455; Metzger, *Prisoner in the American Revolution*, 204–205; "From the Commissioners for Prisoner Exchange" to GW, Apr. 15, 1778, *PGW* 14: 518–523; *Connecticut Gazette*, May 22, 1778.

50. *BJ*, 78–81; Alden, *General Charles Lee*, 190.

51. Sterling, "American Prisoners of War in New York," 383, 384; *BLB*, 95–96. In his *Journal*, Boudinot remembered that the meeting with Lee took place on February 6, but no mention of it is in his diary on that or any other day (Jordan, "Colonel Elias Boudinot in New York City," 456–458). Alden, *General Charles Lee*, 335–436, cites the diary's silence to cast doubt on Boudinot's veracity, but as Boudinot told Lee, and as every American prisoner knew, some things must not be set to paper lest they fall into enemy hands.

52. *Allen Narrative*, 142–144; Duffy, *Ethan Allen and His Kin* 1: 76. Washington was actually rather impressed by Allen. "There is an original something in him that commands admiration," he admitted (GW to Laurens, May 12, 1778, *PGW* 15: 109). Predictably, Allen let it be known that no prisoner had suffered more than he: "the Melevolent Cruelty Inflicted on me by the Brittish in the Course of my Captivity is Scarcely to be Paralled in History" (Allen to Henry Laurens, May 9, 1778: *PGW* 15: 110).

53. Boudinot, *Journal*, 1: 118–119; Boudinot to GW, May 13, 1778, *PGW* 15: 114–115.

54. Parsons to Webb, Feb. 8, 1778, *SBW* 2: 8–9; Conway, "From Fellow-Nationals to Foreigners," 94. Howe to GW, May 10, 1778, *PGW* 15: 92–93; GW to Laurens, May 18 and 24, June 15, 1778, *PGW* 15: 154–155, 194–195, 210–211; GW to Boudinot, May 23, June 2, 1778, *PGW* 15: 299, 310–311; GW to Hamilton, June 4, 1778, *PGW* 15: 333–334; Boudinot to GW, June 18, 28, 1778, *PGW* 15: 402–403, 419–420; GW to General Henry Clinton, June 6, 1778, *PGW* 15: 433; GW to Gates, June 17, 1778 *PGW* 15: 569–573; "Declaration on Prisoners [June 4, 1778]," *PAH* 1: 493; [Peebles], *John Peebles' American War*, 189; Burgoyne, *Enemy Views*, 249–255. See also the pension application by John Chenoweth (RWPA: W18899), and John Hoope to Joseph Howell, Assistant Commissioner of Army Accounts, Mar. 11, 1786, NARA, RG93 (accessed Aug. 3, 2006 via PWD). Boudinot and Loring did eventually resolve the outstanding dispute over the prisoners released over the winter of 1776, 1777 by agreeing that 900 British prisoners, half the total, would settle the account (Boyd, *Elias Boudinot*, 64–66; *BJ* 116–134; *Serle Journal*, 308; *Pennsylvania Packet*, June 10, 1778).

55. Lengel, *General George Washington*, 300–306; Shy, "Charles Lee," 41–48; Alden, *General Charles Lee*, passim. Hamilton's letter described Lee's behavior as "truly childish." Boyd, *Elias Boudinot*, 68.

56. *BLL* 1: 110–111; Boyd, *Elias Boudinot*, 64, 159; *BJ*, 69; Boudinot to GW, Mar. 2, 1778, *PGW* 14: 17.

57. *BJ*, 70, 71; *BLL*, 160, 161; Dixon, "Divided Authority," 100; Boudinot erroneously remembered this letter as coming from Pintard (Boyd, *Elias Boudinot*, 72; also Haffner, "Treatment of Prisoners of War by the Americans," 317–318).

58. Ogden to GW, Apr. 9, 1778, *PGW* 14: 440–441; GW to Ogden, Apr. 13, 1778, *PGW* 14: 498–499.

59. Conway, *War of American Independence*, 103–108; Black, *War for America*, 168–169; Smith, *Loyalists and Redcoats*, esp. 79–94. *The New-Jersey Gazette*, Oct. 21, 1778, reported the departure of ten full regiments from the city, in addition to the evacuation of Fort Washington and all enemy forts in New Jersey *The New York*

Journal, Nov. 5, 1778, said that "near ten thousand" troops had left town on board 150 transports.

60. Jones, *History of New York* 1: 266–269; Onderdonk, *Revolutionary Incidents of Suffolk and Kings*, 71–78; Ward, *Between the Lines*, 33–49; and Meyer, *Irony of Submission*; *Serle Journal*, 301; *New-York Gazette*, Sept. 14, 1778. For a similar raid on Staten Island, see *New-Jersey Gazette*, June 10, 1778. See *PGW* 14: 366–367, for the case of John Chace, a prisoner in New York whose father grabbed a few Tories to exchange for him.

61. *Graydon Memoirs*, 316, relaying information later provided him by Lieutenant Andrew Forrest, who in turn heard it from Captain John Flahaven, a prisoner in the Provost with Marriner. In his *Memoirs*, John Adlum mentions (p. 115) that his landlady, Mrs. Carroll, asked General Robertson to put one "Mariner" in the Provost for attempting to kill "a British colonel who visited her occasionally after dark." If this was the same individual, the story has melodramatic complexities that can only be imagined. The rendition of Marriner's exploits in Cook, *What Manner of Men*, 275–283, is an unusual blend of fiction and faulty research.

62. Strong, *History of . . . Flatbush*, 159–161. Colonel Samuel Webb's return of American officers, prepared for Commissary Beatty in 1778, shows a "William Marrener" and eight others as having "deserted their Parole" (Ford, *Prisoners of War*, 23).

63. The *New-Jersey Gazette*, June 17, 1778, places Mathews in the city that night, whereas the *Royal Gazette* of the same date (which in this instance probably had better information) has the mayor in residence at Melrose Hall (*Pennsylvania Evening Post*, June 20, 1778). Predictably, the *Royal Gazette*'s account of the raid alleges that Marriner and his crew—"shabby Cordwainers"—stole Bache's silver and roughed up his wife. The *New-Jersey Gazette*, on the other hand, applauded him and his men for behaving "with greatest bravery and prudence." Forrest told Graydon that Marriner also wanted to liberate Captain John Flahaven, with whom he had spent time in the Provost (*Graydon Memoirs*, 316). Strong, *History of . . . Flatbush*, 160, claims that Marriner also intended to capture Colonel William Axtell of Melrose Hall, the grandest home in the village. "Old Van Pelt," Marriner's former host in New Utrecht, was subsequently arrested by British cavalry and taken to the Provost, presumably on the grounds that he knew of the raid but did not raise the alarm (*Royal Gazette*, June 20, 1778).

64. *Graydon Memoirs*, 317–318. Graydon says that Forrest was in fact exchanged shortly thereafter, although Webb's return of American officers still on Long Island in August 1778 has Forrest among the men who had "deserted their Parole" (Ford, *Prisoners of War*, 23).

65. "Privateer Bond for William Marriner and Henry Remsen," Aug. 18, 1778, *PWL* 1: 415–416.

66. *New-Jersey Gazette*, Nov. 11, 1778; see also *New-York Gazette*, Nov. 9, 1778, which puts the take at "Cash to the Amount of 200l. [£200], besides a large Quantity of Linen, Blankets, &c." Many years later, Simon Cortelyou's son allegedly found his father's silver tankard in an old inn on Staten Island (Bangs, *Reminiscences of Old New Utrecht*, 52–54). For one of Marriner's most famous exploits, the capture of the *Blacksnake*, see *New-York Gazette*, Apr. 24, 1780; Salter and Beekman, *Old Times in Old Monmouth*, 127.

67. *New-Jersey Gazette*, July 22, 1778; *Pennsylvania Packet*, July 16, 25, 1778; *Pennsylvania Evening Post*, July 30, 1778; *Independent Ledger* (Philadelphia), Aug. 3, 1778; *Continental Journal*, Aug. 13, 1778; Burgoyne, *Enemy Views*, 276–278; Wertenbaker, *Father Knickerbocker Rebels*, 172ff.; Schecter, *Battle for New York*, 314–320. Rumors

made the rounds all fall that the British would soon evacuate New York and perhaps burn it to the ground (see, e.g., *Independent Chronicle*, Sept.17, 1778; *Connecticut Courant*, Nov. 24, 1778). It was eventually understood that these rumors stemmed from misunderstanding preparations for the attacks on Savannah and St. Lucia (see, e.g., the *Pennsylvania Packet*, Oct. 10, 1778).

68. *Royal Gazette*, Aug. 29, 1778; *New-York Gazette*, Sept. 7, 1778; *Independent Chronicle*, Sept. 24, 1778; *Kemble Journal*, 167; Burgoyne, *Enemy Views*, 274.

69. *New-York Gazette*, Sept. 7, 14, 21, Oct. 5, 1778; *New-Jersey Gazette*, Oct. 7, 1778; *Continental Journal*, Oct. 8, 1778; *Pennsylvania Ledger*, Jan. 1, 1779. General Robert Pigot, the British commander in Rhode Island, told General Sullivan that he shipped all his prisoners down to New York (*Mackenzie Diary* 1: 296; Ritchie, "New York Diary," 256, 261, 263).

70. Ingersoll's story is in RWPA: S4425. Ingersoll was vague about the date of his incarceration on the *Scorpion*, but the fact that he describes her lying in the Hudson suggests 1778 or 1779. There were, he said, about 200 prisoners on the *Huntress*, which was anchored in Buttermilk Channel between Governors Island and Long Island. On Sheffield, see *Connecticut Gazette*, July 10, 1778; *Pennsylvania Packet*, July 23, 1778; *Independent Ledger*, Aug. 10, 1778. For similar stories, see *Connecticut Gazette*, Dec. 18, 1778; *New London Gazette*, Dec. 25, 1778. John Adams, in Paris, got word that Admiral James Gambier "has treated Our people with great humanity," but no surviving evidence confirms that verdict (Isaac Smith Sr. to Adams, Nov. 9, 1778: Butterfield, *Adams Family Correspondence*, 3: 117–118; Footner, *Sailor of Fortune*, 53–59).

71. *Connecticut Courant*, Aug. 4, 1778, and Jan. 6, 1779; *Independent Ledger* (Philadelphia), Aug. 24, 1778; *Massachusetts Spy*, Oct. 8, 1778. For more limited (and believable) numbers, see the *Pennsylvania Evening Post*, Aug. 18, 1778, which has twenty-two prisoners arriving in New London at the beginning of August; *Independent Chronicle*, Oct. 15, 1778; *Independent Ledger*, Oct. 19, 1778; "General State of the Prisoners, New York, Dec. 26, 1778," Frederick Mackenzie Papers, WLCL, quoted in Bowman, *Captive Americans*, 30; also Bowman, "New Jersey Prisoner Exchange Conferences," 151.

CHAPTER 6

1. Van Buskirk, *Generous Enemies*, 21–35, 129–147; Burrows and Wallace, *Gotham*, 245–246; Barck, *New York City*, 75–78; Lorenz, *Hugh Gaine*, chap. 12. On the "Black American Revolution" in New York, see Hodges, *Root and Branch*, 139–161; Foote, *Black and White Manhattan*, 210–216.

2. Barck, *New York City*, 203–204; Randall, *Little Revenge*, 161–162, 411–427, 461–790, and passim; Burgoyne, *Enemy Views*, 257.

3. [Smith], *Historical Memoirs*, 250–251; "Letter from Mr. Peter Dubois in New-York, to Mrs. Dubois," *New-Jersey Gazette*, June 9, 1779. After Billy Parsons escaped from New York in mid-April 1780, he gave his father, the general, a report blaming Refugees for the mistreatment of prisoners (Hall, *Parsons*, 286, 288).

4. Shy, "Armed Loyalism"; Calhoon, "Civil, Revolutionary, or Partisan"; Tebbenhoff, "Associated Loyalists"; Ranlet, *New York Loyalists*, 106–119; Wertenbaker, *Father Knickerbocker Rebels*, 222ff.; Barck, *New York City*, 194–195; Ward, *Between the Lines*, 20–21. Of course, Germain and others had been preaching the gospel of predatory war for years. What was new after 1778 was the idea of getting provincials and auxiliaries to do the dirty work.

5. [Smith], *Historical Memoirs*, 59; [Peebles], *John Peebles' American War*, 241, 243; Ritchie, "New York Diary," 263; Uhlendorf, *Revolution in America*, 247; Burgoyne, *Enemy Views*, 274, 324; Schaukirk, *Occupation of New York City*, 9.

6. *Massachusetts Spy*, Jan. 7, 14, 1779; *Boston Post*, Jan. 11, 1779; *Continental Journal* (Boston), Feb. 4, 1779, repr., *New Hampshire Gazette*, Feb. 9, 1779; *Independent Ledger* (Boston), Feb. 1, 1779; and elsewhere. At one point, a rumor got started that the prisoners were all gone and the prison ships would be refitted as transports, but that was erroneous. See, e.g., *Independent Ledger*, Jan. 4, 1779. On the Connecticut General Assembly, see *Connecticut Courant*, Feb. 9, 1779. New London residents were said to have contracted a "distemper" from the prisoners (*Pennsylvania Evening Post*, Feb. 2, 1779).

7. Beatty to GW, Feb. 24, 1779, *SBW* 3: 154. Major Baurmeister referred in mid-May to "352 rebel officers at Flatbush," by which he undoubtedly meant all the paroled officers in Kings County (Uhlendorf, *Revolution in America*, 276). Not all paroled American officers were on Long Island, however. Thomas Hughes, an ensign in the British Army, found "a number" of them living in New York in December 1778. See [Hughes], *Journal*, 57. For Loring, see Bowman, *Captive Americans*, 30; "Weekly Report of Prisoners, March 1, 1779," Clinton Papers, WLCL; and *Connecticut Courant*, May 4, 1779. The list in the *Connecticut Courant* revealed that the largest block of prisoners came from Massachusetts (81), followed by Maryland (22), Virginia (19), Connecticut (8), Rhode Island (7), Pennsylvania (4), and New Jersey (3). All these tallies, however, are of *American* prisoners; there were always French prisoners as well, sometimes a lot of them. It is, as always, difficult to judge mortality rates, but a concerted American effort to inoculate soldiers against smallpox in 1777 must have brought them down somewhat (Fenn, *Pox Americana*, 92–103, and passim; Ann Becker, "Smallpox in Washington's Army," 428ff).

8. Hillard, *Last Men of the Revolution*, 48–51; RWPA: S14782. For another example, see the pension application filed by the son and widow of Isaac Crane, an adjutant in the New York State militia (RWPA: W18980).

9. General Parsons to Mumford, July 20, 1779: Hall, *Parsons*, 256–257; *Connecticut Courant*, Mar. 2, 9, July 13, 1779; *Connecticut Journal*, Mar. 3, 1779; Uhlendorf, *Revolution in America*, 296.; Burgoyne, *Enemy Views*, 329–330; *Royal Gazette*, July 7, 1779. The American reaction is in *New-England Chronicle*, July 15, 1779. Stuart to the Earl of Bute, Sept. 16, 1778, *NRAR*, 58–60, 99.

10. For the Crompond prisoners, see Ritchie, "New York Diary," 278; Burgoyne, *Enemy Views*, 325; Peckham, *Toll of Independence*, 58; Bowman, *Captive Americans*, 30; *American Journal* (Providence), July 8, 1779; and the account by Henry Charlick in RWPA: S23569. (Charlick was captured in September of the following year and spent ten weeks in the Sugar House.) On Pound Ridge, see *New-York Gazette*, July 5, 1779. On Simcoe, see Simcoe, *Journal*, 116–117, 264; Uhlendorf, *Revolution in America*, 316–317; *New-York Gazette*, Oct. 30, Nov. 1, 1779. Two accounts of Simcoe's raid appeared in the *Royal Gazette* for Nov. 3, 1779, one of which has the dragoons taking between twenty and thirty prisoners. American accounts make no mention of prisoners (see, e.g., *Pennsylvania Packet*, Nov. 6, 1779). On Simcoe's reputation, see *New-Jersey Gazette*, Nov. 3, 1779. Marriner prevented Simcoe from being killed as he lay stunned on the ground—a favor that Simcoe would repay the following year when Marriner himself was captured and applied to General Clinton for a parole. Clinton consented after Simcoe put in a good word for him. For other examples of the mayhem that raged in 1779, see Ward, *Between the Lines*, 22–23, 41–43, and passim;

Ritchie, "New York Diary," 280, 302; Uhlendorf, *Revolution in America*, 276; *New-Jersey Gazette*, Feb. 17, 1779; *Pennsylvania Evening Post*, Sept. 18, 1779; *Connecticut Journal*, Oct. 20, 1779; *Norwich Packet*, Oct. 26, 1779; *Royal Gazette*, Dec. 22, 1779.

11. On Tye's exploits, see Ward, *Between the Lines*, 61–64, and Hodges, *Slavery and Freedom in the Rural North*, 92–106.

12. For Silliman: *Connecticut Journal*, May 5, 1779; Ritchie, "New York Diary," 273; Uhlendorf, *Revolution in America*, 275; Ward, *Between the Lines*, 43–44; Cummin, *Connecticut Militia General*, 58–66; Buel and Buel, *Way of Duty*, 145–171. In letters to his wife, General Silliman lavished praise on Loring for his "complaisance, kindness, and friendship," though it is worth remembering that a prisoner's mail was read in Loring's office before it went out. Among other things, Loring agreed to exchange Samuel Silliman, the general's cousin, who had spent seven months already in the Sugar House (Jones, *History of New York*, 2: 425). Jones, who became quite friendly with Silliman on Long Island, was subsequently abducted by Connecticut partisans and exchanged for the general in April 1780 (*New-Jersey Gazette*, Dec. 15, 1779; *PRC*, 2: 503). Connecticut partisans later raided Long Island and captured a man named Glover, said to have led the party that took Silliman (*Pennsylvania Evening Post*, Sept. 29, 1779). [Smith], "Diary of Colonel Josiah Smith," 347. On the Hempstead militia: *New-York Gazette*, July 5, 1779.

13. Ritchie, "New York Diary," 262; Israel Putnam to General Parsons, May 7, 1779: Hall, *Parsons*, 236–237; *Connecticut Journal*, May 19, 1779.

14. The Greenwich raid is described in *Royal Gazette*, June 23, 1779. For Mather, see *Connecticut Journal*, Sept. 8, 1779; July 26, Oct. 18, 1781; *Massachusetts Spy*, Aug. 16, 23, 1781; *Norwich Packet*, Mar. 29, 1781; Hall, *Parsons*, 400–401; Noll, "Moses Mather"; Phoenix, *Whitney Family*, 1: 107; "Revolutionary Records"; pension application of John Clock's widow, RWPA: W17623.

15. William Livingston (WL) to Elisha Boudinot, Nov. 2, 1779: *PWL* 3: 190–191. Fitz Randolph's predations on Staten Island are described in Papas, *Ever Loyal Island*, 85–86. For other examples, see accounts of the capture of Joseph Young (or Youngs), a prominent Westchester County committee-man, in *Royal Gazette*, Dec. 30, 1778; *Pennsylvania Packet*, Feb. 4, 1779; and Uhlendorf, *Revolution in America*, 248. Young was caught by James De Lancey's "cowboys," who also scooped up Captain Daniel Williams, a notorious rebel partisan, and his twelve-man crew. Peckham, *Toll of Independence*, 56, estimates that only five rebels were captured. See also *New-Jersey Gazette*, June 9, 1779: "a party of tories from Staten Island landed at Middletown, in Monmouth, plundered several houses, and carried off four or five of the inhabitants prisoners." A combined force of regulars and Tories attacked Rahway and Woodbridge in late June, rounding up fifteen inhabitants, some of whom were militia officers (*Pennsylvania Packet*, July 13, 1779). Additional cases of captured civilians from New Jersey can also be traced in Governor Livingston's correspondence (e.g., *PWL* 3: 377; 4: 16n4, 371n1, and passim).

16. *New-York Gazette*, June 14, 1779; *Pennsylvania Packet*, June 19, 1779; *New-Jersey Gazette*, June 23, 1779. On the *Oliver Cromwell*, see Abel Woodward's pension application, RWPA: S23496; *Independent Ledger*, Aug. 30, 1779; *Connecticut Journal*, Sept. 8, 1779.

17. Peckham, *Toll of Independence*, 57–66, 121–123, shows a grand total of 416 American prisoners taken in the New York area during 1779, 298 on land and 118 at sea. As explained earlier, his data do not include political (state) prisoners or reflect a mass of unsubstantiated reports about prisoners carried to New York. Nor does

Peckham's tally appear to include cases like those of General Silliman and his son, surprised at home rather than captured in battle. There appear to have been more than a few of these. In July 1779, for example, Lieutenant Jacob Van Tassell (or Tassel) and four kinsmen were seized by regulars while they slept in a private house and were marched down to the Provost (RWPA: S23465). See also the account of Elnathan Finch (RWPA: W7267), captured in Bedford, New York, in June 1781, between stints in the state militia. Often, however, the sources supply no numbers at all. "A Party of Col. Baskerts Regiment from Paulus Hook, took & brought in some Prisoners" is all we will probably ever know about a minor action in late July 1779 (Ritchie, "New York Diary," 287). All things considered, the actual number of prisoners in all categories may be as much as 30 to 50 percent higher than Peckham's figures indicate.

18. *New-Jersey Gazette*, June 16, 1779; *Pennsylvania Packet*, June 19, July 1, 1779; *Massachusetts Spy*, July 1, Aug. 12, 1779; *Providence Gazette*, July 17, 1779. See also Abel Woodworth's recollection that 15 of the 118 men from the *Cromwell* perished during their stint on the *Good Hope*. Her subsequent cleaning, however, made her "tolerable healthful"—for a while (RWPA: S23496).

19. Governor Livingston of New Jersey believed that the threat of retaliation had made the enemy "more indulgent" to prisoners taken in arms, but captured civilians continued to be treated badly (WL to British Prisoners, Mar. 17, 1779: *PWL* 3: 42–43). Also *Massachusetts Spy*, Mar. 11, 1779; *Connecticut Gazette*, Aug. 25, 1779; *New Hampshire Gazette*, Mar. 16, 1779; Syrett, "'Penurious Old Reptile,'" 74; Willcox, "Arbuthnot, Gambier, and Graves"; *Independent Chronicle*, Sept. 2, 1779. See also the *Pennsylvania Packet*, Nov. 11, 1779, reporting on the condition of 238 prisoners recently delivered to Boston. American papers occasionally carried news of prisoners who had been well-treated elsewhere (see *New-Jersey Gazette*, Sept. 6, 1780).

20. *American Journal and General Advertiser*, Oct. 14, 1779; *Pennsylvania Evening Post*, Oct. 19, 1779; *Massachusetts Spy*, Oct. 28, 1779; *Norwich Packet*, Oct. 19, 1779; *Independent Ledger*, Oct. 25, 1779. One of the escapees that day was Thomas Dring. Dring later had the misfortune of being taken prisoner a second time and incarcerated in the *Jersey*.

21. Ranlet, "Tory David Sproat," 187; Banks, *David Sproat*, 116, 124–127, and passim.

22. Ranlet, "Tory David Sproat," 188, 190. I am not persuaded by Ranlet's argument that Sproat pursued a "humanitarian policy" toward American prisoners (ibid., 189–192), much less by Banks's absurd claim that the mistreatment of Americans on the New York prison ships cannot be proved (see Banks, *David Sproat*, 1, 25, and passim). During his previous posting at Halifax, Arbuthnot tolerated conditions on the prison ships *Bellona* and *Lord Stanley* that allegedly dismayed even British observers (*New Hampshire Gazette*, June 28, 1777; see also the testimony that followed when American prisoners seized the *Royal Bounty* en route from Halifax to Providence early the next year, e.g., *NDAR* 11: 288–291). Also *NDAR* 9: 254–255, and the *Independent Chronicle*, Feb. 13, 1777. Sproat's predecessors were James Dick (1778–1779) and then William Burton (1779), a local merchant (see *Royal Gazette* for Nov. 21, 1778; Jan. 23, Apr. 21, 1779; *New-York Gazette*, July 3, 1780).

23. Sproat to the Commissioners for Sick and Hurt Seamen, Oct. 31, 1780: PRO 30/20/12.

24. Uhlendorf, *Revolution in America*, 337, 340–341; *Kemble Papers* 1: 168; *Pennsylvania Packet*, Jan 27, 1780; *New-York Gazette*, Jan. 31, 1780; *Royal Gazette*, Feb. 16,

1780; *New-Jersey Gazette*, Feb. 9, 1780; [Smith], *Historical Memoirs*, 211, 214–215, 217, 220, 221, 232; Ford, *Journals of Hugh Gaine*, 2: 74–77; [Peebles], *John Peebles' American War*, 313ff.; [Greenman], *Diary of a Common Soldier*, 161; Burgoyne, *Enemy Views*, 411–413; Barck, *New York City During the War for Independence*, 197–199; Schecter, *Battle for New York*, 330; Papas, *Ever Loyal Island*, 89–90.

25. [Webb], "William Webb, of the Continental Frigate 'Trumbull.'" Abner Webb remembered his father as having said he was a captive on the *Jersey*, but the subsequent account makes it clear that he was on the *Good Hope*. Sproat's absurd comment was made in the course of his public dispute the next year with Skinner. On the 40 percent survival rate, see "Argus," *American Citizen*, Apr. 21, 1808. The dying prisoner described by Pintard was Joseph Hedden, Jr., a civilian captured during a British raid into New Jersey some days earlier. "Reminiscences of Pintard," NYPL; *Royal Gazette*, Jan. 29, Feb. 9, 1780; *New-York Gazette*, Jan. 24, 31, 1780; *New-Jersey Gazette*, Feb. 2, 1780; Ford, *Journals of Hugh Gaine*, 2: 76–77.

26. *New-Hampshire Gazette*, Jan. 1, 1780; "Extract of a letter from a gentleman at New York. Prison ship, April 2, 1780," *Connecticut Gazette*, June 30, 1780; *Norwich Packet*, July 6, 1780.

27. *New-York Gazette*, Jan. 24, 1780; Schaukirk, *Occupation of New York*, 12; [Smith], *Historical Memoirs*, 217.

28. *Royal Gazette*, Mar. 8, 1780; *New-Jersey Gazette*, Apr. 5, 1780. The *Royal Gazette* said the incendiaries were led by a Connecticut man named Woodbury. The only firsthand account of the fire is Webb's, though as noted his son erroneously placed him aboard the *Jersey*. The prisoners from the *Good Hope* were held on the *Woodland*, a transport and then transferred to the fire ship *Strombolo* and the *Scorpion*, a sloop. Both had been stationed in the Hudson River on the city's west side but were shifted to Wallabout Bay after the *Good Hope* burned (Armbruster, *Wallabout Prison Ships*, 26). On February 24, Hugh Gaine recorded the destruction of another hospital ship in Wallabout Bay, apparently a separate event (*JHG* 2: 81).

29. Thompson's outburst was triggered by the decision to trade former Governor William Franklin of New Jersey for John McKinly, the president of Delaware. Thompson believed that he should have been exchanged ahead of McKinly and almost came to blows with Thomas McKean, a member of Congress and Chief Justice of Pennsylvania (*Pennsylvania Packet*, Dec. 29, 1778; Feb. 2, 25, 1779; Beatty to Laurens, Sept. 15, 1778, SPL, Misc. MSS.). The frustration of the Long Island officers emerges with particular clarity in the correspondence of Samuel B. Webb (see esp. *SBW* 1: 398–401; *SBW* 2: 6, 13, 87–88, 97–98, 106, 107–108, 117, 119, 120, 124, 126, 130–132, 134, 142–143, 147, 152–161, 165; *SBW* 3: 277, 348–351; also SBW to GW, Dec. 29, 1777, *PGW* 13: 53–54; Ford, *Family Letters of Samuel Blachley Webb*, 36–37, 85–86, 109–110, 134, 408–412; Bowman, "New Jersey Prisoner Exchange Conferences"; Dixon, "Divided Authority," 278–281). For one of a growing number of altercations between American officers and British officers on Long Island, see Richard Drakeford to [Alexander] Leslie, July 18, 1778: SFDL.

30. Phillips to Germain, Mar. 25, 1780, quoted in *SBW* 2: 258. Phillips to Clinton, Dec. 20, 1779, *PGC* 7: 229–230; Phillips to Magaw, Dec. 25, 1779, *PGC* 7: 234–235; "Proposition for an Exchange," n.d. *PGC* 7: 236–240; Bowman, "Prisoner Exchange Conferences," 157–158; Dixon, "Divided Authority," 283–284.

31. Dixon, "Divided Authority," 105, 107; Bowman, *Captive Americans*, 72. Lewis Pintard, too, soon resigned as the American agent in New York, explaining that threats had been made against his life and that he would put himself in "great personal

danger" by remaining in the city, even though Washington and Clinton had agreed that resident commissaries were to be protected and treated with "suitable respect." See Pintard to GW, Dec. 6, 16, 1780, and "Propositions Respecting the Agents to be Appointed for Prisoners" [Oct. 21, 1780]: *PGW,* LC. On Skinner, see Thompson, *History of Long Island,* 397–398. Skinner was one of several candidates nominated for the post, and although his appointment was not official until September, he was on the job by midyear (*JCC* 16: 319; *JCC* 17: 789; *JCC* 18: 828, 832; Skinner to Livingston, Sept. 9, 1780: *NJGC,* 260–261; Skinner to WL, Sept. 9, 1780, *PWL,* 4: 56–58; *New-Jersey Gazette,* Nov. 22, 1780). See Dixon, "Divided Authority," 287–289, on the communications between Washington and Clinton that preceded the exchange. There are twenty-two names on the "List of American Officers remaining on Long Island (on Parole) & Elsewhere, after the Exchanges of the 25th & 26th Octbr 1780": *GWP,* LC. Metzger, *Prisoner in the American Revolution,* 212–215. Saffell's RRW, 320–323, lists 101 officers from nine states who were released between November 1780 and April 1781. The high number from Pennsylvania strongly suggests that those men had been captured in the fighting around Philadelphia during the campaigns of 1777 and 1778: Pennsylvania—37; Maryland—15; Connecticut—10; Virginia—10; New Jersey—7; Massachusetts—7; New York—7; S. Carolina—1; N. Carolina—1; Unknown—6.

32. Sproat to the Commissioners for Sick and Hurt Seamen, Oct. 31, 1780, PRO 30/20/12. Admiral Lord Rodney to the Commissioners for Sick and Hurt Seamen, Oct. 12, 1780, [Rodney], *Letter-Books and Order-Book,* 1, 33–34; Certificate of Admiral Rodney, May 12, 1787: Banks, *David Sproat,* 120–121, 125–126; *Royal Gazette,* Oct. 20, Nov. 13, 1779.

33. Arbuthnot's proclamation initially appeared in the *Royal Gazette* for Sept. 18. It was frequently reprinted in that paper and the *New-York Gazette* over the next several months—an indication, arguably, that it failed to have the desired effect. A report of Arbuthnot's losses on the passage from England is in *Connecticut Gazette,* Oct. 13, 1779. It did not help matters that provincial units such as the Queen's Rangers, Colonel Simcoe's regiment, were industriously recruiting in the city at the same time (Memorial of David Sproat to the Right Honorable The Lords Commissioners of the Treasury, Aug. 15, 1785, PRO T 1/624).

34. Usher, "Royal Navy Impressment"; *Independent Ledger,* May 22, 1780. For presses on Long Island, see Burgoyne, *Enemy Views,* 480, and *Pennsylvania Packet,* Oct. 1, 1778. See also *New-Jersey Gazette,* June 21, 1780, for a similar event in Barbados. Another "very hot press" took place in November and another the following May, during which over 300 seamen were taken off the prison ships (*New-Jersey Gazette,* Nov. 15, 1780; *New-Jersey Gazette,* May 9, 16, 1781; *Freeman's Journal* [Philadelphia], May 16, 1781; *Massachusetts Spy,* May 24, 1781). Three more presses would be reported before the end of the war—in November 1781, April 1782, and March 1783 (*Connecticut Journal,* Oct. 11, 1781; *Connecticut Courant,* Apr. 16, 1782; *Pennsylvania Packet,* Mar. 4, 1783). The only previous "hot press" in the city seems to have occurred two years earlier, when a fever of unknown origin incapacitated many crewmen on the warships and transports in the harbor at the very moment the French fleet was expected to arrive (*Independent Ledger,* June 29, 1778). For Grinnell, see *Pennsylvania Packet,* Aug. 22, 1780; *New-Jersey Gazette,* Aug. 23, 1780; *Pennsylvania Evening Post,* Aug. 25, 1780; *New England Chronicle,* Sept. 7, 1780. Grinnell also said that at the time he escaped, there were about 120 American prisoners still on the *Scorpion* and 200 on the *Strombolo.* The master of the *Strombolo* from August to De-

cember 1780 later said he never had fewer than 150 and "frequently above two hundred" prisoners on board (*New-York Gazette*, Feb. 12, 1781).

35. [Rodney], *Letter-Books and Order Book*, 1: 34, 63–64.

36. Peckham, *Toll of Independence*, 67–78, shows 440 prisoners taken in the vicinity of New York that year. A report from the Board of War in mid-August found 720 American *military* prisoners in New York, including 270 officers paroled on Long Island (*JCC* 17: 753). For Marriner's arrest, see *Royal Gazette*, Aug. 9, 1780. Marriner was sent to the Provost and his men to the Wallabout prison ships (*JHG* 2: 96).

37. For the many civilian prisoners confined there as well, see *New-Jersey Gazette*, Mar. 29, May 31, June 7, Aug. 9, 16, 30, Nov. 29, Dec. 20, 1780; *New-York Gazette*, Mar. 27, Apr. 16, 1780; *Royal Gazette*, Feb. 16, Aug. 9, 1780; and *Connecticut Journal*, Feb. 24, 1779. See also the frequent mention of prisoners taken in *JHG* 2: 78–105. For soldiers and officers captured out of the line of duty, see 2 *PA* 11: 581, 618; and the obituary of Joel David in the *Farmer's Cabinet* (Amherst, NH), Aug. 31, 1859. On the oyster gatherers, see *New-Jersey Gazette*, Feb. 9, Mar. 27, 1780. See also Jones, "From War to Peace"; Platt, *Old Times in Huntington*, 56–57, 64–65.

38. André's advocacy of "fire as well as the sword" can be traced back to his unpleasant experiences as a captive of the rebels in Pennsylvania in 1776 (Flexner, *Traitor and the Spy*, 137–160).

39. Board of Loyalists to Clinton, Dec. 1, 1778, *DAR* 18: 239–244; Tebbenhoff, "Associated Loyalists"; Skemp, *William Franklin*, 250; Barck, *New York City*, 203–206; Flexner, *Traitor and the Spy*, 263–267; Wertenbaker, *Father Knickerbocker Rebels*, 228–231; [Smith], *Historical Memoirs*, 464 (Clinton says "he disapproves of nor indeed will ever prosecute a predatory war"). The Associators were organized into three "societies": one, based at Kingsbridge, to operate against rebels in the Hudson Highlands; a second, based at Lloyd's Neck on Long Island, to raid the Connecticut shore; a third, operating out of Bergen Point and Paulus Hook, to harass the coast of New Jersey. For criticism of the Associators from within Loyalist ranks, see Jones, *History of New York* 1: 301–304.

40. The total number of Americans held at Forton and Mill prisons usually hovered around the 1,000 mark (Bowman, *Captive Americans*, 59; and Cohen, *Yankee Sailors*, esp. 30–39). Handfuls of Americans were also held at Kinsale, Kilkenny, Edinburgh, Pembroke, Liverpool, Falmouth, and other ports at various times during the war (Moyne, "Reverend William Hazlitt"; Lemisch, "Listening to the 'Inarticulate,'" 7n14,18 and 12n31). According to Lemisch, the mortality rate in both prisons never exceeded 5 percent; see also Cogliano, *Maritime Prisoners*, 69. On the activities of English reformers, widely covered in American papers, see *NDAR* 9: 611–613; *NDAR* 11: 861, 891–892, 902, and passim; *PHE* 19: 463; Sainsbury, *Disaffected Patriots*, 141–142; *New-Jersey Gazette*, May 13, June 3, 1778; *Connecticut Journal*, May 20, 1778; *Providence Gazette*, May 23, 1778; *Pennsylvania Packet*, Oct. 19, 1779; *Norwich Packet*, Nov. 23, 1779; "Ode to Charity," *American Journal*, Jan. 20, 1780. On aiding fugitives, see Cohen, *Yankee Sailors*, 77–84, 111–114; Cogliano, *Maritime Prisoners*, 105ff.; Lemisch, "Listening to the 'Inarticulate,'" esp. 10–11, 18–19; Prelinger, "Benjamin Franklin and American Prisoners," esp. 283.

41. Prelinger, "Benjamin Franklin and American Prisoners," is the authoritative guide in this matter. See also Bowman, *Captive Americans*, 81, 112; "John Thornton's Memorandum for the American Commissioners in France," [Jan. 5–8, 1778], *NDAR* 11: 885–891. More than a few American prisoners wrote Franklin directly about conditions in Forton and Mill. See, e.g., John Porter to Franklin, June 6, 1777, *NDAR* 9:

381–382, 390–391; or the letter "From Two Hundred Eighty American Prisoners" to Franklin, Feb. 3, 1780, *PBF* 31: 442–444.

42. Franklin to Hartley, Oct. 14 [–Dec. 11], 1777, *PBF* 25: 65; see also Franklin to Hartley, Feb. 12, 1778; *PBF* 25:650–652; Franklin to Hartley, Sept. 3, 1778; *PBF* 27: 342. Franklin seems to have been quite well informed about the uproar in America over prisoner abuse. As noted earlier, he knew about the essay by "Miserecors" within months of its initial appearance (Dumas to Franklin, May 23, 1777; Arrenberg to Franklin, May 24, 1777, *PBF* 24: 68–69, 72). See also the protest that Franklin and the other American commissioners, Silas Deane and Arthur Lee, sent to Lord North in December 1777, *NDAR* 10: 1095–1096.

43. Lafayette to Franklin, May 19, 1779, *PBF* 29: 521–522; "List of Prints to Illustrate British Cruelties" [c. May 1779], *PBF* 29: 590–593. It also occurred to Franklin that engravings of British "Barbarity" could be used on coinage (*PBF* 29: 430). Who first came up with the idea for the atrocity book is not clear, but John Adams is a leading candidate. Adams had had a similar idea back in 1777, and during the time he lived with Franklin in Paris, from February 1778 through May 1779, he would have had ample opportunity to discuss it with both Franklin and Lafayette.

44. Lafayette to Franklin, July 12, 1779, *PBF* 30: 99–100; Franklin to Hartley, Feb. 2, 1780, *PBF* 31: 436–439; *LLP* 3: 256–267, 305–306.

45. Quoted in Prelinger, "Franklin and Prisoners of War," 294. For a similar argument that prisoner abuse and other "horrid enormities" made reconciliation impossible, see William Henry Drayton to the Carlisle Peace Commission, Sept. 4, 1778, *LDC* 10: 568. Americans, Drayton wrote, have been too "deeply impressed" by "the agonies of her sons in the prisons and prison-ships at New-York" to want anything but complete independence. See also the "Manifesto" adopted by Congress on Oct. 13, 1778, *JCC* 12: 1080–1082.

46. Schiff, *Great Improvisation*, 383–386.

CHAPTER 7

1. *Pennsylvania Packet*, July 27, 1779; Jellison, *Ethan Allen*, 219, has the *Narrative* serialized in the *Packet* in the late spring of 1779, prior to its publication in book form, but I have been unable to locate the issues in question. The *Narrative* was extensively serialized *after* the book appeared, and was reprinted a total of nineteen times before 1860. (Denn, "Prison Narratives," 1–2; Doyle, *Voices from Captivity*, 12.)

2. For this and the following paragraphs, I made liberal use of Colley, *Captives*; Purcell, *Sealed with Blood*; Doyle, *Voices from Captivity*, 60–73; Walzer, *Exodus and Revolution*; McWilliams, "Faces of Ethan Allen"; Williams, "Zealous in the Cause of Liberty"; Sieminski, "Puritan Captivity Narrative."

3. Colley, *Captives*, esp. 137–202; Strong, *Captive Selves, Captivating Others*, esp. 211–217, which identifies twenty-two captivity narratives printed in America before the Revolution; Sayre, *American Captivity Narratives*, esp. 1–20.

4. Winfield, *50-Gun Ship*, 42 and passim. "Extract of a Letter from Spithead, May 2 [1776]," *Freeman's Journal* (Portsmouth, NH), Aug. 10, 1776; "British Ships of War on the American Station," *Connecticut Journal*, Mar. 25, 1778, shows only six larger vessels, all third-rates, mounting more than sixty-four guns. The *Jersey*'s prominence on the waterfront is suggested by a notice that the brig *Three Friends* could be found "at Tolmie's Wharf, near the Jersey Hospital Ship" (*Royal Gazette*, Feb. 24, 1779). Her hull, like that of most British warships, was painted black (Greene, *Recollections of the Jersey Prison-Ship*, 26.

5. Charles Bushnell's annotations to [Hawkins], *Adventures of Hawkins*, 212-213, have the *Jersey* converted to a prison ship over the winter of 1779-1780, then moved to Wallabout Bay in the spring. Captain David Laird's log has her only "laying off Long Island." See also Greene, *Recollections of the Jersey Prison-Ship*, 13-14. I have been unable to determine what became of the *Huntress*, a hospital ship anchored in Buttermilk Channel as of 1778 or 1779. The hulks of *Strombolo*, *Scorpion*, and *Hunter* were offered for sale in December (*Royal Gazette*, Dec. 9, 1780). Bushnell says that when no one came forward to buy the *Strombolo*, she was refitted as a hospital ship and moved to Wallabout Bay the following year. *Strombolo* and *Scorpion* may also have been too small to accommodate a sufficient number of guards—their prisoners absconded with embarrassing frequency. See, e.g., *American Journal*, June 28, 1780, describing the escape of thirty-five prisoners at one time from one or the other at the beginning of the month. An earlier mass escape from "the Prison Ship in the East River" is described in *Connecticut Gazette*, Feb. 16, 1780. On that occasion, a number of the fugitives, "unable to endure the severity of the Weather," turned themselves in. This was probably the event described to a Brooklyn audience 110 years later by the granddaughter of one of the escapees, an indication of how long oral traditions of the Revolution sometimes survived in families. See *Brooklyn Daily Eagle*, May 26, 1890.

6. This description derives primarily from drawings of the *Jersey* and the layout of its decks in Greene, *Recollections of the Jersey Prison-Ship*, 16-18. Greene said that the drawings were based on sketches in Dring's manuscript and that the explanatory material was "given almost in his own words."

7. *New-York Packet*, Dec. 29, 1783 (sale notice for the hulls of *Perseverance* and *Bristol Pacquet*, "now lying in the Wallabacht"); Fox, *Adventures*, 106.

8. Colonel Lewis Nicola to Joseph Reed, June 17, 1779, 1 *PA* 7: 492-493. Nicola spoke of the *Jersey* as a prison ship, but he got his information secondhand and was mistaken. According to John van Dyke, the *Jersey* was anchored off the Fly Market in the East River when he came aboard, which is not consistent with other sources suggesting that she may already have been moved to Wallabout Bay ("Narrative of Confinement in the Jersey Prison Ship"). Six-man messes were standard in the navy for the distribution of rations.

9. On Van Dyke's later life, see his pension application, RWPA: S42592.

10. *Pennsylvania Packet*, Jan. 16, 1781. After ten weeks on the *Jersey*, Batterman was released in December 1780, presumably in an exchange worked out by Massachusetts authorities, who then arranged to have his deposition taken in Boston and sent it off to the new commissary, Abraham Skinner, in Philadelphia. Except for handfuls of soldiers, civilians, and a larger number of foreign seamen, the majority of prisoners on the *Jersey* were privateers taken in and around New York waters. Peckham, *Toll of Independence*, 124-125, records only fifty-eight men captured in naval engagements during 1780.

11. A couple of months later, on Admiral Rodney's orders, Talbot and seventy other American officers were removed to the Provost, then sent to Dartmoor prison in England (Fowler, *Silas Talbot*, 56-57; Tuckerman, *Life of Silas Talbot*, 91-97). For "wild beasts," see War, "Germantown Road," 123, quoting Joseph Martin; and *Connecticut Journal*, Nov. 16, 1780. For other accounts of the *Jersey*, see *New England Chronicle*, Jan. 17, 1781; *Connecticut Journal*, Feb. 8, 1781; *American Journal*, Feb. 17, 1781. One highly improbable account had prisoners drinking their own urine and going blind from eating condemned provisions (*New-England Chronicle*, Feb. 3, 1781). No other source, published or unpublished, corroborates such allegations, and

contemporary skepticism is suggested by the fact that only two other printers in the country elected to copy them, the *New-Jersey Gazette*, Feb. 21, 1781, and the *Norwich Packet*, Feb. 20, 1781.

12. Leary, *That Rascal Freneau*, is still the most reliable guide to the poet's life, but see also Axelrad, *Philip Freneau*, and Bowden, *Philip Freneau*.

13. "To the Americans, on the Rumoured Approach of the Hessian Forces, Waldeckers, &c., 1775," in [Freneau], *Poems*, 2. The poem was initially published as "Reflections on Gage's Letter to General Washington, of Aug. 13," *Constitutional Gazette* (New York), Oct. 18, 1775.

14. [Freneau], *Poems of Philip Freneau*, 1: 271–282.

15. His pension application (RWPA: W23069) is conveniently transcribed and printed in [Freneau], *Prose of Philip Freneau*, 492–493.

16. Freneau's extensive revision of the poem in 1786, the first of several, merged the second and third cantos and added many new lines of dialogue. For this and other details of its publication history, see Bowden, "In Search of Freneau's Prison Ships." First appearing as a pamphlet in 1781, "The British Prison Ship" was then copied in the newspapers. My discussion is based on the version printed in the *Independent Ledger*, June 25 and July 2, 1781.

17. On the capture of the *Aurora*, see *New-York Gazette*, June 5, 1780; *Royal Gazette*, May 31, July 1, 1780. Freneau's own footnotes to Canto I date the capture on May 26 and have the narrator's confinement beginning on June 1. Throughout this discussion I am closely following Bowden's "In Search of Freneau's Prison Ships," a fine piece of detective work. Bowden notes that the muster book of the *Iris* lists a "Philip Perno" among the men taken off the Aurora—a possible, if unlikely, error that is really the only reason to believe that Freneau *might* have been aboard. Bowden also builds a strong case that Freneau could not have been the author of *Some Account of the Capture of the Ship "Aurora,"* a prose narrative carefully copied into his log book but mistakenly attributed to him when it was first published at the end of the nineteenth century.

18. GW to Arbuthnot, Jan. 25, 1781, *WW* 21: 133–134. For the congressional re-action, see *JCC* 19: 27–28.

19. Dawson to GW, Feb. 2, 1781, *PGW*, LC. The report itemized the prisoners' weekly food allowance as 66 oz. of bread, 43 oz. of pork, 22 oz. of butter, 1 1/6 pints of peas, and 2 pints of oatmeal. If correct, that was truly a starvation diet, guarantee-ing that an average-sized man would lose at least two pounds of body weight per week (see Appendix A).

20. See, *Royal Gazette*, Feb. 7, 10, 14, and 17, 1781; and *New-York Gazette*, Feb. 12, 1781. These materials are conveniently reprinted in Banks, *David Sproat*, 34–54.

21. Baurmeister's remark is in Uhlendorf, *Revolution in America*, 416. For new tes-timony collected by Congress, see *JCC* 19: 187–188, 517, 620–623, 829; McKean to Washington, Aug. 7, 1781, *LDC* 17: 481; Washington to "The Officer Commanding His Britannic Majesty's Ships of War," Aug. 21, 1781, *WW* 21 (http://etext.lib.vir-ginia.edu/washington); Edmund Affleck to GW, Aug. 30, 1781, GWP. On Novem-ber 10 of that year, the *Pennsylvania Packet* ran an advertisement, purportedly copied from Gaine's *New-York Gazette*, alerting readers to the publication of *A New and Complete System of Cruelty; containing a variety of modern improvements in that art, em-belished with an elegant frontispiece, representing the inside view of a prison ship.* Though a parody, gleefully reprinted in many American papers over the next several months, historians have been fooled into thinking that the ad really did originate with the

Gazette and was an attempt to mock American complaints about the prison ships (see Denn, "Prison Narratives," 30; Colley, *Captives*, 223).

22. *Boston Gazette*, Aug. 20, 1781; repr., *New Hampshire Gazette*, Aug. 27, 1781; *Pennsylvania Packet*, Sept. 4, 1781; and elsewhere. For similar reports, see *Connecticut Gazette*, June 29, 1781; *American Journal*, July 7, 1781; *Pennsylvania Packet*, Aug. 30, 1781; *New-Jersey Gazette*, Sept. 5, 1781; *Massachusetts Spy*, Sept. 21, 1781. Brown's account appeared initially in *New-England Chronicle*, Sept. 6, 1781; repr., *Connecticut Courant*, Sept. 11, 1781. See also the letter from "A Late Prisoner," in *New-Hampshire Gazette*, Sept. 22, 1781; and a letter written by William Drowne aboard the *Jersey* on Sept. 25, 1781, in Greene, *Recollections of the Jersey Prison-Ship*, 171–172. Tradition has it that the *Jersey* was reserved for naval prisoners, but it is clear that she often held military prisoners as well. When Benedict Arnold raided New London in September 1781, some of the Americans captured in the action at Fort Griswold were put on the *Jersey*. See the pension applications filed by the widows of Nathan Burrows and Caleb Burrows, RWPA: W1764 and W25311. The other Fort Griswold prisoners were in the Sugar House (*PRC*, 3: 549). For "fever and small pox," see *Norwich Packet*, Nov. 8, 1781.

23. Sands, "Christopher Vail," 71. According to Captain Roswell Palmer, "a deal of trouble" existed between the Americans on the *Jersey* and 400 or 500 French and Spanish prisoners who occupied her orlop, or lowest deck, and were treated much better than the Americans (Greene, *Recollections of the Jersey Prison-Ship*, 179; see also *Painter Autobiography*, 67–69).

24. [Hawkins], *Adventures*, 67–70. Hawkins wrote in 1834 but his manuscript was not published by Bushnell until 1864, so it is impossible that he and Vail knew of the other's observations ([Fox], *Adventures*, 68 [1847 edition, which I have used throughout]).

25. 22 Geo. 3, c. 10; BF to Jay, Apr. 24, 1782, 37: 205; Mackesy, *War for America*, 433–436, 460–470; Bowman, *Captive Americans*, 114; Anderson, "Treatment of Prisoners," 67; Weintraub, *Iron Tears*, 300–330; Klein and Howard, *Twilight of British Rule*, 242n.

26. [Smith], *Historical Memoirs*, 461–462, 502, and passim; Skemp, *Franklin*, 251–256; Randall, *Little Revenge*, 476; Schaukirk, *Occupation of New York City*, 22; *Royal Gazette*, Oct. 31, 1781; *Pennsylvania Packet*, May 2, 1782. On atonement, see Azel Roe to WL, Jan. 29, [1782], *PWL*, 4: 375.

27. *Massachusetts Spy*, Jan. 10, 1782; *New-Jersey Gazette*, Mar. 6, 1782. Skinner's warning to GW is in letters on Dec. 23, 1781; and Feb. 18, 1782: GWP. See Schaukirk, *Occupation of New York City*, 23; Lorenz, *Hugh Gaine* 2: 141–143; [Peebles], *John Peebles' American War*, 505; Abraham Skinner to Robert Morris, Jan. 11, 1782, *RMP*, 4: 6. Robert Morris, the superintendent of finance for Congress, was working on an arrangement that allowed British merchants captured at Yorktown to exchange their goods for tobacco, then ship the tobacco up to the city for sale. One-half of the net proceeds were to be used for the American prisoners there. What came of the idea is not clear. Conditions on the *Jersey* in the spring of 1782 are described in *New-Jersey Gazette*, Mar. 3, 1782; *Boston Gazette*, May 6, 1782; *Boston Evening-Post*, May 4, 1782; *Continental Journal*, May 9, 1782; *Pennsylvania Packet*, May 21, 1782; *Massachusetts Spy*, May 9, 1782; *Providence Gazette*, May 25, 1782.

28. The Huddy affair has not been explored since Mayo, *General Washington's Dilemma*, but there are authoritative brief accounts of more recent vintage in Ward, *Between the Lines*, 63–68; Skemp, *Franklin*, 256–265; Randall, *Little Revenge*, 470–479. See also Klein and Howard, *Twilight of British Rule*, 243–244.

29. For reactions to Huddy's murder, see Thacher, *Military Journal*, 312–314; *Freeman's Journal*, Apr. 17, 24, May 1, 1782; *New-Jersey Gazette*, Apr. 24, 1782; *New England Chronicle*, Apr. 11, 1782; *Providence Gazette*, May 4, 1782; *Connecticut Journal*, May 16, 1782; *Pennsylvania Packet*, June 1, 1782. Six months earlier, the execution in Charleston of Colonel Isaac Hayne, an officer of the South Carolina militia, had also caused an uproar, but the two cases were quite different. Hayne's case turned on a difference of opinion about the murky terms of his parole, and he was condemned to die after a proper army court-martial—not, like Huddy, simply handed over to Associators to be strung up without even a pretense of legality (Bowden, *Execution of Isaac Hayne*; Knight, "Prisoner Exchange and Parole," 210–211).

30. Ford, *Journals of Hugh Gaine* 2: 148; GW to Clinton, Apr. 21, 1782: *WW* 24 (http://etext.lib.virginia.edu/washington). William Smith's attempts to sort out the legal complications of the case occupy many pages of his *Historical Memoirs*. Before releasing Livingston, Carleton tried to pry information out of him by planting Sir James Jay, John Jay's Tory brother, in the same room. (*Freeman's Journal*, Apr. 24, 1782; *Royal Gazette*, May 4, 1782; *New-Jersey Gazette*, May 15, 1782; *PWL*, 4: 171).

31. *JCC* 23: 715, 847–848; *LDC* 19: 366, 370, 378, and passim.

32. GW to Forman, Dec. 3, 1782, *WW* 25: 388–390; Randall, *Little Revenge*, 477–479.

33. Sproat to Skinner, June 1, 1782. Sproat's correspondence with Skinner was published in the *Royal Gazette*, June 12, 1782; see also Greene, *Recollections of the Jersey Prison-Ship*, 138ff.

34. *New-Jersey Gazette*, Mar. 13, 1782; GW to Knox and Morris, Mar. 11, 1782, *WW* 24: 53–57; Gouverneur Morris to Robert Morris, *RMP* 4: 438–441; Robert Morris to Nathanael Greene, May 10, 1782, *RMP* 5: 158–159. Another sticking point for the American negotiators was money—who owed what to whom for the upkeep of prisoners on both sides since the beginning of the war. Though unable to resolve that question, they did agree to give up General Burgoyne for 1,047 American officers and soldiers currently in prison or on parole. They also agreed to trade General Cornwallis for Henry Laurens, captured at sea early in 1780 en route to the Netherlands and confined in the Tower of London. For a comprehensive review of the issues, see Casino, "Elizabethtown 1782"; and Dixon, "Divided Authority," 59ff., 292ff. In July 1781 Congress appointed Superintendent Morris agent of marine and authorized him to carry out exchanges of naval prisoners, but only those belonging to the United States, not privateers (*RMP* 2: 3–4, and passim). Yet another difficulty was that because small-time privateers often had neither the ability nor inclination to hold prisoners, they simply turned them loose on parole without any kind of formal record keeping. Who they were, and where they were, was anyone's guess. Washington wanted Congress to require that all prisoners taken by privateers be handed over to U.S. authorities, but nothing had been done as yet (Skinner to GW, Dec. 23 and 24, 1781, Feb. 18, 1782; GW to the President of Congress, Dec. 27, 1781, Feb. 18, 1782: *GWP*). Among the ships bringing in new prisoners was the *Belisarius*, which on one occasion returned to port with over 200 rebels in custody (*Royal Gazette*, May 22, 1782).

35. Skinner to Sproat, June 9, 1782; Sproat to Skinner, June 9, 1782; *Royal Gazette*, June 26, 1782.

36. *Royal Gazette*, June 26, 1782; *Providence Gazette*, July 27, 1782. Carleton visited the prison ships only the day before and had some of the sickest prisoners removed to Blackwell's (now Roosevelt) Island in the East River (Greene, *Recollections of the*

Jersey Prison-Ship, 109; cf. *New-Jersey Gazette*, July 24, 1782, erroneously reporting that *all* the prisoners had been put ashore there).

37. *Continental Journal*, Aug. 8, 1782. The author of the statement, a Captain Rover, described himself as having had "the misfortune to be more than once a prisoner in England, and in different prison ships in New-York." In Philadelphia, Robert Morris had already received similar information indicating that the statement was bogus (*RMP* 5: 583–585; see also *Pennsylvania Packet*, Sept. 10, 1782). For Cochran, see *Massachusetts Spy*, Oct. 3, 1782.

38. For a succinct account, consult *RMP* 5: 426–432. Also *JCC* 22: 421–422; *JCC* 23: 461–464, 555–556, 558–559, 580–582, 660–661.

39. Skinner's statement was widely reprinted. See *Providence Gazette*, July 13, 1782. For the *Chance*, see *Boston Evening-Post*, Sept. 14, 1782. On Coffin, see [Coffin], "Destructive Operation," 120. For the anonymous author, see *New-York Gazetteer*, Dec. 30, 1782. See also the appeals of Pennsylvania prisoners for food and clothing in the summer and fall of that year in 1 *PA* 9: 470–471, 667–668. Governor William Livingston soon informed the New Jersey legislature that some citizens from that state held on the *Jersey* had petitioned him for assistance ("To the Assembly," Dec. 9, 1782: *PWL*, 4: 496–497; *Connecticut Journal*, Feb. 13, 1783). The Massachusetts seaman William Russell is quoted in Paine, *Ships and Sailors*, 169. See also Cogliano, *Maritime Prisoners*, 161–166. For a strikingly different recollection of the *Jersey* early in 1783, see *Painter Autobiography*, 66–67.

40. GW to Cornwallis, Oct. 18, 1781, *WW*, 23: 237–238, Evans, *Discourse*; "Justice," *Connecticut Gazette*, Apr. 19, 1776; "Miserecors," *Connecticut Journal*, Jan. 30, 1777; EB to GW, Nov. 13, 1777, *PGW* 12: 236–237; EB to James Wilson and Christian Forster, July 5, 1777, *BLB* 14; BJ 251; see also Clinton to Putnam, Dec. 12, 1777, *PGC* 2: 572; *JCC* 10: 71, 77; *JCC* 19: 27; *New-Jersey Gazette*, Nov. 18, 1778; *Providence Gazette*, July 17, 1779; and Haffner, "Treatment of Prisoners of War by the Americans," 174 and passim.

41. *PGW* 8: 454; Alan Cameron to Congress, Feb. 27, 1776: quoted in Pabst, *American Revolutionary War Records*, 13; see also Boyd, *Elias Boudinot*, 57 and passim; *PGW* 13: 179; Fingerhut, *Survivor*, 55–56. The deplorable handling of William Franklin, David Mathews, Henry Hamilton, and others is described in Skemp, *Franklin*, 221ff.; Randall, *Little Revenge*, 476ff.; and Haffner, "Treatment of Prisoners of War by the Americans," 244–470, 340–360. Wileman's deposition, dated Feb. 18, 1778, is in BHP, NYPL, no. 948. On Troup, see *Royal Gazette*, Dec. 27, 1777; GW to Livingston, Jan. 20, 1778, *PGW* 13: 296–297; *RAM* 1: 195; Burgoyne, *Enemy Views*, 193; Casino, "Elizabethtown 1782," 17, summarizing many other reports of abuse in *RAM* vols. 3 and 4.

42. Sampson, *Escape in America*; Dabney, *After Saratoga*; [Bense], "Brunswick Grenadier," 436, 439, 441, and passim; Dixon, "Divided Authority," 201–243; Haffner, "The Treatment of Prisoners of War by the Americans," 194–240, esp. relating to the ordeal of Ensign Thomas Hughes. Under the terms of the "convention" agreed to at Saratoga, Burgoyne and his army were technically not prisoners of war. But as a practical matter, that was a distinction without a difference, especially after Congress suspended the agreement in 1778. On the Baroness von Riedesel, see Berkin, *Revolutionary Mothers*, 89; for similar experiences, see Uhlendorf, *Revolution in America*, 265–266.

43. For Morris, see *JPC* 1: 842. Moody's exploits are chronicled in Shenstone, *So Obstinately Loyal*. See also Ward, *Between the Lines*, 84–101; *New-Jersey Gazette*, Aug.

9, 1780. For Arnold, see Van Buskirk, *Generous Enemies*, 92–105, and [Smith], *Historical Memoirs*, 334. For Moody's "jail," see his *Narrative*, as quoted in Crary, *Price of Loyalty*, 211. Crary's chapter entitled "Cruelties, Imprisonments, and Executions" provides an abundance of examples in the same vein. John André's travails as a prisoner in 1775–1776, a likely explanation for his later advocacy of waging a predatory war against the rebels, are described in Colley, *Captives*, 207, and Flexner, *Traitor and the Spy*, 139–160.

44. Phelps, *History of Newgate*, 49 and passim; *PRC* 2: 184–185.

45. Fingerhut, *Survivor*, 71–78; Dixon, "Divided Authority," 156–157; Crary, *Price of Loyalty*, 203–204; Jones, *History of New York*, 1: 648, 705–710. For conditions aboard a prison ship in Boston harbor in 1777, see [Sandwich], *Private Papers*, 1: 315–316. Congress sanctioned the use of prison ships in mid-July 1779 (*JCC*, 14: 837; *New-Jersey Gazette*, Aug. 4, 1779).

46. *Pennsylvania Packet*, Sept. 16, 1779; cf. *New England Chronicle*, Oct. 7, 1779.

47. [Bense], "Brunswick Grenadier," 440. Early in 1778, the deputy commissary in charge of the British prisoners at Easton, Pennsylvania, wrote Boudinot that "the poor wretches under my care are almost all sick & dead." The numbers involved are not apparent, however, and this seems to have been a highly unusual case (Boyd, *Elias Boudinot*, 57; Burgoyne, *Enemy Views*, passim; *NDAR* 8: 585, 594–595). At no time was the lax supervision of prisoners more apparent than after Yorktown, when many of the prisoners captured with Cornwallis got away while they were being marched back north, sloppiness that caused Governor Livingston of New Jersey "inexpressible Anxiety" (WL to Benjamin Lincoln, Dec. 24, 1781, *PWL*, 4: 355). The ineffectual American system for handling prisoners is described in Haffner, "Treatment of Prisoners of War by the Americans," 11–25, 176, 368, 369–370, 376–377, 498–508, and passim. Haffner also documents the generally better condition of enemy captives, see ibid., 56, 164–175, 319, 513; Bolton, *Private Soldier Under Washington*, 192–193.

48. SBW to Joseph Barrell, Aug. 10, 1779; *SBW* 2: 192–193; *PWL* 3: 190n1; WL to Benjamin Lincoln, Dec. 24, 1781, *PWL* 4: 354–355; WL to GW, May 14, 1782; ibid., 412–413; WL to Carleton, Aug. 10, 1782; ibid., 4: 449; "Message to the Assembly," Nov. 21, 1782: *SBW* 4: 487–488. See Sampson, *Escape in America*, 119 and passim, for numerous stories of escape and evasion. The incoherence and inefficiency of American policy is a major theme of Dixon, "Divided Authority." Haffner found "no conclusive evidence of deliberate brutality" in the handling of captured Tories ("Treatment of Prisoners of War by the Americans," 166–169, 269, 273–283).

49. Fischer, *Washington's Crossing*, 375–379; Bowman, *Captive Americans*, 84; Metzger, *Prisoner in the American Revolution*, 6–7; Haffner, "Treatment of Prisoners of War by the Americans," 166–169, 273–283; *PWL* 3: 190–191; WL to Benjamin Lincoln, Dec. 24, 1781, *PWL* 4: 354–355; WL to GW, May 14, 1782: *PWL* 4: 412–413; WL to Carleton, Aug. 10, 1782: *PWL* 4: 449; "Message to the Assembly," Nov. 21, 1782: *PWL* 4: 487–488; Simcoe, *Journal*, 273–285; Van Buskirk, *Generous Enemies*, 77.

50. Virtually the only account is Chandler, *American Criminal Trials*, 2: 59–153; but see also Sampson, *Escape in America*, 91–96. For a sample of contemporary press reports, see *New-England Chronicle*, Jan. 15, 1778; *Royal Pennsylvania Gazette*, Mar. 27 and Apr. 24, 1778; *Royal Gazette*, Apr. 11, 1778; *New-York Gazette*, Apr. 13, 1778. A trial record was published later that year as *The proceedings of a general court-martial held at Cambridge . . . upon the trial of Colonel David Henley* (Boston, 1778).

51. *JCC*, 14: 837; 15: 1262; 19: 25; Haffner, "Treatment of Prisoners of War by the Americans," 337–338.

CHAPTER 8

1. Bowman, *Captive Americans*, 114–115. *New-Jersey Gazette*, Jan. 1, 1783. On improved conditions, see the letter from nine American officers to Carleton on March 17, 1783: BHPL. It was mistakenly bruited about town on at least two occasions that all the prisoners had been set free. See Schaukirk, *Occupation of New York City by the British*, 26; Uhlendorf, *Revolution in America*, 546–547. For the dwindling population of the Provost, see *Royal Gazette*, Feb. 5, Mar. 5, Apr. 2, June 1, and July 2, 1783. The forty-one prisoners reported in February came from eight states as well as Ireland and Cuba. See [Fisher], *Elijah Fisher's Journal*, 22 (hereafter *Fisher's Journal*); Carleton to GW, Apr. 6, 1783; *DAR* 19: 384; Ranlet, "Tory David Sproat," 197. Fisher's name does not appear among the twenty-eight on the *Royal Gazette* list of Apr. 2, 1780, suggesting there were more—possibly captured privateers still not being counted as prisoners of war.

2. Miller, *Treaties and Other International Acts*, 2: 162–183. The treaty was signed in 1785 and ratified the following year. Neither Adams nor Franklin ever had a British prisoner in his power, but during a brief stint as governor of Virginia during the war, Jefferson had a number of chances to take the high road and chose otherwise. His handling of Henry Hamilton, formerly the British superintendent at Detroit, was egregious (Haffner, "Treatment of Prisoners of War by the Americans," 340–360).

3. "A Last Advice to the Tories and Refugees in New-York," signed "Steady Whig," *New-Jersey Gazette*, Apr. 16, 1783.

4. *Connecticut Journal*, July 11, 1782; *Massachusetts Spy*, Mar. 6, 1783.

5. *Continental Journal*, Apr. 17, 1783. By my reckoning, the notice was reprinted in at least ten different papers within five weeks of its initial appearance in the *Continental Journal*. They were, by date of publication, *New-Hampshire Gazette*, Apr. 19; *Massachusetts Spy*, Apr. 24; *Connecticut Gazette*, Apr. 25; *Providence Gazette*, Apr. 26; *Pennsylvania Packet*, Apr. 29; *Freeman's Journal* (Philadelphia), Apr. 30; *Independent Gazetteer* (Philadelphia), May 3; *New-Jersey Gazette*, May 7; *New York Packet*, May 8; *South-Carolina Weekly Gazette*, May 24. [Heath], *Memoirs of Major-General Heath*, 388–389; on Stiles, see Thornton, *Pulpit of the American Revolution*, 451. Henry Onderdonk mistakenly claimed in 1849 that the *New York Packet* was the first paper to run the notice by "An American" (Onderdonk, *Revolutionary Incidents of Suffolk and Kings*, 245). In fact, it was one of the *last* to do so. Onderdonk's error has spawned much confusion, however. See Ranlet, "Tory David Sproat," 197ff., which attributes the 11,644 number to Heath, though Heath was simply remarking on what he had just read in the May 8 issue of the *Packet*. Colley, *Captives*, 220, citing Denn, "Prison Narratives," 61–62, even suggests that the *New York Packet* itself may have "invented" the number (c.f. Armbruster, *Wallabout Prison Ships*, 21).

6. TJ to Démeunier, June 26, 1786, *PTJ* 10: 61–64; Ranlet, "Tory David Sproat," 198. Riddy's identification of Sproat as the army's commissary of prisoners was correct, for when Loring left for England in November 1782, Sproat became responsible for both military and naval prisoners (Ranlet, "Tory David Sproat," 198). But why would Sproat show the "registers" to Riddy? Ranlet speculates that Sproat "must have become a very anguished man," owing to the deaths of so many prisoners, and that when Riddy turned up in New York, Sproat took the opportunity to unburden himself with a friend he had known in pre-Revolutionary Philadelphia. That the two men knew each other seems likely, the rest anything but. Given Sproat's hatred of the rebels, it is much more probable that he was *bragging* to Riddy.

7. Sproat required that when a navy ship or privateer came into port with prisoners, her captain or master come at once to his office on Maiden Lane and give him the prisoners' names and other particulars. What Riddy saw may well have been the now-vanished office "ledgers" kept by Sproat, as distinct from the logs of the *Jersey*. See the notice from Sproat in the *Royal Gazette*, Dec. 12, 1781. For other evidence, see Ranlet, "Tory David Sproat," 198. In its 1806 celebration of Evacuation Day, the Tammany Society toasted "the patriotic Female who during the American revolution kept a register of the names of 11000 martyrs of liberty" who perished on the *Jersey*. I have no idea who she might have been, but it is tempting to think that the existence of ledgers or lists of the dead had by this time become an urban legend of sorts (see "Tammanial Toasts," *Republican Watch-Tower* [New York], Nov. 28, 1806). Jefferson eventually sent Riddy's deposition back to New York, where the Confederation government had recently come to roost. There, the Under Secretary for Foreign Affairs, Henry Remsen, Jr., read the document and scrawled a note on the back, testifying to its accuracy. "There is a person living now on Long Island," Remsen wrote, "who informed me that the number of American prisoners who were buried from on board the Jersey prison ship, along the shore on his land, could not be less in number than 10,000." Remsens had owned property adjacent to Wallabout Bay since the mid-seventeenth century. Henry's informant was probably either Rem Remsen or Abraham Remsen, both of whom reportedly made a practice of trying to rebury bodies uncovered on the shore by the wind and tides. It is unlikely, however, that either one had access to official records. "Not less in number than 10,000" sounds like a lucky guess, perhaps prompted by the now widely known announcement by "An American" (*PTJ* 10: 269 [Johnson], "Recollections of . . . General Jeremiah Johnson," part 2, 24).

8. For death rates in other wars, see Doyle, *Voices from Captivity*, 308; and Ferling, *Almost a Miracle*, 428. The surviving logbooks of the *Jersey* identify 7,773 captives by name and only irregularly indicate those who died and thus are wildly incomplete (Lemisch, "Listening to the 'Inarticulate,'" 9n20 and 10n21). The Society of Old Brooklynites published the names of the captives in *A Christmas Reminder*. Lemisch notes two gaps in the logs: from November 21, 1777, to August 2, 1778 (nine months), and December 25, 1780, to February 14, 1781 (seven weeks), the latter covering the period when the *Jersey* was a prison ship.

9. It is impossible to be precise, but the following annualized summary of the evidence presented in previous chapters probably errs on the conservative side.

Military and Civilian Prisoners brought to NYC (est.)

1776	c. 5,000
1777	c. 1,000
1778	700–1000
1779	600–800
1780	700–800
1781	400–500
1782	700–800
1783	50–100
Total	9,150–10,000

10. Recall that over the winter of 1776–1777, fully two-thirds of the Fort Washington prisoners died of disease and malnutrition, and there was at least one report of as many as 100 burials a day. In later years, as conditions became less crowded and the smallpox epidemic tailed off, the mortality rate undoubtedly came down, but by all ac-

counts it rarely if ever fell below 50 percent. No one ever suggested, moreover, that places like the Sugar House or the Provost were markedly healthier than the *Jersey*.

11. On rebel captives detained in South Carolina, Georgia, and the West Indies, see Ranlet, "In the Hands of the British"; Bowman, *Captive Americans*, 42; Dodge, *A Narrative*; and the depositions of James Butterfield and John Brown, describing in detail "the most wanton cruelty" they endured on an island in the St. Lawrence, now known, appropriately enough, as Prisoners Island (*Connecticut Journal*, Aug. 1, 1782). [Segar], *Brief Narrative*, 34–35, mentions "forty or fifty" prisoners on the island over the winter of 1781–1782; see also Phoenix, *Whitney Family*, 1: 103. There may have been more prisoners in these places than is sometimes realized. For example, as of January 1783 ninety-three Americans were still being held in Antigua. *Newport Mercury*, Mar. 1, 1783. Lemisch, "Listening to the 'Inarticulate,'" 7n15, cites John Howard's celebrated report, *The State of the Prisons in England and Wales* (1792) for the numbers of Americans held at Mill (1,296) and Forton (1,200). On the mortality rates at Forton and Mill, see Cogliano, *Maritime Prisoners*, 69.

12. The figures for battle deaths (6,824) and deaths in camp (c. 10,000) come from Howard Peckham's classic study, *The Toll of Independence*. For the total of all fatalities, I combined those two numbers with my guesstimates of how many prisoners died in New York (18,000) and elsewhere (1,000). Peckham believed that no more than 18,152 Americans became prisoners during the war, of whom 8,500 (47 percent) did not survive captivity. All told, he put the number of in-service deaths at 25,324. The marked difference between his tally of prisoners and mine stems in part from his admittedly cautious methodology, which often led him to discard *all* conflicting reports of the number of prisoners taken. More important, Peckham greatly underestimated the mortality rates among prisoners, and he excluded several categories that have figured prominently in the present account: rebel officers and men seized by vigilantes or (like General Lee) not captured in battle; the throngs of civilians confined every year in New York or, less frequently, aboard Wallabout prison ships; and, finally, the large number of men taken as privateers, not wearing the uniform of either the fledgling Continental Navy or one of the so-called navies of individual states. For other estimates, less careful than Peckham's, see Armbruster, *Wallabout Prison Ships*, passim; and Bowman, *Captive Americans*, 30–31, 60–61, and passim.

13. Bureau of the Census, *Statistical History*, Series A 6–8 (p. 8), Series A 119–134 (p. 6), Series A 143–157 (p. 19), and Series Z 1–19 (p. 1168); Boatner, *Encyclopedia of the Revolution*, 262–264, which follows Heitman, *Historical Register of the Continental Army*; see also Clodfelter, *Warfare and Armed Conflicts*, 1: 196–197. The apparent addition of 965,000 whites and 185,000 blacks between 1780 and 1790 may reflect undercounting in the prefederal sources, overcounting in the 1790 census, or some combination of the two. Dramatic increases are certainly believable, however. The movement of peoples all around the Atlantic basin had increased sharply in the years just before the war, and immigration to the United States would accelerate after the war. For a sample of many other attempts to estimate the numbers involved, see Mackesy, *War for America*, 29; Higginbotham, *War of American Independence*, 389; and Stephenson, *Patriot Battles*, 30–31. See Colley, *Captives*, 214, who proposes that from 50,000 to as many as 100,000 Britons, including American Tories and civilians as well as regular military and naval personnel, were imprisoned by the rebels during the war.

14. Wilson, *Loyal Blacks*, 21; Quarles, *Negro in the Revolution*, ix and passim. There would have been many more if panicked planters in South Carolina and Georgia had not forced Congress to abandon a plan for enlisting an additional 3,000 southern

slaves. In any event, the increasing presence of African American soldiers reflected the army's growing reliance on poor and propertyless men, generally after 1777 or 1778 (Neimeyer, *America Goes to War*, 65–88; Martin and Lender, *Respectable Army*, esp. 87–97; Horton and Horton, *In Hope of Liberty*, 62; Higginbotham, *War of Independence*, 395–397; Robinson, *Slavery in the Structure of American Politics*, 113–122; Miller, *Triumph of Freedom*, 508–510). As it happened, one of the African American seamen taken on the *Royal Louis* was a fourteen-year-old powder boy named James Forten. Young Forten could have avoided imprisonment by agreeing to accompany the son of *Amphion*'s captain back to England, but he declined to abandon the cause. Although it would be a comfort to know that his stalwart patriotism earned young Forten the attention and respect of his white shipmates, not a single one of those who left accounts of life (and death) aboard the *Jersey* over the autumn of 1781 even *remembered* the presence of what must have been scores of African Americans incarcerated with them. Indeed, as we have seen, white prisoners often cited the indiscriminate mixing of races as another example of the British penchant for cruelty. Possibly by 1781 color no longer mattered in the sweltering, gloomy hold of a prison ship, but it is more likely that the erasure of blacks from the memories of *Jersey* survivors makes more sense as yet another indication of what the Revolution did not change. Surely that partly explains why that fourteen-year-old powder boy later became one of the country's most determined abolitionists (see Winch, *Gentleman of Color*, 46). Americans began to complain about race mixing in British prisons very early in the war. For example, on January 9, 1777, the executive committee of Congress told Washington that American seamen were held in New York without "distinction between Masters, Mates, Foremast Men & Negroes which surely is an unnecessary cruelty" (*PGW* 8: 21–23).

15. "New High in U.S. Prison Numbers," *Washington Post*, Feb. 29, 2008.

16. Peckham, *Toll of Independence*, 132–133, calculated that 0.9 percent of the population as of 1780 died in service, without—inexplicably—taking into account the number of Tories killed.

17. Quarles, *Negro in the American Revolution*, 172; Brown, *Good Americans*, 227, makes the case for 100,000 exiles. Calhoon, *Loyalists in Revolutionary America*, 500–502, suggests a figure between 60,000 and 80,000 white exiles, as does Norton, *British-Americans*. On the number of runaway slaves, see Frey, *Water from the Rock*, 174–175; see also Raphael, *People's History*, esp. 330–337; Horton and Horton, *In Hope of Liberty*, 62 and passim.

CHAPTER 9

1. *LDC* 22: 442; *JCC* 28: 320–321.

2. *JCC* 4: 89–90; 32: 270. On "gratitude" as an argument for commemoration, see Purcell, *Sealed with Blood*, 26–33, 102–07, and passim. Also Silverman, *Cultural History of the Revolution*, 314–316. For memorials to other officers, see *JCC* 7: 242–243, 258, 369; *JCC* 8: 472; *JCC* 9: 770, 861; *JCC* 15: 1324; *JCC* 18: 923; *JCC* 21: 978; *JCC* 30: 395. In several instances, Congress stipulated that the monuments be put up at state rather than federal expense.

3. *LDC* 3: 113–114; *Daily Advertiser*, Nov. 23, 1787; Doyle, *Voices from Captivity*, 89–116; Purcell, *Sealed with Blood*, 86–91; Savage, *Standing Soldiers, Kneeling Slaves*, esp. 166–169; Newman, *Parades and the Politics*, 55–57; Gabriel, *Major General Montgomery*, 188.

4. Burrows and Wallace, *Gotham*, 265–266; Pomerantz, *New York*, 19–21.

5. Burrows and Wallace, *Gotham*, 266–279.

6. *Independent Journal*, Dec. 29, 1784; Pomerantz, *New York*, 90. In his notes to [Hawkins], *The Adventures of Christopher Hawkins*, 215, Bushnell says that a hostile crowd of ex-prisoners "assembled on the wharf" when David Laird, a former captain of the *Jersey*, returned to New York "a short time after the peace of 1783." The story appears to be apocryphal, however.

7. Rosenwaike, *Population History*, 16; *New-York Packet*, Oct. 3, 1785. For boys finding bones, see Cozzens, *Geological History of Manhattan*, 22. Jonathan Livingston put the damages to his sugar house at £500 and said the prisoners destroyed "many Thousand Earthen Potts and pans, brass & Copper pans and Kettles and other Impliments." Livingston to Carleton, Nov. 7, 1782: BHP, NYPL. When offered for sale in 1784, it was described only as "large, well, and substantially built"—nary a word of its recent use as a prison. *New-York Packet*, June 28, 1784.

8. [Johnson], "Recollections," Part 2: 24; "Description of Hell-Gate," *Pennsylvania Packet*, Dec. 21, 1789. Fears of contagion reportedly discouraged vandals and souvenir hunters from disturbing the *Jersey* while she disintegrated. What became of the other hospital ships and prison ships still anchored in Wallabout Bay at the end of the war is not clear. Seaworthy vessels probably left with the fleet on or before Evacuation Day; the hulls of the *Perseverance* and *Bristol Pacquet* were later sold and presumably removed. *New-York Packet*, Dec. 29, 1783. On events in 1792, see Stiles, *Account of the Interment*, 2: 14–15.

9. "A Lover of His Country," *Columbian Gazetteer*, Mar. 31, 1794. Mushkat (*Tammany*, 35) identifies Davis, an editor of the *Columbian Gazetteer*, as the author. See also Mushkat, "Matthew Livingston Davis"; Cray, "Commemorating the Prison Ship Dead"; and Link, *Democratic-Republican Societies*, 18n. For similar ideas, see "Junius Americanus," *Argus*, June 9, 1795; "Old Soldier," *National Gazette*, May 8, 1793; *The Time Piece*, Aug. 8, 1798; and *Claypool's American Daily Advertiser*, Sept. 21, 1799. Russell's *Oration* was frequently reprinted as a pamphlet, the last time in 1830. The prison ship passages were often excerpted, as in the *American Mercury*, Mar. 10, 1803. For a warm local reaction, see *Providence Journal*, July 9, 1800.

10. "A Soldier of '76," *New-York Evening Post*, May 1, 1802; *Daily Advertiser*, July 17, 20, 1802; *American Citizen*, Jan. 8, 1803. The historian Nathaniel Prime, one of those who went to watch the excavations, later recalled "skulls and feet, arms and legs, sticking out of the crumbling bank in the wildest disorder" (*History of Long Island*, 367). On the origins of the Navy Yard, see Burrows and Wallace, *Gotham*, 340–341. The partisan appropriation of public festivals and other forms of commemoration was of course an old story by 1800—and one explored creatively in a number of recent studies. See Newman, *Parades and the Politics of the Street*; Waldstreicher, *In the Midst of Perpetual Fetes*; Hoffer, *Revolution and Regeneration*.

11. *Public Advertiser*, Mar. 5, 1808. See also *Washington Federalist*, Feb. 16, 1803; *Annals of Congress*, 12: 507–508 (Feb. 10, 1803). The version reprinted in Stiles, *Account of the Interment*, 8–12, differs slightly from the original. Also Ostrander, *History of Brooklyn*, 2: 15–16; Cray, "Commemorating," esp. 578–579; Purcell, *Sealed with Blood*, esp. 144–149; Mitchill, *Picture of New-York*, 162–163, 188. Mitchill, at the time a member of Congress from New York, identified two reasons why his colleagues did not approve the proposal: "Some are of opinion that Congress out not to appropriate public money for such purposes. Others think that the art of Printing has superceded the use and intention of monuments" (Stiles, *Account of the Interment*, 15).

12. Although Talbot was not identified as its author, the book was substantially constructed from Talbot's own words. See Fowler, *Talbot*, 190; Tuckerman, *Life of*

Silas Talbot, 91–101; *Evening Post*, Mar. 7, 1803; Burrows and Wallace, *Gotham*, 378, 395. Altogether, only a dozen Revolutionary War memoirs were published in the United States up to 1800, but the market for personal narratives would expand steadily thereafter (Purcell, *Sealed with Blood*, 150). Philip Freneau, now one of the country's best-known Republican editors, weighed in at this time with a new poem, "Reflections on Walking over the ground on Long-Island, New York, where many Americans were interred in Prison Ships, during the war with Great-Britain." *New-York Weekly Museum*, Apr. 13, 1803; Marsh, *Works of Philip Freneau*, 152–153.

13. Barnes, *Fanning's Narrative*, 17–18, 166, and passim. Although early publication notices identified Fanning as the author (e.g., *New-York Spectator*, Mar. 18, 1807), his name was not on the title page until a second edition appeared the following year.

14. Mitchill published the letter in the *Medical Repository*, 11 (New York, 1807), 260–267. It was later reprinted as an addendum to Bushnell's edition of *The Narrative of John Blatchford* (117–127). Six months after writing Mitchill, Coffin repeated his story to the Tammany Society. In this second communication he contended that many prisoners had been killed by poison (Stiles, *Account of the Interment*, 44–59). The society also heard from one William Burke of Delaware, who claimed that many Americans on the *Jersey* were "put to death by the bayonet" while trying to get on deck at night—"sometimes five, sometimes six, and sometimes eight or ten" at a time (Stiles, *Account of the Interment*, 146n).

15. *Public Advertiser*, Jan. 23, May 15, July 11, and (quoting the Petersburg paper) Aug. 18, 1807. For other examples, see the *Republican Watch-Tower* (New York), Aug. 8, 1807; *American Citizen*, Aug. 7, 1807; *The Repertory*, Aug. 11, 1807; *United States Gazette*, Aug. 17, 1807.

16. [Barlow], *The Columbiad*, 180–181, 388. Publication of the American edition was announced in the *Republican Watch-Tower*, Nov. 3, 1807. Barlow also noted that his information came, at least in part, from Elias Boudinot, who told him "that in one prison ship alone, called the Jersey, which was anchored near Newyork, *eleven thousand* American prisoners died in eighteen months."

17. Rock, *Artisans of the New Republic*, 77–82; Burrows and Wallace, *Gotham*, 411.

18. *Public Advertiser*, Feb. 12, 1808. It was around this time, too, that being a former prisoner of war seems to have become a qualification for political office. See *Republican Watch-Tower*, Feb. 19, 1808; "The Alms-House," *Public Advertiser*, Feb. 19, 1808; and "Jersey Prison Ship," ibid., Feb. 18, 1808. For opinion elsewhere, see "How Sleep the brave who sink to rest," *New-Hampshire Gazette*, Mar. 1, 1808.

19. In the *Public Advertiser*, Feb. 2, 1808; *Independent Chronicle*, Mar. 10, 1808; Cray, "Commemorating," 582–583. For samples of the enthusiastic mail generated by Tammany's announcement, see Stiles, *Account of the Interment*, 33–44. For Federalist reactions, see *New-York Evening Post*, Feb. 19, 1808; *American Citizen*, Apr. 22, 1808; *New-York Commercial Advertiser*, Apr. 6, 20, 1808 ("Will not the bones of these heroes at Wallabout, rise up and upbraid the hypocrites who are now shedding Crocodile tears over them . . . ?"); *New-York Herald*, Apr. 9, 23, 1808. "Danbury Farmer," in the *Public Advertiser*, Feb. 26, 1808; "Adherents of Britain versus The Bones at the Wallabout," ibid., Mar. 3, 1808; and "Amicus IV: To the Republican Representatives in Congress," ibid., Mar. 8, 1808.

20. Stiles, *Account of the Interment*, 64–65. The council also endorsed the plan but contributed no money: see ibid., 59–62, and *Public Advertiser*, Apr. 21, 1808. For the event on Apr. 6, see ibid., Apr. 5, 1808. Both Stiles (*Account of the Interment*, 79) and Cray ("Commemorating," 58) mistakenly date the event on April 13. Benjamin Ro-

maine is one of those characters in post-Revolutionary New York about whom one would like to know more. Born in Poughkeepsie in 1762, he was preparing to enter King's College when the British takeover forced his family to flee to Hackensack, New Jersey. He enlisted with his brother's militia company in 1777 and took part, by his own account, in no fewer than twenty-seven "affairs of arms" during the war. In 1781 he was captured and spent seven weeks as a prisoner in New York—where, exactly, he didn't say, but it was not on a prison ship, as often reported. After the war, he returned to the city and opened what became a well-known school for boys and girls whose alumni included, among others, Washington Irving. Apparently, he did well enough in the booming Manhattan real estate market to quit teaching in 1797, after which his close association with the Tammany Society won him various political appointments. His wartime experiences left him with an abiding hatred of the English, and according to Henry Stiles, "amusing stories are yet related of the rough manner in which he would absolutely refuse to treat with any Englishman who applied to become a tenant of any of his houses" (RWPA: W18839; Stiles, *History of Brooklyn*, 1: 373n).

21. *American Citizen*, Apr. 12, 1808; *Public Advertiser*, Apr. 7, 1808. The Wallabout Committee quickly issued a pamphlet describing the ceremony and Fay's speech: *An Account of the procession, together with copious extracts of the oration, delivered at the Wallabout (L.I.), April 6th, 1808.* Fay helped introduce the British reformer John Howard to American readers. See his *Essays of Howard*.

22. *American Citizen*, Apr. 27, 1808. For press coverage of the event elsewhere, see *Guardian* (Albany), Apr. 16, 1808; *New-Hampshire Gazette* (Portsmouth), Apr. 19, 1808; *The Democrat* (Boston), Apr. 30, 1808; *The Olive-Branch* (Norwich, NY), Apr. 30, 1808; *Essex Register* (Salem, Massachusetts), May 11, 1808; *American Mercury* (Hartford), May 12, 1808. On preparations for the second ceremony, see *Public Advertiser*, May 6, 24, 25, 26, 1808; *American Citizen*, May 14, 16, 1808. Cray, "Commemorating," 584. Sixty years later, the vault was described as "about fifteen feet long, twelve feet wide, and eighteen feet deep; constructed of granite, arched with brick." *Brooklyn Daily Eagle*, June 3, 1869.

23. *Republican Watch-Tower*, May 31, 1808. McNamara, *Day of Jubilee*, 17–22 and passim; Burrows and Wallace, *Gotham*, 292–296.

24. This account of the procession draws on the detailed reports in *Public Advertiser*, May 25, 27, and 28, 1808; *Republican Watch-Tower*, May 31, 1808; *Essex Register*, June 4, 1808; and the Wallabout Committee's *Account of the Interment of the Remains of 11,500 American Seamen, Soldiers and Citizens, Who Fell Victims to the Cruelties of the British, on Board their Prison Ships at the Wallabout* . . . (New York, 1808), extensively annotated and republished by Stiles as *Account of the Interment*. See also Charles E. West, "Prison Ships in the American Revolution"; and Cray, "Commemorating," 584–585.

25. For reactions elsewhere, see *The Monitor*, June 21, 1808; *City Gazette and Daily Advertiser* (Charleston, SC), June 8, 10, 11, 1808; *Olive-Branch* (Norwich, NY), June 11, 1808; *Otsego Herald* (Cooperstown, NY), June 11, 1808; *Political Observatory* (Walpole, NH), June 13, 1808; *The World* (Bennington, VT), June 13, 1808. The Sag Harbor event was reported in the *Public Advertiser*, June 2, 1808.

26. For Federalist reactions, see *New-York Evening Post*, May 26, 1808; see the *Federal Republican*, July 22, 1808, ridiculing the Republicans in Philadelphia who toasted victims of the "*New*-Jersey prison ship" [emphasis added]. The mockery went on for years. See "Chemical discovery," *Portland Gazette*, June 20, 1808; *Commercial Advertiser*, July 8, 1808; "11,500 *Dry Bones*," in the *Washington Republican or, True American* (New York), Aug. 12, 1809; "Democracy Run Mad," the *Portsmouth Oracle*, Sept. 15,

1810 (from the *Connecticut Courant*); the *Political Bulletin and Miscellaneous Repository* (New York), Dec. 22, 1810; *The Balance*, June 28, 1808 ("Burlesque"). For the English agent, see David W. Parker, "Secret Reports of John Howe," 83; Cray, "Commemorating," 586.

27. *Public Advertiser*, May 28, July 7, Sept. 16, 1808; May 15, 1811; *American Citizen*, Jan. 5, 1809; *The Democrat*, June 1, 8, 1808.

28. Mushkat, *Tammany*, 32–45.

29. *New-York Columbian*, July 2, 3, 8, 9, 1818; *National Advocate*, July 3, 1818; *Commercial Advertiser*, July 7, 1818; *New-York Spectator*, July 10, 1818. Gabriel, *Major General Montgomery*, 193–197; and Francis, *New York During the Last Half Century*, 39. The Tammany Society's decision to participate in the ceremony was noted in the *Daily Advertiser*, July 8, 10, 1818. Papers all over the country covered Montgomery's re-interment.

30. *New-York Spectator*, Feb. 16, 20, 23, 1821; and the *New-York Evening Post*, Feb. 17, 1821. In 1826, no monument having appeared, the legislature told the Tammany Society to give the money back or face legal action. If it did, there is no record of the fact. Myers, *History of Tammany*, 22–23.

31. A summary that barely conveys the rich literature on these matters. I have learned much from Kammen, *Season of Youth*; Burstein, *America's Jubilee*; Harris, *Public Lives, Private Virtues*; Caspar, *Constructing American Lives*, esp. chap. 1; Young, *The Shoemaker and the Tea Party*, esp. chap. 5; Resch, *Suffering Soldiers*; Callcott, *History in the United States*; van Tassel, *Recording America's Past*; and Knouff, *The Soldiers' Revolution*, esp. chap. 7.

32. Sherburne, *Memoirs*, preface (pages not numbered), 113, 114, 123, 132–139, 147, 151, and passim; *Rhode-Island American*, May 15, 1829; Jan. 4, 1831; *New-Hampshire Patriot*, Dec. 7, 18, 29; Aug. 29, 1831. Sherburne's hardscrabble existence after the war is apparent from his 1818 pension application, initially filed in Ohio, where he was living in a cabin in the woods (RWPA: S42275). Thomas Painter, also aboard the *Jersey* in the spring of 1783, had almost certainly read Sherburne by the time he composed his own autobiography in 1836 (not published until 1910). He too said nothing of British cruelty and ascribed his "miraculous preservation" to "the kind care, and protection of my Heavenly Father." *Autobiography of Painter*, 72, 90–91, 98–101, 127.

33. Andros, *Old Jersey Captive*, 11–13, 16, 24, 33, 34, 35, 49, 61, 63, 65, 79. Andros had served as pastor of the church in Berkeley, Massachusetts, since 1788 (White, "Thomas Andros: Captive"). Cf. *Autobiography of Painter*, 47.

34. *Old Jersey Captive*, 16, 19–20, 56. The scriptural quotation is from Titus 3:3.

35. Greene, *Recollections of the Jersey*, 4–5, 19–20, 23n. It has been reprinted, by my count, at least a half dozen times, most recently in 1992, and served as the basis for the 1904 novel by Mary C. Francis, *Dalrymple*. Greene mistakenly placed Dring's death in August 1825, five months after the fact. He may also be responsible for having Dring say he spent "nearly five months" on the *Jersey*, whereas the text indicates that he spent less than two, from May to early July 1782. Though minor, these errors suggest that Greene did not know Dring well, if at all—notwithstanding his assurances that Dring's "faculties were then perfect and unimpaired, and his memory remained clear and unclouded." For Dring's death on Mar. 8, 1825, see *Rhode-Island American*, Mar. 11, 1825. Greene also said that Dring's manuscript had been authenticated by a number of gentlemen who were themselves survivors of the *Jersey*—a claim repeated by Greene's publisher, Hugh H. Brown, in advertisements for the book (*Rhode Island American*, Feb. 6, 1829).

36. Greene, *Recollections of the Jersey*, 26, 38, 82. The unidentified snippets of verse on p. 51 are probably Greene's.

37. Ibid., 86.

38. Ibid., 88, 91–94; Sherburne, *Memoirs*, 83–85; see Lemisch, "Listening to the 'Inarticulate,'" 21. In fact, virtually everyone who described conditions on the *Jersey* alluded to the enervating despair that gripped men with less than one chance in three of surviving—not an environment likely to promote the creation of "governments" among her prisoners. Anyone healthy enough or optimistic enough to think about making rules would be more likely to escape, or die trying. Recall, too, Andros's description above of the *Jersey* prisoners as "hateful and hating one another."

39. Greene, *Recollections of the Jersey*, 13–14, 48–50, 56–57; see Sherburne, *Memoirs*, 110–111. It appears that Greene actually knew little about the ship or its history and got most of the details wrong, as he did in this notably inaccurate sentence: "At the commencement of the American Revolution, being an old vessel, and proving to be much decayed, she was entirely dismantled; and, soon after, was moored in the East River at New-York, and converted into a Store-ship."

40. *Adventures of Fox*, iii–vi, 87–88, 96, 111, 112, 131–134, 229. Fox also said he was serving aboard the American privateer *Protector* when she was overtaken off Sandy Hook in May 1781 by two enemy frigates, *Roebuck* and *May-Day*. Actually, the *Protector* was captured by the *Roebuck* and *Medea* (*Pennsylvania Packet*, Oct. 16, 1781). This and other lapses suggest that Fox absorbed Greene's version of the story so easily because his own grip on the details was fading, not that he was deliberately lying.

41. *Adventures of Fox*, 102, 103, 115–130, 146–149. Cf. Coffin: "I never knew, while I was on board, but one instance of defection, and that person was hooted at and abused by the prisoners till the boat was out of hearing." *Destructive Operation of Foul Air*, 127.

42. Thorburn, *Fifty Years' Reminiscences*, 9–10, 166–170; Dunshee, *As You Pass By*, 98–99, and passim; Lucey, "History of City Hall Park," esp. 35ff. *New-York Mirror,* Apr. 8, 1826; Sept. 17, 1831. On these and other changes in the city's built environment during the first half of the 19th century, see Burrows and Wallace, *Gotham*, passim. Today, *every* tangible link with Revolutionary New York has vanished, except for St. Paul's Chapel on Broadway (completed in 1766), Bowling Green (enclosed by the same cast iron fence it had in 1776), and the Morris-Jumel mansion in upper Manhattan (built in 1765 when the city still lay far to the south). The so-called "Governor's House" on Governors Island, once thought to date from the early eighteenth century, is now believed to be a full century younger. Fraunces Tavern, though often represented as having held its ground on Pearl Street since 1719, is in fact the product of early-twentieth-century guesswork as to what the original building might have looked like. Demolition of the Rhinelander Sugar House in 1892 gave rise to stories—completely unsubstantiated—that it had served as a prison during the Revolution. Windows from the building are nonetheless preserved at One Police Plaza and at the Van Cortlandt House in the Bronx as relics of the "sugar house-prison." On the relentless transformation of the city's built environment, see Page, *Creative Destruction of Manhattan*, esp. chap. 1; and Domosh, *Invented Cities*.

43. Hood, "Journeying to 'Old New York'"; Tuckerman, *Life of Talbot*, 94. In 1851, a local merchant named Jonathan Gillet, Jr., advertised his wish to give a cane to a survivor, if one could be found. Several replied, lots were drawn, and the cane went to Levi Hanford, who had spent seventeen months in the Liberty Street sugar house. Hanford's family kept the cane for years "as a precious relic" (Stiles, *Letters from the*

Prisons and Prison-Ships, 38; *Walton Reporter,* Apr. 4, 1883). It was no coincidence that by 1840, gentlemen like Philip Hone were bemoaning the loss of interest in Evacuation Day, once an occasion for public hoopla rivaling Independence Day (McNamara, *Day of Jubilee,* 38–39).

44. Moss, *American Metropolis,* 2: 160–161; *New York Daily Times,* Feb. 17, 1854.

45. Moss, *American Metropolis,* 3: 161; *New York Daily Times,* Feb. 18, 1854.

46. *New York Daily Times,* Feb. 4, 15, 17, Mar. 1, 11, 28, 1854. Cutler's highly regarded peroration was later issued as a pamphlet. See also *Remarks of Judge Wendell.*

47. *New York Daily Times,* Mar. 31, 1854.

48. *New York Daily Times,* May 6, 1854.

49. See esp. Romaine's *Review. The tomb of the martyrs*—a peculiar, rambling manifesto that combined Romaine's wish for a permanent memorial with his horror of states' rights. His 1834 pension application is in RWPA: W18839. Also, Stiles, *History of Brooklyn* 1: 375; Ostrander, *History of Brooklyn* 2: 8, 21–23; Thompson, *History of Long Island* 1: 247; *Brooklyn Daily Eagle,* Feb. 11, 1842; July 5, 1843; Jan. 30, Feb. 15, 1845; Jan. 20, 1895; *Hudson River Chronicle,* Mar. 2, 1841. *Journal of the House of Representatives,* 28th Cong., 2nd. sess., 288–289, 468. The story of the skeleton with iron manacles was widely reprinted (e.g., the *Barre Gazette,* Feb. 26, 1841). In 1841, Congressman Henry C. Murphy, a Brooklyn Democratic boss, former mayor of the City of Brooklyn, and the founder of the *Brooklyn Daily Eagle,* got the House Committee on Military Affairs interested in a Wallabout monument, but Congress adjourned without taking action.

50. Reynolds, *Walt Whitman's America,* esp. 11–15; *Brooklyn Daily Eagle,* July 2, 1846.

51. See *Brooklyn Daily Eagle,* Feb. 9, Nov. 15, 27, Dec. 1, 3, 1847. Washington Park, Brooklyn's first, had been laid out in 1847. Even before then, however, it had been the site of the city's annual Independence Day festivities (*Brooklyn Daily Eagle,* June 15, 1900).

52. *Brooklyn Daily Eagle,* May 28, Oct. 1, 2, 1850; Mar. 7, July 5, 12, 26, 1851; May 31, 1852; July 9, 1853; May 28, June 1, 15, 18, 19, 1855; Jan. 20, 1895. [Taylor], *Martyrs to the Revolution,* 13ff. Taylor, who was president of the Martyr Monument Association, constructed this pamphlet almost entirely out of excerpts from Dring, Andros, and Sherburne. The appendix conveniently reprinted the association's charter and bylaws as well as its standard fund-raising letter. There are hints in the *Eagle's* coverage of the Association that it had become—or was thought to have become—a front for the nativist Know-Nothing (American) party, which backed ex-President Millard Fillmore's bid for reelection in 1856. Indeed, when Fillmore campaigned in Brooklyn that year, he referred pointedly to the Wallabout martyrs and the association's effort to preserve their memory. "Can it be possible—can reasonable men for a moment suspect that the descendants of these martyrs can basely sacrifice the patrimony which they have inherited, which their descendants left them?" In response to which the large and enthusiastic crowd chanted, "No, never!" *Brooklyn Daily Eagle,* June 26, 1856. On the association's inability to raise money by private contributions, see ibid., Dec. 14, 1859; May 21, 1860.

53. *Brooklyn Daily Eagle,* June 18, 1873. Twenty years later the man in charge of the move published an account of the event, complete with a diagram of how the coffins were stacked up in the mausoleum. Ibid., May 29, 1895.

54. See *Brooklyn Daily Eagle,* Mar. 8, Apr. 11, May 30, June 17, 28, July 5, 1876; May 29, 1882; May 26, 1884; May 25, 1885; May 31, 1886; May 30, July 2, 1887; May 26, 1888; May 22, 26, 1890; May 27, 1895; May 25, 1896.

55. Ibid., Jan. 21, 1877.

56. Ibid., May 31, 1886; May 6, 1887; Jan. 13, Feb. 9, Oct. 5, Nov. 2, 1888; Jan. 2, Apr. 9, 1893. See also the Society's 1890 *Appeal to the Congress of the United States.*

57. Ibid., Jan. 7, Feb. 6, 1891; Mar. 24, 1898. The DR was formed by disgruntled members of the DAR who advocated more restrictive qualifications for membership (direct lineal descent from a Revolutionary patriot rather than collateral descent). In Brooklyn, competition between the two was the source of considerable confusion and acrimony. See *Brooklyn Daily Eagle*, Dec. 10, 1893; May 1, 6, 1895; June 25, July 1, 2, 1896. For a brief history of the Association, see *Dedication of the monument*, 58–62. In an effort to raise additional monies, Mrs. Stephen V. White, a founder of the Brooklyn DAR, arranged for the publication of *Prison ship martyr: Captain Jabez Fitch: his diary in facsimile, 1776* ([New York], 1897). Alas, Fitch never set foot on any of the Wallabout prison ships. Neither was he a martyr, reaching the ripe old age of seventy-five before his death of natural causes in 1812. It would appear, in other words, that Mrs. Smith neglected to read the document before sending it to the printer. Odder still, the book was reissued in 1907 as *The diary (in facsimilie) of Jabez Fitch, a prison-ship martyr of 1776: discovered by Mrs. S.V. White of Brooklyn, N.Y., and sold for the benefit of the Martyrs' Monument Fund* (New York, 1897). No "discovery" was necessary, however, since portions of the diary had already appeared in print and its existence was hardly a secret. See *Fitch Diary*, 132–134; *New York Times*, Mar. 21, 1903. For a happier example of fund-raising publications by another founding member of the Brooklyn DAR, see Alice Morse Earle's very capable *Martyrs of the prison-ships of the Revolution.*

58. *Brooklyn Daily Eagle*, Jan. 24, 29, Feb. 1, Mar. 23, May 22, June 5, 1900. Discoveries of this sort were not uncommon, even at the end of the nineteenth century. See ibid., July 24, 1886. More bones were in fact turned up a few months later and yet again in 1902. Ibid., Mar. 24, 1900; June 19, 1902; *New York Times*, May 15, 1903.

59. *Brooklyn Daily Eagle*, June 17, 1900.

60. *Brooklyn Daily Eagle*, June 27, Oct. 13, 14, 16, 25, 1902. The City of New York contributed $50,000 and the state an additional $25,000. The Tammany Society chipped in $1,000. *New York Times*, May 10, 27, June 9, 1903; Apr. 22, 1904; Feb. 15, 1905; Mar. 11, 1907. *Dedication of the monument*, 29–30, 33, 62; *New York Times*, Oct. 27, 1907. Whether the timbers found in 1902 did in fact belong to the *Jersey* is open to question.

61. *Dedication of the monument*, 3–4; *New York Times*, Nov. 15, 1908; and *Program of Dedicatory Ceremonies.*

62. *Dedication of the monument*, 9–18.

63. *Dedication of the monument*, 18–19.

EPILOGUE

1. George Louis Beer quoted in Novick, *That Noble Dream*, 83. Cf. James A. Woodburn's introduction to Lecky, *American Revolution, 1763–1783*, vi–vii: "The intelligent reading of our Revolution should lead us to see that . . . it has in no sense destroyed the essential unity of the Anglo-Saxon race."

2. *Graydon Memoirs*, 269–270.

3. Coggeshall, *History of the American Privateers*, 342–343; Stiles, *History of the City of Brooklyn*, 1: 361–362; Dandridge, *American Prisoners*, 1; Banks, *David Sproat*, 1–2. Stiles also observed that the Civil War had made "rebels" and "rebellion" seem rather less attractive than they had before. The Brahmin Anglophilia of American historians at the end of the nineteenth century is described in Wish, *American Historian*,

109–132; Higham, Krieger, and Gilbert, *Development of Historical Studies in the United States*, 161–167, and passim; and Novick, *Noble Dream*, 112–116.

4. Janvier, *In Old New York*, 243; see Hood, "Journeying to 'Old New York'"; Andreasen, "Treason or Truth." In its issue of Apr. 29, 1893, the *New York Times* pronounced the previous day's naval parade "a significant commentary on the extremely friendly relations which exist between the United States and Great Britain" (*New York Times*, Nov. 26, 1905; Nov. 26, 1902). See McNamara, *Day of Jubilee*, 158, 171; Novick, *Noble Dream*, 83–85. By 1918, Boston, too, had suspended its annual Evacuation Day celebration because the soldiers who once took part were off fighting alongside the British on European battlefields (*New York Times*, Mar. 18, 1918).

5. Ian Hay, *Getting Together* (New York, 1917), quoted in Squires, *British Propaganda*, 73. On Anglophobia in textbooks, see Altschul, *American Revolution in Our School Text-Books* and Moreau, *Schoolbook Nation*, esp. 191ff. Blakey, *Historians on the Homefront*, chronicles the eagerness of many professional historians to get on the war bandwagon. See also Novick, *Noble Dream*, 116–132.

6. Many of the essential sources are compiled in Slide, *Robert Goldstein and "The Spirit of '76*," esp. 10, 42, 48, 63–65, and 92–104. See also Mock, *Censorship 1917*, 179–181. Bledsoe's decision in the civil forfeiture proceeding was reported in the *New York Times*, Feb. 3, 1918, which also noted that the Justice Department had printed up the decision as a pamphlet "for general circulation" and sent copies to Sinn Fein newspapers for their "future guidance." Goldstein appealed but his conviction was upheld by the Ninth Circuit in 1919 (*Goldstein v. United States* 258 Fed. 908). President Wilson subsequently commuted Goldstein's sentence to three years. For a recent survey of the legal issues, see Stone, "Origins of the 'Bad Tendency' Test," 411–452. No copies of the film have survived.

7. Armbruster, *Prison Ships*, 4, 14, 17, and passim.

8. Quoted in Andreasen, "New York City Textbook Controversy," 406. See also Zimmerman, "'Each "Race" Could Have Its Heroes Sung.'" Other textbooks coming under fire were authored by Albert Bushnell Hart, Willis M. West, Andrew C. McLaughlin, and Claude H. Van Tyne (*New York Times*, Dec. 7, 1921; June 4, 6, 1923). The postwar revival of Anglophobia is described fully in Moser, *Twisting the Lion's Tail*, but see also Blakey, *Historians on the Homefront*, 133–152; and Nash, Crabtree, and Dunn, *History on Trial*, 26–39.

9. Van Tyne, *England and America*, 2, 11, 15, 17, 23, and passim. Long excerpts from Van Tyne's address were reprinted in the *New York Times*, May 14, 1927—not surprising inasmuch as the paper had repeatedly editorialized against the textbook critics, one of whom was Mayor John F. Hylan.

10. Abbott, *New York in the American Revolution*, and Barck, *New York City During the War for Independence*. An important exception to the trend was Wertenbaker, *Father Knickerbocker Rebels*, which devoted one (albeit thinly researched) chapter to "Corruption and Cruelty." On prisoner abuse stories as "propaganda," see Davidson, *Propaganda*, 369–371; Adams, *New England in the Republic, 1776–1850* (Boston, 1926), 60; Ralph Adams Brown, "New Hampshire Editors"; Anderson, "The Treatment of Prisoners of War in Britain"; and Morison, *John Paul Jones*, 165–166.

11. Bowman, *Captive Americans*, 124; Baxter, "American Revolutionary Experience," 5, 7, 58–59, 64, 78–79, 162, and passim; Denn, "Prison Narratives," 4, 24, 26, 32, 58, and passim. One reviewer complained that Metzger, *Prisoner in the American Revolution*, had a "decidedly whiggish bias" because it seemed less inclined to excul-

pate the British (*JAH* 58 [Dec. 1971], 724–725). For evidence that the Cold War revived Anglophilia in the academy, see Billington et al., *Historian's Contribution*.

APPENDIX A

1. We commonly use "calories" to describe the energy potential of food, and I have done so in the text for the sake of clarity. But those "calories" are properly referred to "kilocalories"—the amount of heat required to raise the temperature of one kilogram of water by one degree centigrade. "Kilocalorie" is the term employed by nutrition scientists, and the data in the table reflect that usage. To estimate the caloric content of the foods in question, I used the Basal Energy Calculator, Cornell University Medical Center (http://www-users.med.cornell.edu/~spon/picu/calc/beecalc.htm); Pennington, *Bowes and Church's Food Values of Portions Commonly Used*; and the USDA National Nutrient Database (http://www.nal.usda.gov/fnic/foodcomp). I am grateful to my colleague, Kathleen V. Axen, for her expert guidance in these matters.

APPENDIX B

1. The oddly heart-shaped formatting was adopted by the *Daily Advertiser* but not the *Independent Gazetteer.* The latter added a line at the top, "Inserted by particular request," and omitted "taken from his own mouth by the ordinary of Newgate" at the end. Otherwise the two pieces were identical.

2. Black pioneers were fugitive slaves who had joined the British Army in return for the promise of emancipation at the end of the war. They worked as scouts, spies, personal servants, and laborers. A Pennsylvania runaway named Richmond had the job of public hangman and as such functioned as Cunningham's assistant at the Provost, until he ran off in 1781. See *Royal Gazette*, Aug. 4, 1781; Hodges, *Root and Branch*, esp. 147–158.

3. See, among others, *Federal Gazette* (Philadelphia), Feb. 1, 1792; *Washington Spy* (Elizabeth Town, MD), Feb. 8, 1792; *Vermont Gazette* (Bennington), Feb. 13, 1792; *Western Star* (Stockbridge, MA), Feb. 14, 1792; *Essex Journal* (Newburyport, MA), Feb. 15, 1792. For typical nineteenth-century embellishments, see Watson, *Historic Tales of Olden Time*, 179; Lossing, *Hours with the Living Men and Women of the Revolution*, 235–239.

4. That Cunningham's name did not appear on the Newgate Calendar was a problem first noted by George Bancroft, who did extensive research in British archives for his multivolume *History of the United States* (1834–1876). London's gallows had been moved from Tyburn to Newgate in 1782. The Newgate Calendar is now available online (http://tarlton.law.utexas.edu/lpop/etext/completenewgate.htm) as are the records of the Old Bailey (http://www.oldbaileyonline.org). To pay his debts, Cunningham allegedly said that he "mortgaged my half pay"—the pension he would have received *after* leaving the army. Binns's reference to Cunningham is in [Binns], *Recollections of the Life of John Binns*, 147–148.

5. The last ship to have arrived in Philadelphia from Britain seems to have been the *Camilla* out of Bristol, which came in on January 3. The brig with London newspapers was the *Peter,* which dropped anchor in New York on January 17.

6. See "Gaine's Marine List," in the *New-York Gazette*, Aug. 8, 1774, and advertisements in the *New-York Journal* and Rivington's *New York Gazetteer,* both Aug. 11, 1774.

7. Bailyn, *Voyagers to the West*, 592ff.; *New-York Journal*, Mar. 9, 1775.

8. *Rivington's New-York Gazetteer,* Mar. 9, 1775. Local patriots denounced this version of what happened as "false and malicious" in the *New-York Gazette*, Mar. 13,

1775. John Hill may have been the same John Hill, "late of the town of Omagh, in Ireland," who advertised the opening of his "New Beef Steak and Oyster House" a year earlier (*New-York Gazetteer,* March 17, 1774). See also Becker, *History of Political Parties in the Province of New York,* 182–183.

9. "Cives," *Independent Gazetteer* (Philadelphia), Aug. 23, 1783; *Connecticut Courant,* Nov. 4, 1783. The activities of the Wallaces can be traced in Harrington, *New York Merchant.* For Wetherhead, see Crary, *Price of Loyalty,* 44–45.

10. [Edes], *Diary of Peter Edes,* 99, 101, and passim. For additional glimpses of Cunningham's tyrannical behavior in Boston, see also Newell, "Journal kept during the time yᵗ Boston was shut up in 1775–6."

11. This description of Oswald draws on the only modern study of his life and career, Stumpf, "Colonel Eleazer Oswald." Possibly Philip Freneau knew something about Oswald; on the Liberty Pole incident, see Leary, *That Rascal Freneau,* 54ff.

12. Boudinot's version of the "French doctor" story (see chapter 4) appears to conflate details of the mysterious "Debuke" or "Debute" with Cunningham's "Confession." Boudinot later wrote that he "saw an acct in the London Paper of this same Frenchman being taken up in England for some Crime and condemned to dye.—At his Execution he acknowledged the fact of his having murdered a great number of Rebels in the Hospital at New York, by poyson" (BJ, 35–36). As with Cunningham, however, no such person appears in the records of Newgate Prison or the Old Bailey.

WORKS CITED

Account of the procession, together with copious extracts of the oration, delivered at the Wallabout (L.I.), April 6th, 1808. New York, 1808.

American National Biography. New York, 1999.

Appeal to the Congress of the United States from the Society of Old Brooklynites for the erection of a monument over the remains of 11,500 prisoners who died on board the British prison ships during the Revolutionary War. Brooklyn, 1890.

Argument of Peter Y. Cutler, Esq., before the Street Committee of the Board of Aldermen of the city of New-York: delivered March 1st, 1854, in the matter of extending Albany Street to Broadway, through Trinity Church Yard. New York, 1854.

Calendar of Historical Manuscripts Relating to the War of the Revolution, in the Office of the Secretary of State, 2 vols. Albany, 1868.

Christmas Reminder. Being the Names of About Eight Thousand Persons, a Small Portion of the Number Confined on Board the British Prison Ships During the War of the Revolution. Brooklyn, 1888.

Dedication of the monument and other proceedings. New York, 1913.

History of Litchfield County, Connecticut. Philadelphia, 1881.

History of Northampton County, Pennsylvania. Philadelphia, 1877.

Journal of the House of Representatives, 28th Congress, 2nd Session (Washington, DC, 1844–1845).

Journals of the Provincial Congress, Provincial Convention, Committee of Safety, and Council of Safety of the State of New York, 1775–1776–1777, 2 vols. Albany, 1842.

Letters of the Two Commanders in Chief; Generals Gage and Washington and Major Generals Burgoyne and Lee; with the Manifesto of General Washington to the Inhabitants of Canada. New York, 1775.

Minutes of the Committee and of the first Commission for detecting and defeating conspiracies in the state of New York, December 11, 1776–September 23, 1778. 2 vols. Albany, 1924–1925.

New Records of the American Revolution. London, 1927.

Papers of the War Department, Center for History and New Media, George Mason University. http://wardepartmentpapers.org.

Program of Dedicatory Ceremonies of the Prison Ship Martyrs' Monument, Fort Greene Park, Brooklyn, N.Y., Saturday, Nov. 14, 1908, and History of the Prison Ship Martyrs. Brooklyn, 1908.

Public Records of the State of Connecticut, 16 vols. Hartford, 1894.

329

Remarks of Judge Wendell, before the Street Committee of the Board of Alderman. March 14, 1854. New York, 1854.

Report on American Manuscripts in the Royal Institution of Great Britain. Historical Manuscripts Commission, 4 vols. London, 1904–1909.

Report on the Manuscripts of Mrs. Stoppford-Sackville. Historical Manuscripts Commission, 2 vols. London, 1904.

"Revolutionary Records." *American Monthly Magazine* 19 (Nov. 1901), 501–502.

"Revolutionary Reminiscences by an Old Soldier." *The United States Review* (Dec. 1854), 508–513.

Selections from the Correspondence of the Executive of New Jersey from 1776 to 1786. Newark, 1848.

Some Account of the Capture of the Ship "Aurora" (1899; repr., New York, 1971).

Abbott, Wilbur C. *New York in the American Revolution.* New York, 1929.

Abell, Francis. *Prisoners of War in Britain 1756 to 1815: A Record of their Lives, their Romance and their Sufferings.* London, 1914.

Adams, James T. *New England in the Republic, 1776–1850.* Boston, 1926.

[Adams, John]. *Diary and Autobiography of John Adams,* ed. L. H. Butterfield. 4 vols. Cambridge, MA, 1962.

[Adlum, John]. *Memoirs of the Life of John Adlum in the Revolutionary War,* ed. Howard H. Peckham. Chicago, 1968.

Alden, John R. *General Charles Lee: Traitor or Patriot?* Baton Rouge, 1951.

———. *General Gage in America.* Baton Rouge, 1948.

[Allen, Ethan]. *A Narrative of Colonel Ethan Allen's Captivity Written by Himself.* Burlington, VT, 1838.

Altschul, Charles. *The American Revolution in Our School Text-Books.* New York, c. 1917.

Ammerman, David. *In the Common Cause: American Response to the Coercive Acts of 1774.* New York, 1974.

[Anderson, Enoch]. *Personal Recollections of Captain Enoch Anderson, an Officer of the Delaware Regiments in the Revolutionary War.* Wilmington, DE, 1896.

Anderson, Olive. "The Treatment of Prisoners of War in Britain During the American War of Independence." *BIHR* 28 (1955), 63–83.

Andreasen, Bethany. "Treason or Truth: The New York City Textbook Controversy, 1920–1923." *NYH,* 66 (Oct. 1985), 397–419.

Andros, Thomas. *The Old Jersey Captive.* New York, 1833.

Anthon, Charles. "Anthon's Notes." *SIIP* 5 (Oct. 1927–May 1929), 1–20; (Oct. 1929–May 1930), 71–160.

Arch, Stephen Carl. "Writing a Federalist Self: Alexander Graydon's *Memoirs of a Life.*" *WMQ* 52 (July, 1995), 415–432.

Armbruster, Eugene L. *The Wallabout Prison Ships, 1776–1783.* New York, 1920.

[Atlee, Samuel]. "Extract from the Journal of Col. Atlee." 2 *PA* 1: 512–516.

Atwood, Rodney. *The Hessians: Mercenaries from Hessen-Kassel in the American Revolution.* Cambridge, MA, 1980.

Axelrad, Jacob. *Philip Freneau: Champion of Democracy.* Austin, 1967.

Backus, Isaac. *A Church History of New England.* 2 vols. Providence, RI, 1784.

Bailyn, Bernard. *Voyagers to the West: A Passage in the Peopling of America on the Eve of the Revolution.* New York, 1996.

Balderston, Marion, and David Syrett, eds. *The Lost War: Letters from British Officers During the American Revolution.* New York, 1975.

Bancroft, George. *History of the United States.* 1834–1876. 10 vols. Boston, 1834–1875.

Bangs, Charlotte R. (Mrs. Bleecker). *Reminiscences of Old New Utrecht and Gowanus.* Brooklyn, 1912.

Banks, James Lenox. *David Sproat and Naval Prisoners in the War of the Revolution.* New York, 1909.

Barck, Oscar. *New York City During the War for Independence.* New York, 1931.

Barker, A. J. *Prisoners of War.* New York, 1975.

Barlow, Elizabeth. *Forests and Wetlands of New York City.* Boston, 1969.

[Barlow, Joel]. *The Columbiad, a Poem. By Joel Barlow.* London, 1809.

Barnes, Samuel C. *Wallabout and the Wallabouters.* New York, c. 1888.

Baxter, Beverly V. "The American Revolutionary Experience: A Critical Study of Diaries and Journals of American Prisoners During the Revolutionary Period." Ph.D. dissertation, University of Delaware, 1976.

Baugh, Daniel A. *British Naval Administration in the Age of Walpole.* Princeton, NJ, 1965.

Becker, Ann M. "Smallpox in Washington's Army: Strategic Implications of the Disease During the American Revolutionary War." *JMH* 68 (Apr. 2004), 381–430.

Becker, Carl. *The History of Political Parties in the Province of New York, 1760–1776.* Madison, 1909; reprinted 1960.

Bellesiles, Michael A. *Revolutionary Outlaws: Ethan Allen and the Struggle for Independence on the Early American Frontier.* Charlottesville, 1993.

[Bense, Johann]. "A Brunswick Grenadier with Burgoyne: The Journal of Johann Bense, 1776–1783." Trans. Helga Doblin and ed. Mary C. Lynn. *NYH* 65 (Oct. 1985), 421–444.

Berkin, Carol. *Revolutionary Mothers: Women and the Struggle for America's Independence.* New York, 2005.

Bernard, John. *Retrospections of America, 1797–1811.* Orig. pub. 1887; repr. New York, 1969.

Bickham, Troy O. "Sympathizing with Sedition? George Washington, the British Press, and British Attitudes During the American War of Independence." *WMQ* 59 (Jan. 2002), 39–64.

Bill, Alfred H., and Walter F. Edge. *A House Called Morven.* Rev. ed. Princeton, NJ, 1978.

Billias, George A., ed. *George Washington's Generals.* New York, 1964.

———, ed. *George Washington's Opponents: British Generals and Admirals in the American Revolution.* New York, 1969.

Billington, Ray A., et al. *The Historian's Contribution to Anglo-American Misunderstanding.* New York, 1966.

[Binns, John]. *Recollections of the Life of John Binns: Twenty-Nine Years in Europe and Fifty-Three in the United States. Written by Himself.* Philadelphia, 1854.

Black, Jeremy. *Culloden and the '45.* New York, 1990.

———. *War for America: The Fight for Independence, 1775–1783.* New York, 1991.

Blake, John L. *A Biographical Dictionary: Comprising a Summary Account of the Lives of the Most Distinguished Persons of All Ages, Nations, and Professions.* Philadelphia, 1859.

Blakey, George T. *Historians on the Homefront: American Propagandists for the Great War.* Lexington, KY, 1970.

Blatchford, John. *Narrative of Remarkable Occurrences, in the Life of John Blatchford, of Cape Ann, Commonwealth of Massachusetts.* New London, 1788.

[Blatchford, John]. *The Narrative of John Blatchford*, ed. Charles I. Bushnell. New York, 1865.

Bliven, Bruce, Jr. *Battle for Manhattan*. New York, 1955.

Boatner, Mark. *Encyclopedia of the American Revolution*. New York, 1966.

Bolton, Charles K., ed. *Letters of Hugh Earl Percy from Boston and New York, 1774–1776*. Orig. pub. 1902; repr. Boston, 1972.

——. *The Private Soldier Under Washington*. Orig. pub. 1902; repr. Port Washington, NY, 1964.

Booth, Mary L. *History of the City of New York*. New York, 1859.

[Boudinot, Elias]. "Colonel Elias Boudinot's Notes of Two Conferences Held by the American and British Commissioners to Settle a General Cartel for the Exchange of Prisoners of War." *PMHB* 24 (1900), 291–305.

——. *The life, public services, addresses, and letters of Elias Boudinot*, ed. Jane J. Boudinot. 2 vols. Boston, 1896.

——. *"Their Distress is almost intolerable": The Elias Boudinot Letterbook, 1777–1778*, ed. Joseph Lee Boyle. Bowie, MD, 2002.

Boudinot, Elias. *Journal or Historical Recollections of American Events during the Revolutionary War*. Philadelphia, 1894.

Bowden, David K. *The Execution of Isaac Hayne*. Lexington, SC, 1977.

Bowden, Mary Weatherspoon. "In Search of Freneau's Prison Ships." *EAL* 14 (Sept. 1979), 174–192.

——. *Philip Freneau*. Boston, 1976.

Bowler, Arthur. *Logistics and the Failure of the British Army in America, 1775–1783*. Princeton, NJ, 1975.

Bowman, Larry G. *Captive Americans: Prisoners During the American Revolution*. Athens, OH, 1976.

——. "Lewis Pintard: Agent to American Prisoners, 1777–1780." *Journal of the Great Lakes History Conference* 1 (1976), 38–49.

——. "Military Parolees on Long Island, 1777–1782." *JLIH* 18 (1982), 21–29.

——. "The New Jersey Prisoner Exchange Conferences, 1778–1780." *NJH* 97 (Autumn 1979), 149–158.

Boyd, George A. *Elias Boudinot: Patriot and Statesman, 1740–1821*. Princeton, NJ, 1952.

Breen, T. H. "Ideology and Nationalism on the Eve of the American Revolution: Revisions Once More in Need of Revising." *JAH* 84 (June 1997), 13–39.

Brewer, John. *The Sinews of Power: War, Money and the English State, 1688–1783*. New York, 1989.

Brigham, Clarence S., ed. *British Royal Proclamations Relating to America*. Orig. pub. 1911; repr. New York, 1968.

Brown, Gerald S. *The American Secretary: The Colonial Policy of Lord George Germain, 1775–1778*. Ann Arbor, MI, 1963.

Brown, Ralph A. "New Hampshire Editors Win the War: A Study in Revolutionary Press Propaganda." *NEQ* 12 (Mar. 1939), 35–51.

Brown, Wallace. *The Good Americans: The Loyalists in the American Revolution*. New York, 1969.

Bruce, Anthony. *The Purchase System in the British Army, 1660–1871*. London, 1980.

Buchanan, John. *The Road to Valley Forge: How Washington Built the Army That Won the Revolution*. Hoboken, NJ, 2004.

Buel, Joy D., and Richard Buel. *The Way of Duty: A Woman and Her Family in Revolutionary America*. New York, 1984.

Buel, Richard, Jr. *Dear Liberty: Connecticut's Mobilization for the Revolutionary War.* Middletown, 1980.

[Bureau of the Census]. *The Statistical History of the United States from Colonial Times to the Present*. New York, 1976.

Burgoyne, Bruce E., ed. *Enemy Views: The American Revolutionary War as Recorded by the Hessian Participants*. Bowie, MD, 1996.

Burnett, Edmund C. *The Continental Congress*. Orig. pub. 1941; repr. New York, 1965.

Burrows, Edwin G. "Kings County." In Joseph S. Tiedemann and Eugene R. Fingerhut, eds., *The Other New York: The American Revolution Beyond New York City*. Albany, 2005, 21–42.

———. "The News from Occupied Flatbush." *America in Britain* 43 (2005), 4–6.

———, and Mike Wallace. *Gotham: A History of New York City to 1898*. New York, 1999.

———, and Michael Wallace. "The American Revolution: The Ideology and Psychology of National Liberation," *Perspectives in American History* 6 (1972), 167–306.

Burstein, Andrew. *America's Jubilee: How in 1826 a Generation Remembered Fifty Years of Independence*. New York, 2001.

Butterfield, L. H., ed. *Adams Family Correspondence*. 7 vols. Cambridge, MA, 1963–2005.

———. *Diary and Autobiography of John Adams*. 4 vols. Cambridge, MA, 1962.

Callcott, George H. *History in the United States, 1800–1860: Its Practice and Purpose*. Baltimore, 1970.

Calder, Angus. *Revolutionary Empire: The Rise of the English-Speaking Empires from the Fifteenth Century to the 1780s*. New York, 1981.

Calhoon, Robert McC. "Civil, Revolutionary, or Partisan: The Loyalists and the Nature of the War for Independence." In R. Calhoun, ed., *The Loyalist Perception and Other Essays*. Columbia, SC, 1989, 147–162.

———. *The Loyalists in Revolutionary America, 1760–1781*. New York, 1973.

Campbell, Charles F. *The Intolerable Hulks: British Shipboard Confinement, 1776–1857*. 3rd ed. Tucson, AZ, 2001.

Carp, Benjamin L. "The Night the Yankees Burned Broadway: The New York City Fire of 1776." *EAS* 4 (Fall 2006), 471–511.

Casino, Joseph J. "Elizabethtown 1782: The Prisoner-of-War Negotiations and the Pawns of War" *NJH* 102 (Spring–Summer 1984), 1–35.

Caspar, Scott. *Constructing American Lives: Biography and Culture in Nineteenth-Century America*. Chapel Hill, NC, 1999.

Chandler, Peleg W. *American Criminal Trials*. 2 vols. Boston, 1844.

Clark, William B. et al., eds., *Naval Documents of the American Revolution*. 11 vols. Washington, DC, 1964.

[Clinton, George]. *Public Papers of George Clinton*, ed. Hugh Hastings and J. A. Holden. 10 vols. Albany, 1899–1914.

Clodfelter, Micheal. *Warfare and Armed Conflicts: A Statistical Reference to Casualty and Other Figures, 1618–1991*. 2 vols. Jefferson, NC, 1991.

Cobbett, William, and T. C. Hansard, eds. *The Parliamentary History of England, from the Earliest Period to the Year 1803*. 36 vols. London, 1806–1820.

Cochran, Hamilton. *Scudders in the American Revolution.* Privately printed, 1976.

[Coffin, Alexander]. "The Destructive Operation of Foul Air, Tainted Provisions, Bad Water, and Personal Filthiness, upon Human Constitutions; exemplified in the unparalleled Cruelty of the British to the American Captives at New-York during the Revolutionary War, on Board their Prison and Hospital Ships. By Captain Alexander Coffin, Jun., one of the surviving Sufferers: In a Communication to Dr. Mitchill, dated September 4, 1807." In Charles I. Bushnell, ed., *The Narrative of John Blatchford.* New York, 1865, 117–127.

Coggeshall, George. *History of American Privateers.* Privately printed, 1856. [New York]

Cogliano, Francis D. *American Maritime Prisoners in the Revolutionary War: The Captivity of William Russell.* Annapolis, 2001.

Cohen, Paul E., and Robert T. Augustyn. *Manhattan in Maps.* New York, 1997.

Cohen, Sheldon. *Yankee Sailors in British Gaols: Prisoners of War at Forton and Mill, 1777–1783.* Newark, NJ, 1995.

Colley, Linda. *Britons: Forging the Nation, 1707–1837.* New Haven, CT, 1992.

———. *Captives: Britain, Empire and the World, 1600–1850.* London, 2002.

Collins, Varnum L. *President Witherspoon.* 2 vols. Princeton, NJ, 1925.

Conway, Stephen. *The British Isles and the War of American Independence.* New York, 2000.

———. "From Fellow-Nationals to Foreigners: British Perceptions of the Americans, circa 1739–1783." *WMQ* 59 (Jan. 2002), 65–100.

———. "'The great mischief Complain'd of': Reflections on the Misconduct of British Soldiers in the Revolutionary War." *WMQ* 47 (July 1990), 370–390.

———. "To Subdue America: British Army Officers and the Conduct of the Revolutionary War," *WMQ*, 43 (July 1986), 381–407.

———. *The War of American Independence, 1775–1783.* London, 1995.

Cook, Fred J. *What Manner of Men: Forgotten Heroes of the American Revolution.* New York, 1959.

[Cornelius, Elias]. *Journal of Dr. Elias Cornelius, A Revolutionary Surgeon. Graphic Description of His Sufferings while a Prisoner in Provost Jail, New York, 1777 and 1778.* Washington, DC, 1903.

Cox, Caroline. *A Proper Sense of Honor: Service and Sacrifice in Washington's Army.* Chapel Hill, NC, 2004.

Cozzens, Issacher. *A Geological History of Manhattan or New York Island.* New York, 1843.

Crary, Catherine S. *The Price of Loyalty: Tory Writings from the Revolutionary Era.* New York, 1973.

Cray, Robert E., Jr. "Commemorating the Prison Ship Dead: Revolutionary Memory and the Politics of Sepulture in the Early Republic, 1776–1808." *WMQ* 56 (July 1999), 565–590.

[Cresswell, Nicholas]. *The Journal of Nicholas Cresswell, 1774–1777.* New York, 1924.

Cummin, Katharine H. *Connecticut Militia General Gold Selleck Silliman.* Hartford, CT, 1979.

[Cutler, Peter]. *The argument of Peter Y. Cutler, Esq., before the Street Committee of the Board of Aldermen of the city of New-York: delivered March 1st, 1854, in the matter of extending Albany Street to Broadway, through Trinity Church Yard.* New York, 1854.

Dabney, William M. *After Saratoga: The Story of the Convention Army.* Albuquerque, 1954.

Dandridge, Danske. *American Prisoners of the Revolution.* Charlottesville, SC, 1911.

Dankers, Jasper, and Peter Sluyter. *Journal of a Voyage to New York.* Orig. pub. 1867; privately reprinted, 1966.

Dann, John C., ed. *The Revolution Remembered: Eyewitness Accounts of the War for Independence.* Chicago, 1980.

Daughan, George C. *If By Sea: The Forging of the American Navy from the American Revolution to the War of 1812.* New York: Basic Books, 2008.

Davidson, Philip. *Propaganda and the American Revolution, 1763–1783.* Chapel Hill, NC, 1941.

Davies, K. G., ed. *Documents of the American Revolution, 1770–1783.* Colonial Office Series 12. Dublin, 1976.

Delafield, Julia. *Biographies of Francis Lewis and Morgan Lewis.* New York, 1877.

Denn, Robert J. "Prison Narratives of the American Revolution." Ph.D. dissertation, Michigan State University, 1980.

Devine, Francis E. "The Pennsylvania Flying Camp, July–November 1776." *PH* 46 (Jan. 1979), 59–78.

Dixon, Martha W. "Divided Authority: The American Management of Prisoners in the Revolutionary War, 1775–1783." Ph.D. dissertation, University of Utah, 1977.

Dohla, Johann. *A Hessian Diary of the American Revolution,* trans. Bruce E. Burgoyne. Norman, OK, 1990.

Dodge, John. *A Narrative of the Capture and Treatment of John Dodge, By the English at Detroit. Written by Himself.* Philadelphia, 1779.

Domosh, Mona. *Invented Cities: The Creation of Landscape in Nineteenth-Century New York and Boston.* New Haven, CT, 1996.

Douglas, David C., et al., eds. *English Historical Documents.* 12 vols. New York, 1950.

Doyle, David N. *Ireland, Irishmen, and Revolutionary America, 1760–1820.* Dublin, 1981.

Doyle, Robert C. *Voices from Captivity: Interpreting the American POW Narratives.* Lawrence, KS, 1994.

Draper, Theodore. *A Struggle for Power: The American Revolution.* New York, 1996.

Duffy, Christopher. *The Military Experience in the Age of Reason.* New York, 1988.

Duffy, John J., ed. *Ethan Allen and His Kin: Correspondence, 1772–1819.* 2 vols. Hanover, 1998.

Dunlap, William. *A History of the American Theater from Its Origins to 1832.* Orig. pub. 1832; repr. Chicago, 2005.

Dunshee, Kenneth H. *As You Pass By.* New York, 1952.

Earle, Alice M. *Martyrs of the prison-ships of the Revolution.* Philadelphia, 1895.

Eddis, William. *Letters from America,* ed. Aubrey C. Land. Cambridge, MA, 1969.

[Edes, Peter]. *A Diary of Peter Edes, The Oldest Printer in the United States, Written During His Confinement in Prison, By the British, in the Year 1775.* Bangor, ME, 1837, ed. and repr. by Samuel L. Boardman as *Diary of Peter Edes.* Bangor, ME, 1901.

Ekirch, A. Roger. *Bound for America: The Transportation of British Convicts to the Colonies, 1718–1775.* Oxford, 1987.

Evans, Israel. *A Discourse, Delivered, On the 18th Day of December, 1777, the Day of Public Thanksgiving, Appointed by the Honourable Continental Congress.* Lancaster, PA, 1778.

Evans, Mary T. "Letters of Dr. John McKinly to His Wife, while a Prisoner of War, 1777–1778." *PMHB* 34 (1910), 9–20.

Fanning, Nathaniel. *Fanning's Narrative, Being the Memoirs of Nathaniel Fanning, An Officer of the Revolutionary Navy, 1778–1783*, ed. by John S. Barnes. New York, 1912.

[Fanning, Nathaniel]. *Narrative of the adventures of an American navy officer.* New York, 1806.

[Fell, John]. *Delegate from New Jersey: The Journal of John Fell*, ed. Donald W. Whisenhunt Port Washington, NY, 1973.

Fenn, Elizabeth. *Pox Americana: The Great Smallpox Epidemic of 1775–1782.* Unpublished manuscript, 2001.

Ferling, John. *Almost a Miracle: The American Victory in the War of Independence.* New York, 2007.

Fernow, Berthold. *The Battle of Long Island.* Brooklyn, 1869.

———. *Historic and Antiquarian Scenes in Brooklyn and Its Vicinity.* Brooklyn, 1868.

———. *New York in the Revolution.* Orig. pub. 1887; repr. Cottonport, LA, 1972.

Field, Thomas W. *The Battle of Long Island.* Brooklyn, 1869.

———. *Historic and Antiquarian Scenes in Brooklyn and Its Vicinity.* Brooklyn, 1868.

Fingerhut, Eugene R. *Survivor: Cadwallader Colden II in Revolutionary America.* Washington, DC, 1983.

Fischer, David Hackett. *Washington's Crossing.* New York, 2004.

[Fisher, Elijah]. *Elijah Fisher's Journal while in the War for Independence.* Augusta, 1880.

[Fitch, Jabez]. *The New-York Diary of Lieutenant Jabez Fitch*, ed. W. H. W. Sabine. New York, 1954.

Flexner, James Thomas. *The Traitor and the Spy: Benedict Arnold and John André.* Boston, 1975.

Foley, William E. *Wilderness Journey: The Life of William Clark.* Columbia, MO, 2004.

Fooks, Herbert C. *Prisoners of War.* Federalsburg, MD, 1924.

Foote, Thelma W. *Black and White Manhattan: The History of Racial Formation in Colonial New York City.* New York, 2004.

Footner, Hulbert. *Sailor of Fortune: The Life and Adventures of Commodore Barney, U.S.N.* New York, 1940.

Force, Peter, comp., *American Archives.* 9 vols. Washington, DC, 1837–1853.

Ford, Paul L., ed. *Journals of Hugh Gaine: Printer.* New York, 1902.

Ford, W. C., ed. *Family Letters of Samuel Blachley Webb, 1764–1807.* New York, 1912.

———, ed. *Journals of the Continental Congress.* 34 vols. Washington, 1906.

———. *Prisoners of War (British and American), 1778.* Philadelphia, 1893.

Foulke, Joseph. *Memoirs of Jacob Ritter, A Faithful Minister in the Society of Friends.* Philadelphia, 1844.

Fowler, William M., Jr. *Silas Talbot: Captain of Old Ironsides.* Mystic, CT, 1995.

[Fox, Charles James]. *The Speeches of the Right Honourable Charles James Fox, in the House of Commons.* 6 vols. London, 1815.

[Fox, Ebenezer]. *The Adventures of Ebenezer Fox, in the Revolutionary War.* Orig. pub. 1838; repr. Boston, 1847.

Francis, John W. *New York During the Last Half Century: A Discourse in Commemoration of the Fifty-Third Anniversary of the New York Historical Society.* New York, 1857.

Francis, Mary C. *Dalrymple: A Romance of the British Prison Ship, the Jersey.* New York, 1904.

[Franklin, Benjamin]. *The Papers of Benjamin Franklin*, ed. Leonard W. Labaree et al. 39 vols. New Haven, 1959.

Frazer, Persifor. *General Persifor Frazer: A Memoir*. Philadelphia, 1907.

Freeman, Joanne B. *Affairs of Honor: National Politics in the New Republic*. New Haven, CT, 2001.

[Freneau, Philip]. *The Poems of Philip Freneau: Poet of the Revolution*, ed. Fred Lewis Pattee. 3 vols. Princeton, NJ, 1902.

———. *Poems Relating to the American Revolution*, ed. Evert A. Duyckinck. New York, 1865.

———. *The Prose of Philip Freneau*, ed. Philip M. Marsh. New Brunswick, 1955.

Frey, Sylvia R. *The British Soldier in America: A Social History of Military Life in the Revolutionary Period*. Austin, TX, 1981.

———. *Water from the Rock: Black Resistance in a Revolutionary Age*. Princeton, NJ, 1991.

Furman, Gabriel. *Antiquities of Long Island*. New York, 1875.

Gabriel, Michael P. *Major General Richard Montgomery: The Making of an American Hero*. Madison, NJ, 2002.

Gallagher, John J. *The Battle of Brooklyn, 1776*. Rockville Centre, NY, 1995.

Gilmour, Ian. *Riots, Risings, and Revolution: Governance and Violence in Eighteenth-Century England*. London, 1992.

Gould, Eliga H. "American Independence and Britain's Counter-Revolution." *P&P* 154 (Feb. 1997), 107–141.

———. *The Persistence of Empire: British Political Culture in the Age of the American Revolution*. Chapel Hill, NC, 2000.

Graydon, Alexander. *Memoirs of His Own Time, with Reminiscences of the Men and Events of the Revolution*. Philadelphia, 1846.

Green, Ashbel. *The Life of the Revd. John Witherspoon*, ed. Henry L. Savage. Privately printed, 1973.

Greene, Albert G. *Recollections of the Jersey Prison-Ship, from the Original Manuscript of Captain Thomas Dring, One of the Prisoners*, ed. Henry Dawson. New York, 1865.

Greene, Donald J., ed. *Samuel Johnson: Political Writings*. New Haven, CT, 1977.

[Greenman, Jeremiah]. *Diary of a Common Soldier in the American Revolution, 1775–1783: An Annotated Edition of the Military Journal of Jeremiah Greenman*, ed. Robert C. Bray and Paul E. Bushnell. DeKalb, 1978.

Gruber, Ira D. *The Howe Brothers and the American Revolution*. New York, 1972.

Grumman, William E. *The Revolutionary Soldiers of Redding, Connecticut, and the Record of their Services*. Hartford, NJ, 1904.

Guttridge, G. H. *English Whiggism and the American Revolution*. Berkeley, 1963.

———, ed. *The American Correspondence of a Bristol Merchant, 1766–1776: Letters of Richard Champion*. Berkeley, 1934.

Haffner, Gerald O. "The Treatment of Prisoners of War by the Americans During the War of Independence." Ph.D. dissertation, Indiana University, 1952.

Hall, Charles S. *Life and Letters of Samuel Holden Parsons*. New York, 1968.

Hall, Edward H. *The Old Martyrs' Prison*. New York, 1902.

[Hamilton, Alexander]. *The Papers of Alexander Hamilton*, ed. Harold C. Syrett et al. 27 vols. New York, 1961–1987.

[Hanford, Levi]. *A Narrative of the Life and Adventures of Levi Hanford, a Soldier of the Revolution*, ed. Charles I. Bushnell. New York, 1863.

Harrington, Virginia D. *The New York Merchant on the Eve of the Revolution*. New York, 1935.

Harris, Christopher. *Public Lives, Private Virtues: Images of American Revolutionary War Heroes, 1782–1832*. New York, 2000.

Hawke, David Freeman. *Benjamin Rush: Revolutionary Gadfly*. Indianapolis, 1971.

[Hawkins, Christopher]. *The Adventures of Christopher Hawkins, Containing Details of His Captivity. Escape From the Jersey Prison Ship*, ed. Charles I. Bushnell. New York, 1864.

Hay, Ian. *Getting Together*. New York, 1917.

Hayes, Michael. "General Nathaniel Woodhull and the Battle of Long Island." *LIHJ* 7 (Spring 1995), 166–177.

[Heath, William]. *Memoirs of Major-General Heath*. Boston, 1798.

Heitman, Francis B. *Historical Register of the Continental Army*. Washington, DC, 1914.

Henry, John Joseph. *Account of Arnold's Campaign Against Quebec*. Albany, 1877.

Hibbert, Christopher. *Redcoats and Rebels: The American Revolution Through British Eyes*. New York, 1990.

Higginbotham, Don. *War and Society in Revolutionary America: The Wider Dimensions of Conflict*. Columbia, SC, 1988.

———. *The War of American Independence: Military Attitudes, Policies, and Practice, 1763–1789*. New York, 1971.

Higham, John, Leonard Krieger, and Felix Gilbert. *History: The Development of Historical Studies in the United States*. Englewood Cliffs, NJ, 1965.

Hill, George B., ed. *Boswell's Life of Johnson*, rev. L. F. Powell. 6 vols. Oxford, 1934–1950.

Hillard, E. B. *The Last Men of the Revolution: A Photograph of Each From Life, Together With Views of Their Homes Printed in Colors. Accompanied by Brief Biographical Sketches of the Men*. Hartford, CT, 1864.

Hinman, Royal R. *A Historical Collection, from Official Records, Files, &c., of the Part Sustained by Connecticut during the War of the Revolution*. Hartford, CT, 1842.

Hodges, Graham R. *Root and Branch: African-Americans in New York and East Jersey, 1613–1863*. Chapel Hill, NC, 1999.

———. *Slavery and Freedom in the Rural North: African Americans in Monmouth County, New Jersey, 1665–1865*. Madison, WI, 1997.

Hoffer, Peter Charles. *Revolution and Regeneration: Life Cycle and the Historical Vision of the Generation of 1776*. Athens, GA, 1983.

Hollister, G. H. *The History of Connecticut*. 2 vols. Hartford, CT, 1857.

Hood, Clifton. "Journeying to 'Old New York': Elite New Yorkers and Their Invention of an Idealized History in the Late Nineteenth and Early Twentieth Centuries." *JUH* 28 (Sept. 2002), 699–719.

Horton, James Oliver, and Lois E. Horton. *In Hope of Liberty: Culture, Community, and Protest Among Northern Free Blacks, 1700–1860*. New York, 1997.

Howard, John. *The State of the Prisons in England and Wales*. 1792.

Howard, John. *Essays of Howard, or, Tales of the prison*. New York, 1811.

Howard, Michael, George J. Andreopoulos, and Mark R. Shulman, eds. *The Laws of War: Constraints on Warfare in the Western World*. New Haven, CT, 1994.

Hughes, Robert. *The Fatal Shore: The Epic of Australia's Founding*. New York, 1987.

[Hughes, Thomas]. *A Journal by Thos: Hughes for His Amusement, & Designed Only for His Perusal by the Time He Attains the Age of 50 If He Lives So Long (1778–1789)*. Cambridge, MA, 1947.

Huguenin, Charles A. "Ethan Allen, Parolee on Long Island." *VH* 25 (1957), 103–125.

Hunt, Freeman. *Lives of American Merchants*. 2 vols. New York, 1858.

Hutson, James H., ed. *Letters from a Distinguished American: Twelve Essays by John Adams on American Foreign Policy, 1780*. Washington, DC, 1978.

Idzerda, Stanley J., ed. *Lafayette in the Age of the American Revolution: Selected Letters and Papers, 1776–1790*. 5 vols. Ithaca, NY, 1977.

Janvier, Thomas A. *In Old New York: A Classic History of New York City*. Orig. pub. New York, 1894; repr. 2000.

[Jefferson, Thomas], *The Papers of Thomas Jefferson*, ed. Julian P. Boyd et al. 34 vols. Princeton, NJ, 1950.

Jellison, Charles A. *Ethan Allen: Frontier Rebel*. Syracuse, NY, 1969.

Jensen, Merrill. *The Founding of a Nation: A History of the American Revolution, 1763–1776*. New York, 1968.

[Johnson, Jeremiah]. "Recollections of . . . General Jeremiah Johnson," ed. Thomas W. Field. Part 1, *JLIH* 12 (Spring, 1976), 5–21; Part 2, *JLIH* 13 (Fall 1976), 21–41.

Johnson, William Branch. *The English Prison Hulks*. London, 1957.

Johnston, Henry P. *The Battle of Harlem Heights*. Orig. pub. 1897; repr. New York, 1970.

———. *The Campaign of 1776 Around New York and Brooklyn*. Brooklyn, 1878.

Jones, Daniel P. "From War to Peace: The Revolutionary War Letters of William Peartree Smith, 1780–83." *NJH* 104 (1986), 49–77.

Jones, Maldwyn A. "Sir William Howe: Conventional Strategist." In George A. Billias, ed., *George Washington's Opponents: British Generals and Admirals in the American Revolution*. New York, 1969, 39–72.

Jones, Thomas. *History of New York During the Revolutionary War*, ed. E. F. De Lancey, 2 vols. New York, 1879.

Jordan, Helen, ed. "Colonel Elias Boudinot in New York City, Feb., 1778." *PMHB* 24 (1900), 453–466.

Kammen, Michael. *A Season of Youth: The American Revolution and the Historical Imagination*. New York, 1978.

Karsten, Peter. *Law, Soldiers, and Combat*. Westport, CT, 1978.

[Kemble, Stephen]. *The Kemble Papers*. 2 vols. *NYHC*. New York, 1884–1885.

Kipping, Ernst. *The Hessian View of America*. Monmouth Beach, NJ, 1971.

———, and Samuel S. Smith, eds. *At General Howe's Side, 1776–1783: The Diary of General William Howe's aide de camp, Captain Friedrich von Muenchhausen*. Monmouth Beach, NJ, 1974.

Klein, Milton, and Ronald W. Howard, eds. *The Twilight of British Rule in Revolutionary America: The New York Letter Book of General James Robertson, 1780–1783*. Cooperstown, NY, 1983.

Knapp, Samuel L. *The Life of Thomas Eddy*. New York, 1834.

Knapp, Shepherd. *A History of the Brick Presbyterian Church in the City of New York*. New York, 1909.

Knight, Betsy. "Prisoner Exchange and Parole in the American Revolution." *WMQ* 48 (Apr. 1991), 201–222.

Knouff, Gregory T. *The Soldiers' Revolution: Pennsylvanians in Arms and the Forging of Early American Identity*. University Park, PA, 2004.

Labaree, Benjamin Woods. *The Boston Tea Party*. New York, 1964.

———. "The Idea of American Independence: The British View, 1774–1776." *MHSP* 82 (1970), 3–20.

Landesman, Alter F. *A History of New Lots, Brooklyn*. Port Washington, NY, 1977.

[Laurens, John]. *The Army Correspondence of Colonel John Laurens*, ed. W. G. Simms. New York, 1867.

[Lawrence, Robert]. *A Brief Narrative of the Ravages of the British and Hessians at Princeton in 1776–1777*, ed. Varnum Lansing Collins. Princeton, NJ, 1906.

Leary, Lewis. *That Rascal Freneau: A Study in Literary Failure*. Orig. pub. 1941; repr. New York, 1964.

Lecky, W. E. H. *The American Revolution, 1763–1783*, ed. J. A. Woodburn. New York, 1929.

[Lee, Andrew]. "Sullivan's Expedition to Staten Island in 1777: Extract from the Diary of Captain Andrew Lee." *PMHB* 3 (1879), 167–173.

[Lee, Charles]. *The Lee Papers, 1754–1811*. 4 vols. *NYHC*. New York, 1872–1875.

[Leggett, Abraham]. *The Narrative of Major Abraham Leggett*, ed. Charles I. Bushnell. New York, 1865.

Leiby, Adrian. *The Revolutionary War in the Hackensack Valley: The Jersey Dutch and the Neutral Ground, 1775–1783*. New Brunswick, 1991.

Lemisch, Jesse. "Listening to the 'Inarticulate': William Widger's Dream and the Loyalties of American Revolutionary Seamen in British Prisons." *JSH* 3 (1969), 1–29.

Lender, Mark E. "The Social Structure of the New Jersey Brigade: The Continental Line as an American Standing Army." In Peter Karsten, ed., *The Military in America: From the Colonial Era to the Present*. New York, 1986, 27–44.

Lengel, Edward G. *General George Washington: A Military Life*. New York, 2005.

Lenman, Bruce. *The Jacobite Risings in Britain, 1689–1746*. London, 1980.

Lindsey, William R. "Treatment of American Prisoners of War During the Revolution." *Emporia State Research Studies* 22 (Summer 1973), 5–32.

Link, Eugene P. *Democratic-Republican Societies, 1790–1800*. New York, 1942.

[Livingston, William]. *The Papers of William Livingston*, ed. Carl Prince and Dennis P. Ryan. 4 vols. Trenton, 1980.

Lorenz, Alfred R. *Hugh Gaine: A Colonial Printer-Editor's Odyssey to Loyalism*. Carbondale, IL, 1972.

Lossing, Benson J. *Hours with the Living Men and Women of the Revolution*. New York, 1889.

Lowell, Edward J. *The Hessians and the Other German Auxiliaries of Great Britain in the Revolutionary War*. New York, 1884.

Lucey, Mark C. "A History of City Hall Park in New York City, 1652–1838." Master's thesis, Brooklyn College, 2004.

Luke, Myron, and Robert W. Venables. *Long Island in the Revolution*. Albany, NY, 1976.

Lutnick, Solomon. *The American Revolution and the British Press, 1775–1783*. Columbia, MO, 1967.

Lydenberg, Harry M. *Archibald Roberson, Lieutenant-General Royal Engineers: His Diaries and Sketches in America, 1762–1780*. New York, 1930.

[Mackenzie, Frederick]. *Diary of Frederick Mackenzie, Giving a Daily Narrative of His Service as an Officer of the Regiment of Royal Welch Fusiliers During the Years 1775–1781 in Massachusetts, Rhode Island and New York*. 2 vols. Cambridge, MA, 1930.

Mackesy, Piers. *The War for America, 1775–1783*. Orig. pub. 1964; repr. Lincoln, 1993.

Manders, Eric I. *The Battle of Long Island*. Monmouth Beach, NJ, 1978.

Marsh, Philip. *The Works of Philip Freneau: A Critical Study.* Metuchen, NJ, 1968.

Martin, James K., and Mark E. Lender. *A Respectable Army: The Military Origins of the Republic, 1763–1789.* Wheeling, IL, 1982.

Mather, Frederick G., et al., eds. *New York in the Revolution.* 2 vols. Albany, 1904.

Mather, Frederick G. *The Refugees of 1776 from Long Island to Connecticut.* Albany, 1913.

Mayo, Katherine. *General Washington's Dilemma.* New York, 1938.

Mayo, Robert, comp., *Army and Navy Pension Laws and Bounty Land Laws of the United States.* Washington, DC, 1852.

McGeachy, Robert A. "The American War of Lieutenant Colonel Archibald Campbell of Inverneill." www.earlyamerica.com/review /2001_summer_fall/ amer_war.html.

[McMichael, James]. "Diary of Lieutenant James McMichael." 2 *PA* 15, 195–203.

McNamara, Brooks. *Day of Jubilee: The Great Age of Public Celebrations in New York, 1788–1909.* New Brunswick, NJ, 1997.

McWilliams, John. "The Faces of Ethan Allen: 1760–1860." *NEQ* 49 (June 1976), 257–282.

Mercantile Library Association. *New York City during the American Revolution.* New York, 1861.

Metzger, Charles H. *The Prisoner in the American Revolution.* Chicago, 1962.

Meyer, Lois J. *The Irony of Submission: The British Occupation of Huntington and Long Island, 1776–1783.* Privately printed, 1992.

Miller, Hunter, ed. *Treaties and Other International Acts of the United States of America.* 8 vols. Washington, DC, 1931.

Miller, John C. *Triumph of Freedom: 1775–1783.* Boston, 1948.

Mitchell, Broadus. *Alexander Hamilton: Youth to Maturity, 1755–1788.* New York, 1957.

Mitchill, Samuel L. *The Picture of New-York; or The Traveller's Guide through the Commercial Metropolis of the United States.* New York, 1807.

Mock, James R. *Censorship 1917.* Princeton, NJ, 1941.

Moody, James. *Narrative of His Exertions and Sufferings in the Cause of Government Since the Year 1776.* London, 1783.

Moore, Frank, ed. *Diary of the American Revolution.* 2 vols. New York, 1860.

Moore, George H. *The Treason of Charles Lee.* New York, 1860.

Moore, John Bassett. "A Hundred Years of American Diplomacy." *Harvard Law Review* 14 (November 1900), 165–183.

Moreau, Joseph. *Schoolbook Nation: Conflicts over American History Textbooks from the Civil War to the Present.* Ann Arbor, 2002.

Morison, Samuel Eliot. *John Paul Jones: A Sailor's Biography.* Boston, 1959.

[Morris, Robert]. *The Papers of Robert Morris,* ed. E. James Ferguson et al. 9 vols. Pittsburgh, 1973–.

Moser, John E. *Twisting the Lion's Tail: American Anglophobia between the World Wars.* New York, 1999.

Moss, Frank. *The American Metropolis.* 3 vols. New York, 1897.

Moyne, Ernest J. "The Reverend William Hazlitt: A Friend of Liberty in Ireland During the American Revolution." *WMQ* 21 (Apr. 1964), 288–297.

Mulford, Carla. "Annis Boudinot Stockton." *American National Biography.* New York, 1999.

———, ed. *Only for the Eye of a Friend: The Poems of Annis Boudinot Stockton.* Charlottesville, 1995.

Mushkat, Jerome. "Matthew Livingston Davis and the Political Legacy of Aaron Burr." *NYHQ*, 59 (Apr. 1975), 123–148.

———. *Tammany: The Evolution of a Political Machine, 1789–1865*. Syracuse, NY, 1971.

Muzzey, David S. *An American History*. 1911.

Myers, Gustavus. *The History of Tammany Hall*. New York, 1901.

Namier, Lewis, and John Brooke. *England in the Age of the American Revolution*. 2nd ed. New York, 1961.

———. *The House of Commons, 1754–1790*. 3 vols. New York, 1964.

———. *The Structure of Politics at the Accession of George III*. 2nd ed. London, 1957.

Nash, Gary B., Charlotte Crabtree, and Ross E. Dunn. *History on Trial: Culture Wars and the Teaching of the Past*. New York, 1997.

Neimeyer, Charles P. *America Goes to War: A Social History of the Continental Army*. New York, 1996.

Nelson, Paul David. *William Alexander, Lord Stirling*. University, AL, 1987.

Newell, Timothy. "A journal kept during the time y^t Boston was shut up in 1775–6." *MHSC* 4th ser. (Boston, 1852), 1: 261–276.

Newman, Simon. *Parades and the Politics of the Street: Festive Culture in the Early American Republic*. Philadelphia, 1997.

Newton, Caroline G. *Rev. Roger Newton, Deceased 1683, and One Line of His Descendants*. Privately printed, 1912.

[Nice, John]. "Excerpts from the Diary of Captain John Nice." *PMHB* 16 (1892), 392411.

New-York Historical Society. *Narratives of the Revolution in New York*. New York, 1975.

[Nichols, Francis]. "Diary of Lieutenant Francis Nichols." *PMHB* 20 (1896), 512–513.

Noll, Mark A. "Moses Mather (Old Calvinist) and the Evolution of Edwardseanism." *CH* 49 (Sept. 1980), 273–285.

Norton, Mary Beth. *The British-Americans: The Loyalist Exiles in England, 1774–1789*. Boston, 1972.

Novick, Peter. *That Noble Dream: The "Objectivity Question" and the American Historical Profession*. Cambridge, 1988.

Onderdonk, Henry, Jr. *Documents and Letters Intended to Illustrate the Revolutionary Incidents of Queens County*. New York, 1846.

———. *Revolutionary Incidents of Suffolk and Kings Counties*. New York, 1849.

O'Shaughnessy, Andrew Jackson. "'If Others Will Not Be Active, I Must Drive': George III and the American Revolution." *EAS* 2 (Spring 2004), 1–46.

Ostrander, Stephen M. *A History of the City of Brooklyn and Kings County*. 2 vols. Brooklyn, 1894.

Pabst, Anna C. Smith. *American Revolutionary War Manuscript Records: Elias Boudinot and General Haldimand Papers*. Delaware, OH, 1969.

Page, Max. *The Creative Destruction of Manhattan, 1900–1940*. Chicago, 1999.

Paine, Ralph. *The Ships and Sailors of Old Salem*. Chicago, 1912.

[Painter, Thomas]. *Autobiography of Thomas Painter, Relating His Experiences during the War of the Revolution*. Privately printed, 1910.

Papas, Philip. *That Every Loyal Island: Staten Island and the American Revolution*. New York, 2007.

Parker, David W. "Secret Reports of John Howe, 1808, Part I." *AHR* 17 (Oct. 1911), 70–74.

Peckham, Howard H. *The Toll of Independence: Engagements and Battle Casualties of the American Revolution.* Chicago, 1974.

[Peebles, John]. *John Peebles' American War: The Diary of a Scottish Grenadier, 1776–1782,* ed. Ira Gruber. Mechanicsburg, PA, 1998.

Pennington, Jean A. T. *Bowes and Church's Food Values of Portions Commonly Used.* 17th ed. Philadelphia, 1998.

Perry, Ichabod. *Reminiscences of the Revolution.* Lima, NY, 1915.

Phelps, Richard H. *A History of Newgate of Connecticut.* Albany, 1860.

Phoenix, S. Whitney. *The Whitney Family of Connecticut.* 3 vols. New York, 1878.

Pintard, John. "The Old Jail." *New-York Mirror,* Sept. 10, 1831.

Plank, Geoffrey. *Rebellion and Savagery: The Jacobite Rising of 1745 and the British Empire.* Philadelphia, 2006.

Platt, Henry C. *Old Times in Huntington: An Address.* Huntington, 1876.

Pomerantz, Sidney I. *New York: An American City, 1783–1803.* New York, 1938.

Prelinger, Catherine M. "Benjamin Franklin and the American Prisoners of War in England During the American Revolution." *WMQ* 32 (Apr. 1975), 261–294.

Prime, Nathaniel. *History of Long Island.* New York, 1845.

Purcell, Sara J. *Sealed with Blood: War, Sacrifice, and Memory in Revolutionary America.* Philadelphia Press, 2002.

Quarles, Benjamin. *The Negro in the American Revolution.* Chapel Hill, NC, 1961.

Randall, Willard S. *A Little Revenge: Benjamin Franklin and His Son.* Boston, 1984.

Ranlet, Philip. *The New York Loyalists.* Knoxville, TN, 1986.

———. "British Recruitment of Americans in New York During the American Revolution." *Military Affairs* 48 (Jan. 1984), 26–28.

———. "In the Hands of the British: The Treatment of American POWs During the War of Independence." *Historian* 62 (Summer 2000), 731–757.

———. "Tory David Sproat of Pennsylvania and the Death of American Prisoners of War." *PH* 61 (Apr. 1994), 185–205.

Raphael, Ray. *A People's History of the American Revolution.* New York, 2001.

Resch, John. *Suffering Soldiers: Revolutionary War Veterans, Moral Sentiment, and Political Culture in the Early Republic.* Amherst, 1999.

Reynolds, David S. *Walt Whitman's America: A Cultural Biography.* New York, 1995.

Richards, Eric. "Scotland and the Uses of the Atlantic Empire." In Bernard Bailyn and Philip D. Morgan, eds., *Strangers Within the Realm: Cultural Margins of the First British Empire.* Chapel Hill, NC, 1991.

Riggs, A. R. "Arthur Lee, A Radical Virginian in London, 1768–1776." *VMHB* 78 (July 1970), 268–280.

Ritcheson, Charles H. *British Politics and the American Revolution.* Norman, OK, 1954.

Ritchie, Carson I. A. "A New York Diary of the Revolutionary War." In NYHS, *Narratives of the Revolution in New York.* New York, 1975, 206–303.

Robinson, Donald L. *Slavery in the Structure of American Politics, 1765–1820.* New York, 1971.

Rock, Howard B. *Artisans of the New Republic: The Tradesmen of New York City in the Age of Jefferson.* New York, 1984.

Rodger, N. A. M. *The Insatiable Earl: A Life of John Montagu, Fourth Earl of Sandwich, 1718–1792.* New York, 1993.

———. *The Wooden World: An Anatomy of the Georgian Navy.* Annapolis, 1986.

[Rodney, George]. *Letter-Books and Order-Book of George, Lord Rodney, Admiral of the White Squadron, 1780–1782.* 2 vols. New York, 1932.

Romaine, Benjamin. *Review. The tomb of the martyrs, adjoining the United States Navy Yard, Brooklyn City, in Jackson Street, who died in dungeons and pestilential prisonships, in and about the city of New York, during the seven years of our Revolutionary War.* New York, 1839.

Rose, Alexander. *Washington's Spies: The Story of America's First Spy Ring.* New York, 2006.

Rosenwaike, Ira. *Population History of New York City.* Syracuse, NY, 1972.

Rowe, G. S. "The Travail of John McKinly, First President of Delaware." *DH* 17 (1976), 21–36.

Royster, Charles. *A Revolutionary People at War: The Continental Army & American Character, 1775–1783.* Chapel Hill, NC, 1979.

[Rush, Benjamin]. *The Autobiography of Benjamin Rush,* ed. George W. Corner. Princeton, NJ, 1948.

———. *Letters of Benjamin Rush,* ed. L. H. Butterfield. 2 vols. Princeton, NJ, 1951.

Russell, Jonathan. *An oration, pronounced in the Baptist Meeting-House, in Providence on the anniversary of American independence, July 4, 1800.* Providence, RI, 1800.

Ryan, Dennis P., ed. *A Salute to Courage: The American Revolution as Seen Through Wartime Writings of Officers of the Continental Army and Navy.* New York, 1979.

Sabine, W. H. W. *Murder, 1776, and Washington's Policy of Silence.* New York, 1973.

———. *The Suppressed History of General Nathaniel Woodhull.* New York, 1954.

Saffell, W. T. R. *Records of the Revolutionary War.* Orig. pub. 1913; repr. Baltimore, 1969.

Sainsbury, John. *Disaffected Patriots: London Supporters of Revolutionary America, 1769–1782.* Kingston and Montreal, 1987.

Salter, Edwin, and George C. Beekman. *Old Times in Old Monmouth.* Orig. pub. 1887; repr. Baltimore, 1980.

Sampson, Richard. *Escape in America: The British Convention Prisoners, 1777–1783.* Chippenham, UK, 1995.

Sands, John O. "Christopher Vail, Soldier and Seaman in the American Revolution." *Winterthur Portfolio* 11 (1976), 53–73.

[Sandwich, John]. *The Private Papers of John, Earl of Sandwich,* ed. G. R. Barnes and J. H. Owen. 4 vols. Privately printed, 1932 [London].

Savage, Kirk. *Standing Soldiers, Kneeling Slaves: Race, War, and Monument in Nineteenth-Century America.* Princeton, NJ, 1997.

Savelle, Max. "Nationalism and Other Loyalties in the American Revolution." *AHR* 67 (July 1962), 901–923.

Sayre, Gordon M. *American Captivity Narratives.* Boston, 2000.

Schaukirk, Ewald G. *Occupation of New York City by the British.* Orig. pub. 1887; repr. New York, 1969.

Schecter, Barnet. *The Battle for New York: The City at the Heart of the American Revolution.* New York, 2002.

Scheer, George F., and Hugh F. Rankin. *Rebels and Redcoats.* New York, 1957.

Schiff, Stacy. *A Great Improvisation: Franklin, France, and the Birth of America.* New York, 2005.

Schwartz, Laurens R. *Jews and the American Revolution: Haym Salomon and Others.* Jefferson, NC, 1987.

[Segar, Nathaniel]. *A Brief Narrative of the Captivity and Sufferings of Lieutenant Nathan'l Segar.* Paris, ME, 1825.

Selesky, Harold. "Colonial America." In Michael Howard, George J. Andreopoulos, and Mark R. Shulman, eds., *The Laws of War: Constraints on Warfare in the Western World*. New Haven, 1994, 78–85.

[Serle, Ambrose]. *The American Journal of Ambrose Serle*, ed. Edward H. Tatum, Jr. San Marino, CA, 1940.

Seton, Bruce Gordon, and Jean Gordon Arnot, eds. *The Prisoners of the '45*. 3 vols. Edinburgh, 1928.

Shenstone, Susan B. *So Obstinately Loyal: James Moody, 1744–1809*. Montreal, 2000.

Sherburne, Andrew. *Memoirs of Andrew Sherburne: A Pensioner of the Navy of the Revolution*. Orig. pub. Utica, 1828; repr. Freeport, NY, 1970.

Shy, John. "Armed Loyalism: The Case of the Lower Hudson Valley." In *A People Numerous and Armed: Reflections on the Military Struggle for American Independence*. New York, 1976), 183–192.

———. "Charles Lee: The Soldier as Radical." In George A. Billias, ed., *George Washington's Generals*. New York, 1964, 22–53.

———. "Thomas Gage: Weak Link of Empire." In George A. Billias, ed., *George Washington's Opponents: British Generals and Admirals in the American Revolution*. New York, 1969.

———. *Toward Lexington: The Role of the British Army in the Coming of the American Revolution*. Princeton, NJ, 1965.

Sieminski, Greg. "The Puritan Captivity Narrative and the Politics of the American Revolution." *AQ* 42 (Mar. 1990), 35–56.

Silverman, Kenneth. *A Cultural History of the American Revolution*. New York, 1976.

Simcoe, John Graves. *A Journal of the Operations of the Queen's Rangers*. Orig. pub. 1844; repr. New York, 1968.

Simes, Thomas. *The Military Guide for Young Officers*. 2 vols. Philadelphia, 1776.

Skemp, Sheila L. *William Franklin: Son of a Patriot, Servant of a King*. New York, 1990.

Slade, William. "The Revolutionary War Diary of William Slade." HSM, unpublished manuscript.

Slide, Anthony, ed. *Robert Goldstein and "The Spirit of '76."* Metuchen, NJ, 1993.

Smith, Thomas E. V. *The City of New York in the Year of Washington's Inauguration, 1789*. Orig. pub. 1889; repr. 1972.

[Smith, Josiah]. "Diary of Colonel Josiah Smith, July 23–Sept. 7, 1776." In Frederick G. Mather, *The Refugees of 1776 from Long Island to Connecticut*. Albany, NY, 1913, 1010–1012.

Smith, Paul H., et al., eds. *Letters of Delegates to Congress, 1774–1789*. 26 vols. Washington, DC, 1976–.

———. *Loyalists and Redcoats: A Study in British Revolutionary Policy*. New York, 1964.

[Smith, William]. *Historical Memoirs from 26 August to 12 November 1783 of William Smith*, ed. W. H. W. Sabine. New York, 1971.

Squires, James Duane. *British Propaganda at Home and in the United States from 1914 to 1917*. Cambridge, MA, 1935.

Starkey, Armstrong. "War and Culture, a Case Study: The Enlightenment and the Conduct of the British Army in America, 1755–1781." *W&S* 8 (May 1990), 1–28.

Starr, Edward C. *A History of Cornwall, Connecticut: A Typical New England Town*. New Haven, CT, 1926.

Stedman, Charles. *The History of the Origin, Progress, and Termination of the American War*. 2 vols. London, 1794.

Steele, Ian K. "Surrendering Rites: Prisoners on Colonial North American Frontiers." In Stephen Taylor, Richard Connors, and Clyve Jones, eds., *Hanoverian Britain and Empire: Essays in Memory of Philip Lawson*. Rochester, NY, 1998, 137–157.

Steiner, Bernard C. *The Life and Correspondence of James McHenry*. Cleveland, 1907.

Stephenson, Michael. *Patriot Battles: How the War of Independence Was Fought*. New York, 2007.

Sterling, David L., ed. "American Prisoners of War in New York: A Report by Elias Boudinot." *WMQ* 13 (1956), 376–393.

Stevens, John A. *Progress of New York in a Century, 1776–1786*. New York, 1876.

Stiles, Henry R. *A History of the City of Brooklyn*. 2 vols. Brooklyn, 1867.

———, ed. *Letters from the Prisons and Prison-Ships of the Revolution*. New York, 1865.

———, ed. *Account of the Interment of the Remains of American Patriots, Who Perished on Board the British Prison Ships during the American Revolution*. New York, 1865.

Stokes, I. N. Phelps. *The Iconography of Manhattan Island, 1498–1909*. 6 vols. New York, 1915–1928.

Stone, Geoffrey R. "The Origins of the 'Bad Tendency' Test: Free Speech in Wartime." *Supreme Court Review* (2002), 411–452.

Stone, Hiram, ed. "The Experiences of a Prisoner in the American Revolution." *JAH* 2 (1908), 527–529.

Stone, William L., ed. *Letters of Brunswick and Hessian Officers During the American Revolution*. Albany, 1891.

Strickland, Matthew. *War and Chivalry: The Conduct and Perception of War in England and Normandy, 1066–1217*. Cambridge, MA, 1996.

Strong, Pauline T. *Captive Selves, Captivating Others: The Politics and Poetics of Colonial American Captivity Narratives*. Boulder, CO, 1999.

Strong, Thomas M. *The History of the Town of Flatbush*. New York, 1842.

Stumpf, Vernon O. "Colonel Eleazer Oswald: Politician and Editor." Ph.D. dissertation, Duke University, 1968.

Syrett, David. "'This penurious old reptile': Rear-Admiral James Gambier and the American War." *HR* 74 (Feb. 2001), 63–76.

Taaffe, Stephen R. *The Philadelphia Campaign, 1777–1778*. Lawrence, KS, 2003.

[Talbot, Silas]. *An Historical Sketch, to the End of the Revolutionary War, of the Life of Silas Talbot, Esq. of the State of Rhode Island, Lately Commander of the United States Frigate, the Constitution, and of an American Squadron in the West-Indies*. New York, 1803.

[Taylor, George]. *Martyrs to the Revolution in the British Prison-Ships in the Wallabout Bay*. New York, 1855.

Tebbenhoff, Edward H. "The Associated Loyalists: An Aspect of Militant Loyalism." *NYHQ* 63 (April 1979), 115–44.

Thacher, James. *Military Journal of the American Revolution*. Hartford, CT, 1862.

Thomas, Peter D. G. *Lord North*. New York, 1976.

Thompson, Benjamin. *A History of Long Island*. New York, 1839.

Thorburn, Grant. *Fifty Years' Reminiscences of New-York*. New York, 1845.

[Trumbull, Benjamin]. "Journal of the Campaign at New York, 1776–7." *CHSC* 7 (1899), 177–220.

[Trumbull, Jonathan]. *The Trumbull Papers*. 2 vols. Boston, 1888.

Tuckerman, Henry T. *The Life of Silas Talbot*. New York, 1850.

Uhlendorf, Bernhard A., ed. *Revolution in America: Confidential Letters and Journals, 1776–1784, of Adjutant General Major Baurmeister of the Hessian Forces*. New Brunswick, 1957.

Usher, Roland G., Jr. "Royal Navy Impressment During the American Revolution." *MVHR* 37 (Mar. 1951), 673–688.

Valentine, Alan C. *Lord George Germain*. Oxford, 1962.

Van Buskirk, Judith. *Generous Enemies: Patriots and Loyalists in Revolutionary New York*. Philadelphia, 2002.

[Van Dyke, John]. "Narrative of Confinement in the Jersey Prison Ship, by John van Dyke, Captain in Lamb's Regiment, N.Y.S.A." *HM* 7 (May 1863), 147–151.

Van Tassel, David D. *Recording America's Past: An Interpretation of the Development of Historical Studies in America 1607–1884*. Chicago, 1960.

Van Tyne, Claude H. *England and America: Rivals in the American Revolution*. New York, 1927.

Vincitorio, Gaetano L. "The Revolutionary War and Its Aftermath in Suffolk County, Long Island." *LIHJ* 7 (Fall 1994), 68–85.

Wade, Herbert T., and Robert A. Lively. *This Glorious Cause: The Adventures of Two Company Officers in Washington's Army*. Princeton, NJ, 1958.

Wahrman, Dror. "The English Problem of Identity in the American Revolution." *AHR* 106 (Oct. 2001), 1236–1262.

[Waldo, Albigence]. "Diary Kept at Valley Forge by Albigence Waldo." *HM* 5 (May 1861), 129–134, 169–172.

Waldstreicher, David. *In the Midst of Perpetual Fetes: The Making of American Nationalism, 1776–1820*. Chapel Hill, NC, 1997.

Walzer, Michael. *Exodus and Revolution*. New York, 1985.

[Wansey, Henry]. *Henry Wansey and His American Journal: 1794*, ed. David John Jeremy. Philadelphia, 1974.

War, Townsend. "Germantown Road and Its Associations." *PMHB* 5 (1881), 1–18.

Ward, Harry M. *Between the Lines: Banditti of the American Revolution*. Westport, CT, 2002.

[Washington, George]. *The Papers of George Washington: Revolutionary War Series*, ed. Philander D. Chase et al. 17 vols. Charlottesville, 1985–2008.

———. *The Writings of George Washington*, ed. John C. Fitzpatrick. 39 vols. Washington, DC, 1931–1944.

Watson, John F. *Historic Tales of Olden Time: Concerning the Early Settlement and Advancement of New-York City and State for the Use of Families and Schools*. New York, 1832.

[Webb, Samuel B.]. *Correspondence and Journals of Samuel Blachley Webb*, ed. Worthington C. Ford. 3 vols. Orig. pub. 1893; repr. New York, c. 1969.

[Webb, William]. "William Webb, of the Continental Frigate 'Trumbull'—Statement of his Son, Rev. Abner Webb." *NYGB* 29 (Oct. 1888), 242–243.

Weintraub, Stanley. *Iron Tears: America's Battle for Freedom, Britain's Quagmire: 1775–1783*. New York, 2005.

Wertenbaker, Thomas J. *Father Knickerbocker Rebels: New York City During the Revolution*. New York, 1948.

West, Charles E. "Prison Ships in the American Revolution." *JAH* 5 (Jan. 1911), 121–128.

White, Joseph E. "Thomas Andros: Captive." *NEQ* 10 (Sept. 1937), 516–526.

Whittemore, Henry. *The Heroes of the American Revolution and Their Descendants*. Brooklyn, 1897.

Willard, Margaret Wheeler, ed. *Letters on the American Revolution, 1774–1776*. Boston, 1925.

Willcox, William B. "Arbuthnot, Gambier, and Graves: 'Old Women' of the Navy." In George A. Billias, ed., *George Washington's Opponents: British Generals and Admirals in the American Revolution*, 260–290. New York, 1969.

Williams, Daniel E. "Zealous in the Cause of Liberty: Self-Creation and Redemption in the Narrative of Ethan Allen." In Leslie E. Brown and Patricia Craddock, eds., *Studies in Eighteenth-Century Culture*, Vol. 19. East Lansing, MI, 1989, 325–347.

Wilson, Ellen G. *The Loyal Blacks*. New York, 1976.

Winch, Julie. *A Gentleman of Color: The Life of James Forten*. New York, 2002.

Winfield, Charles H. *History of the County of Hudson, New Jersey*. New York, 1874.

Winfield, Riff. *The 50-Gun Ship*. London, 1997.

Wish, Harvey. *The American Historian: A Social-Intellectual History of the Writing of the American Past*. New York, 1960.

Young, Alfred F. *The Shoemaker and the Tea Party: Memory and the American Revolution*. Boston, 1999.

Young, Philip. *Revolutionary Ladies*. New York, 1977.

Zimmerman, Jonathan. "'Each 'Race' Could Have Its Heroes Sung': Ethnicity and the History Wars in the 1920s." *JAH* 87 (June 2000), 92–111.

INDEX

Page locators in bold indicate photographs or charts.